DATE DUE

OC 14 '97			
NO 17 '97			
DE 1 97			
AP 23 '98			
DE 26 98			
Mar 7			
OC 14 04			

DEMCO 38-296

The story of shattered life
can be told only in bits and pieces

Rilke

Life in Fragments
Essays in Postmodern Morality

Zygmunt Bauman

BLACKWELL
Oxford UK & Cambridge USA

Copyright © Zygmunt Bauman, 1995

)e identified as author of this work has
ιe Copyright, Designs and Patents Act
988.

ɔlished 1995
ted 1995

Publishers Ltd
108 Cowley Road
Oxford OX4 1JF
UK

Blackwell Publishers Inc.
238 Main Street
Cambridge, Massachusetts 02142
USA

Library of Congress Cataloging-in-Publication Data
Bauman, Zygmunt.
Life in fragments : Essays in Postmodern Morality / Zygmunt
Bauman.
p.   cm.
ISBN 0–631–19266–2 (alk. paper); 0–631–19267–0 (paperback).
1. Ethics, Modern – 20th century.   2. Postmodernism.
3. Civilization, Modern – 20th century.   I. Title.
BJ319.B38   1995
170—dc20   94 – 19673
                                                          CIP

British Library Cataloguing in Publication Data
A CIP catalogue record for this book is available from the British Library.

Typeset in $10\frac{1}{2}$ on 12 pt Bembo
by Graphicraft Typesetters Ltd., Hong Kong
Printed in Great Britain by T. J. Press Ltd., Padstow, Cornwall

This book is printed on acid-free paper

Contents

Introduction: In Search of Postmodern Reason

In *Postmodern Ethics* (Oxford: Blackwell, 1993) – the book to which the present essays refer and whose motifs they develop – I considered the changes which the new, postmodern perspective has brought or may bring to our orthodox understanding of morality and moral life. I proposed there that the breaking up of certain modern hopes and ambitions, and the fading of illusions in which they wrapped social processes and the conduct of individual lives alike, allow us to see the true nature of moral phenomena more clearly than ever. What they enable us to see is, above all, the 'primal' status of morality: well before we are taught and learn the socially constructed and socially promoted rules of proper behaviour, and exhorted to follow certain patterns and to abstain from following others, we are already in the situation of *moral choice*. We are, so to speak, ineluctably – *existentially* – moral beings: that is, we are faced with the challenge of the Other, which is the challenge of responsibility for the Other, a condition of *being-for*. Rather than being an outcome of social arrangement and personal training, this 'responsibility for' frames the primal scene from which social arrangements and personal instruction start, to which they refer and which they attempt to reframe and administer.

This proposition is not, emphatically, a part of the ancient and, on the whole, fruitless debate about the 'essential goodness' or 'essential evil' of humans. 'To be moral' does not mean 'to be good', but to exercise one's freedom of authorship and/or actorship as a choice between good and evil. To say that humans are 'essentially moral beings' does not mean to say that we are basically good; and to say that socially constructed and taught rules are secondary regarding that primal moral condition does not mean to say that evil comes from the distortion or incapacitation of the original goodness by unwholesome social pressures or flawed social arrangements. To say that the human condition is moral before it is or may be anything else means: well before we are told authoritatively what is 'good' and what 'evil' (and, sometimes,what is neither) we face the choice between good and evil; we face it already at the very first, inescapable moment of encounter with the Other. This means in its turn that, whether we choose it or not, we confront our situation as a moral problem and our life choices as moral dilemmas. What follows is that we bear moral responsibilities (that is, responsibilities for the choice between good and evil) well before we are given or take up any concrete responsibility through contract, calculation of interests, or enlisting to a cause. What follows as well is that such concrete responsibilities are unlikely to exhaust and replace in full the primal moral responsibility which they strive to translate into a code of well tempered rules; that the fact of moral responsibility may be only concealed, but not revoked.

This primal fact of our being-in-the-world as, first and foremost, a condition of moral choice, does not promise a happy-go-lucky, carefree life. On the contrary, it makes our predicament acutely uncomfortable. Confronting the choice between good and evil means finding oneself in a situation of ambivalence. This would be a relatively minor worry, were the ambiguity of choice limited to the straightforward preference for good or evil, each clearly, unmistakably defined; in particular, to the choice between acting on one's responsibility for the Other or desisting from such action – again with a pretty clear idea of what 'acting on responsibility' involves. This is not, however, the case. Responsibility for the Other is itself shot through with ambivalence: it has no obvious limits, nor does it easily translate into practical steps to be taken or refrained from – each such step being instead pregnant with consequences that are notoriously uneasy to predict and even less easy to evaluate in advance. The ambivalence that pertains to the condition of 'being for' is permanent and incurable; it can be taken away only together with whatever is 'moral' in the moral condition. One is tempted to say that facing the ambivalence of good and evil (and thus, so to speak, 'taking responsibility for one's own responsibility') is the *meaning* (the sole meaning) of being moral.

This means, though, rubbing the salt of loneliness into the wound of ambivalence. Dilemmas have no ready-made solutions; the necessity to choose comes without a foolproof recipe for proper choice; the attempt to do good is undertaken without guarantee of goodness of either the intention or its results. The realm of responsibility is frayed on all sides; it is equally easy to underdo as it is to overdo what 'acting responsibly' may ideally require. Moral life is a life of continuous uncertainty. It is built of the bricks of doubt and cemented with bouts of self-deprecation. Since the dividing lines between good and evil have not been drawn before, they are drawn in the course of action; the outcome of these efforts at drawing lines is akin to a string of footprints rather than a network of charted roads. And thus loneliness is as permanent and unevictable a resident of the house of responsibility as is ambivalence.

When unmitigated and unassuaged, that loneliness in the face of endemic ambivalence of moral condition is excruciatingly painful to live with. No wonder much of human inventiveness was dedicated throughout history to designing ways of alleviating the burden. In pre-modern times the principal designs were religious in character. The hub of every religious system was not the idea of sin, but that of the *repentance* and *redemption*. No religion considered sinless life a viable prospect nor proposed a way towards a life without evil. On the whole, religions realistically accept the inevitability of sin (that is, of pangs of conscience, unavoidable in view of the incurable uncertainty of the moral situation), and concentrate their efforts instead on ways to assuage the pain through the clear-cut prescription for repentance, tied to the promise of redemption. The essence of religious solutions to moral ambivalence, is, so to speak, dealing with it retrospectively – by providing the means of balancing out the burden of a wrong choice. What has been done, may be undone – the wrong may be made good again. Responsibility for choice is still a lonely matter – it rests fairly and squarely on the individual's shoulders, as do the consequences of choosing evil over good; but an *ex post facto* cure is provided, and it is provided collectively, in the name of an authority transcending the power and the understanding of the sinner, and thus guaranteeing freedom from worry in exchange for obedience.

It was only the modern project of remaking the world to the measure of human needs and capacities, and according to a rationally conceived design, that promised life free from sin (now renamed as guilt). Legislation was to be the principal tool of the rebuilding (seen as a 'new beginning' in the fullest sense of the term; a beginning unbound by anything which went on before, a virtual 'starting from scratch'). In the case of the moral condition, legislation meant designing an ethical code: one that (unlike the religious strategies of repentance and forgiveness) would actually *prevent* evil from being done, lending the actor an *a priori* certainty as to what is to be done, what can be left undone and what must not be done. (The feasibility of the project was assured in advance, tautologically; following the ethical rules could produce nothing but good, since 'good' has been defined in unambiguous terms as obedience to the rules.) The modern project postulated the possibility of a human world free not only from sinners, but from sin itself; not just from people making wrong choices, but from the very possibility of wrong choice. One may say that in the last account the modern project postulated a world free from moral ambivalence; and since ambivalence is the natural feature of the moral condition, by the same token it postulated the severance of human choices from their moral dimension. This is what the substitution of ethical law for autonomous moral choice amounted to in practice.

In effect, the focus of moral concerns has been shifted from the self-scrutiny of the moral actor to the philosophical/political task of working out the prescriptions and proscriptions of an ethical code; meanwhile the 'responsibility for the responsibility' – that is the responsibility for deciding what practical steps the responsibility requires to be taken and what steps are not called for ('go beyond the call of duty') – has been shifted from the moral subject to supra-individual agencies now endowed with exclusive ethical authority.

From the moral actor's point of view, the shift had much to be commended. (Indeed, this shift was one of the main reasons why the surrender of autonomy could be credibly represented as emancipation and increase of freedom.) Having reduced the vague, notoriously underdefined *responsibility* to a finite list of duties or *obligations*, it spares the actor a lot of anxious groping in the dark, and helps to avoid the gnawing feeling that the account can never be closed, the work never finally done. The agony of choice (Hannah Arendt's 'tyranny of possibilities') is largely gone, as is the bitter aftertaste of a choice never ultimately proved right. The substitution of rule-following for the intense, yet never fully successful, listening to infuriatingly taciturn moral impulses results in the almost unimaginable feat of not just absolving the actor from the personal responsibility for the wrongs done, but freeing the actor from the very possibility of *having* sinned. More promptly than the equivalent religious remedies – because *in advance*, before the act has been committed – the guilt is eliminated from choice, which is now simplified to the straightforward dilemma of obedience or disobedience to the rule. All in all, the modern shift from moral responsibility to ethical rulings offered a compensatory drug for an ailment induced by another modern accomplishment: the foiling of many determinants that once kept the actor's actions within tight and strictly circumscribed limits, so producing an 'unencumbered', 'disembedded' personality that is allowed (and forced to) self-define and self-assert. To the moral self, modernity offered freedom complete with patented ways of escaping it.

In what are commonly called 'postmodern' times the modern ailment of autonomy persists, while the compensatory drug is no longer available on National Ethical Service prescriptions. It can be purchased only in the free market, in the thick of the cutthroat publicity war between drug companies calling each other's bluff, extolling their own products and undercutting the claims of the competition. With the state ethical monopoly (and indeed, the state's desire for monopoly) in abeyance, and the supply of ethical rules by and large privatized and abandoned to the care of the marketplace, the tyranny of choice returns, though this time it taxes not so much the moral competence, as the shopping skills of the actor. The actor is responsible not for the contents with which the responsibility has been filled, but for the choice of an ethical code from among many, each of which sports expert endorsement and/or the credentials of box-office success. True, the 'responsibility for the responsibility' is no more lodged with central powers (or powers aspiring to centrality), having been shifted back to the actor; but this privately owned and managed meta-responsibility Mark II is not a responsibility for listening to the moral instinct or following moral impulse, but for putting one's bets on an ethical pattern likely to emerge victorious from the war of expert promises and/or popularity ratings. In the volatile atmosphere of flashing fames, flickery fads and freak franchises, this is not an easy matter – no more secure than speculating on the stock exchange. The consequences of choice outlive, as a rule, the authority on whose advice the choice had been made . . .

The tendency of permit-issuing authorities to depart prematurely takes quite a lot of weight out of the consequences, though. The essence of the episode is that it leaves no lasting traces; life lived as a succession of episodes is a life free from the worry about consequences. The prospect of living with the results of one's actions, be they what may, seems somewhat less daunting if remote and uncertain; less daunting, at any rate, than the *immediate* prospect of challenging the authority currently most vociferous and commanding most troops. Modernity extolled the delay of *gratification*, in the hope that the gratification will be still gratifying when the delay is over; the postmodern world in which authorities spring up, unannounced, from nowhere, only to vanish instantly without notice, preaches *delay of payment*. If the savings book was the epitome of modern life, the credit card is the paradigm of the postmodern one.

One possible interpretation of what is happening is that post-modernity preserves the precious gain of modernity – the 'unencumbered' autonomy of the actor – while simultaneously removing the price tag and the strings that modernity attached to it. Now, at long last, you may eat your cake and have it. (Or, rather, as cakes tend to get stale and unappetizing faster than before – you may eat your cake and *recycle* it.) Postmodernity (or, more appropriately still in this context, 'late modernity'), one hears time and again, is the ultimate crowning of the modern dream of freedom and of the long and tortuous effort to make the dream come true. So let us celebrate the world unencumbered by imagined obligations and fake duties. With universal principles and absolute truths dissipated or kicked out of fashion, *it does not matter much* any more what personal principles and private truth one embraces (the embrace must be never tight anyway) and follows (the following need not be too loyal and committed, to be sure).

Does it or does it not matter? – this is the question. And it remains a question – perhaps the crucial, constitutive question of postmodern (late modern) life. One might say with considerable conviction that precisely the opposite to the postmodernist account of postmodernity is the case: that *the demise of the power-assisted universals and absolutes has made the responsibilities of the actor more profound, and, indeed, more* consequential, *than ever before.* One might say with still greater conviction, that, between the demise of universal absolutes and absolute universals on the one hand and 'everything goes' licence on the other, there is a jarring *non sequitur*. As Steven Connor recently pointed out, 'the lack of absolute values no more makes all other values interchangeable than the absence of an agreed gold standard makes all world currencies worth the same.'[1]

Or, as Kate Soper suggests, it is quite conceivable (though it still remains to be seen whether it is realistic as well) to give up on 'the grand narrative idea of a single truth, without giving up on the idea of truth as a regulative ideal'.[2] If one translates Soper's proposition into the language of ethics, one may say that it is possible to give up on the grand narrative idea of a single ethical code, without giving up on the idea of moral responsibility as a regulative ideal. After the translation, though, the proposition looks unduly modest and meek.

[1]   Steven Connor, 'The Necessity of Value', in *Principled Positions: Postmodernism and the Rediscovery of Value*, ed. Judith Squires (London: Lawrence & Wishart, 1993), pp. 39–40.
[2]   Kate Soper, 'Postmodernism, Subjectivity and the Question of Value', in *Principled Positions*, ed. Squires, pp. 28–9.

One would rather say that it is precisely *because of* the demise of the allegedly unified and ostensibly unique ethical code, that the 'regulative ideal' of moral responsibility may rise into full flight. Choices between good and evil are still to be made, this time, however, in full daylight, and with full knowledge that a choice has been made. With the smokescreen of centralized legislation dispersed and the power-of-attorney returned to the signatory, the choice is blatantly left to the moral person's own devices. With choice comes responsibility. And if choice is inevitable, responsibility is unavoidable. No secure hiding place is left, and such shelters from responsibility as are on offer tend to be withdrawn from the supermarket shelves before the attached warranty expires, so that there is nowhere to which complaints can be addressed if the commodity proves faulty. One is left with the product and its defects and has only oneself to blame.

Will this new condition make us do good things more often than before and evil things less often? Will it make us better beings? Neither a 'yes' nor a 'no' answer can be responsibly given to those questions. As always, the moral situation is one of inherent ambivalence, and it would not be moral without a choice between good and evil. (Before eating from the tree of knowledge of good and evil, Adam and Eve were not moral beings, and the Garden of Eden was a place without morality.) What this new condition does spell out, however, is a prospect of a greater awareness of the moral character of our choices; of our facing our choices more consciously and seeing their moral contents more clearly.

It has to be repeated again and again: even that last prospect – of eyes opened wider to the 'for' in every 'with', of resurrecting the consideration of the Other temporarily elbowed out or suspended by the obedience to the norm – does not necessarily augur the arrival of a better world populated by better people. Even if that prospect became true, there is no guarantee of any sort that morality will gain by exposing itself point-blank to the moral self abandoned to her or his own moral sense. No one has, perhaps, given this uncertainty (nay fear) a more poignant voice than Gillian Rose:

> *New ethics* [by which Rose means such a postmodern view of morality as repudiates 'any politics of principle' and takes the Other, rather than the moral subject, for its centre point] is waving at 'the Other' who is drowning and dragging his children under with him in his violent, dying gestures. *New ethics* cares for 'the Other'; but since it refuses any relation to law, it may be merciful, but, equally, it may be merciless. In either case, having renounced principles and intentions, *new ethics* displays 'the best intentions' – the intention to get things right this time. In its regime of sheer

mercy, *new ethics* will be as implicated in unintended consequences as its principled predecessor.[3]

This is, roughly, the idea I wished my own book on *Postmodern Ethics* to convey: that *postmodernity is the moral person's bane and chance at the same time*. And that *which of the two faces of the postmodern condition will turn out to be its lasting likeness, is itself a moral question*.

The essays collected in the present volume follow up these ideas – as they draw life-juices from, or dry up and wilt in, the daily life of postmodern men and women. Unlike their predecessors collected in the previous volume, these essays are less concerned with the question of how morality can be narrated in the absence of the 'politics of principle', and more – mainly – with the question what aspects of life conditions make the 'politics of principle' redundant or impossible to conduct. It would be unfair to blame the philosophers for abandoning principles and refusing to seek unshakeable foundations of human goodness; it would be presumptuous to propose that what is worrying about the moral plight of postmodern humans is that philosophers 'got it wrong' and neglect their duty. Philosophy always was and remains an informed, thoughtful commentary on being, and the being it is a commentary on is the kind of being lived under the conditions which happen to be the fate of men and women of their time and part of the world. There must be something in that time and that part of the world which makes some familiar commentaries sound hollow while supplying new motifs and new tunes. These essays attempt to unravel this 'something'.

Christopher Lasch observed in his recent study that society is 'no longer governed by a moral consensus'. He also points out that our social order no longer requires 'the informed consent of citizens'. I propose that the two observations are not unconnected, and the two phenomena they report have common roots. And that there is an intimate link between both and a third phenomenon, located seemingly on an entirely different level of experience – 'our impatience with anything that limits our sovereign freedom of choice . . . our preference for "nonbinding commitments".'[4] I propose that the study of postmodern morality(ies) must be a study in the context of postmodern life and postmodern life strategies. It is the guiding theme of these essays that the roots of postmodern moral problems go down

---

[3]   Gillian Rose, *Judaism and Modernity: Philosophical Essays* (Oxford: Blackwell, 1993), p. 6.
[4]   Christopher Lasch, *The True and Only Heaven: Progress and its Critics* (New York: W. W. Norton, 1991), pp. 30, 31, 34.

to the fragmentariness of the social context and the episodicity of life pursuits.

These are studies not so much in 'unintended consequences', as in the endemic and incurable ambivalence of the primal moral scene – the scene of moral choices and the scene of discovery of the morality of choices – in which any consequences are begotten, by design or by default. These essays attempt to take stock of the dangers and opportunities inherent in this scene – and, above all, of those ambivalent appurtenances of postmodern life of which we do not yet know whether they are hurdles or springboards; and which, for all we know, may yet become either.

1

Morality without Ethics

Ethics is the concern of philosophers, educators and preachers. They make ethical statements – when they speak of the ways people behave towards each other and toward themselves. They would not say, though, that any description of that behaviour deserves to be counted among ethical statements. To say merely what people do to each other and to themselves does not yet mean speaking ethics: it means at the utmost making statements that belong to the sociology or ethnography of moral behaviour. If not only common conduct, but also its common *evaluation* is described (that is, information is included about whether the people in question approve of, or condemn certain actions), the statements belong to 'ethnoethics' – which tells us about the views of right and wrong held by the people described, but not necessarily shared by those who describe them, and certainly not deemed acceptable merely for the fact of being held by those described; 'ethnoethics' tells us what certain people ('ethnos') *believe* to be right or wrong, without telling us whether those beliefs themselves *are* right or wrong. But philosophers, educators and preachers will insist that to make an ethical statement it is not enough to say that some people believe something to be right or good or just. If philosophers, educators, and preachers make ethics their concern, this is precisely because none of them would entrust judgement of right and wrong to the people themselves or would recognize, without further investigation, the authority of their beliefs on that matter.

Ethics is therefore something more than a mere description of what people do; more even than a description of what they believe they ought to be doing in order to be decent, just, good – or, more generally, 'in the right'. Properly ethical statements are such as do not depend for their truthfulness on what people are actually doing or even on what they believe they ought to be doing. If what ethical statements say and what people do or believe are at odds with each other, this is assumed to mean, without need of further proof, that it is the people who are in the wrong. Only ethics can say what *really* ought to be done so that the good be served. Ideally, ethics is a code of law that prescribes correct behaviour 'universally' – that is, for all people at all times; one that sets apart good from evil once for all and everybody. This is precisely why the spelling out of ethical prescriptions needs to be a job of special people like philosophers, educators and preachers. This is also what casts these special people, the ethical experts, in a position of authority over ordinary people who just go on doing things while applying rules of thumb they cling to (often without as much as being able to tell clearly what those rules are like). The authority of ethical experts is legislative and juridical at the same time. The experts pronounce the law, and judge whether the prescriptions have been followed faithfully and correctly. They claim to be able to do it because they have access to knowledge not available to ordinary people – by speaking to the spirits of the ancestors, studying the holy scriptures, or unravelling the dictate of Reason.

The derogatory view of the 'ethical competence' of ordinary people in ordinary circumstances, and the authority bestowed in advance on what the experts say, may say, or would wish to say on the subject, presume that properly ethical judgements are not 'founded' (that is, authoritative and binding) as long as the only evidence that may be called on their behalf is the fact that 'people do this sort of thing'. True foundations must be stronger and less volatile than ordinary people's erratic habits and their notoriously unsound and mercurial opinions. What is more, those foundations must be placed at a distance from the hurly-burly of daily life, so that ordinary people will not see them from the places in which they conduct their ordinary business, and will not be able to pretend that they know them unless told, taught or trained by the experts. Lay people's ethical impotence and the experts' ethical authority explain and warrant each other: and the postulate of a 'properly founded' ethics supports them both.

Let us note that it is not exactly the people's need for guidance and reassurance that sent the ethical expert to work. Most of the people, most of the time (and that includes the ethical experts themselves whenever they take a break from their professional pursuits and occupy themselves with their own mundane daily tasks) can do very well without a code and without official stamps certifying its propriety. Indeed, they need the code and its authorizations so seldom that they hardly ever have a chance to discover its absence – just as we do not notice the theft of household items we never use. Most people – most of us – follow most of the time the habitual and the routine; we behave today the way we behaved yesterday and as the people around us go on behaving. As long as no one and nothing stops us from doing 'the usual', we may go on like this without end. So rather it is the other way around: it is the ethical experts who cannot remain what they are – the experts bearing authority, in a position to tell others what to do, to reproach them for doing wrong and to force them to do what is right – without asserting the need for rock-hard foundations and foolproof reassurance we allegedly miss; without insisting in theory, and better still demonstrating in practice, that without such foundations and the reassurances they found we 'cannot go on', or, at least, we cannot go on as we *should* – as truly decent, *moral* people should. If stated repeatedly, with authority, and with the support of adequate resources, propositions tend to become true in the end – and the training aimed at making us 'expert-dependent' cannot but bring its fruit; sooner or later, we start seeking keenly and of our own accord reliable guidance from 'people in the know'. Once we stop trusting our own judgement, we grow susceptible to the fear of being in the wrong; we call what we dread sin, guilt or shame – but whatever name we use we feel the need of the helpful hand of the expert to fetch us back into the comfort of certainty. It is out of such a fear that the dependency on expertise grows. But once the dependency has settled and taken root, the need of ethical expertise becomes 'self-evident', and above all self-reproducing.

This also means that the need for ethical experts depends little, if at all, on whether the experts can or cannot deliver on their promise. (Just as we need medical experts whatever the effectiveness of the services they offer.) The need depends solely on the condition in which one cannot do without seeking such delivery. Paradoxically, the need grows even bigger as the goods delivered are not fully up to the expectations and thus do not satisfy the need they were hoped to quell.

Society: the operation cover-up

The idea of chaos, says the Polish sociologist of culture Elżbieta Tarkowska, refers 'to a certain state, a primal state that precedes the creation; a state marked by fluidity, formlessness, indetermination, indifferentiation, total confusion of all elements'. Since in the state of chaos 'change is permanent', this state 'appears to those cast into it (as well as to observers and students) as unclear, illegible, unpredictable'. Let us explain that the chaos described by Tarkowska is a state in which everything can happen (just as order, chaos's antonym, is a state in which certain events are practically excluded, while certain others are more than randomly probable); in which the probability of no event is higher than the probability of any other – and even if it was, we would not be able to tell this beforehand. Chaotic being is devoid of structure – if 'structure' means precisely an uneven distribution of probabilities, non-randomness of the events. In the course of the discussion that followed her attempt to add the concept of 'chaos' to the vocabulary of cultural studies, Tarkowska noted that the extant language of the social sciences resists the addition; even when the participants of the debate agreed to describe as 'chaos' the (temporary, as they hoped) states of theoretical confusion and uncertainty occurring at the time of the so-called 'paradigmatical crisis', they showed distinctly their unwillingness (more intuitive than reasoned) to deploy the concept of 'chaos' in the description of the human condition rather than of the theory of that condition. In their resistance to the representation of social reality as 'chaotic in its own right' the participants of the learned debate were in full agreement with the commonsensical intuition, cultivated by our language, which assumes and implies the discrete nature, differentiation, classification and general 'orderliness' of the world. They preferred to speak of 're-structuring' or simply 'transformation' of culture. A state of 'objective' structurelessness, if at all thinkable, appeared to them only as a temporary weakening of structure – or, more exactly, as that brief, dramatic and pregnant moment that divides one order from another which is to replace it. They could speak of 'chaos' only as of *departure from the norm*, disturbance of the normal state of affairs – and thus as of an abnormal and exceptional state, a dangerous state, a state of 'crisis' or disease. Much like 'crime' or 'illness', the idea of chaos seemed to be burdened from the start with a stigma no definitional efforts could wash off.

'Human beings', noted Cornelius Castoriadis in 1982, 'cannot accept Chaos and accept it as Chaos, they cannot stand up straight and confront the Abyss.' That they cannot do that, cannot be 'explained', 'given sense' – represented as the effect of something else, of a cause, is itself the source and the cause of all sense-making bustle and all explanatory effort, itself being senseless and inexplicable. It is, we may say, a pristine and 'brute' fact that human beings exist in the never-ending, since never fully successful, effort to escape from Chaos:

society, its institutions and their routines, its images and their compositions, its structures and their managerial principles, are all facets of that forever inconclusive and relentless escape. Society, we might say, is a massive and continuous cover-up operation. And yet the best the escape ever succeeds in coming up with is a thin film of order that is continuously pierced, torn apart and folded up by the Chaos over which it stretches: that Chaos 'is constantly invading alleged immanence – the given, the familiar, the apparently domesticated'. And the invasion is, like the 'immanence' itself, a daily, familiar, though never completely domesticated event: it manifests itself 'through the emergence of the irreducibly new, of radical alterity', and 'through destruction, annihilation, death'.[1]

We may say though that the cover-up operation called Society is on the whole effective enough for the 'Chaos', the 'Abyss', the 'groundlessness', of which Castoriadis speaks, to appear to us humans, not as the primal scene from which we busy ourselves to run away and hide, but dressed up as the break in 'the given', an irruption, a crevice in the otherwise solid rock of normality, a hole in the smoothly flowing routine of being. It bursts into our lives as a signal of defeat and a notice of bankruptcy, as a reminder of the laughable arrogance of ambition and the flimsiness of the efforts that follow it. Chaos is all the more terrifying for the promises brandished by the routine of the given. Society is an escape from fear; it is also the breeding ground of that fear, and on that fear it feeds and from it the grip in which it holds us draws its strength.

Birth and death, the entry of the new and the exit of the familiar, are two gaping holes in the pretence of order which no effort ever did or ever will plug. The being locked in the brief/narrow time/ space between the entry and the exit, and daily reminded of the stubborn contingency and ineluctability of both limits as it travels between the limits of its own, cannot stretch the meanings it spins far enough to cover the '*before*' and the '*beyond*'. From that unsupervised and uncontrolled *elsewhere*, from that *otherwise than being*, comes the novelty and the unexpected; and in it all that is usual and homely ultimately sinks. Meanings are islands in the sea of meaninglessness, albeit wobbly and drifting islands, unanchored to the sea-bottom – if that sea has a bottom, that is. Without an anchor of

---

[1]   Cornelius Castoriadis, 'Institution of Society and Religion', trans. David Ames Curtis, in *Thesis Eleven*, vol. 31 (1993), pp. 1–17. For Elżbieta Tarkowska's findings, consult her 'Chaos kulturowy, albo o potrzebie antropologii raz jeszcze', in *Kulturowy wymiar przemian społecznych*, ed. Aldona Jawłowska, Marian Kempny and Elżbieta Tarkowska (Warsaw: IFiS Pan, 1993), pp. 34–5.

its own, the self-grown islands of meaningfulness need support from the outside: a foundation is needed where the anchor is absent. Says Nietzsche:

> Natural death is independent of all reason and is really an irrational death, in which the pitiable substance of the shell determines how long the kernel is to exist or not; in which, accordingly, the stunted, diseased and dull-witted jailer is lord, and indicates the moment at which his distinguished prisoner shall die. Natural death is suicide of nature – in other words, the annihilation of the most rational being through the most irrational element that is attached thereto. Only through religious illumination can the reverse appear; for then, as is equitable, the higher reason (God) issues its orders, which the lower reason has to obey.[2]

The inscrutable reason of God covers up for the non-reasonability of Chaos; now the principle meant to make the short/narrow time/space of being liveable reaches beyond the limits that make that time/space unendurable, pacifying the beyond. Reason monitors the armistice between the logical and the absurd, the pretensions of order and its brevity/narrowness. Chaos is baptized with a name that denies its groundlessness, and Being is excused from the need to account for itself, for its purpose and for its meaning. Human order is never forced to admit that it can draw on nothing but itself to explain either its presence or its limitations; society remains secure where it rules, as long as it signs over the management of what it does not rule. It can even, for a time, keep secret its own signature on the act of renunciation, and mask its own impotence as the omnipotence of God, its own incomprehension as God's omniscience, its own mortality as God's eternity, its own insularity as God's omnipresence.

There is nothing contingent about the link between society and religion. It would be futile to go on accounting for that link by a collection of historical accidents and choices. Religion and society are one; society without religion is incomplete and doomed, unable to defend itself in any court. The warrant of all meanings, yet itself meaningless; the endorser of all purposes, but itself purposeless; unable to suppress the evidence of that incongruence, society would lose the case the moment it was called as the defendant, charged with the authorship and responsibility for its deeds.

If one cannot confront the Abyss, the best thing is to chase it out of sight. This is exactly what society/religion achieves. Society needs God. Best of all, a 'personal' God, a God like you and me, only infinitely more resourceful – one who sees clearly order and meaning

---

[2] Friedrich Nietzsche, *Human All-too-human: A Book for Free Spirits*, part 2, trans. Paul V. Cohn (Edinburgh: T. W. Foulis, 1991), pp. 286–7.

and plan where you and I can only see or suspect a mockery of sense and purpose. A non-personal God, like Reason or the Laws of History, is but a second-best solution – a distant second, to be sure. The 'Invisible Hand' or the 'Cunning of Reason' or 'Historical Inevitability' all share with a personal God the crucial attributes of inscrutability and unaccountability – but what they leave aside unattended and unsupervised are those stubborn qualities of Being that made God necessary in the first place: first of all, the brevity/narrowness of existence, mortality, death – 'the annihilation of the most rational being by the most irrational of elements'. Where they deputize, death becomes an offence, a challenge, and an aperture through which the Absurd seeps into life; an unlockable window in the cosy yet cramped house of sensible existence – opening onto the infinite expanses of non-sense. Once it 'cannot be made sense of', death must be belied, suppressed by a cultural secrets act, or deconstructed[3] – and this proves to be an excrutiatingly difficult task.

In the absence of God, without His assistance, 'not confronting the Abyss' is not easy. What one is then staring in the face is the brute fact that, as Arthur Schopenhauer noticed a long time ago – from within a still young, exuberant and self-confident modernity – 'existence is merely accidental':

> if anyone ventures to raise the question why there is not nothing at all rather than this world, then the world cannot be justified from itself; no ground, no final cause of its existence can be found in itself; it cannot be demonstrated that it exists for its own sake, in other words, for its own advantage.

What is, then, the answer to the question?

> Death is the result, the *résumé*, of life, or the total sum expressing at one stroke all the instruction given by life in detail and piecemeal, namely that the whole striving, the phenomenon of which is life, was a vain, fruitless, and self-contradictory effort, to have returned from which is a deliverance.[4]

---

[3] I have described these expedients in *Mortality, Immortality, and Other Life Strategies* (Cambridge: Polity Press, 1992).

[4] Arthur Schopenhauer, *The World as Will and Representation*, trans. E. F. J. Payne (New York: Dover, 1966), pp. 579, 637. Hegel served Schopenhauer as the epitome of all attempts to belie the ultimate vanity – groundlessness – of being; the author of the most elaborate, standard-setting attempt to enthrone Reason in the controlling seat vacated by God was dismissed by Schopenhauer as 'a commonplace, inane, loathsome, repulsive, ignorant charlatan, who with unparalleled effrontery compiled a system of crazy nonsense' (*Parerga and Paralipomena*, vol. 1, trans. E. F. J. Payne (Oxford: Clarendon Press, 1974), p. 96.

At that time, Schopenhauer's voice was a cry in wilderness; or, rather the site from which voices of that sort could be heard was cast as wilderness by the civilization still confident that it could do the job that God had failed, or was no more allowed, to perform. Nineteenth-century philosophy successfully marginalized and anathematized Schopenhauer-style insights. It started with a grandiose optimistic utopia of Hegel; it proceeded by the all-bounds-out-of-bounds confidence of scientism; it ended up with Nietzsche's confinement to a madhouse. Throughout that dreaming century (perhaps best symbolized by Count Saint-Simon, who instructed his valet to wake him up each morning with the words: 'Arise, your highness, great deeds are to be done') the hope was never allowed to be extinguished that not only what is to be done will be done but that it will also become clear and indisputable that what is being done is what must be done *und kann nicht anders*. ('The modern times' – says E. M. Cioran – 'begins with two hysterics: Don Quichote and Luther.').[5] What is peculiar about the views expressed in the above quotations from Castoriadis is not their novelty (Schopenhauer said it all, and with exemplary force), but that they are no longer marginal. What used to be the voice of dissent is fast becoming an orthodoxy. What was whispered in condemned slums is now shouted in city squares; what was smuggled surreptitiously in the dark of night is now traded in the open in brightly lit and crowded shopping malls. And this difference makes all the difference.

Facing the unfaceable

Now, at long last, we 'stand up straight and confront Chaos'. We have never done it before. Merely to confront Chaos would be off-putting and upsetting enough. But the novelty of the act – the total absence of any precedent to go by, be reassured by, be guided by – makes the situation totally unnerving. The waters we leaped into are not just deep, but uncharted. We are not even at the crossroads: for crossroads to be crossroads, there must first be roads. Now we know that we *make* roads – the only roads there are and can be – and we do this solely by *walking* them.

[5] E. M. Cioran, *The Temptation to Exist*, trans. Richard Howard (London: Quartet Books, 1987), p. 35. At that era, says Cioran, 'even her [Europe's] doubts were merely convictions *disguised*' (p. 55). Much unlike the present one: 'The ancient historian who remarked of Rome that she could no longer endure neither her vices nor their remedies did not so much define his own epoch as anticipate ours.' (p. 63)

Or, to say the same in the language of philosophers and educators (though still not in the language of preachers, whatever remains today of that category): no foundations have been found nor are likely to be found for being; and no efforts to lay such foundations have succeeded nor are likely to succeed. There is neither cause nor reason for morality; the necessity to be moral, and the meaning of being moral, can neither be demonstrated nor logically deduced. And so morality is as contingent as the rest of being: it has no ethical foundations. We can no more offer ethical guidance for the moral selves, no more 'legislate' morality, or hope to gain such ability once we have applied ourselves more zealously, or more systematically, to the task. And since we have convinced ourselves and everyone willing to listen that the case of morality is safe only if set on solid ground built by forces stronger than those of the moral selves themselves – such forces as both precede and outlive the brief/narrow time/space of the moral selves – we find it exceedingly difficult, nay impossible, to comprehend why the self should be moral and how we would recognize it to be moral when or if it is moral.

It is one thing to believe the ethical foundations to be *not-yet*-found or *as-yet*-unconstructed, and an altogether different thing not to believe in ethical foundations at all. Dostoevsky's blunt 'if there is no God, everything is permissible' shouted out the innermost fears of the modern builders of godless (or, perhaps, 'post-divine') order. 'There is no God' means: there is no force stronger than human will and more powerful than human resistance, capable of coercing human selves to be moral; and no authority more ennobled and trustworthy than humans' own cravings and premonitions, to assure them that deeds they feel to be decent, just and proper – moral – are indeed such, and to lead them away from error in case they go wrong. If there is no such force and such authority, humans are abandoned to their own wits and will. And these, as the philosophers kept and the preachers keep hammering home, can give birth solely to sin and evil, and as theologians explained to us so convincingly, cannot be relied upon to cause right behaviour or pass the right judgement. There can be no such thing as 'ethically unfounded morality'; and 'self-founding' morality is, blatantly and deplorably, ethically unfounded.

Of one thing we can be sure: whatever morality there is or there may be in a society which has admitted its groundlessness, lack of purpose and the abyss bridged by just a brittle gangplank of convention – can be only *an ethically unfounded morality*. As such, it is and will be uncontrollable and unpredictable. It builds itself up, as it may dismantle itself and rebuild itself in a different fashion, in the course of *sociality*: as people come together and take their leave, join forces and fall apart, come to agreement and fall out, patch up and tear down the bonds and loyalties and solidarities that unite them. So much we know. The rest, however – the consequences of all that – is far from being clear.

Or perhaps the despair is unfounded, the ignorance exaggerated. One may say: the self-constitution of society is not new, only 'news'; society has existed through self-constitution since the beginning of time, *only we did not know about it* (or, rather, we managed to turn our eyes away from that truth). But quite a lot hangs on that 'only'. In Castoriadis's terms: while always self-constituting, society has in addition until now been 'self-occultating'. 'Self-occultation' consists in denying or disguising the fact of self-constitution, so that society may confront the precipitate of its own self-creation as an outcome of a heteronomous command or the extraneous order of things. Presumably, a heteronomous command is easier to follow than one's own untested project; the consequences are less difficult to bear, sufferings are easier to endure, the pangs of conscience are muffled, the salt of responsibility is not rubbed into the wound of failure. (Every perpetrator of crime, brought to trial and pleading innocence by pointing his finger to those 'up there' who gave the command, knows the difference very well.) The agony of 'disoccultation' derives first and foremost from coming face to face with responsibility that cannot be given up and for which there are no takers.

This agony is the plight of *autonomous society*; that is, to quote Castoriadis again,

> one that self-constitutes itself explicitly. This amounts to saying: it knows that the significations in and through which it lives and exists as society are its *oeuvre* and that they are neither necessary nor contingent[6]

– which means, let us add, that they are neither non-negotiable nor coming unannounced and from nowhere. To the autonomous society, significations (also the meanings of 'being moral') do not appear groundless, though they are blatantly devoid of 'foundations' in the sense implied by ethical philosophers; they are 'founded' all right, but their foundations are made of the same stuff as the significations they found. They are, also, the sediments of the ongoing process of

---

[6] Castoriadis, 'Institution of Society and Religion'. Castoriadis hails the advent of autonomy as the chance of humanity. What it comes to replace is, after all, the jarring inhumanity of all assumption of heteronomy: 'the true Revelation is the one from which we have benefited, our society is the sole true society or is society par excellence, the other ones do not truly exist, are lesser, are in limbo, are in expectation of being – of evangelization' (ibid.).

self-creation. Ethics and morality (if we insist on separating them still) grow of the same soil: moral selves do not 'discover' their ethical foundations, but (much like the contemporary work of art which must supply its own interpretive frame and standards by which it is to be judged) build them up while they build up themselves.

Now take this new-look world, and populate it with the all-too-familiar bugbear of the normatively un- or under-regulated, lonely 'asocial' monster of a Hobbes or a Durkheim, and there will be every reason to fear for the future of humanity. Or, rather, there would have been, were it not for a fact which deserves to be repeated once more (and many times yet), that it is not so much the way we live together that has changed, as our understanding of how we go on achieving this remarkable feat. And so we know that in the same way as the heteronomous ethical foundations of humane order, the scarecrow of the asocial ogre was a fiction of the self-occultating society. (In fact, the two fictions needed each other, generated each other and corroborated each other in the same way that self-fulfilling prophecies do.) The task of self-creation remains as excruciatingly difficult as it used to be, but there are no immediately obvious reasons for it to be *more* difficult now than it was before. What has changed is that we know now just how difficult the task is and suspect that no easy escape from the difficulty can be found: no subterfuge or closing of one's eyes will help.

One can as well go along with Max Horkheimer, who selected Schopenhauer as 'the teacher for our time'. ('There are few ideas' – wrote Horkheimer in 1961 – 'that the world today needs more than Schopenhauer's – ideas which in the face of utter hopelessness, because they confront it, know more than any others of hope.') Schopenhauer's

> doctrine of blind will as an eternal force removes from the world the treacherous gold foil which the old metaphysics had given it. In utter contrast to positivism, it enunciates the negative and preserves it in thought, thus exposing the motive for solidarity shared by men and all beings – their abandonment. No need is ever compensated in any beyond. The urge to mitigate it in *this* world springs from the inability to look at it in full awareness of this curse and to tolerate it when there is a chance to stop it. For such solidarity that stems from hopelessness, knowledge of the *principium individuationis* is secondary . . .
>
> To stand up for the temporal against merciless eternity is morality in Schopenhauer's sense.[7]

[7] Max Horkheimer, *Critique of Instrumental Reason*, trans. Matthew O'Connell et al. (New York: Seabury Press, 1974), pp. 83, 82.

Weaving the veil

It was a most salient characteristic of the modern spirit that it never reconciled itself to that 'abandonment', nor for a moment admitted 'hopelessness'. In this respect it was at one with the pre-modern, theologically inclined occultation. Modern 'disenchantment' was partial at all times: decrying and disavowing old strategies and jaded generals, yet extolling the potency of the younger officers who took their place, the need for strategy and the promise that the right strategy will be eventually produced. The priests of science replaced the priests of God; the progress-guided society was to achieve what the pre-ordained society failed to do. Doubts as to the ultimate success were recast as the critique of the imperfect past. The weaknesses and errors of yesterday would be undone under the new management – and the priests of the progressive movement differed from the priests of eternal God in their continuous self-renewing. The modern critique was incomplete unless leading to the 'positive' programme; only a 'positive' critique was acceptable; however fearful and shocking, the critique had to point toward a happy end. The modern critique drew its energy and its legitimation from the unshaken belief that a 'solution' can be found, that a 'positive' programme is certainly possible and most certainly imperative. In retrospect, the lauded modern disenchantment seems more like passing the baton in the relay race of magicians. The modern disenchantment came in a package-deal that contained a new, fully operative enchantment kit.

The magic formulae were now History and Reason: Reason of History, or History as the work of Reason, or History as the process of self-purification of Reason, of Reason coming through History into its own. In such formulae, Reason and History were Siamese twins, not to be cut apart. Reason came as History, as the perpetual not-yet, as the *elsewhere* of any place and the *some other time* of any moment. 'Reason' was a curious noun, behaving like a verb and always used in the future tense – and the purpose-minded present was expected to surrender to Reason as it drew its meaning from the purpose it was meant to achieve, from the project it served. Reason-about-to-rule lent meaning to the present, which was to partake in the time-binding, future-controlling effort. Modern narrative, in Jean-François Lyotard's words, sought its legitimation 'in a future it was to make to come, that is in an idea to be implemented'. The immortality of hope seemed to have been assured by the inextinguishable tension between the future, always not-yet-reached, and the present, forever bringing it closer: the tension between 'the particularity, the contingency, the opacity of the present, and universality, self-determination, transparency of the future it promised'.[8]

Modernity was an incessant effort to fix the goals: to bind the self-same future that lent the effort its meaning. It was an effort to make sure that in the end it would be proven that it had not been in vain; to force the legitimation in advance to confirm itself *ex post facto*. Unlike the old, pre-modern, theological rendition of self-occultation, the modern version could take change and uncertainty and contingency in its stride: it wrapped in the cloud of meaning not just *what is and must be*, but also *what is about to vanish* and thus could not be made sense of if not for the fact that the site has been cleared by its disappearance. The sense that modernity wove to cover up the groundlessness of being, also of modern being, was that of *creative destruction*.

'Given the spectacle of their teeming successes', says Cioran,

> the nations of the West had no trouble exalting history, attributing to it a meaning and a finality. It belonged to them, they were its agents: hence it must take a rational course . . . Consequently they placed it under the patronage, by turns, of Providence, of Reason, and of Progress.[9]

The local law of Western civilization that called itself modernity could be articulated as universal and *felt* like universal thanks to the universality of the embrace in which the West squeezed the rest of the human globe: it was the globality of their domination that allowed Europeans to project '*their* civilization, *their* history, *their* knowledge

---

[8] Jean-François Lyotard, *Le Postmoderne expliqué aux enfants: Correspondance 1982–1985* (Paris: Galilée, 1988), pp. 36, 47. In contrast, says Lyotard, 'postmodernity is the end of the people-king of histories' (p. 39).

[9] Cioran, *The Temptation to Exist*, pp. 48–9. If 'a definition is always the cornerstone of a temple', 'the god in whose name one no longer kills is dead indeed' (E. M. Cioran, *A Short History of Decay*, trans. Richard Howard (London: Quartet Books, 1990), pp. 18, 172). When a civilization stops defining, erecting temples, killing in the name of a god, and reverts to defensive battles – when 'Life becomes its sole obsession' instead of being a means of realizing the values the civilization had committed itself to serve – the era of decline is entered (p. 111). It happens when the sense of fatality dawns; nothing can be done to improve the world as a whole, 'no more collective crusades, no more citizens, but wan and disabused individuals' who 'abandon themselves now to a frenzy of small claims' (*The Temptation to Exist*, p. 49). The fruit cannot be made juicier; there is no certainty that juice will be flowing tomorrow; let everybody do their best to squeeze the fruit to the last drop. Such a sense of fatality, complete with its 'everyone for himself' consequences, descends upon civilizations to which, one may say, history 'belongs' no more.

as civilization, history and knowledge *überhaupt'*.[10] Perspectives from which perceptions are made are fixed by the power differential. The object of perception is as feeble and accidental as the power to change it or move it out of the way is overwhelming. From the pinnacle, the objects at the bottom of the hierarchy look minuscule. To the gun-wielding pioneers colonizing America, Australia or New Zealand the land they took possession of must have seemed empty: a zero-point of history, a site for a fresh start and a new beginning.

The specifically modern form of self-occultation was the perception of the world as a frontier; modernity is, first and foremost, a *frontier civilization*. It can survive only as long as some frontier is still left as a site for the promised, hoped for, beginning; or, rather, as long as the world allows itself to be perceived – and, above all, treated – as a frontier. 'The West', says Castoriadis, 'is a slave to the idea of absolute freedom', understood as 'pure arbitrariness (Willkür)', 'absolute void' yet to be filled with qualities.[11] Whatever can be done, must be done. It is *the ability to act*, not the action itself, that counts in the first place. The content of action, the purpose of action, the consequences of action are all derivative, secondary.

Modern existence is only ostensibly purpose-oriented. What truly matters is the self-confidence derived from 'having the means' – since it is the trust that one can go on trying (that no failure is definite) which feeds the 'History is the progress of Reason' type of self-occultation. Thus, contrary to its self-awareness and/or self-aggrandizing propaganda, modern civilization is and always has been not *action*-oriented, but *ability-to-act*-oriented. That ability, though, was the joint product of the tools one can muster and the resistance of the raw material (that is, the unreadiness of the stuff to be treated as raw material): of the power differential, in short. It is reasonable to suppose that the flattening out of the power differential between the West and the rest was among the principal reasons of the history-, progress-, project-oriented version of self-occultation running out of steam; of the crisis of modernity; of the advent of postmodernity; of the growing willingness to admit that not only is Being underpinned by Chaos and Absurdity rather than preordained Order and Meaning, but it is going to stay that way for the duration, and nothing we can do will change it.

---

[10] David E. Klemm, 'Two Ways of Avoiding Tragedy', in *Postmodernism, Literature and the Future of Theology*, ed. David Jasper (New York: St Martin's Press, 1993), p. 19.
[11] Cornelius Castoriadis, *Philosophy, Politics, Autonomy: Essays in Political Philosophy*, ed. David Ames Curtis (Oxford University Press, 1991), pp. 196–7.

The veil pierced

Modernity once deemed itself *universal*. It now thinks of itself instead as *global*. Behind the change of terms hides a watershed in the history of modern self-awareness and self-confidence. Universal was to be the rule of reason – the order of things that would replace slavery to passions with the autonomy of rational beings, superstition and ignorance with truth, tribulations of the drifting plankton with self-made and thoroughly monitored history-by-design. 'Globality', in contrast, means merely that everyone everywhere may feed on McDonald's burgers and watch the latest made-for-TV docudrama. Universality was a proud project, a herculean mission to perform. Globality, in contrast, is a meek acquiescence to what is happening 'out there'; an admission always tinged with the bitterness of capitulation even if sweetened with an 'if you can't beat them, join them' self-consoling exhortation. Universality was a feather in philosophers' caps. Globality exiles the philosophers, naked, back into the wilderness from which universality promised to emancipate them. In David E. Klemm's words:

> [A] law is built into the competitive system of global economy, which ends up making the philosophical discourse quite irrelevant: maximise economic benefits. This law plays the role of norm for directing and constraining action, not by appealing to truth but by determining actual outcomes of life. The law itself selects the successful from the failures, along the lines of a kind of economic Darwinism. The appeal to truth cannot challenge the law . . .[12]

In other words, it does not matter much now what philosophers say or do not say, however strongly they would wish the opposite to be the case; and however stubbornly they insist, from Hegel to Habermas, that history and modernity, and above all history progressing/maturing to its modern stage, is a *philosophical* problem – a task *waiting* (even if, like Habermas believes, it does not know or would not admit that) for philosophical adjudication. Chaos and contingency, which were to be chased away beyond the borders of societal islands of rational order, are back with a vengeance; they rule inside what was meant and hoped to be the safe house of Reason, managed by the legislated laws, not the law of nature; and when contingency rules, the sages are demoted from the high table of history-makers to the menial jobs of court chroniclers. To add bafflement to humiliation, it is not at all clear that the high table itself has survived the shift from universality to globalization (or, rather, the unmasking

---

[12] Klemm, 'Two ways of Avoiding Tragedy', pp. 18–9.

of universality as globalization; or debasing the *project* of universality as the *practice* of globalization). Society does not pretend any more to be a shield against contingency; in the absence of powers strong and wilful enough to attempt the taming of the wild beast of spontaneity, society itself turns into the site of chaos – the battlefield and/or grazing ground for the herds each pursuing its own route, though they are all in the same search for food and a secure home. Chronology replaces history, 'development' takes the place of progress, contingency takes over from the logic of plan that was never to be. It is not the philosophers who failed to place the groundless and contingent being on secure foundations; it is rather that the building gear has been snatched from their hands, not in order to be given to others, less deserving and trustworthy, but to join the dreams of universal reason in the dustbin of dashed hopes and unkept promises.

The demotion of legislators would have provoked political anger; the dismantling of the legislative process breeds philosophical despair. It is not just that the hoped-for lasting marriage between truth and power ended up in divorce; much worse than that, the philosophers' truth ran short of eligible bachelors to be married to; there seems to be no escape from spinsterhood. Simply, there are no powers in sight eager to don the 'enlightened despot' mantle sewn by the philosophers for truth's bridegroom, however desperately one may seek them or sniff them out in the tribal chiefs – today's rebels, yet unmasked as tomorrow's petty tyrants. (For those who display the latter inclination, Cioran has the following warning: 'a definition is always the cornerstone of a temple'; all 'fiery eyes presage slaughter'; 'the man who proposes a new faith is persecuted, until it is his turn to become a persecutor: truth begins by a conflict with the police and ends by calling them in'.)[13] The postmodernist (as distinct from postmodern) discourse of philosophers in the grip of legislative nostalgia follows faithfully the agenda of all narratives of frustration. Expectedly, it is the carriers of the news who are blamed with venom, while the news itself is strenuously rebutted or disdainfully dismissed.

In doing so, philosophers blame reality for not rising to the standard of guided rationality they set as the horizon of progressive history. What has in fact happened is that the processes set afoot with the advent of modernity, mistaken for a progress towards co-ordinated and/or guided (universal) rationality, gave birth to the multitude of uncoordinated and self-guided (local, parochial) rationalities which turned into the principal obstacle to universal rational order. At the far end of the modern saga looms Ulrich Beck's 'risk society', which can hope, at best, that some local, and globally risky, initiatives will

[13] Cioran, *A Short History of Decay*, pp. 18, 4, 74.

be undertaken in time to limit the harm left by yesterday's local, globally damaging, undertakings.

The 'sour grapes' feeling reverberates in the often voiced opinion that our present age is afflicted and enfeebled by the petering out of the ability of 'forward thinking', and in particular by the waning of utopias. One wonders, though, whether the diagnosis is correct; whether it is not the fading of a certain *kind* of utopia that is bewailed here, concealed in the overly generalized proposition. Postmodernity is modern enough to live by hope. It has lost little of modernity's boisterous optimism (though philosophers are unlikely to partake of it; they find too few crumbs under the festive table – not much room has been left for *their* type of skills and credentials in the specifically postmodern vision of 'new and improved' future). Postmodernity has its own utopias, though one may be excused for failing to recognize in them what one has been trained to seek and find in the utopias that spurred and whipped the modern impatience with the forever imperfect realities of the present.

Joe Bailey describes well the two mutually complementary postmodern utopias: that of the wondrous healing capacity of the free market, and that of the infinite capacity of the 'technological fix'. The first, neo-liberal utopia visualizes the paradise of the fully liberated, deregulated market competition which unfailingly finds the shortest and cheapest way to riches and happiness.

> Basically society is seen as a *natural* order in which satisfactory social institutions arise unintentionally. Interference, conscious design via planning and 'politicization' of social provision are all seen as dangerous disruptions of a spontaneous social order.

The second, technological, utopia

> states that social, political and even moral problems of society are susceptible to a technical solution, that progress in all spheres is only guaranteed by technological change and that the society in which we now live is accelerating into new qualitative improvements through technological development.

Bailey concludes:

> These are prominent, and, I would suggest, powerful new utopias which project an optimism into public discourse. More, they dominate and colonise optimism.[14]

[14] See Joe Bailey, *Pessimism* (London: Routledge, 1988), pp. 73, 75, 76.

Postmodern utopias are anarchistic – only seldom anarcho-syndicalistic. They envisage a world with rights, without duties, and above all without rulers and *gens d'armes*, except such as are needed to guarantee a secure promenade stroll and protect shopping bags against the muggers. They put their trust in the wisdom of absent reason. They militate against design and plan, against sacrifice in the name of future benefits, against the delay of gratification – all these rules-of-thumb of yore deemed effective thanks to the belief that the future can be controlled, bound, forced to conform to the likeness painted in advance, and hence what one does now matters for later – is 'pregnant with consequences'. Postmodern wisdom recognizes only one planning, of the type called 'family planning' (so called perversely and duplicitously, in truly Newspeak style, as its essence consists precisely in preventing families from being created) – one preoccupied with the *prevention* of 'pregnancy', with the cleansing of acts from consequences – as if the new axiom was the exact reversal of the old one: namely, that instead of actors binding the future, it is the future which binds and constrains and oppresses the actors. The spontaneity of the world which postmodern utopias conjure up makes nonsense of all concern with the future except the concern with being free from concern with the future – and able to act, accordingly, in an unconcerned fashion.

The chaos and contingency which modernity spent two centuries to occlude out of the business of life is not just back in the field of vision, but appears there (perhaps for the first time so blatantly, and for so many viewers) naked, without cover or adornment, and without shame that would prompt it to seek clothing. Groundlessness is no more the guilty, shameful secret of being for which society tried its best to repent and atone. It is hailed instead as the beauty and joy of being, as the sole ground of real freedom. Postmodernity means dismantling, splitting up and deregulating the agencies charged in the modern era with the task of pulling humans, jointly and individually, to their ideal state – that of rationality and perfection, of rational perfection and perfect rationality. Postmodern utopias want us to rejoice in that dismantling, to celebrate the surrender of (demanding, stretching, vexing) ideals as the final act of emancipation.

It is not at all clear how the cause of morality, goodness, justice can be seriously promoted in a world which has seemingly come to terms with its own groundlessness, does not seem to mind it any more and is little perturbed by the absence of agencies charged with the task of keeping Chaos at bay. No wonder ethical philosophy is losing its nerve, and prefers to stay inside the enchanted circle of the learned commentaries on ancient texts to its traditional, but now

increasingly adventurous and unpopular, business of ethical legislation and adjudication. Having taken a good look at the current
intellectual preoccupation on both the left and the right of the political spectrum, Castoriadis found an 'appalling ideological regression
among the *literati*'.

Defining and legislating is always, overtly or indirectly, a critique
of the extant reality – and the present reluctance to do either coin-
cides, not by chance, with almost total extinction of critical thought
– indeed of the ability to imagine, let alone suggest, a type of society
different from the one seemingly left today without a plausible and
viable alternative. 'The present period is thus best defined as the
general retreat into conformism' – concludes Castoriadis, with sad-
ness and anger; but even he, demanding an injection of new life into
the fast wilting project of social and individual autonomy, ends up
with an observation not much different from the opinion blamed
(and with good reason) for the numbness and ideological impoverishment of present-day literati: 'New political objectives and new
human attitudes are required, of which, for the time being, there are
but few signs.'[15]

The veil torn up

Even if it is responsible for the 'bad press' presently blighting and
crippling all determined ethical commitment, the widespread and
prospectless blindness to an alternative seems more a symptom than
the cause of ethical weariness and caution. The reticence of ethical
arbitration seems to stem from genuine uncertainty as to the merits
of the 'Chaosgate' operation in the specifically modern form in
which it has previously been conducted. While certainly successful in
establishing numerous local islands of order, that operation neither

[15] Cornelius Castoriadis, 'The Retreat from Autonomy: Post-modernism as
Generalized Conformity', in *Thesis Eleven*, no. 31 (1992). In Castoriadis's view,
as long as the alternative attitudes do not show, 'it would be absurd to try to
decide if we are living through a long parenthesis, or if we are witnessing the
beginning of the end of Western history as a history essentially linked with the
project of autonomy and codetermined by it'. This intellectual indecision is,
however, precisely what makes many a commentator condemned by Castoriadis
so reticent of commitment. One can comment that legislating for reality without reality stretching itself towards what is being legislated for it would not
necessarily augur well for the 'project of autonomy' and might not usher in the
kind of alternative society Castoriadis has in mind.

managed to keep chaos out of bounds (or out of mind, for that matter) nor did it secure the hoped-for 'ethical progress'. On reflection, the medicine looks no more (if not less) prepossessing than the ailment it was meant to heal. 'The general progress of mankind', both in the sense of effective control over the elemental, contingent and potentially disastrous, and in the sense of growing social and individual autonomy, simply failed to arrive – while the effort to bring it about bore quite a few poisonous fruits. The question by which any reflective mind must be haunted is whether the effort *could* bring other than poisonous fruits. Until there is a plausible answer to that question, it is not immediately obvious that 'ideological regression' is a matter of betrayal or cowardice, rather than prudence and a sense of responsibility. As Jean-François Lyotard put it,

> after these two last centuries we have become more sensitive to the signs which imply an opposite [to progress] movement. Neither liberalism, economic or political, nor the diverse forms of Marxism emerged from those gory centuries without incurring a charge of crimes against humanity.

Two doubts more than anything else sap the ethical confidence and self-righteousness of the West.

The first is the suspicion, stubbornly refusing to be dispelled, that Auschwitz and the Gulag (much as the later, and quite recent, resurgence of the resentment of strangers, in its many forms – ranging from ethnic cleansing, through surreptitiously rejoiced assaults on foreigners, and up to the publicly applauded 'new and improved' anti-immigration and nationality laws) were legitimate products, rather than aberrations, of the typically modern practice of 'ordering by decree'; that the other face of 'universalization' is divisiveness, oppression and a leap toward domination, while the allegedly 'universal' foundations all too often serve as masks of intolerance to otherness and licences for the smothering of the alterity of the Other; that, in other words, the price of the project of humanization is more inhumanity. The tentacles of this doubt reach deep – in fact to the very heart of the modern project. What is being questioned is whether the wedlock between the growth of rational control and the growth of social and personal autonomy, that crux of modern strategy, was not ill-conceived from the start, and whether it can ever be consummated.

The second doubt is similarly fundamental; it concerns another essential assumption of the modern project: that modernity is an intrinsically universal civilization, indeed the first civilization in the long tormented history of mankind which is fit for global application.

The corollary of that belief was the self-portrayal of the modern part of the world as 'advanced' – as a sort of avant-garde which blazes the trail for the rest of mankind to follow; the ruthless eradication of 'pre-modern' ways of life at the most distant corners of the globe could be then seen as an overture to a truly global unity of equal partners, a sort of Kantian *civitas gentium*, guided by *jus cosmopoliticum* – a federation of free peoples pursuing the same values and sharing in the same ethical principles. None of these closely correlated creeds passed the test of time with flying colours. The signals are multiplying that far from being endemically universal, modern civilization is eminently unsuitable for universal application; that to remain buoyant in some places it must devastate and impoverish other localities – and that it may well run out of steam once it runs short of localities on which to dump the waste-products of order-building and chaos-conquering at home. To quote Lyotard again:

> humanity is divided into two parts. One confronts the challenge of com-plexity, the other confronts the ancient, terrible challenge of survival. This is perhaps the principal aspect of the failure of the modern project . . .
>   It is not the absence of progress, but on the contrary the development – techno-scientific, artistic, economic, political – which made possible the total wars, totalitarianisms, the widening gap between the riches of the North and poverty of the South, unemployment and the 'new poor' . . .

Lyotard's conclusion is blunt and damning: 'it has become impossible to legitimize development by the promise of the emancipation of humanity in its totality.'[16] Yet it was exactly that 'emancipation' – from want, 'low standards of life', paucity of needs, doing what the community has done rather than 'being able' to do whatever one may still wish in the future ('able' in excess of present wishes) – that loomed vaguely behind Harry Truman's 1947 declaration of war on 'underdevelopment'. Since then, unspeakable sufferings have been visited upon the extant 'earth economies' of the world in the name of happiness, identified now with the 'developed', that is modern, way of life. Their delicately balanced livelihood which could not survive the condemnation of simplicity, frugality, acceptance of human limits and respect for non-human forms of life, now lies in ruin, yet no viable, locally realistic alternative is in sight. The victims of 'development' – the true Giddensian juggernaut which crushes everything and everybody that happens to stand in its way – 'shunned by the advanced sector and cut off from the old ways . . . are

[16]   Lyotard, *Le Postmoderne expliqué aux enfants*, pp. 116, 118, 124, 141.

expatriates in their own countries.'[17] Wherever the juggernaut has passed, know-how vanishes, to be replaced by a dearth of skills; commodified *labour* appears where *men and women* once lived; tradition becomes an awkward ballast and a costly burden; common utilities turn into under-used resources, wisdom into prejudice, wise men into bearers of superstitions. Not that the juggernaut moves of its own accord only, aided and abetted by the crowds of its future victims eager to be crushed (though this is also the case; on many occasions one would be tempted to speak of a Moloch, rather than a juggernaut – that stone deity with a pyre in its belly, into which the self-selected victims jumped with joy, singing and dancing); it is also, once started, pushed from behind, surreptitiously yet relentlessly, by uncounted multitudes of experts, engineers, contractors, merchants of seeds, fertilizers, pesticides, tools and motors, scientists of research institutes and native as well as cosmopolitan politicians in search of prestige and glory. Thus, the juggernaut seems unstoppable, and the impression of unstoppability makes it yet more unstoppable. From this 'development', 'naturalized' into something very close to a 'law of nature' by the modern part of the globe desperately searching for new supplies of virgin blood it needs in order to stay alive and fit, there seems to be no escape. But what is that 'development' developing?

One may say that the most conspicuously 'developing' under 'development' is the distance between what men and women make and what they need to appropriate and use in order to stay alive (however the 'staying alive' may translate under the circumstances). Most obviously, 'development' develops the dependency of men and women on things and events they can neither produce, control, see nor understand. Other humans' deeds send long waves which, when they reach the doorsteps, look strikingly like floods and other natural disasters; like them they come from nowhere, unannounced, and like them they make a mockery of foresight, cunning and prudence. However sincerely the planners may believe that they are, or at least can be, in control, and however strongly they believe that they see order in the flow of things – for the victims (the 'objects' of development) the change opens up the floodgates through which chaos

[17] See Wolfgang Sachs's Introduction in *The Development Dictionary: A Guide to Knowledge as Power*, ed. Wolfgang Sachs (London, 1992). See also particularly the entries by Gustavo Esteva, Vandana Shiva, Majid Rahnema, Gerald Berthaud and Ivan Illich in this remarkable, passionate yet closely argued book. See also the perceptive discussion of the book (Walter Schwarz 'Beware the Rich Bearing Gifts') in *The Guardian*, 11 July 1992.

and contingency pour into their, once orderly, lives. They feel lost now where once they felt at home. For the planners a disenchantment – for them enchantment; a mind-boggling mystery now wrapping tightly the once homely, transparent and familiar world. Now they do not know how to go on; and they do not trust their feet – not steady enough to hold to the shifting and wobbly ground. They need props – guides, experts, instructors, givers of commands.

This is not, though, what is understood as 'development' in economic and political narratives. There, development is measured by the volume of products consumed – by the scope of effective demand for goods and services. As far as economic science and political practice are concerned, development occurs when that scope increases. In a characteristically pleonastic reasoning, this is represented as progress in the satisfaction of needs (as Robert E. Lane of Yale University points out, for orthodox economists 'satisfaction with something is revealed by the very fact that it was bought, regardless of the joy or sorrow that something may bring or of alternative uses of a person's time and effort outside the market'[18] – so that it goes without saying that people buy what they need and that they buy it *because* they need it); a reasoning which glosses over the vast problem of the offer preceding demand and commodities 'buying' their own prospective customers, of the wants being industrial products in the same way as are the marketed goods deemed to satisfy them. The unspoken premise which makes the above equation credible – even 'evident' – is that happiness comes in the wake of the satisfaction of desires (a belief with strong commonsensical roots, in spite of being repeatedly discredited by a chain of eminent thinkers from Schopenhauer to Freud). The conclusion of this quasi-syllogism, based on one tautological and one false premise, is that development is necessary and desirable and ethically correct because it increases the volume of human happiness; while in another bout of circular reasoning that conclusion is over and over again corroborated by the statistics of increased income and volume of trade in the 'developed' part of the world.

Surveying the available findings about the level of life-satisfaction as perceived and defined by those supposed to be satisfied, Robert Lane comes to a conclusion jarringly at odds with the orthodox economic wisdom:

> Studies in advanced economies show, as one would expect, that for every thousand pounds increase in income there is, indeed, an increased sense of

---

[18]   Robert E. Lane, 'Why Riches Don't Always Buy Happiness', in *The Guardian*, 9 August 1993.

well-being – but only for the poorest fifth of the population. Beyond that, there is almost no increase in people's satisfaction with their lives as income levels increase . . . [I]n the US and England there is only a trivial and erratic relationship. The rich are no happier than the middle classes and the upper middle class is no happier than the lower middle class. Beyond poverty and near-poverty levels of income, if money buys happiness, it buys very little and often it buys none at all.

Increased income adds happiness to life only among those who are in poverty; but, as all statistics show, it is precisely people in poverty who may expect little income increase as the result of 'development'; if anything, their ranks grow, and their relative share in the old and new riches falls. (And let us note first of all that it is 'development' itself that recasts frugal existence as 'material deprivation', thus producing, rather than resolving, the socio-psychological 'problem of poverty' in the form deployed in its self-legitimation.) Those whose happiness may increase thanks to a greater income have the least chance of expanding their gains, while whose who do earn more (and spend more) fail to notice that their well-being improves . . .

And finally, there is the 'snake eating its tail' phenomenon, more visible by the day as the growth so buoyant during post-war reconstruction grinds to a halt, and yesteryear magnanimity is fast translated from the language of ethics into that of economics and redefined as 'counter-productive'. One can expect the grand vision of the worldwide development – of making *everybody* modern and happy – to sink without trace in the quicksands of local protectionisms, in the universal scramble for a greater share of vagrant capital, and national governments' efforts to steal other peoples' jobs and dump abroad home unemployment. On all accounts, little is left to galvanize the old creed of emancipation-through-development and to keep alive the old hope that at the far end of the development saga an orderly, rationally designed and managed world awaits.

Morality uncovered

Modernity knew where it was going and was determined to get there. The modern mind knew where it wished to arrive and knew what it needed to do to find out how to get there. If modernity was obsessed with self-legislating and the modern mind was a legislative mind, it was not for its cupidity or imperial appetites, but arrogance and self-confidence. Global imperialism and unbounded voraciousness were but the pragmatic reflections of the mind-boggling task of conjuring up an order where chaos ruled, and to do it by its own efforts, with no external help and no guarantee of success other than its own determination. That task called for cool heads and powerful hands. Much needed to be destroyed on the way, but that *destruction was creative*. Ruthlessness was needed to pursue and reach the goal, but the loftiness of the goal made mercy into a crime and unscrupulousness into humanitarianism. The shining prospect of health required medicine to be bitter, the dazzling project of universal freedom called for close surveillance and strict rules. The radiant vision of the rule of reason forbade trust in the rational powers of those destined to bask in its benevolence.

One may say that legislative obsession is the feature of all civilizations ('this was a world that had been civilised for centuries, had a thousand paths and roads' – wrote Michael Ondaatje in *The English Patient*, meaning that one can recognize a civilization by travellers following laid tracks rather than blazing their own trails, and by tracks having been laid for them to be followed), but only modernity recognized *itself* as civilization, called itself that name and made a consciously embraced destiny out of its discovered fate (and only retrospectively construed others as inferior variants of itself, thus presenting its own particularity as universal modality – much like the education-obsessed pedagogues of the Enlightenment appointed old wives and parish priests their predecessors in the history of the teaching profession). Modernity defined itself as *civilization* – that is as an effort to tame the elements, and create a world that would not be like that if not for the work of creation: an artificial world, an art-work world, a world which like any work of art must seek and build and defend and protect its own foundations. Unlike other civilizations, modernity legislated itself into legislation – legislation as a vocation and duty and as the matter of survival.

Law stood between order and chaos, human existence and animal free-for-all, the habitable and the uninhabitable world, meaning and meaninglessness. Law was for everybody and for everything: also for everything anybody may do to anybody else. The incessant search for ethical principles was a part (an expectable part, an inexorable part) of legislative frenzy. People had to be told of their *duty* to do good and that doing their duty is goodness. And people needed to be prevailed upon to follow that line of duty, which without being taught or goaded or coerced they would hardly do. Modernity was, and had to be, *the Age of Ethics* – it would not be modernity otherwise. Just as the law preceded all order, ethics must precede all morality. Morality was a *product* of ethics; ethical principles were the means of production; ethical philosophy was the technology, and ethical preaching was the pragmatics of moral industry; good was its planned yield, evil its waste or sub-standard produce.

If ordering and creation were the battle-cries of modernity, de-regulation and recycling became the catchwords of postmodernity. Meditations on Nietzschean 'eternal return' came to fill the blank pages of the guidebooks from which the story of progress had been deleted. We are still going, but we no longer know where; we cannot be sure whether we move in a straight line or run in a circle. 'Forward' and 'backward' lost much of their meaning, unless they apply to short trips and confined spaces where the curvature of time-space can be for a moment forgotten. The new is but a recycling of the old, the old is awaiting resurrection and dusting-off to become new. (As I tried to show in *Mortality, Immortality, and Other Life Strategies*, there is no mortality – not 'ultimate death', not in the sense of once-for-allness, of no return, of irrevocability; there is just the disappearing act, the temporary falling into oblivion – being forgotten, which means being put in cold storage to be reclaimed when need be. But without mortality there is no immortality either, not in the sense of the 'forever and ever', of permanence, of no aging nor falling into obsolescence – only an instant immortality, immortality *for an instant*, as given to the vagaries of fate as mortality once was. And so there is little to earn, gain, win – nothing to spur into the effort of master-ing the fate, conquering the blight, preserving the ephemeric, making the transitional durable. Mortality cannot become revocable without rendering immortality revocable as well.) History falls apart; once more, as before the dawn of modernity, it reminds one of a string of events, rather than of a 'building up', cumulative process. Things *happen*, instead of following and binding each other. Yet unlike in pre-modern times, there is no superior mind or higher force to *make* them happen, to deputize for the absent bonds.

In the time-space of episodes and localities *phronesis*, the practical know-how, the skill to tackle things within reach, takes over from objective truth and rock-steady principles; concern with the ability to move on replaces the worry about foundations; and rules of thumb put paid to universal principles. In that time-space, any but until-further-notice and within-these-limits legislation is vanity (and total-itarian nightmare). And so there is no room left for ethical legisla-tion, except inside the nostalgia-soaked hideaways of academia.

For everybody who is used to consider morality as the end-prod-uct of ethical industry (that is, for all of us, habituated to think of morality in such a way), the end of the Age of Ethics (that is, the age of *legislating for morality*) portends the end of morality. With the pro-duction lines phased-out, the supply of goods will surely dry up. In the wake of the world kept in bounds by God's commandment, and another one administered by Reason, here comes a world of men and women left to their own smartness and cunning. Men and women let loose . . . Loose men, loose women? Life, again, nasty, brutish and short?

This is what the fear-mongering age of legislation prepared us to expect. The strategy of order-building inevitably spawns a no-alternative, without-us-a-deluge policy. It is always *our* type of civilized life, or barbarism. A replacement for this order is total randomness, not another order. Out there is a jungle, and the jungle is frightening and *unliveable* because in the jungle *everything is allowed to happen*. But even that unspeakable horror of the free-for-all was represented by the fear-mongering propaganda of the civilized order as 'the *law* of the jungle'. In the age of built-up orders and of order-building, the entity most difficult, nay impossible, to contemplate was a world in which there was no 'order' – however spurious, contorted or perverse (just as it was difficult to imagine 'superstitions' without bad teachers, or dissent without ringleaders of rebellion). Today, however, we are confronting the unimaginable: not the questioning of one set of legislated principles in the name of another set – but the questioning of the very legislating of principles as such. A jungle deprived even of the jungle law . . . Morality without ethics . . . This is not just the prospect of replacing one morality with another; not even of promoting a wrong kind of morality, based on false principles, or on not-universalizable, backwoods or backwater principles. Ours is the unthinkable prospect of society *without* morality.

Legislators cannot imagine an orderly world without legislation; the ethical legislator or preacher cannot imagine a moral world without a legislated ethics. In their terms, they are right. Little wonder that it takes such an enormous effort to envisage the vocabulary in which to conceive of, articulate and discuss the moral issues of the post-ethical, post-legislative human condition; even less wonder that such an effort meets with vehement intellectual resistance.

And yet it is solely because of the modern promotion of 'no morality without ethical law' principle that *the world without ethics* seems to be necessarily self-evidently *a world without morality*. But try to shake off the mental sediments of that promotion, delete the identity mark forced between morality and the ethically legislated morality – and it may well occur to you that with the demise of effective ethical legislation morality does not vanish, but, on the contrary, comes into its own. It may well be that the power-assisted ethical law, far from being the solid frame which protected the wobbly flesh of moral standards from falling apart, was a stiff cage that prevented those standards from stretching to their true size and passing the ultimate test of both ethics and morality – that of guiding and sustaining inter-human togetherness. It may well be that once that frame has fallen apart, the contents it was meant to embrace and contain will not dissipate, but on the contrary gain in solidity, having now nothing to rely on but their own inner strength. It may well be that with attention and authority no more diverted to the concerns with ethical legislation, men and women will be free – and obliged – to face point-blank the reality of their own moral autonomy – and that means also of their own non-get-riddable, inalienable moral responsibility. It may happen (just may) that in the same way as modernity went down in history as *the age of ethics*, the coming post-modern era will come to be recorded as *the age of morality* . . .

Ethical laws, moral standards

Whatever passes as 'good' or 'bad', explained Friedrich Nietzsche, has something to do with hierarchy, superiority and inferiority, domination and rule. There is no 'natural', intrinsic relationship between certain conduct and goodness (for instance, 'there is no *a priori* necessity for associating the word *good* with altruistic deeds'); the link needs to be decreed first to be seen. And those who have the power to decree and make the decree hold – do:

> the judgment *good* does not originate with those to whom the good has been done. Rather it was the 'good' themselves, that is to say the noble, mighty, highly placed, and high minded who decreed themselves and their actions to be good, i.e., belonging to the highest rank, in contradistinction to all that was base, low-minded and plebeian. It was only the *pathos of distance* that authorised them to create values and name them . . .
>   The basic concept is always *noble* in the hierarchical, class sense, and from this has developed, by historical necessity, the concept *good* embracing nobility of mind, spiritual distinction. The development is strictly parallel to that other which eventually converted the notions *common, plebeian, base* into the notion *bad*.[19]

[19] Friedrich Nietzsche, *The Genealogy of Morals*, trans. Francis Golffing (New York: Doubleday, 1956), pp. 160, 162, 171. The happy-go-lucky spontaneity of aristocratic self-confirmation makes even the contempt for the common, its other and less prepossessing face, benign and but half-serious: 'There is in all contempt too much casualness and nonchalance, too much blinking of facts and impatience, and too much inborn gaiety for it ever to make of its object a downright caricature and monster . . . They did not have to construct their happiness factitiously by looking at their enemies, as all rancorous men are wont to do.' (pp. 171–2)

One may say that Nietzsche's portrayal of the primeval (in his
view 'natural', inborn, undistorted)[20] aristocratic vision of good and
bad is one of morality without ethics, spontaneity of goodness and
goodness of spontaneity that resent and shake off all codification by
rules . . . But freedom of the noble is, let us observe, un-freedom of
the common; spontaneity of the high and mighty reverberates as
alien, uncontrolled fate of the low and powerless. No wonder that
the counter-morality of the 'humble and base' appeals to rules: it
cries for the rules, constraining rules, hand-binding rules – rules whose
coercive might would make up for the impotence of the dominated.
Nietzsche sniffs out in all rule-bound morality, in all ethics, a conspiracy of the slaves. It was, says Nietzsche, the rancour of resentful,
jealous yet impotent slaves that challenged and in the end sapped the
aristocratic equation between good, noble, powerful, beautiful, happy
and favoured-of-the-gods, and pushed through the contrary idea that
'only the poor, the powerless, are good; only the suffering, sick, and
ugly, truly blessed'. It is just the weak, the ordinary, the untalented,
the impotent, who invented rule-guided morality and go on using it
as a battering ram against the true morality of the noble.[21]

Nietzsche identifies all ethics – all rule-bound morality – with the
lowly and the downtrodden, since he conceives of their polar opposite, the aristocracy of will and spirit, as having no use for rules;
Nietzsche's aristocracy asserts itself, it becomes itself – the nobility
that it is – through disregard and disdainful rejection of the levelling-
up pressure of the 'norm'. It was, though, the aristocracy of fenced
manors and walled castles that served Nietzsche as the prototype for
his model of nobility: cut off from the *hoi polloi* in life and thought,

[20] Friedrich Nietzsche, *Twilight of the Idols*, trans. R. J. Hollingdale
(Harmondsworth: Penguin, 1968). '[E]ven when the moralist merely turns to
the individual and says to him: "*You* ought to be thus and thus" he does not
cease to make himself ridiculous. The individual is, in his future and in his past,
a piece of fate, one law more, one necessity more for everything that is and
everything that will be.' (p. 46)

[21] Nietzsche's is not an impartial analysis of ethical history, of course. His
purpose is partisan, guided by the commitment to the salvage from ruin of what
he considers to be the original, pristine, aristocratic self-assertion that loftily
dismisses all critique of itself as a vulgar and dastardly expression of *ressentiment*.
To the readers of *The Anti-Christ*, Nietzsche had the following advice to give:
'One must be superior to mankind in force, in *loftiness* of soul – in contempt . . .'
And the following summary of his own positive morality: 'What is good? – All
that heightens the feeling of power, the will to power, power itself in man.
What is bad? – All that proceeds from weakness. What is happiness? – The
feeling that power *increases* – that a resistance is overcome.' (*The Anti-Christ*, trans.
R. J. Hollingdale (Harmondsworth: Penguin, 1968), pp. 114–5)

infinitely remote and neither building nor needing to build bridges over the abyss that separated them, attending to no communication from the common and the base, nor feeling the need to communicate anything to them. Such aristocracy might have been, perhaps, able to construe freely its opposite as a pure projection of disengaged, carefree thought, not the object of practical engagement – and do it perfunctorily and unthinkingly without fear of the consequences of error.

Modern elites which replaced it did not have such advantage. From the start of the new era, they had been entangled and locked in the twists of the master–slave dialectics and thus dependent on the pliability of the 'masses' for their own privilege and mindful of the need to reassert that privilege so that the masses could go on casting them as their masters. Like the aristocracy of old, the modern elite were rulers – but unlike that aristocracy they had to be also teachers, guardians and wardens if they wished to sustain their rule. Their political and economic *domination* had to be endorsed by spiritual *hegemony*. Not for a single moment could they forget the presence of the masses; absent-mindedness or error of judgement could be costly, their consequences irreparable and in the end suicidal. The modern elite could not afford the genuine or putative playfulness, the child-like, self-centred and lighthearted gaiety of the Nietzschean elites. Their plight was not a game – not an adventure of free-roaming errant knights, nor the troubadour's poetic fantasies. Modern domi-nation was a no-joking, deadly serious matter. It was a full-time job, calling for high skills and constant concentration.

Whatever Nietzsche's aristocracy might have needed or done without, it was the elites, the dominant, which needed rules in times of modernity. Strict rules, preferably unambiguous rules, enforce-able rules, effective rules. They needed ethics – a code of rules for everyone and every life occasion; rules ubiquitous, reaching every nook and cranny of the dominated space, steering or arresting, as the case may require, every move of whoever inhabits that space. Noth-ing and nobody could be left alone, to itself, to chance. That much the dominant needed to secure in order to perpetuate their domination – to bind and control the dark forces emanating from unruly and erratic masses, to 'tame the beast', to hold in check the *mobile vulgus* or *les classes dangereuses*. To achieve all this, however, they needed a kind of law which would present the order of their domination – the order that is their domination and can be nothing else – not in terms of their own peculiarity, but in terms of the universality of the prin-ciples which make the dominant dominant and the dominated domi-nated, and oblige both to stay as they are. And so they needed an ethics well and truly grounded, universal or universalizable, and beckoning to the authority of Reason – that wondrous faculty like no other, that pronounces on the matter only once and recognizes no right to appeal.

It was the dominated who, on the contrary, felt no need of such rules. The dominated would hardly feel the inclination to account for their lives in terms of universal and principally arguable 'oughts'. It was always the case that the rules, framed by the dominant as postulates of Reason, would resurface at the dominated end as brutal force and 'blind necessity'. To the dominated it felt more like being buffeted, than swimming; pushed, rather than moving freely; 'having to', rather than choosing. The question whether there was a pattern in the series of the 'musts' and 'no choices', and the question of rationality or irrationality of that pattern, is, from the perspective of the dominated, a purely academic matter; and the dominated, notoriously, are not fond of, nor have time for, academic pastimes. Were the dominated to theorize the universe they live in, taking their own life experience as the starting-point and the benchmark, they would not end up with an elegant code of ethical principles and moral injunctions, but with a tangled mesh of irresistible forces and no-questions-asked inevitability.

It could well be an illusion of their appointed and self-appointed spiritual guides, that in the modern era, which happened to be as well the era of capitalism (and if not of capitalism, then of totalitarianism), 'the masses' chose, embraced, and *followed* 'values', so that their conduct could be explained by the fact of that choice. Such a view imputes to 'the masses' more freedom of manoeuvre than they ever had and could have. 'Ordinary' men and women endowed with 'ordinary' measures of resources and power seldom faced situations of genuine choice between values. As Joseph A. Schumpeter observed long ago,

> whether favourable or unfavourable, value judgments about capitalist performance are of little interest. For mankind is not free to choose. This is not only because the mass of people are not in a position to compare alternatives rationally and always accept what they are being told. There is a much deeper reason for it. Things economic and social move by their own momentum and the ensuing situations compel individuals and groups to behave in certain ways whatever they may wish to do – not indeed by destroying their freedom of choice but by shaping the choosing mentalities and by narrowing the list of possibilities from which to choose.[22]

[22] Joseph A. Schumpeter, *Capitalism, Socialism and Democracy* (London: George Allen & Unwin, 1976), pp. 129–30.

The collapse of ethical legislation, the event so horrifying for the philosophers, educators and preachers, may well have passed unnoticed for those many to whom life was all along a string of 'musts' rather than 'oughts', necessities rather than principles. Much like before, the many are more often pushed around than walking – and even if they walk, they aim where they expect the next push to goad them. Like before, they are seldom given time to sit down and ruminate about principles; survival is the name of the game, and the survival in question is as a rule survival till the next sunset or the one after next. Things are taken as they come, and forgotten as they go. For those many, ethical principles did not vanish; they were never there in the first place. The philosophers' loss of nerve and the cacophony of sermons and exhortations of the market-place that replaced the universal law of the philosophers make little change. People do not get less moral than before; they are now 'immoral' only in a kind of ethical/philosophical sense, which if applied to their real life practice would oblige one to describe them as 'immoral' also in the bygone era of high ethical hopes.

People sunk up to their ears in the daily struggle for survival were never able, nor felt a need, to codify their understanding of good and evil in the form of an ethical code. After all, principles are about the future – about how much that future should differ from the present. By their nature, principles fit well the emancipated, 'disembedded', 'unencumbered', self-constructing, self-improving modern individual, who got off his chest the banausic worries of being fed, shod and sheltered, and thus could dedicate his time to 'transcending' all that; principles are needed to (hopefully) prevent the transcendence from running out of hand. Survival, on the contrary, is essentially conservative. Its horizon is drawn with yesterday's paints; to stay alive today means not losing whatever it was that secured one's livelihood yesterday – and not much more than that. Survival is about things not getting worse than before.

What follows is that whatever moral judgements might be made by people overwhelmed by the task of survival, tend to be negative, rather than positive: they would take the form of condemnation, not exhortation, proscription rather than prescription. As Barrington Moore Jr. found out, the downtrodden throughout the ages were morally aroused by the experience of *injustice*, rather than any prospective model of justice with which they wished to replace the shape of quotidianity; and they experienced as unjust whatever was the *departure* from the oppression they faced daily and routinely, however severe and inhuman that 'habitualized' misery could be and how 'unjust' it could be proclaimed as being when sized up by some abstract 'objective' principles of decency; it was the crude reality of feudal exploitation which peasants rose to defend as their *Rechtsgewohnenheiten*. Moral outrage was prompted by driving the screw of oppression a turn or two further down, rather than by a disaffection with the daily level of oppression, unmasked, exposed and standing condemned by a forward-looking project of perfect justice.[23] On that view of 'popular morality' – which tends to refer to benchmarks rather than principles – Axel Honneth commented that it implies the need to seek the structure of popular morality through the manifested 'standards for moral condemnation':

> the social ethics of the suppressed masses contains no ideas of a total moral order or projections of a just society abstracted from particular situations, but is instead a highly sensitive sensorium for injuries to intuitively recognized moral claims . . . [T]he inner morality of the consciousness of social injustice can be grasped only indirectly on the basis of standards posed by the moral disapproval of social events and processes.[24]

If one is to trust the seminal discovery of Barrington Moore, popular morality at no time resembled the code of universal principles at which the true ethics, according to modern philosophy, ought to aim. It does not mean that 'the masses' were strangers to moral sentiments and moral sensitivity and had to be taught morality, or forced to be moral. It only means that whatever morality they might have had was by and large neither enhanced nor diminished by the expert efforts or the lack of efforts to install the heteronomous principles of the good/evil distinction.

Hence, let us repeat, the crisis of ethics does not necessarily augur a crisis of morality; even less obviously does the end of the 'era of ethics' herald the end of morality. A convincing case could be constructed on behalf of the opposite supposition: that the end of the 'ethical era' ushers in the 'era of morality' – and that postmodernity could be viewed as such an era. Not in the sense of necessarily producing more good and less evil than the principles-seeking and universality-promoting, ethically legislating modernity; not even in the sense of simplifying moral choices or making moral dilemmas less haunting; and certainly not in the sense of making the life of morality easier, facing odds less overwhelming and resilient than before. One

---

[23] See Barrington Moore Jr., *Injustice: The Social Basis of Obedience and Revolt* (London, George Allen & Unwin, 1979).
[24] Axel Honneth, 'Moral Consciousness and Class Domination: Some Problems in the Analysis of Hidden Morality', trans. Mitchell G. Ash, in *Praxis International*, April 1992.

might say that postmodernity is an 'era of morality' in one sense only: *thanks to the 'disocclusion'* – the dispersal of ethical clouds which tightly wrapped and obscured the reality of moral self and moral responsibility – *it is possible now, nay inevitable, to face the moral issues point-blank, in all their naked truth, as they emerge from the life experience of men and women, and as they confront moral selves in all their irreparable and irredeemable ambivalence.*

Paradoxically, it is only now that actions appear to the moral selves as matters of responsible choice – of, ultimately, moral conscience and responsibility. On the one hand, inside the polyphony of diverse, often dissenting, voices and conflicting, shifting loyalties which mark the 'deregulated', fragmented postmodern condition, it is no more credible that the divide between good and bad has been predetermined, thus leaving to the acting individual solely the task of learning and applying an unambiguous ethical principle suitable for the occasion. On the other hand, the blatant contingency of being, the episodicity of life occasions and the instability of each and any aspect of social existence result in the fast-changing standards of 'normalcy' which once – when solid and persistent – offered the benchmark against which injustice, the violation of the 'normal' and 'habitual', could be measured, thereby confirming in a round-about way the stable and 'objective' standards of popular morality. In the event, *both* sources of past heteronomy of moral behaviour seem to be drying up. The denizens of the postmodern era are, so to speak, forced to stand face-to-face with their moral autonomy, and so also with their moral responsibility. This is the cause of moral agony. This is also the chance the moral selves never confronted before.

2

Forms of Togetherness

Togetherness comes in many kinds.

There is a *mobile* togetherness of the busy street or the shopping mall. A site of passing by, of momentary closeness and instant parting. A mobile site with liquid contents; as the site moves, shapes move (or are sucked) into it and pass out of (or are shaken off) it – some shapes ostensibly self-propelling, some others set in virtual motion solely by the movement of the mobile space itself. Only some shapes stand a chance of condensing into strangers – into *the beings with intentions*, beings whose intentions count though unknown, and count *because* unknown. (It is the ignorance of intentions that counts, as it may interfere with the mobility and liquidity of the site.) Most shapes never make it that far, as they flash through the periphery of attention. (It helps when attention itself is kept at the 'peripheral register'.) Peripheral shapes are but the outer boundaries of the trajectory of the mobile site: obstacles to be avoided or be steered between. A swift and skilful navigation may keep all shapes safely at the periphery; a seasoned (and lucky) walker can pass from there to here without encountering *anybody* and without being met. The few shapes that do condense into strangers (either by an attention too eager or the shapes too obtrusive) intersperse the progress with *encounters*: instead of one trajectory and the space it forms through its own progress, there are two trajectories now and two (uncoordinated) spacings. Such shapes turn now into *intruders*. They cannot be relied upon to stay put or proceed in a steady and monotonous fashion. Their moves can no longer be plotted in advance: they need to be *guessed*. Navigation turns into *risk-management*. In the street-style togetherness, the stranger is an obstacle; encounter is a nuisance and a delay. In the street, being *aside* each other cannot be escaped. But one tries hard not to be *with* each other.

This is what one tries as well in another unwanted though unavoidable togetherness – the *stationary* togetherness of the railway carriage, or the aircraft cabin, or the waiting room. The gathering of strangers who know that they will soon go, each one's own way, never to meet again – but that before that happens they are bound to share this space here and now; not 'for the sake of' anything in particular, not because what they have to do needs them to stay in physical reach of each other. None of the strangers-among-the-strangers really needs the presence of any other. That presence is totally fortuitous, accidental and redundant whichever way you look at it. The purpose of one's own presence here would not suffer a whit were all the others to disappear or never to have been here in the first place. True, the others are not obstacles (not unless they enforce an encounter, refuse to be invisible, and otherwise make a nuisance of themselves) – but neither are they of use. This is a site of suspended animation, of refrigerated encounters. And once cast in the situation of stationary togetherness we do what we can, and with exquisite skills, to keep the animation suspended; in one witty description, 'given half the chance we'll stuff the seat next to ours in a café with raincoats and umbrellas, stare unremittingly at posters about measles in a doctor's waiting room . . . Anything but invite encounter; anything but get involved.' All this to keep 'the stranger at arm's length'.[1] Skilful design may help to keep it like that – in up-to-date carriages, coaches, aircraft the passengers gaze at the neck of the passenger in the seat before, while the rest of the seats, together with their occupiers, are hidden from sight altogether; the crowded place pretends to be empty, the spacing transforms physical fullness into a spiritual void. But where the design fails, personal skills of void-enacting come to the rescue: a newspaper or a paperback hastily

---

[1] Michael Schluter and David Lee, *The R Factor* (London: Hodder & Stoughton, 1993), pp. 15, 14. The fear of rising above the level of suspended animation reaches deep, penetrating places which once were seats of intense relationship. In the authors' words, 'the home itself has grown lean and mean, wider families being broken into nuclear and single-parent units where the individual's desires and interests characteristically take precedence over those of the group. Unable to stop treading on each other's toes in the mega-community, we have stepped into our separate houses and closed the door, and then stepped into our separate rooms and closed the door. The home becomes a multi-purpose leisure centre where household members can live, as it were, separately side by side. Not just the gas industry but life in general has been privatised.' (p. 37)

bought before boarding are the portable moats of the overcrowded age. One can bury one's eyes in the printed page, or turn them away, or close them. Ears are a different matter. The passenger-style togetherness thrives in a complicity of silence, and loud speech pierces the protective shell of conspiracy.

There is a measured, *tempered* togetherness of an office building or a factory floor. This is a togetherness on purpose, though the purposes that prompted people to come together may not be at one with the purpose of their being together. Whatever the purpose of this togetherness, staying together is the condition of reaching it; as there is no other reason for its perpetuation, the purpose of togetherness determines the form the togetherness needs to assume, while other purposes – notably those which motivate the gathered to come and stay together – need to be either enlisted to serve and support that form or be forced into irrelevance. Such togetherness is a matrix of (and for) structured encounters – normatively regulated, rule-governed, pre-emptively circumscribed and preferably sharp and short, lest they should spill over other encounters which need to be kept in a different register, lose focus, or grow receptive to purposes other than the one at hand. The skilful design of the office-type togetherness needs balancing between the tasks of enabling the structured encounters and disabling the unstructured ones, while at the same time making the stay-together attractive enough for all involved – a preliminary condition of both tasks to be undertaken with a chance of success. This is a tall order under the best of circumstances, as the condition continuously undermines the very tasks which it is the condition of; however strict may be the declared opposition between structured (desired) encounters and unstructured (undesirable) ones, between reports and leaks, loyalty and cliquishness – the borderlines are difficult to draw and virtually impossible to guard, since the encounters, however fragmentary, tend to grow multi-sided and even whole when often enough repeated. The continuity which the office-type togetherness can hardly do without tends also to transform the matrix intended for structured encounters only into a matrix for unintended, spontaneously and 'rhyzomically' growing solidarities.

There is a *manifest* togetherness of a protest march, a football crowd, a disco – togetherness only masquerading as instrumental; it needs an outside reason only as a pretext or a rallying call, since first and foremost it is its own goal and purpose. The purpose of this togetherness is being together, and being together in large numbers, numbers which do not normally inhabit the space of that size, numbers which exceed the ordinary, prescribed or daily experienced density.

The higher-than-usual physical density gestates a similar density of sensual impressions: the overflow of sights and sounds, a higher-than-usual level of sensual stimulation, but more importantly yet a *condensed*, concentrated stimulation – reaching the elsewhere unreachable pitch thanks not only to the massive volume, but also to the monotonous homogeneity of stimuli: the same colour scarves wrapped around thousands of necks, the same jingle or ditty chanted, the same words shouted out rhythmically by thousands of breasts, the same twists and turns gone through by thousands of bodies. A mass, but a uniform mass – in which everything idiosyncratic and private may dissolve (albeit, and comfortingly, for a time only) or be strangled into silence. The routine of quotidianity is suspended for the duration, together with its bittersweet little freedoms and big dependencies, the daily tyranny of possibilities and sorrowful joys of decision-making. A successful manifest togetherness numbs through over-stimulation: ecstasy leads to (borders on, melts with) nirvana. Nietzsche would call this kind of togetherness dionysian; Maffesoli would call it orgiastic; Durkheim would perhaps spy out in it the collective commemoration of the long-gone mechanical solidarity; Victor Turner could speak of a bank-holiday trip to *communitas* hidden on working days in the seams of the *societas*. All would agree that whatever its name, togetherness of this kind is mostly about the unloading of the burden of individuality. Ostensibly, the masks are torn off to uncover the grimace of a bare face; in fact, it is faces that are wiped clean of their identities so that another identity may rule supreme which is no one's identity, no one's responsibility and no one's task. With identity, at least for the duration, not an individual property – the manifest togetherness nips encounter in the bud. There are no selves capable of meeting the others in their selfhoods, and so the manifest togetherness is a space without encounters; in that togetherness one seeks, and finds, or finds without seeking, a leave of absence from the wearisome and worrisome, taxing and testing gamble of encounter.

The opposite is true of a *postulated* togetherness (of the brotherhoods and sisterhoods of nations, races, classes, genders and other shadowy and abstruse dream-communities) – though the latter is all too often confused with the one described above by practitioners and theorists alike. Postulated togetherness is always a work of imagination spurred by *homesickness*. (Homesickness, as Jonathan Matthew Schwartz points out, needs to be distinguished from 'the nostalgic yearning'; it is 'the experience of home at a distance'; it is 'an urge to feel at home, to recognize one's surroundings and belong here'. But, let us note, and note well, the 'home' of the 'homesickness' is 'feeling in the future perfect tense';[2] no real house of brick and mortar, not even a house tightly woven of the yarn of human bonds, would meet the standards set by the 'homesickness home'. Homesickness is not just about the absence of home, but – albeit unknowingly – about the impossibility of ever finding one; it is about keeping the hope alive by the expedient of infinite postponement). True, the building site of identity, with its daily chores and sweat and weariness of the builders, is the soil on which both manifest togetherness and postulated togetherness grow; but here the affinity ends, as one togetherness seeks to destroy what the other seeks to establish. Manifest togetherness allures by the emancipation from encounters; the postulated togetherness seduces by its promise of intimate encounters guaranteed to be consummated before even attempted. 'Feeling at home', 'belonging', means encounters plentiful and unproblematic, encounters invariably satisfying, the comforts of being with others cleansed of the dangers of having the 'with' withdrawn, or of the cosiness turning into oppression. Real, familiar houses hover awkwardly half-way between homes and prisons; the 'home' of 'homesickness' is one house with a money-back guarantee in case it veers uncomfortably close to the prison end. Such a home is a dream of permanent abode; but permanence is the nightmare part of the dream. The 'home' of 'homesickness' keeps its seductive powers as long as it keeps its portability. Residing in the future perfect tense helps: frustrated encounters are not subpoenaed to testify at the trial of hope; the case never comes to the court anyway, as it stays endemically inconclusive, none of its many tests is awarded the status of *experimentum crucis*.

There is a *meta*-togetherness, a *matrix-like* togetherness of a pub, a holiday beach, a dance-hall. Not so much togetherness in its own right, as a matrix for the 'real thing' – a weaver's workshop where filaments may be knitted into a tissue, solitary lives entwined and braided. Whoever comes here is a weaver-to-be and/or a fibre-to-be, and knows that all the others around yearn to weave and/or serve as the yarn for other weavers' fabrics. Meta-togetherness is designed as a scene for encounters; facilitating encounters is the measure of good design. Here the waiting has been taken out of the wanting; the mere fact of being here takes care of the first hurdles and cuts the first ice. Here, unlike in other places, one can be reasonably sure that the offer of togetherness will not be rejected offhand, that the gambits

---

[2] Jonathan Matthew Schwartz, *In Defence of Homesickness: Nine Essays on Identity and Locality* (Københavns Universitet Akademisk Forlag, 1989), pp. 15, 13, 32.

will be responded to, that the snubbing of advances is one thing the convention of the place would not allow. Ultimate success is not guaranteed, of course; but the amount of courage and skills one needs to muster to try for success has been cut down considerably. Encounters are available at a reduced price, which is good news. The bad news is that, like in the case of many other commodities purchased on sale, the durability of the goods is less than fully guaranteed and the customer's rights are less than fully honoured. Few fabrics stay in one piece for long after leaving the premises; few encounters survive the last-order call or the end of the holiday season. Meta-togetherness is first and foremost a land of endless experiments, of trials and errors – but errors that do not pre-empt further trials, and trials that do not aim at being foolproof.

The brands of togetherness listed thus far have been presented in the ideal-typical form, of course. And – please note – not in any intrinsically logical or preferable order, suggested by increasing or decreasing value of any particular variable. It is better to assume that the sequence has been fully random. (It is not even clear whether the list is exhaustive; readers surely can, and are invited to, add the missing types that escaped the author's attention or for one reason or another were deemed unworthy of inclusion.) In particular, it is advisable not to plot the successive models on any straight line, ascending or descending, leading to 'more' of togetherness, to a more 'intimate' togetherness or a 'better' togetherness, however the last quality could be measured. On the other hand, it is vital to note that all their peculiar features notwithstanding, the forms of togetherness so far discussed share certain remarkable characteristics, perhaps decisive for their moral consequences.

Being-aside, being-with, being-for

The most salient among the common traits are two: within each of the listed settings, encounters (if at all allowed) are *fragmentary*, or *episodic*, or both. They are fragmentary in as far as only a part of the multi-sided selves and their manifold desires and interests is engaged in the encounter – the rest being temporarily suspended, put surreptitiously aside, or manifestly held back as *private* (that is, presumed irrelevant to this encounter here and now). And they are episodic, in as far as the encounters are enacted as if they had no past history and no future; whatever there is to the encounter, tends to be begotten and exhausted in the span of the encounter itself – starts, develops and ends in the course of it; each encounter is given the appearance of a self-enclosed, even self-sustained, entity. The most important consequence of the episodic nature of the encounter is the *lack* of consequences – encounters tend to be *inconsequential* in the sense of not leaving a lasting legacy of mutual rights and/or obligations in their wake. Or, at least, most of the art of fragmentary/episodic encounters is aimed at preventing such a legacy from being left; encounters are played with the *intention* of inconsequentiality.

In the settings marked by the above-listed forms of togetherness persons are cast *aside* each other; their co-presence has the modality of *being-aside*. Obviously, from a birds-eye view the presence of others, even an aside-presence, matters – the field of action is not empty, the resources it contains must be shared, and what the others do or may do somehow, indirectly, determines the feasibility of purposes and the range of viable strategies; but people immersed in the state of togetherness are not birds, can ill afford a birds-eye view and have little time for it. From the inside of their togetherness, most other person-like entities are seen as, mostly, just being 'on the side'. They furnish the space through which one moves, but for most practical purposes they just flicker at the periphery of vision and vanish or are glossed over as soon as their position has been plotted, rarely stopping for enough time to command a share of attention. It is from this largely indiscriminate and poorly mapped backcloth that certain entities are picked up by shifting attention and made into persons – that is, into the partners of an encounter.

The nature of togetherness, however, lends its flavour to encounters entered within its framework. Encounters tend to be as fragmentary and episodic as the togetherness itself. From being aside, the selected others move into the modality of being-with. Now they are objects of attention; now the mutual dependencies that precede the interaction, arise during the interaction and/or are negotiated and modified in the course of the encounter, come into the field of view, are given topical relevance, turn into objects of thought and decision. Let us emphasize, though, that the relevance offered is but *topical*, and that it is as a rule the topic-at-hand, the *ad hoc* interest, that both generates and limits the relevance. The constraining impact of topicality engraves itself on both sides. No more of the self tends to be deployed in the encounter than the topic-at-hand demands; and no more of the other is highlighted than the topic-at-hand permits. Being-with is a meeting of incomplete beings, of deficient selves; in such a meeting, highlighting is as crucial as concealing, engagement must be complemented by disengagement, deployment of some resources must be paired with withdrawal of others. The intermittence of revelation and secrecy is, as a matter of fact, the major building technique of the being-with type of encounter. When compared with a meeting of complete selves – a meeting that is neither fragmentary nor episodic – the being-with type of encounter can be justly dubbed a *mis*-meeting. What is, however, that non-deficient meeting against which the deficiency of mis-meeting is measured, that meeting-of-complete-selves, which serves as an imaginary horizon by which to plot all other meetings, and redefines all other meetings as mis-meetings? Apparently, it cannot be found in togetherness of any of the thus far enumerated types (not as its legitimate resident at any rate; as a freak happening at the utmost). So to find it, one needs to explore the possibility of another kind of togetherness; one that, hopefully, proves hospitable and conducive to encounters *other* than of the being-with kind.

Think of conditions which must be met by a togetherness concerned not with keeping distance and cutting time; one that is, or becomes, or tends to be, *whole* and *continuous*. Such togetherness must have assumed, though more often than not counter-factually, that it is bound to last forever; only in infinite time is wholeness feasible. And it must have assumed, again counter-factually in many cases, that it is all-embracing; only between complete beings may communication be truly continuous. Whether this togetherness proves to be in practice as whole and as continuous as it pretends to be is a different matter; and a matter that is never resolved conclusively, never receives the final, irrevocable answer. What counts, however, is that the assumption of its being such (permanent and all-embracing) must be made; that the partners should relate to each other as if the assumption was true, and true in a definite fashion – subject neither to negotiation nor to further tests.

And so the partners must relate in some other way than being-with. (One is tempted to say, dismissively, 'some other way than *mere* being-with'; the sought-after 'other way' needs to be, after all, 'more perfect' – in the core sense of the idea of perfection as *wholeness*.) Such another way of relating is *being-for*; it breaks decisively that endemic separation, which under the condition of being-with remains the baseline from which every encounter is but a temporary departure and to which partners return (or are pushed back) after every episode of encounter; and a baseline from which no full departure, however momentary, is plausible, as long as the intrinsic fragmentariness of being-with encounters persists. Being-for is a leap from isolation to unity; yet not towards a *fusion*, that mystics' dream of shedding the burden of identity, but to an *alloy* whose precious qualities depend fully on the preservation of its ingredients' alterity and identity. Being-for is entered for the sake of safeguarding and defending the uniqueness of the Other; and that guardianship undertaken by the self as its task and responsibility makes the self truly unique, in the sense of being irreplaceable; no matter how numerous the defenders of the Other's unique otherness may be, the self is not absolved of responsibility. Bearing such a task without relief is what makes a unique self out of a cipher. Being-for is the act of transcendence of being-with.

Unlike the passage from being-aside to being-with, this transcendence is not offered as a prefabricated chance of the setting – of *any* setting, any empirically given form of togetherness. None of the known forms of togetherness privileges the being-for; but none wards off its happening either. There is no causal connection, not even an 'elective affinity', between the state of being-for and any particular social setting – and if a positive or negative correlation between the two were found, one may well consider it coincidental. Much in human existence determines various forms of being-with and renders them inevitable. Nothing, though, decides the emergence of being-for in any comparably 'deterministic' or 'probabilistic' way. Being-for is not an output, an outgrowth, an outcome, an issue or a fruit of being-with – since the spatial and temporal fragmentation on which being-with depends and which it reasserts in each successive episode cannot be repaired, not with the resources and strategies available to being-with; it can only be pushed aside, dismissed, by-passed, ignored. Being-for may only come, so to speak, from behind the back of being-with.

Neither can the self plan, plot, design, calculate the passage from being-with to being-for. Being-for is not born of judgement; nor is it a matter of choice. It is not entered because it is preferred – as more useful, more pleasurable, more prudent or generally more satisfying. It is not even clear how one could decide the problem of preference, which already presumes that what is being preferred and (all the rest above which it is preferred) has a function which can be prised off the being as such and thus made into an object of assessment; all knowledge one could use to deal with the issue of choice and preference is already a fragmented knowledge presupposing fragment-ariness of being; while being-for is precisely about wholeness and indivisibility. Being-for has not much to recommend itself in the courthouse of Reason, since the court of Reason asks questions like why?, what for?, on what ground?, on whose authority? – questions to which being-for has no good answers and cannot have answers, being the being-for it is. Being-for is a scandal of Reason; *the* scandal of Reason, as a matter of fact, since Reason had asserted itself and goes on reasserting in the opposition to, and struggle against, every-thing that escapes the net of judgement. And being-for is the biggest fish that escapes the net – so big and unruly that it tears up the net on its way out.

A person-to-person encounter, says Arne Johan Vetlesen (he uses this term more or less synonymically with my usage of being-for, or of *meeting* as opposed to *mis*-meeting),

> the look meeting look, the face facing a face, amounts to a relation that is shot through with a moment of commitment. But this commitment is unlike all others; it is not a product of the subject's intentionality; it is not wanted, it simply imposes itself as a property pertaining to the very structure of this dyad of proximity.[3]

Eyes stop wandering around and glossing over moving shapes, eyes meet other eyes and stay fixed – and a *commitment* shoots up, apparently from nowhere, certainly not from previous intention, instruction, norm; the emergence of commitment is as much surprising as its presence is commanding. Encounters are pregnant with commitment, and there seems to be no way of controlling this particular pregnancy . . . One can only try abortion; or the confinement of commitment-bearing meetings in private homes, cloisters or orphanages.

Its obstreperous and threatening opposite, that 'shooting and being shot', that sudden opening up to the Other, the unplanned explosion of non-indifference, the abrupt closing of distance – Reason calls by the names of sentiment, emotion, feeling, passion.

Reason tries and tries again to describe and define those 'others of itself' 'in their own terms', in reference to their allegedly endemic and immanent traits, thereby construing them into object-like entities with their own identity. Not to much avail, though, since the only hard-core meaning of sentiment/emotion/feeling/passion is the defiance, disregard and snubbing of Reason. Reason and sentiment define each other: it is only their opposition which carries meaning, not each term alone, independently of its opposite. For Reason to be rule-governed – its opposite, the unruly, must be the unreason – sentiment. When Kant says that emotions (that is, *all* emotions except the passion for moral law – that law forbidden to be undermined by personal, subjective, I and Thou motives) must not be allowed to interfere with the work of Reason since they becloud and impair judgement, he commits tautology: 'emotions' stand exactly for what 'impairs' 'judgement' – and not for much beside. If the rules and the norms which Reason excels in legislating did hold human

---

[3] Arne Johan Vetlesen, *Perception, Empathy, and Judgment: An Inquiry into the Preconditions of Moral Performance* (Pennsylvania State University Press, 1993), p. 202.

togetherness in a complete and unqualified grip, there would be hardly an occasion for the notion of passion to be conceived. But Reason's supervision stops well short of fullness, human conduct well short of monotony, human intercourse well short of predictability. Sentiment/ emotion/feeling/passion is the name of this unpredictability which opens where the arm of Reason, however long, cannot reach (while having provided, originally, the *casus belli*, the pretext for stretching the arm). In the garden of Reason, sentiments are weeds – plants that seed themselves in unexpected and inconvenient spots. The spots are inconvenient because they have not been allocated in advance – they are random from the point of view of the master plan, and hence undermine the design because the design is, first and foremost, about the impossibility of randomness.

From the start of modernity, with its universal otherhood called the 'public sphere', with its incessant effort to conjure up order out of the chaos of otherhood – emotions were the 'ubi leones' of reason-controlled order; they were things yet to be tamed and mastered, listed on the agenda of unfinished business appended to every successive career biography of Reason. The public sphere – the site of togetherness – was to be ruled by *civility* (which took *intimacy* for its dark, unprepossessing, and shameful side). And civility, according to numerous teachers' texts and teach-yourself handbooks, 'opposed point by point the moves of heart and body in their intimate passions' (Philippe Ariès).[4] Civility was the question of mostly negative, not positive learning: of what one should hide, what one should not speak about, what one should be ashamed of. Every spontaneity, every gesture or grimace unplanned and uncontrolled disclosed and betrayed the thinness of civilized veneer and the wantonness of passions boiling underneath; all spontaneity was, therefore, destructive of the civil order, and for the sake of that order had to be 'shamed out of existence', proclaimed degrading and embarassing and made to be experienced that way. In a text dedicated to planting civilized manners, Erasmus wrote at the threshold of modernity, that in a child 'fierce eyes indicate violence, fixated eyes are signs of arrogance, eyes wandering and unfocused show stupidity' (and so on);[5] the

---

[4]   Philippe Ariès, *Histoire de la vie privée*, ed. Philippe Ariès and Georges Duby, vol. 3 (Paris: Seuil, 1986), p. 165. Civility, says Ariès, is a 'strictly regulated manner of conduct', designed to convey in public an identity (or a side of it) one wished to present to anonymous others constituting the 'public sphere', and thus command 'enforced separation between intimate affections' and public intercourse.

[5]   Quoted from *La Civilité puérile* (1530), after Jacques Revel, 'Les Usages de la civilité', in *Histoire de la vie privée*, p. 172.

eyes were windows allowing a glimpse of the private interior, which the rules of civility did not reach and which they did not control. Those windows had to be made opaque, so that uncontrolled things would never interfere with the controlled environment of civility. 'The wild man inside' needed to be kept on a leash and preferably never paraded in public; conversely, 'the wild' in man was precisely all that which the rules of public life prohibited parading. And the rules forbade everything they did not rule and could not rule.

Knud E. Løgstrup writes of the *spoken* and *unspoken* demands immanent in the encounter, and suggests that all correspondence between the two 'is purely coincidental; usually they are not at all alike'. 'The demand which is present in any human relationship is . . . unspoken and is not to be equated with a person's expressed wish or request.'[6]

Convention and commitment

The spoken demand (the articulated demand, the verbalizable demand) has the modality of a rule. Like the rule, it spells out what is to be done, and – by commission or by omission – what must not or need not be done; obliquely it also exonerates the rule-follower from not thinking beyond the spelled-out instruction, supplying him with the uncontentious probe of 'the duty fulfilled', 'the obligation met', 'the job well done'. The spoken demand saves the actor a lot of trouble; whether coming in the form of a universal rule, or in the shape of a request from the partner of the encounter who invokes such a rule, it can be weighed according to the merit of the case. The only worry is whether the application (or invocation) of the rule is justified by the nature of the case (whether the partner 'deserves' a peculiar treatment envisaged by the rule, and just how much of it s/he deserves). In a rule-governed encounter, the actor is not confronted with another person, but with a 'spoken demand'; the true relationship is between the actor and the rule, while the other person, the cause or the target of action, is but a pawn moved around the

---

[6] Knud E. Løgstrup, *The Ethical Demand*, trans. Theodor J. Jensen (Philadelphia: Fortran Press, 1971), pp. 20–1. 'No one is more thoughtless', says Løgstrup, 'than he who makes a point of applying and realizing once-delivered directions . . . Everything can be carried out very mechanically; all that is needed is a purely technical calculation. There is no trace of thinking and imagination that are triggered only by uncertainty and doubt.'(p. 121)

chessboard of rights and duties. The rule-governed area is an area of *convention*, and convention can not only do without emotional commitment but considers all sentiment except loyalty to the rule and all commitment except commitment to rule-following as potentially dangerous impostors. Convention substitutes concern with the rule for the concern for the partner of encounter (the latter being not just unnecessary, but one that 'beclouds the judgement' and thus creates the possibility that the rule will not be observed in full, will be set aside, or downright violated). Says Lévinas: 'Marvellous alterity of the Other has been banalized and dimmed in a simple exchange of courtesies which became established as an "interpersonal commerce" of customs.'[7] We use convention, concludes Løgstrup, 'as a means of keeping aloof from one another and for insulating ourselves.' The rule-governed togetherness, the being-with exhausted in the observance of rules, is a colony of hermits, an archipelago of one-resident islands. It also allows for interaction devoid of sentiment save the sentiments focused on the procedure of interaction.

Paul Ricoeur suggested that 'l'homme entre dans le monde éthique par la peur et non par l'amour.'[8] This holds true as long as we identify the 'world of ethics' with the rule-governed 'being-with' togetherness. The fear in question is not the fear of the licentious, savage and unbridled Other, but of the stringent and severe Law – though it is the opposite that the texts promoting the rule of Law usually intimate. The wildness of the Other (and of oneself, within) is here the ultimate incarnation of the severity of Law reprocessed and recast; what could be the cause of resentment towards the Law is – through a cunning subterfuge – redeployed in Law's service. The ethics – the law-like spelling out of the difference between moral and immoral – ushers into the world it defines as moral through the gate of fear: the double fear of the world without Law, and of the Law's punishment for disobedience.

But there is another gate, one of love, fellow-feeling, concern: of *commitment*; only it seems to usher into a different building, one of morality, whose correspondence to the house of ethics (to paraphrase Løgstrup) is 'purely coincidental' (though ethics aims at invading and annexing that building and expelling all its inhabitants who resist the *Anschluss*). In this building of morality entered by commitment it is the *unspoken* demand that guides the residents. This building is also

---

[7]   Emmanuel Lévinas, 'La Souffrance inutile', in *Entre-nous: Essais sur le penser-à-l'autre* (Paris: Grasset, 1991).

[8]   Paul Ricoeur, *La Symbolique du mal*, vol. 2 of *Philosophie de la volonté: finitude et culpabilité* (Paris: Aubière Montaigne, 1960), p. 35.

plagued by loneliness, though of a different kind than the loneliness of being-with togetherness. While the ethical loneliness is contrived, the loneliness of the moral person is uncontrived; the first is the loneliness of counselled indifference and non-commitment, the second is the loneliness of wayward commitment and concern.

In his splendid exploration of sentiments as preconditions of moral performance, Vetlesen objects to Hannah Arendt's interpretation of evil (as implied by her influential account of Eichmann's case) as a product of *thoughtlessness* – suggesting instead that 'Eichmann was *not* merely thoughtless, but first of all *insensitive*'; that what truly set the evil loose was Eichmann's '*indifference* to the meaning of suffering, to the infliction of pain'; 'Insofar as he adopts an objectifying attitude towards his fellows, as opposed to a participatory-empathic one, Eichmann for all practical purposes *prevents the domain of moral phenomena from being disclosed to him.*'[9] Which, let us make clear, does not necessarily mean that Eichmann and other perpetrators of 'legal crimes' were unethical. On the contrary: the participatory-empathic stance is always, irreparably a personal stance personally taken – it is endemically erratic, shuns codification, cannot be taught or obtained by rote learning, and for this very reason the world of ethics, the world of regularity, codes, teaching and learning has no room for empathy and emotional participation in the sufferings of the Other. The 'participatory-empathic attitude' is inside the ethically organized world an alien body, and the 'objectifying' stance taken by Eichmann was a triumph, not a defeat, of ethics. (It was Hannah Arendt again who alerted us to the fact that it is the 'ethically correct' paterfamilias – the law-abiding citizen, the honest tradesman, the loyal husband and the caring father – on whom rests the possibility that 'one fine day a highly organized and mechanized humanity will conclude quite democratically – namely by majority decision – that for humanity as a whole it would be better to liquidate certain parts thereof'.)[10] As Vetlesen rightly points out, those who turn to reason's capacity for

---

[9] Vetlesen, *Perception, Empathy, and Judgment*, p. 305. Vetlesen concludes: 'There is no disinterested access to the phenomenon of suffering; if one bars the capacity to feel from morality, one bars humanity from it.'

[10] Hannah Arendt, *The Origins of Totalitarianism* (London: André Deutsch, 1985), p. 299. Hannah Arendt was at pains to show that Hitler's 'abnormality' has its roots sunk deeply into the formal/legal fabric of modern society. 'Hitler's motto that "Right is what is good for the German people" is only a vulgarized form of a conception of law which can be found everywhere' (p. 299). Hitler 'proved his supreme ability for organizing the masses into total domination by assuming that most people are . . . first and foremost job holders and good family men' (p. 338). 'Intellectual, spiritual, and artistic [one can add: moral] initiative is as

logical proof in their search for the safeguards against humanity, are bound to end up empty-handed, if not worse. Thus, for instance, Karl-Otto Apel, who places his bets on the 'responsibility of reason, which must take the place of a consciousness of sin based to some extent on instinct',[11] speaks, even though unknowingly, in the name of the self-same modern strategy which spawned the new, modern type of legally blessed, organized criminality no more dependent on the moral mobilization of its perpetrators.

What is legally condemned (and legally prevented or legally persecuted) is action on authority other than that of the legal/ethical code. It is against this awesome might of the allowing/disallowing legislation of reason that rebellious moral sentiments (rebellious by the very fact of being sentiments instead of calculations) are up against. This makes the rebel lonely. The rebel has nothing reputable for a guide, neither authoritative teachers nor power-assisted rules to vouch for being-in-the-right and having-done-what-duty-demands. The rebel is lonely *because* the demand which s/he follows is *unspoken*. Social norms, says Løgstrup, 'give comparatively precise directives about what we shall do and what we shall refrain from doing.' The unspoken, and hence radical, demand 'gives no directions whatever . . . It specifies nothing . . . but leaves it entirely to the individual.'

This 'unspokenness' is not a 'givenness' of a sort – a voice nudging one to act yet refusing to articulate what it is that the action should be about. The 'unspokenness' stands for silence, which is audible only in contrast to the hubbub of counsels and vociferous promptings. The 'unspokenness' means that the command as we know it and as we used to expect it to be has not been given; we would not know of the unspoken demand at all were we not used to hear many demands spoken. There is little point in the attempts to describe and define the 'unspoken demand' in its own terms, as 'another kind' of demand (and still less in trying to argue the 'reasons' for the unspoken demand logically, as Løgstrup gratuitously undertook). The

---

dangerous to totalitarianism as the gangster initiative of the mob, and both are more dangerous than mere political opposition' (p. 339). *All* initiative is to be weeded out; initiative born of hatred is as dangerous as one born of love; in this sense, one may say, the conception of the ethical substitute for morality is 'totalitarian by heart'; at any rate, it enters into no conflict with collective cruelty – if anything, it is one of the latter's necessary conditions.

[11]   Karl-Otto Apel, *Diskurs und Verantwortung* (Frankfurt-Main: Suhrkamp, 1989), pp. 17–18. What Apel says is said in one form or another by all contemporary followers of 'discursive ethics'. The criticism aimed at Apel applies therefore in large measure to 'discursive ethics' as such, notably to the propositions of Jürgen Habermas, its foremost proponent.

'unspokenness' is a pure negativity, pure absence of guidance. (And since one can speak of nothingness only obliquely, speaking of a being 'which is not', we speak of an 'unspoken command' – but we will be well advised to remember that we use the word 'command', as Derrida would say, *sous rature*, an empty shell made out of linguistic necessity, so to speak. Any attempt to imagine an object at which the term *sous rature* winks – and even more so any attempt to imagine an authority standing behind that object, an authority who *gave the command* – would be the error of hypostasis.) The 'unspokenness' means simply that the actor is now on his/her own, plotting his/her own itinerary without assistance, groping in the dark and never quite sure that the road chosen is the right road. But it also means that the actor *does not know of* his/her ignorance and *does not ask* whether the choice of road was right; if s/he did, s/he would have invoked a command and most certainly found one – there are so many of them jostling for attention. The 'unspokenness' means rather that the authority of command *has not been sought*, that the actor acts without a command and acts as if command was not needed. This carefree spontaneity of action, this undesignedness of action, is called in the parlance of Reason, as we remember, sentiment/emotion/feeling/passion. When sentiments take the lead, demands are numbed and made redundant; and this is, in the end, all the idea of 'unspoken demand' stands for. When acting without command and without asking for one, the self accomplishes what Lévinas characterized as the 'breaking through its form'[12] – breaking through *any socially drawn form*, shedding *any* socially-sewn dress, facing the other as a face, not mask, and facing one's own bare face in the process.

The unbearable uncertainty of being-for

This passage from being-with to being-for, from convention to commitment; this tearing-off the masks until the naked, defenceless

---

[12] See Emmanuel Lévinas. 'Freedom and Command', in *Collected Philosophical Papers*, trans. Alphonso Lingis (The Hague: Martinus Nijhoff, 1987), p. 20. Lévinas points out that the 'encounter with the face' follows a 'command prior to institutions, which the encounter articulates' (p. 21) – in other words, the encounter follows its own rules, constructed 'on the way', as it goes. This is the exercise in freedom, inconceivable in the being-with world of conventions: 'Institutions obey rational order in which freedom no longer recognizes itself ... The will experiences the guarantees that it has provided against its own degradation as another tyranny' (p. 17) – a standing invitation to rebellion as long as the will is prompted by its urge to freedom.

face shows itself and is seen – is more often than not described as the work of love, also by both Løgstrup and Lévinas. For Løgstrup, the 'unspoken demand' is a 'demand for love', a 'demand to take care' of the Other.[13] For Lévinas, the beginning of morality is 'une préoccupation de l'autre jusqu' au sacrifice, jusqu' à la possibilité de mourir pour lui'.[14] Once identified with the realm of being-for, the realm of morality is enclosed in the frame of sympathy, of the willingness to serve, to do good, to self-sacrifice for the sake of the Other. Awakening to the face – Lévinas never tired of repeating – is tantamount to the shock of hearing the inaudible call for assistance, which the vulnerability and weakness of the Other, revealed in the nakedness of the face, issues without speaking; the shock so overpowering that it renders ridiculously insignificant all those rational considerations which bask in self-importance in the world of conventions and contractual obligations. The birth of the moral person is the self-command: s/he is my responsibility, and my responsibility alone. And this means that I, and I alone, am responsible for her/his integrity and welfare.

> At the moment I am responsible for the Other, I am unique. I am unique in as far I am irreplaceable, in as far as I am chosen to respond. Responsibility is lived as election.[15]

Taking moral responsibility means not to consider the Other any more as a specimen of a species or a category, but as unique, and by so doing elevate oneself (making oneself 'chosen') to the dignity of uniqueness.

The long rule of ethical legislation and long indoctrination by ethical legislators have had, however, an overall effect of construing morality after the image of ethics. If ethics is about drawing the boundary of good while sitting on this side of the border, then morality as imagined in the ethically administered world must also be about the distinction between good (what you must do) and evil (what you must not do) and about staying put on the side of goodness. Whether an offshoot or sediment of ethics (as it is depicted in the dominant ethical philosophy, aided and abetted by the dominant sociology), or an alternative to the conventionality of ethical code (as construed in Løgstrup's or Lévinas's rebellion against the dominant

---

[13] See Løgstrup, *The Ethical Demand*, pp. 22, 58.

[14] Lévinas, *Entre-nous*, p. 10; see also 'La Philosophie et l'éveil', in ibid.

[15] Entretiens Emmanuel Lévinas–François Poirié, in François Poirié, *Emmanuel Lévinas – Qui êtes-vous?* (Lyons: La Manufacture, 1987), p. 115.

philosophy), morality remains a reflection of the official portrait of ethics; painted after the likeness and in the image of an ethics self-confident (nay, arrogant) enough to claim the ability to set apart good from wrong-doing and to guide towards good while steering clear of the traps and ambushes of evil.

It seems that the propositions to discuss the non-conventional morality in terms of the 'unspoken' (as distinct from the 'spoken') demand, or an 'unconditional' (as distinct from the 'conditional', contractually defined) responsibility, equally carry the burden of their origins: they are haunted by the spectre of the law-like ethics they have been designed to shake off. Implicitly, they perpetuate mental frames and demarcation lines construed by that ethics – even if only through their explicit negation and hostile engagement. With each foot in a different (and barely compatible) universe of discourse, the two propositions are not fully at home in either. They also generate a categorial confusion which in its turn leads to virtually unresolvable quandaries. The break-through which they propose and embody does not seem radical enough to reopen the issue of morality in a form resonant with the 'post-legitimation' era.[16] Finally, they became hostage to the inherited notions of command or demand which now turn frankly incongruous. If in the ethically legislated morality commands and demands used to be meaningful as long as they referred to a speaking subject (be it God or Reason), today there seems to be no good answer to the persistent and pertinent questioning of the source. Objections to questioning are not likely to sound convincing, let alone conclusive, as the very notion of 'demand' or 'command' is a standing invitation to queries about credentials and reasons for obedience. Attempts to answer the questions lead to yet more

---

[16] In an interview with *Le Monde* on the occasion of the 'International Parliament of Writers' convened at Strasbourg (see 'La Ligne de résistance', in *Le Monde*, 5 November 1993, p. 29), Jean-François Lyotard spoke of the necessity to re-think 'the political outside the two-hundred-years old principle of legitimation' established by the French Revolution. The principle required *legitimacy* of human rights and duties, and assumed that this legitimacy is given by authoritative texts and can be established by consulting those texts. The principle, says Lyotard, no more operates (due to the collapse of legislative reason, we may argue – see my *Intimations of Postmodernity* (London: Routledge, 1992) – which leaves us no choice but 's'avancer sans autorité pour essayer de signifier ce qui n'est pas signifiable ou, du moins, qu'il y a un manque de sens, faire entendre que quelque chose n'est pas clairement audible, qui est même difficile à nommer.' Acting – and thinking – without authority needs among other things a new language, cut off from the umbilical cord that ties it down to the legitimation-focused discourse.

bewildering problems, like in Løgstrup's insistence that the radical demand should be obeyed 'given the fact that life has been received as a gift'.[17]

I propose that the passage from the convention-ruled to the moral condition is not marked by the sudden numbness of the once voluble demand, nor by the dropping of conditions which once circumscribed responsibility, but by the appearance (or reappearance) of what the ethical legislation declares off-limits in the world of morality: namely of the emotional relationship to the Other. I also propose that the kind of emotion which colours the relationship is secondary, regarding the very emotionality of encounter which is primary – and decisive. The being-for is, to start with, neutral in relation to good and evil; it does not find the opposition of good and evil ready-made, less still drawn in a clear-cut, unmistakable and once-for-all way; it is rather that *the opposition itself, the possibility of acts being good or evil, emerges and takes shape in the history of being-for* (though even here it seldom if ever reaches the degree of clarity which the omniscient ethical legislation presupposes).

The being-for, I propose, means an *emotional* engagement with the Other *before* it is committed (and before it can be, conceivably, committed) to a specific course of action regarding the Other. Emotions transform the 'mere being-with' into a being-for through three crucial achievements. First, emotion marks the exit from the state of *indifference* lived among thing-like others. Second, emotion pulls the Other from the world of finitude and stereotyped certainty, and casts her/him into the universe of under-determination, questioning and openness. Third, emotion extricates the Other from the world of convention, routine and normatively engendered monotony, and transmits her/him into a world in which no universal rules apply, while those which do apply are overtly and blatantly non-universal, specific, born and shaped in the self-containment of the face-to-face protected from the outside influence by the wall of sentiment. Through these three feats, emotional engagement makes the Other into a problem and the task of and for the self (precisely the condition which the all-regulating supra-individual ethics strove to prevent); now it is up to the self, and the self alone, to do something (an unspecified something) about the Other. The Other turns into the self's *responsibility*, and this is where morality begins as the possibility of choice between good and evil.

The emotions we are speaking about here need not be necessarily those of sympathy or fellow-feeling; still less of empathy,

---

Løgstrup, *The Ethical Demand*, p. 123.

commiseration or compassion. The sole requisite is that the Other is cast as a target for emotion. What must happen in the first instance, before sympathy or compassion may have their chance, is what Martin Buber described as *the resistance to objectification*:

> The realm of the interhuman goes far beyond that of sympathy . . . The only thing that matters is that for each of the two men the other happens as the particular other, that each becomes aware of the other and is thus related to him in such a way that he does not regard and use him as his object, but as his partner in a living event . . . The essential thing is not that the one makes the other his object, but the fact that he is not fully able to do so and the reason for his failure . . . [I]t is my privilege as man that by the hidden activity of my being I can establish an impassable barrier to objectification.[18]

The object can be handled as objects are: scrutinized, dissected, measured, classified, moved from one place to another. Erecting an obstacle to such handling, a 'barrier to objectification', is a notion synonymical with that of developing an emotional attitude. We dub 'emotional' the act and thought that is not bound by the results of measurement and evaluation. Emotions do not reason, let alone reason logically. They are not consistent and rarely happen to be cohesive, free of inner contradictions. They evade or explode any frame built of norms and rules. Since, as Jean-François Lyotard reminds us, we have come to identify maturity in humans with predictability, reliability and regularity of conduct – emotions cannot but be cast, dismissively, as manifestations of *infantility* (that is, of what the project of maturation, in the form given to it by the modern era, wants us to leave behind). When in the grip of emotion, it is as if we have reverted to the infantile state of defencelessness and abandonment: there are no rules to go by; we move in the world once more uncharted; we chart it anew, as if from scratch, as we go.

This is precisely what 'bearing responsibility' means (the fact belied by the notion of maturation as of gradual surrender to the norms; within that notion, the invocation 'be responsible!' means 'follow the rules!'). Pointing my finger at the rules, re-presenting my bond with the Other as an item in the set of similar bonds, a specimen of a category, a case of a general rule – I avoid all responsibility except a procedural one. Being tied to the Other by emotion means, on the other hand, that I am responsible for her/him, and most of all for what my action or inaction may do to her/him. I am no more a

---

[18] Martin Buber, *The Knowledge of Man: Selected Essays*, trans. Maurice Freedman and Ronald Gregor Smith (New York: Harper, 1965), pp. 73–4.

cipher, an exchangeable item in a set, a refillable slot in the network of relations; what I do, counts – and it counts as well if I desist from doing it. Now the Other becomes my hostage; and I in turn become a hostage to my responsibility.

And so the event of catching the Other in the net of my emotions establishes a bond of mutual dependency: that primal mutuality is also my lonely creation, and my lone responsibility. I am responsible for keeping this mutual dependency alive. This is the sole reality which my emotional 'stretching towards' the Other has founded. The rest is silence; I do not know what the exercising of my responsibility may mean, responsibility comes both empty, waiting to be filled, and infinite, unlikely to be ever ful-filled. And so I am also responsible for reforging the existential responsibility into a practical one, for filling it with the contents it lacks, for struggling to make it, against all odds, fulfillable. This responsibility makes me powerful; it also assumes my power; it presents the Other to me as weak; it also assumes her/his weakness. One is responsible *to* someone stronger than oneself; one is responsible *for* someone weaker than oneself.

Being-for, being responsible-for, is therefore at bottom *a power relationship*. This circumstance cannot be made null and void; it persists, even if pushed to the background or emphatically denied, through the whole interaction that stems from responsibility, also in such action as has the surrender to the Other for its aim. (Even the surrender I have chosen is an exercise in my power of choice.) The connection between responsibility and power is virtually tautological: without power, there would be no responsibility. Without power, filling the responsibility with contents would be inconceivable (and vice versa, that filling is nothing else but manifestation of power).

Which also means that responsibility is synonymical with *freedom*. In fact, one may say that responsibility-for-the-Other, power-over-the-Other and freedom *vis-à-vis* the Other are three terms founded by three different discourses, yet converging on the same realm of the 'primal moral scene'.

At this primal scene, the course of action is not-yet-determined. The dividing line between good and evil is not-yet-drawn. It is only the subsequent actions of the actors that will make the distinction, set apart good from evil, determine the goodness and the evil of what will have been done. There is no scenario written in advance, and the actors write the plot as they proceed, each being his or her own director; and construe the language of writing in the course of writing it.

My responsibility for the other, Lévinas repeatedly insists, includes also my responsibility for determining what needs to be done to exercise that responsibility. Which means in turn that I am responsible for defining the needs of the Other; for what is good, and what is evil for the Other. If I love her and thus desire her happiness, it is my responsibility to decide what would make her truly happy. If I admire her and wish her perfection, it is my responsibility to decide what her perfect form would be like. If I respect her and want to preserve and enhance her freedom, it is again my responsibility to spell out what her genuine autonomy would consist of. 'Evil shows itself to be sin, that is, a responsibility, despite itself, for the refusal of responsibilities',[19] says Lévinas. To which I would add that not-refusing the responsibility does not ward off the spectre of evil. Taking up the responsibility is a necessary but woefully insufficient condition of goodness. The exercise of responsibility means steering forever a course between good and evil without the succour of certainty or authoritative reassurance, without hope of ever drawing the last, definite and uncontestable line between the two. If the refusal of responsibility ushers in the life of sin, its acceptance leads into a life of anxiety and self-deprecation. This is why avoiding the *morality* of relationship, not the avoidance of *doing good* (opting out from morality, not from goodness) is the most alluring of temptations evil may dangle in front of the self despairing of the burden of actorship and authorship.

'What men commonly commend as good or kind' observes Løgstrup, caustically, 'usually represents in reality the kind of accommodation that results in insecure relationship. What men commonly call love is usually an affectation which shuns like plague the truth between people.' But love, Løgstrup contends, is not indulgence. Condoning does not agree with the care for the Other. To care, is to do something about making the lot of the other *better* than it is. (As Lévinas would add, I am responsible also for the faults of the Other.) But this, signals Løgstrup, is pregnant with another perversion. The first of Løgstrup's perversions does not seem, to be sure, a 'perversion' at all, being rather a straightforward *shirking* of responsibility and thus pre-empting the possibility of perverting it (Løgstrup describes the first perversion as 'the kind of animation which, due to laziness, fear of people, or a propensity for cozy relationship, consists in simply trying to please one another while always dodging the issue') and is more akin to Lévinas's sin of omission. The second, though, is a genuine perversion: 'our wanting to change other people. We have a definite opinion about how they ought to

---

[19] Emmanuel Lévinas, 'Language and Proximity', in *Collected Philosophical Papers*, p. 137.

be.' But 'responsibility for the other person never consists in our assuming the responsibility which is his.'[20] Well and fine, but how to do one without the other? How to act upon my own responsibility without having an opinion what is good for her? And if I confine myself to taking what I hear from her at its face value, would it not be equal to the sin of omission?

The Scylla of indifference, of the responsibility abandoned, and the Charybdis of the autonomy stolen, of the responsibility degenerating into coercion – seem too close to each other for safe sailing. Both love and hatred, both goodness and evil seem to be legitimate residents in the house managed by moral responsibility. All are 'inside jobs' of responsibility. The primal moral scene is strewn with ambivalence. All the acting on that scene aims at the reduction of ambivalence. What the acting amounts to, though, is a never-ending string of settlements between mildly attractive or unattractive eventualities. (Settlement, says Lars-Henrik Schmidt, is not a decision; it differs from a rational calculation and proceeds 'without fixed criteria'; it is not 'looking for help in understanding or in reasoning' and is not 'deciding according to concepts or principles'; it has 'no fixed procedure'; in short – 'it differs from the "might-know"ing of understanding, the "dare-hope"ing of judging and the "ought-do"ing of reason.')[21] Most horrifyingly, the sum total of ambivalence seems to be immune to all the efforts to trim it down and, if anything, to grow – much like the fire-spitting heads of the dragon known to multiply through being cut off.

To act morally means to face up to that incurable ambivalence.

The good is in the future

Maurice Blanchot said of poetry: 'It comes from beyond the future and does not cease to come when it has come.'[22] And of the writer:

---

[20]   See Løgstrup, *The Ethical Demand*, pp. 24ff.

[21]   Lars-Henrik Schmidt, *Settling the Values* (Aarhus: Center for Kulturforskning, 1993), pp. 1–8.

[22]   Maurice Blanchot, *The Siren's Song: Selected Essays*, trans. Sacha Rabinovitz (Bloomington: Indiana UP, 1982), p. 241. The same applies to art as a whole. Art, says Blanchot, 'is always in advance of acquired forms of culture, so that, in fact, it is post-cultural' (p. 188). 'Culture requires finished works that can be seen as complete and can be admired in static permanence in those storehouses of culture which are our museums, concert halls, academies, record libraries and libraries . . . So an art which has no answers but only questions, which even questions the existence of art, cannot fail to be seen as disturbing, hostile and coldly violent.' (p. 189)

'You will never know what you have written, even if you have written only to find it out . . . Before the work, the writer does not yet exist; after the work, he is no longer there.'[23] And of the stranger:

> To speak of someone, means to agree not to introduce him into the system of things, that is the things to be known; means to recognize his not-being-known and to admit him as a stranger, without obliging him to stop being different. In this sense, the word is the promised land where the exile is accomplished through the stay, since what is at stake here is not being at home, but always outside, in a movement in the course of which the stranger delivers himself without self-denial.[24]

Art and the Other of moral relationship – the Other of being-for, the Other as *the face* – share the same status: when they are, they are in the future; when they are not in the future, they are no more. They are what they are only as a challenge to what already is and has been. They are always 'outside' (in Lévinas's phrase, 'otherwise than being'). When grasped and given, they lose what makes them what they are. And what they are is akin to the modality of the future:

> What is in no way grasped, is the future; exteriority of the future is totally different from spatial exteriority precisely because the future is absolutely surprising. The future anticipated, future projected, considered to be the essence of time by all theories from Bergson to Sartre, are merely the present of the future and thereby not the authentic future: that which has not been grasped, which falls upon us to overpower. The future is the Other.[25]

The future is full of surprises; and so is the Other, as long as acknowledged in his absolute alterity. The being-for is like living-towards-the-future: a being filled with anticipation, a being aware of the abyss between future foretold and future that will eventually be; it is this gap which, like a magnet, draws the self towards the Other,

---

[23] Maurice Blanchot, *Vicious Circles*, trans. Paul Aster (New York: Station Hill, 1985), pp. 59, 60.
[24] Maurice Blanchot, *L'Entretien infini* (Paris: Gallimard, 1969), p. 187.
[25] Emmanuel Lévinas, *Le Temps et l'Autre* (Paris: PUF, 1991), p. 64. Of the incurably surprising future, Karl Jaspers had the following to say: 'We can envision possibilities and probabilities and impossibilities, but experience tells us that the impossible can happen, that the probable may never happen, and above all, that new, completely unthought of realities may appear . . . Nothing great, nothing fundamental has ever been foretold, nor have its origins been understood in retrospect' (*The Future of Mankind*, trans. E. B. Ashton (University of Chicago Press, 1961), pp. 282–3).

as it draws life towards the future, making life into an activity of overcoming, transcending, leaving behind. The self stretches towards the Other, as life stretches towards the future; neither can grasp what it stretches toward, but it is in this hopeful and desperate, never conclusive and never abandoned stretching-toward that the self is ever anew created and life ever anew lived. In the words of M. M. Bakhtin, it is only in this not-yet accomplished world of anticipation and trial, leaning toward stubbornly an-other Other, that life can be lived – not in the world of the 'events that occurred'; in the latter world, 'it is impossible to live, to act responsibly; in it, I am not needed, in principle I am not there at all.'[26]

Art, the Other, the future: what unites them, what makes them into three words vainly trying to grasp the same mystery, is the modality of possibility. A curious modality, at home neither in ontology nor epistemology; itself, like that which it tries to catch in its net, 'always outside', forever 'otherwise than being'. The possibility we are talking about here is not the all-too-familiar unsure-of-itself, and through that uncertainty flawed, inferior and incomplete being, disdainfully dismissed by triumphant existence as 'mere possibility', 'just a possibility'; possibility is instead 'plus que la réalité' – both the origin and the foundation of being. The hope, says Blanchot, proclaims the possibility of that which evades the possible; 'in its limit, this is the hope of the bond recaptured where it is now lost.'[27]

---

[26] M. M. Bakhtin, 'K filosofii postupka', quoted after P. S. Gurevich, 'Problema drugogo v filosofskoĭ antropologii M. M. Bakhtina', in *M. M. Bakhtin kak filosof* (Moscow: Nauka, 1992), p. 86. Lévinas's intention is strikingly similar. He wants to oppose the 'collectivity' of I–Thou, which is founded in the 'temporal transcendence of a present towards the mystery of the future' to the legacy of post-Platonian 'social' 'which was always sought in the ideal of a fusion', in which 'the subject tended to identify with the Other while sinking in a collective representation or shared ideal. That was a collectivity which said "we" and which – turning towards the Sun of intelligibility, towards the truth, felt the Other aside itself, not *en face*' (Lévinas, *Le Temps et l'Autre*, p. 88).

[27] Blanchot, *L'Entretien infini*, pp. 58–9. In 'Ordo Amoris', Max Scheler writes of the '*unlimitedness of love*, experienced by us as a potentiality; consequently, the striving which is built upon the act of love is unlimited as well . . . A love which is by its essence infinite, however much it is interrupted, however much it is bound to and particularized by the specific organization of its bearer, demands for its satisfaction an *infinite good* . . . Wherever man, individually or communally, believes he has attained in a *finite good* an absolutely final fulfillment and satisfaction of his love-drive, we have a case of *delusion*, a stagnation of his spiritual-ethical development.' This is, says Scheler, not a case of love, but 'infatuation' (*Selected Philosophical Essays*, trans. David R. Lachterman (Evanston: Northwestern University Press, 1973), p. 114).

The hope is always the hope of *being fulfilled*, but what keeps the hope alive and so keeps the being open and on the move is precisely its *unfulfilment*. One may say that the *paradox of hope* (and the paradox of possibility founded in hope) is that it may pursue its destination solely through betraying its nature; the most exuberant of energies expends itself in the urge towards rest. Possibility uses up its openness in search of closure. Its image of the better being is its own impoverishment . . .

The togetherness of the being-for is cut out of the same block; it shares in the paradoxical lot of all possibility. It lasts as long as it is unfulfilled, yet it uses itself up in never ending effort of fulfilment, of recapturing the bond, making it tight and immune to all future temptations. In an important, perhaps decisive sense, it is self-destructive and self-defeating: its triumph is its death.

The Other, like restless and unpredictable art, like the future itself, is a *mystery*. And being-for-the-Other, going towards the Other through the twisted and rocky gorge of affection, brings that mystery into view – makes it into a challenge. That mystery is what has triggered the sentiment in the first place – but cracking that mystery is what the resulting movement is about. The mystery must be unpacked so that the being-for may focus on the Other: one needs to know what to focus on. (The 'demand' is *unspoken*, the responsibility undertaken is *unconditional*; it is up to him or her who follows the demand and takes up the responsibility to decide what the following of that demand and carrying out of that responsibility means in practical terms.)

Mystery – noted Max Frisch – (and the Other is a mystery), is an exciting puzzle, but one tends to get tired of that excitement. 'And so one creates for oneself an image. This is a loveless act, the betrayal.'[28] Creating an image of the Other leads to the substitution of the image for the Other; the Other is now fixed – soothingly and comfortingly. There is nothing to be excited about anymore. I know what the Other needs, I know where my responsibility starts and ends. Whatever the Other may now do will be taken down and used against him. What used to be received as an exciting surprise now looks more like perversion; what used to be adored as exhilarating creativity now feels like wicked levity. Thanatos has taken over from Eros, and the excitement of the ungraspable turned into the dullness and tedium of the grasped. But, as György Lukács observed, 'everything one person may know about another is only expectation, only

---

[28] Max Frisch, *Sketchbook 1946–1949*, trans. Geoffrey Skelton (New York: Harcourt Brace Jovanovich, 1977), p. 17.

potentiality, only wish or fear, acquiring reality only as a result of what happens later, and this reality, too, dissolves straightaway into potentialities'. Only death, with its finality and irreversibility, puts an end to the musical-chairs game of the real and the potential – it once and for all closes the embrace of togetherness which was before invitingly open and tempted the lonely self.[29] 'Creating an image' is the dress rehearsal of that death. But creating an image is the inner urge, the constant temptation, the *must* of all affection . . .

It is the loneliness of being abandoned to an unresolvable ambivalence and an unanchored and formless sentiment which sets in motion the togetherness of being-for. But what loneliness seeks in togetherness is an end to its present condition – an end to itself. Without knowing – without being capable of knowing – that the hope to replace the vexing loneliness with togetherness is founded solely on its own unfulfilment, and that once loneliness is no more, the togetherness (the being-for togetherness) must also collapse, as it cannot survive its own completion. What the loneliness seeks in togetherness (suicidally for its own cravings) is the foreclosing and pre-empting of the future, cancelling the future before it comes, robbing it of mystery but also of the possibility with which it is pregnant. Unknowingly yet necessarily, it seeks it all to its own detriment, since the success (if there is a success) may only bring it back to where it started and to the condition which prompted it to start on the journey in the first place.

The togetherness of being-for is always in the future, and nowhere else. It is no more once the self proclaims: 'I have arrived', 'I have done it', 'I fulfilled my duty.' The being-for starts from the realization of the bottomlessness of the task, and ends with the declaration that the infinity has been exhausted. This is the tragedy of being-for – the reason why it cannot but be death-bound while simultaneously remaining an undying attraction. In this tragedy, there are many happy moments, but no happy end. Death is always the foreclosure of possibilities, and it comes eventually in its own time, even if not brought forward by the impatience of love. The catch is to direct the affection to staving off the end, and to do this against the affection's nature.

What follows is that, if moral relationship is grounded in the being-for togetherness (as it is), then it can exist as a project, and guide the self's conduct only as long as its nature of a project (a not-yet-completed project) is not denied. Morality, like the future itself,

[29]   See György Lukács, 'The Moment and Form', in *Soul and Form*, trans. Ann Bostock (Cambridge, Mass.: MIT Press, 1974), pp. 107–9.

is forever not-yet. (And this is why the ethical code, any ethical code, the more so the more perfect it is by its own standards, supports morality the way the rope supports the hanged man.) It is because of our loneliness that we crave togetherness. It is because of our loneliness that we open up to the Other and allow the Other to open up to us. It is because of our loneliness (which is only belied, not overcome, by the hubbub of the being-with) that we turn into moral selves. And it is only through allowing the togetherness its possibilities which only the future can disclose that we stand a chance of acting morally, and sometimes even of being good, in the present.

3

Broken Lives, Broken Strategies

The 'Middle' in the title of Gillian Rose's book *The Broken Middle*[1] stands for the space that extends, and the time that passes, between the 'Beginning' and the 'End'. The 'Beginning' is the *potentiality*; the 'End' – the *actuality* of being. When contemplated from the Middle, the beginning is remembered as a cluster of possibilities that already begin to vanish or ossify; the end is adumbrated as the foreclosing of possibilities. But it is in the Middle that the potentiality is trimmed and congealed into actuality. It is in the Middle where we, sad alchemists, convert the gold of freedom into the base metal of necessity. It is the Middle, the work done there and the thought that makes the work done, which diffracts the contents of its own compound of freedom and boundedness onto two separate and opposite screens and recasts the beginning as the universe of the possible and the end as the realm of unfreedom. It is the silent or outspoken work done in the Middle that sets the beginning apart from the end and makes both oppose each other.

The Middle is the seat of ambiguity, ambivalence and equivocation – of the oppositions 'which might initiate process and pain' (p. xiii) but which are not resolved in that process, however painful. The reward for pain is the 'risk of coming to know', meaning to know the presence and irresolution of contraries, the 'aporetic' fate of being.

'I am an end or a beginning', noted Franz Kafka. 'I am an end or

---

[1]   Gillian Rose, *The Broken Middle: Out of our Ancient Society* (Oxford: Blackwell, 1992).

a beginning' is the modality of the Middle. Such end and beginning as meet there are the end of the beginning and the beginning of the end: beginning is ending because its hold is loosening, the end is but starting because its grip is still weak. This is the place of loneliness, fear, anxiety – and moral choice. This is the place of responsibility. At the start, anxiety has no anchor, it is just the premonition of the 'possibility of possibility'. Says Rose: 'Not the choosing of good and evil but possibility . . . gives rise to anxiety, the "intermediate" psychological term for this passing of possibility over into actuality which is not logical nor ethical, but existential, "entangled freedom", where freedom is entangled in itself' (p. 95). The 'ethical' is the moral that has been already pre-empted, 'communalized' or divinized. At the time of the Middle, the ethical – the law – is always already there. It helps as little to quell anxiety as the knowledge that God's verdict has been already recorded did to disperse the nightmares of the pious Calvinist. One still confronts freedom suspecting that it is not really as free as it looks and pretends, but knowing little of the nature of bondage. In Maurice Blanchot's words, 'everyone here has his own prison, but in that prison each person is free.'[2] Like Hermann Hesse's Knecht, so the hero of Blanchot's 'Idyll' finds the world unliveable when he is finally allowed to enter it. Can one be free only inside the prison? Is not the delusion of freedom outside the true beginning of bondage? Is not the actor/author (and everyone is an actor/author of one's life) 'the ephemeral character who is born and dies each evening in order to make himself extravagantly seen, killed by the performance that makes him visible'?[3] Before the work is done/word written down, freedom is not yet. When it has been done, it is no more (and so is the actor/author, s/he who works/writes).

Breaking out, into prison

One can read Rose's '*broken* Middle' as the 'broken *prison*' (or, more precisely perhaps, though certainly more perplexingly – breaking the boundary between the prison and the world outside). What has happened on the road to the point where modernity reaches its *post*(humous life?) is the dismantling of the prison walls, with the effect that authorship/actorship, no more 'outside' as there are no walls to demarcate the non-incarceration, finds itself doing the DIY job. The *broken* Middle is the world of private prison huts, each

[2] Maurice Blanchot, 'Idyll', in *Vicious Circles*, trans. Paul Aster (New York: Station Hill, 1985), p. 10.
[3] Maurice Blanchot, 'After the Fact', in *Vicious Circles*, p. 60.

custom-made by its 'singular', 'unique' resident. The Middle has been broken (was there ever an unbroken one?) in the course of the *privatization of the prison service.*

In the colony of one-cell prisons which is the site of the broken Middle, freedom means 'to be always all-ready for anxiety' (p. 87); there, 'anxiety defines sin, not sin anxiety', though 'law precedes desire and intelligibility' (p. 86) – there always has been a beginning *before* the Middle is reached, though in an individual prison everything seems to 'begin from the beginning', to start afresh, inside – in the Middle itself. Sin is the product of anxiety, but anxiety arises from the vague, yet poignant feeling that the sin has been *already* committed, and from the still more harrowing uncertainty as to the exact nature of that sin.

What does this 'already' stand for? More importantly, what power – actorial/authorial power – made that 'already' into a sinful one? From where comes that Law which, if known, would make one's own actorship/authorship intelligible? Kafka's K. struggled in vain to find the answers in the court of law; the court received him when he came and dismissed him when he went. The crime, so it seemed, was to be accused of one – but no one spelled out the charge, no one sat on the prosecutor's bench. Despairing of finding the beginning of his guilt, Kafka wrote: 'My imperfection is . . . not congenital, not earned.' 'The reproaches lie around inside me.'[4] The vagueness, the haunting elusiveness of the Law guided Kierkegaard's pen, when he wrote of the 'continual commandment': 'I hear it, as it were, even when I do not hear it, in such a way that, although it is not audible itself, it muffles or embitters the voice bidding me to do other things.' Rose comments: 'the curse of continual commandment grating against the temporal demands of the opposed and embittered voice . . . The non-intelligible inner commandment which nevertheless insists on being communicated is, in effect, imperative but not comprehendable' (pp. 73–4). A century after Kierkegaard, Emmanuel Lévinas wrote of 'obeying the order before it is formulated', the command which is binding before it has been spoken.[5] And Knud E. Løgstrup concluded that since 'The Command' is 'unconditional, infinite, absolute', and above all 'unspoken', 'a person can never be entirely sure that he has acted in the right manner'.[6]

---

[4]   *The Diaries of Franz Kafka*, ed. Max Brod (Harmondsworth: Penguin, 1964), pp. 18–19.
[5]   Emmanuel Lévinas, *Otherwise than Being, or Beyond Essence*, trans. Alphonso Linges (The Hague: Martinus Nijhoff, 1981), p. 13.
[6]   Knud E. Løgstrup, *The Ethical Demand*, trans. Theodor J. Jensen (Philadelphia: Fortran Press, 1971), pp. 48, 46, 114.

The 'brokenness' of the Middle is lived as uncertainty; an uncertainty from which each act is an attempt to escape (to pass from the Beginning, where everything is but the possibility, to the End, where certainty has been bought at the price of freedom), but which each act only succeeds in deepening. It is as if the Middle laboured under the curse of never ending Beginning; as if the Beginning, that 'tyranny of opportunities' (Hannah Arendt), was never to end . . .

A sociologist would be naturally inclined to decipher the infuriating 'under-determination' of the command never spoken and order never formulated as the emergence of diffuse, de-centred, contradictory social pressures from the secure shelter of the Divine and its one and only Code of Moral Law. Having abandoned all pretence of universality (which could be only construed as supra-human), that 'liberation' left the lonely prisoner of the Middle free to build his own prison . . .

This is the finding brought home from Rose's exploratory expedition to the Middle:

> The agony of authorship is to remain with anxiety of beginning and equivocation of the ethical . . . Because the middle cannot be mended, because no politics or knowledge may be available or employable, it does not mean that no comprehension or representation is possible, or that it is in any case avoidable. (p. 296)

No recipes of repairing the fissure are to be trusted; the more radical they are, the more they need to be suspected. Each attempt to repair (no attempt can do without violence) will but exacerbate the condition meant to be repaired. Residing in the broken Middle is our common fate. We can live at no other place; there is no other place, nor could there be.

Rose offers us serene, dignified philosophy that shuns illusions and – more than anything else – self-delusions. What it rejects is, in the end, the modern hope of the Human replacing the Divine and doing His job. In this sense, the most important of senses, Rose's philosophy, despite the author's own protestations, is *postmodern through and through*. In a fashion so typical of postmodern mind, it still thinks it would be nice if the hopes of modernity came true but it no more believes that they ever will.

Rose's philosophy fits well the present mood of the 'disenchantment mark two': disenchantment with the potency and wisdom of the same *human reason and will* which the first disenchantment, the modern disenchantment, the disenchantment of Nature (the code-name for the Divine), bestowed with magic powers and the gift of infallibility (the act that reforged that disenchantment into a philosophy of optimism and boisterous self-confidence). 'No more salvation by society', wrote Peter Drucker recently. No more social engineering, we all shout, with varying degrees of shrillness. As to the dreamt-of communal alternative to the now universally suspect state – more and more fingers get singed as the heat of communally fanned emotions melts the old civilized solidarities to pour them into the moulds of new, uncivilized ones. Beware the salvation coming from those quarters – this much we may know by now; though whatever we *may* know, many are seeking it and many more still will join them in the search.

Paul Valéry[7] once described our civilization as a 'regime of intense excitations'. To be immersed in such a civilization, said Valéry, means to be 'intoxicated by energy', 'besotted by haste'. Indeed, ours is a kind of civilization characterized more by its curious mode of self-cancelling being, than by any fixed contents; more by attitudes than substances. It does not matter so much what is being done and what targets are chased; what does matter is that whatever is being done be done quickly, and that the chased targets escape capture, move and keep moving. To be 'intoxicated with energy' means to be intoxicated with the *ability* to move and act, not with any particular work to be done or particular destination to be reached. Our civilization is not about the *delay* of gratification (that would be, indeed, contrary to its nature), but about the *impossibility* of being gratified.

Modern life, Valéry pointed out, is energized by the unquenchable thirst for energy, not guided by the need to satisfy 'eternal life needs'. Finding new sources of energy and exploiting them more efficiently means increasing the potentiality of labour, more often than not in excess of any needs already felt. Modernity 'is lavish with needs' ('les prodigue'); it creates new needs as it goes, needs never before experienced, previously unimaginable. 'Having invented a new material, it invents, *to suit its properties*, new diseases it may cure, new cravings it may pacify . . .'

> Men are, therefore, drunk by dissipation. Abuse of speed; abuse of light; abuse of tranquillizers, sedatives and stimulants; abuse of the frequency of impressions; abuse of the formidable means of *decoupling* and *activating*, which puts enormous powers in the hands of a child. All present life is inseparable from that abuse . . . People develop dependency on the poison, require its continuous supply, find each dose insufficient. In the times of Ronsard, the eye was satisfied with a candle. The sages of those times, who willingly worked at night, read (and what illegible scribblings they

[7] See Paul Valéry, 'Sur la crise de l'intelligence', in *Vues* (Paris: La Table Ronde, 1948), pp. 122–4.

read!) and wrote without difficulty in any flickering and miserable light. Today, one needs twenty, fifty, one hundred candles [watts].

Life, one may say, is always – and endemically so – a self-critique. But modern life, Valéry seems to suggest, has accelerated that critique to such an extent that the achievement of the goal previously pursued discredits and ridicules the need (exposing its unforgivable modesty), instead of satisfying it. We may say that when need-gratifying becomes an addiction, no dose of gratification can gratify any more. At some critical speed gratification becomes inconceivable – and then the acceleration itself, rather than accumulation of gains, becomes the motive of the chase. Under the circumstances, the opposition between conservatism and creation, preservation and critique collapses. (The implosion of the opposition is aptly grasped by the idea of *recycling*, which blends preservation with renewal, rejection with affirmation.) To be conservative is to maintain the pace of acceleration. Or better still – to keep, to preserve the acceleration's self-accelerating tendency . . .

Acceleration and its discontents: 'quality of life'

There would be no interest in the 'quality of life' (the concept itself would hardly have been coined), if not for the widespread, often vague, but always acute and unnerving feeling that life as it is 'is not good enough'. Discussion about quality of life is not so much about deciding what a truly good life would be like, as it is about giving that vague, elusive feeling of disaffection some flesh and bone: about spelling out just what makes life as it is not pleasant enough and on the whole unsatisfactory.

For that reason the 'quality of life' discourse is in its innermost core *a critique of daily life*. Only secondarily is it what it pretends to be in the first place – a critique of the principles of social integration and systemic organization, or of moral standards of society, or both (depending on the theoretical frame adopted). It is, therefore, true to the spirit of modern mentality, which from the start felt uncomfortable in the 'broken Middle' ('out of here, that's my goal' – as Kafka noted), but believed that an escape may be plotted; which was inebriated with its own ability to make things different from what they happen to be at the moment (and thus could not conceive of a valid reason for tolerating the things being as they are), and denied the authority of extant reality in the name of what that reality could become if diligently worked on. And yet the critique conducted under the heading of 'quality of life' differs from the mainstream cultural criticism of 'classical' modernity in two important respects. These two differences give it a distinctly *post*modern character.

First, the idea of 'quality of life' came to replace the preoccupation with *self-preservation and survival*, which used to be at the heart of the modern critique. In the most radical, Marxist critique of modern society in the form that society was given under the aegis of capitalism, society stood condemned for inefficiency and lack of moral standards in performing (or not performing) the task of securing human survival. Modernity (at least in its capitalist form) was accused of wasting human creative effort, and of failing to provide for a just distribution of the resources that human survival demanded. Accordingly, 'survival' was the name of the game in which capitalism failed and socialism's success was hoped for. 'Quality of life', on the other hand, becomes the main standard of reality-critique in the part of the world in which survival in its basic, biological sense has been assured for all or almost all humans (or at least so it has been assumed) – so that the future which supplies the criteria for criticizing the present cannot be imagined as 'more *survival*' ('survival more secure'), but only as 'more *happiness*' of those whose survival (as beings capable of pursuing happiness and being happy) has been already guaranteed. As Ulrich Beck pointed out in *Risikogesellschaft*, and more poignantly yet in *Gegengifte*, the issues of survival reappear in contemporary discussion in a changed form: as the problems of detecting and neutralizing the risks inadvertently created by the spectacular achievements of science and technology in *fulfilling* the task of insuring survival. We may note, though, that this concern with survival, mark two, blends completely in practice with the concerns for quality of life; for instance, most support for the ecological movement comes from people worried about the deterioration of the happiness-generating potential of their habitat, rather than about a more abstract issue of the continuation of the human species.

Secondly, and perhaps even more symptomatically, the 'quality of life' differs from 'survival' (and all other goals which modernity set in front of itself) by its endemic *non-finality*. It was the paradox of life bent on survival that the sought-after ideal state, in whatever colours it was painted, appeared as above all the end of struggle and the final resolution of whatever might have been felt as a 'problem' needing 'resolution'; as something like 'the end of history' – a stable, unchanging state of affairs, but even more directly as the end of life itself; the unspoken and unspeakable ideal of life filled with the worry of survival is death ... The horizon of life-for-the-sake-of-self-preservation was the state of *perfection* – and perfection, as we all knew since the times of Alberti, is the no-change state, a state which cannot be improved any further – a state which any change may only make worse than it is. And so the modern reality-critique always used solid standards to measure and expose reality's shortcomings. (The trajectory of progress – one which allowed the critics to depict the present as already backward, 'behind time', and thus doomed to extinction – was invariably imagined as a track with a finishing line.) On the other hand, the contemporary (postmodern) reality-critique, organized around the concept of the quality of life, does not possess, or explicitly rejects, the idea of a 'final state', of a known-in-advance summit to which humans, in search of improvement, may climb. The goal of quality of life is intrinsically open-ended – though not for the sluggishness of imagination, but for the horror of 'mortgaging the future', pre-empting the possibilities it may yet disclose; for the fear of 'being fixed' and for the distaste of constraints which the preference for a specific 'ideal state' would necessarily impose on the pursuit of the good life. One may say, paradoxically, that the defining feature of the postmodern idea of the good life is the lack of definition of the good life.

The successive campaigns conducted in the name of quality of life tend to be, of course, specific. Each campaign is triggered by a particular complaint: by the inconvenience most painful, the danger most fearful, the dream most poignant at a particular time or place for a particular category of people. But the campaign topics do not 'naturally' add up into one overwhelming, exterritorial and extemporal model of an 'ultimate' quality of life which would make all further efforts of improvement gratuitous and redundant. It is, rather, the ability to set ever new goals, and not any goal in particular, which comes closest to the popular (though seldom articulated) image/postulate of the good life. (Already in 1958 Karl Jaspers noted that 'our time thinks in terms of "knowing how to do it", even where there is nothing to be done'.) This emphasis on non-fixity, on freedom of manoeuvre, on fitness to embrace and absorb new experience and new opportunities for pleasure whatever such opportunities may yet prove to be, is after all in tune with the essential contingency, episodicity and fragmented, 'non-systemic' character of postmodern existence.

The concept of 'quality of life' has had such a spectacular career in intellectual discourse precisely because of the resonance between the notorious elusiveness and under-determination of its contents and similar features endemic to the experience of postmodern life. Postmodern life strategies, like the idea of the quality of life, are guided by the heuristic principles of 'keeping the options open', avoidance of commitment and, more generally, being wary of 'mortgaging the future'.

It is for this reason that any definition of what the quality of life – now missing, yet needed to be gained – consists of, is bound to be local and transitory, soon to be forgotten by those who today cling to it, and not at all certain to be understood even by next-door neighbours (though this may seem incredible to people who embrace such a definition 'naturally' and uncritically, as self-evident; as already Schopenhauer discovered and Freud explained, it is the prospect of overcoming a specific unhappiness here and now which always appears to us as 'happiness as such'). *The most prominent feature of 'quality of life' is that it always exists as an image*, and that that image is perpetually *changing*. That credibility, seductive power and mobilizing potential of each image (or the lack of it) depends on its chiming with (or its dissonance with) the locally and historically circumscribed experience. In principle, the images of the 'quality of life' are *resistant to universalization* – and all the more so the more concrete and precisely defined they are.

The area thrown open by the quality-of-life discourse is therefore a territory of endemic and perpetual under-determination (though it was brought into being originally with the intention to cure the vexingly elusive and vague disaffection and anxiety). Ambivalence always generates the *demand for expertise*; lack of orientation attracts experts in road-finding. Experts tend to promise a once-for-all, secure escape route from uncertainty, but what they offer in practice is a decision how to 'settle' the present dilemma without in the least reducing its ambivalence. It is precisely because of the fact that the reduction of ambivalence is not on the cards, that only controversial and inconclusive 'settlements' are feasible, that the need for experts is so acute. We need them above all as *authority*; as someone we can trust because everybody trusts them, so that when accepting their advice we may be less tormented with doubts or guilty feelings than when we act on our own responsibility. The disaffection born of the life-framework defined by consumer society provides for that reason a particularly fertile ground for the growth and propagation of ever new specialisms. The growth is self-perpetuating, as none of the expert 'settlements' can be by definition finite and final; paraphrasing Wittgenstein, one can say that the succesive changes in the quality of life leave everything in the human condition as ambivalent as before.

Acceleration and its discontents: 'identity'

'Identity continues to be the problem it was throughout modernity' – says Douglas Kellner, and adds that 'far from identity disappearing in contemporary society, it is rather reconstructed and redefined'. Just a few paragraphs further down Kellner casts doubts on the feasibility of the selfsame 'reconstruction and redefinition', pointing out that 'identity today becomes a freely chosen game, a theatrical presentation of the self' and that 'when one radically shifts identity at will, one might lose control . . .'[8] Kellner's ambivalence reflects the present ambivalence of the issue itself. One hears today of identity and its problems more often than ever before in modern times. And yet one wonders whether the current obsession is not just another case of the general rule according to which things are noticed only *ex post facto*; when they vanish, go bust or fall out of joint.

I propose that while it is true that identity 'continues to be the problem', this is *not* 'the problem it was throughout modernity'. Indeed, if the *modern* 'problem of identity' was how to construct an identity and keep it solid and stable, the *postmodern* 'problem of identity' is primarily how to avoid fixation and keep the options open. In the case of identity, as in other cases, the catchword of modernity was 'creation'; the catchword of postmodernity is 'recycling'. Or one may say that if the 'media which was the message' of modernity was the photographic paper (think of relentlessly swelling family albums, tracing page by yellowing page the slow accretion of irreversible and non-erasable identity-yielding events), the ultimately postmodern medium is the videotape (eminently erasable and reusable, calculated not to hold anything forever, admitting today's events solely on condition of effacing yesterday's ones, oozing the message of universal 'until-further-noticeness' of everything deemed worthy of recording). The main identity-bound anxiety of modern times was the worry about durability; it is the concern with commitment-avoidance today. Modernity built in steel and concrete; postmodernity – in bio-degradable plastic.

Like 'quality of life', identity as such is a modern invention. To say, as it is commonly said, that modernity led to the 'disembedding' of identity, or that it rendered the identity 'unencumbered', is to assert a pleonasm – since at no time did identity 'became' a problem; it could exist only as a *problem*, it was a 'problem' from its birth – was *born* as a problem (that is, as something one needs do something about – as a task); it was a problem, and thus ready to be born, precisely because of that experience of under-determination and free-floating which came to be articulated *ex post facto* as 'disembeddedment'. Identity would not have congealed into a visible and graspable

---

[8]   Douglas Kellner, 'Popular Culture and Constructing Postmodern Identities', in *Modernity and Identity*, ed. Scott Lasch and Jonathan Friedman (Oxford: Blackwell, 1992).

entity in any other but the 'disembedded' or 'unencumbered' form.

One thinks of identity whenever one is *not sure of* where one belongs; that is, one is not sure how to place oneself among the evident variety of behavioural styles and patterns, and how to make sure that people around would accept this placement as right and proper, so that both sides would know how to go on in each other's presence. *'Identity' is a name given to the sought escape from that uncertainty.* Hence 'identity', though ostensibly a noun, behaves like a verb, albeit a strange one to be sure: it appears only in the future tense. Though all too often hypostatized as an attribute of a material entity, identity has the ontological status of a project and a *postulate*. To say 'postulated identity' is to say one word too many, as there is not nor can there be any other identity but a postulated one. Identity is a critical projection of what is demanded and/or sought upon 'what is', with an added proviso that it is up to the 'what is' to rise, by its own effort, to the 'sought/demanded'; or, more exactly still, *identity is an oblique assertion of the inadequacy or incompleteness of the 'what is'.*

Identity entered modern mind and practice dressed from the start as an individual task. It was up to the individual to find an escape from uncertainty. Not for the first and not for the last time *socially* created problems were to be resolved by *individual* efforts, and *collective* maladies healed by *private* medicine. Not that the individuals were left to their own initiative and that their acumen was trusted; quite the contrary – putting the individual responsibility for self-formation on the agenda spawned the host of trainers, coaches, teachers, counsellors and guides all claiming to hold superior knowledge of what the identities they recommended consisted of and of the ways such identities could be acquired, held, and shown to be acquired and held. The concepts of identity-building and of culture (that is, of the idea of the individual incompetence, of the need for collective breeding and the importance of skilful and knowledgeable breeders) were mutually complementary, gave sense to each other, and thus could only be born together. The 'disembedded' identity ushered simultaneously into the individual freedom of choice and into the individual's dependency on expert guidance.

Modern life as pilgrimage

The figure of the pilgrim was not a modern invention; it is as old as Christianity. But modernity gave it a new prominence and a seminally novel twist.

When Rome lay in ruins – humbled, humiliated and sacked and pillaged by Alaric's nomads, St Augustine jotted down the following observation: '[I]t is recorded of Cain that he built a city, while Abel, as though he were merely a pilgrim on earth, built none.' 'The true city of the saints is in heaven'; here on earth, mused St Augustine, Christians wander 'as on pilgrimage through time looking for the Kingdom of eternity'.[9]

For pilgrims through time, the truth is elsewhere; the true place is always some distance, some time away. Wherever the pilgrim may be now, it is not where he ought to be, and not where he dreams of being. The distance between the true world and this world here and now is made of the mismatch between what is to be achieved and what has been. The glory and gravity of the future destination debases the present, plays down its significance, makes light of it. For the pilgrim, what purpose may the city serve? For the pilgrim, only streets make sense, not the houses – houses tempt the tired wanderer to rest and relax, to forget about the destination or to postpone it indefinitely. Even the streets, though, may prove to be obstacles rather than help, traps rather than thoroughfares. They may misguide, divert from the straight path, lead astray. 'Judeo-Christian culture', writes Richard Sennett, 'is, at its very roots, about experiences of spiritual dislocation and homelessness . . . Our faith began at odds with place.'[10]

'We are pilgrims through time' was under the pen of St Augustine not an exhortation, but a statement of fact. We are pilgrims whatever we do, and there is little we can do about it even if we wished. Earthly life is but a brief overture to the eternality of the soul. Ultimately, it is not where we are destined to be – and only that part of ours that is destined to be elsewhere is worthy of concern and care.

Only a few would wish, and have the ability, to compose that brief earthly overture themselves, in tune with the music of the heavenly spheres – to make their fate into a consciously embraced destiny. These few would need to escape the distractions of the town. The desert is the habitat they must choose. The desert of the Christian hermit was set at a distance from the hurly-burly of daily life, away from the town and the village, from the realm of the mundane, from the *polis*. The desert meant putting a distance between oneself and

---

[9] St Augustine, *The City of God*, trans. Gerald S. Walsh et al. (New York: Image, 1958), p. 325. The meaning of the Early-Christian pilgrimage/hermitage has been exquisitely explored by Judith Adler in her forthcoming book.
[10] Richard Sennett, *The Conscience of the Eye: The Design and Social Life of Cities* (London: Faber and Faber, 1993), p. 6.

'here' – one's duties and obligations, the warmth and the agony of being with others, being looked at by others, being framed and moulded by their scrutiny, demands and expectations. Here, in mundane quotidianity, one's hands were tied, and so were one's thoughts. Here, the horizon was tightly packed with huts, barns, copses, groves and church towers. Here, wherever one moved, one was *in a place*, and being in place meant staying put, doing what the place needed to be done. The desert, on the contrary, was a land not-yet sliced into places, and for that reason it was the land of self-creation. The desert, said Edmond Jabès, 'is a space where one step gives way to the next, which undoes it, and the horizon means hope for a tomorrow which speaks.' 'You do not go to the desert to find identity, but to lose it, to lose your personality, to become anonymous . . . And then something extraordinary happens: you hear silence speak.'[11]

The desert is the archetype and the greenhouse of the raw, bare, primal and bottom-line freedom that is but the absence of bounds. What made the medieval hermits feel in the desert so close to God was the feeling of being themselves god-like: unbound by habit and convention, by needs of their own bodies and other people's souls, by their past deeds and present actions. In the words of the present-day theorists, one would say that the hermits were the first to live through the experience of 'disembedded', 'unencumbered' selves. They were god-like, because whatever they did they did *ab nihilo*. Their pilgrimage to God was an exercise in self-construction. (This is why the Church, wishing to be the sole connecting line to God, resented the hermits from the start – and soon went out of its way

---

[11] Edmond Jabès, *The Book of Questions*, vol. 2, trans. Rosmarie Waldrop (Hanover: Wesleyan University Press , 1991), p. 342. *The Book of Margins*, trans. Rosmarie Waldrop (Chicago University Press, 1993), p. xvi. Jabès quotes the words of Gabriel Bounoure: '. . . The desert, by its exclusion of housing, opens an infinite elsewhere to man's essential wandering. Here, no here makes sense.' (*The Book of Margins*, p. 16) Jean Baudrillard was struck on his fateful American trip by the affinity between the desert and the modern metropolis: 'not only is there a profound and necessary relation between the immorality of the circulation of signs and the primitive scene of the deserts, but it's the same thing . . . The deserts, let's not forget, are the place of an extermination (including that of the Indians), the place of a disappearance of meaning (including that of nature). The metropoles, the megapolises, along with the whole "American way of life", they too are the place of a subtle extermination of man and the ends of man; their prodigious outgrowth, the exact inverse of the desert, is however just as much a subtle extermination of meaning.' ('The End of the End', Interview with John Johnston, in *Baudrillard Live: Selected Interviews*, ed. Mike Gane (London: Routledge, 1993), p. 162)

to force them into monastic orders, under the close supervision of rules and routine.)

The Protestants, as Weber told us, accomplished a feat unthinkable for the lonely hermits of yore: they became *inner-wordly pilgrims*. They invented the way of embarking on pilgrimage without leaving home. This they could do, however, only because the desert stretched and reached deep into their towns, right up to their doorsteps. They did not venture into the desert; it was the world of their daily life which was becoming more and more 'like the desert'. Like the desert, the world became placeless; the familiar features had been obliterated, but the new ones that were meant to replace them were given the kind of permanence once thought unique to sand dunes. In the new post-Reformation city of modernity, the desert began on the other side of the door.

The Protestant, that pattern-setter (or is he but an allegory?) for modern life-strategy, so Sennett tells us, was 'tempted by wilderness, by a place of emptiness which made no seductive demands of its own upon him'. In this he was not different from the hermit. The difference was that instead of travelling to the desert, the Protestant worked hard to make the desert come to him – to remake the world in the likeness of the desert. 'Impersonality, coldness and *emptiness* are essential words in the Protestant language of environment; they express the desire to see the outside as null, lacking value.'[12] This is the kind of language in which one speaks of the desert: of nothingness waiting to become something, if only for a while; of meaninglessness waiting to be given meaning, if only a passing one; of a space without contours, ready to accept any contour offered, if only until other contours are offered; of a space not scarred with past furrows, yet fertile with expectations of sharp blades; of virgin land yet to be ploughed and tilled; of the land of the perpetual beginning; of the place-no-place whose name and identity is not-yet. In such a land, the trails are blazed by the destination of the pilgrim, and there are few other tracks to reckon with.

In such a land, commonly called modern society, pilgrimage is no more a *choice* of the mode of life; less still is it a heroic or *saintly* choice. Living one's life as pilgrimage is no more the kind of ethical wisdom revealed to, or intuited by, the chosen and the righteous. Pilgrimage is what one does *of necessity*, even if the push is miraculously reincarnated as a pull, and a purpose is made of inevitability. One *must* live one's life as pilgrimage in order to avoid being lost in a desert – to invest the walking with a purpose while wandering the

[12] Sennett, *The Conscience of the Eye*, pp. 44, 46.

land with no destination. Being a pilgrim, one can do more than walk – one can *walk to*. One can also look back at the footprints left in the sand and collate them into a road. One can *reflect* on the road past and speak of it as a *progress towards*, an advance, *a coming closer to*; one can make a distinction between 'behind' and 'ahead', and plot the 'road ahead' as a succession of footprints yet to pockmark the land without features. Destination, the set purpose of life's pilgrimage, gives form to the formless, makes a whole out of the fragmentary, lends continuity to the episodic.

The desert-like world commands life to be lived as pilgrimage. But because life has been already made into a pilgrimage, the world at the doorsteps is desert-like, featureless; its meaning is yet to be brought in through the wandering which would transform it into the track leading to the finishing line where the meaning resides. *This 'bringing in' of meaning has been called 'identity building'*. The pilgrim and the desert-like world he walks acquire their meanings *together*, and *through each other*. Both processes can and must go on because there is a distance between the goal (the meaning of the world and the identity of the pilgrim, always not-yet-reached, always in the future) and the present moment (the station of the wandering and the identity of the wanderer).

Both meaning and identity can exist only as *projects*, and it is the distance which enables the projects to be. The 'distance' is what we call, in the 'objective' language of space, the experience which in 'subjective', psychological terms we speak about as dissatisfaction with, and denigration of, the here and now. The 'distance' and 'dissatisfaction' have the same referent, and both make sense within the life lived as pilgrimage.

'It is the difference in amount between the pleasure of satisfaction which is *demanded* and that which is actually *achieved* that provides the driving factor which will permit of no halting at any position attained, but, in the poet's words "Presses ever forward unsubdued" (Faust)' – observed Freud in *Beyond the Pleasure Principle*. Janine Chasseguet-Smirgel[13] offers an extended commentary on that seminal observation, tracing the beginning of self-development, identity-building etc. to the primary condition of delayed gratification, of the never-to-be-bridged distance between the ego-ideal and the realities of the present.

'Distance' translates as 'delay' . . . Passage through space is a function of time, distances are measured by the time needed to cancel

---

[13] Janine Chasseguet-Smirgel, *The Ego-Ideal: A Psychoanalytic Essay on the Malady of the Ideal*, trans. Paul Barrows (London: Free Association Books, 1985).

them. 'Here' is the waiting; 'there' is the gratification. How far is it from here to there, from the waiting to gratification, from the void to meaning, from the project to identity? Ten years, twenty? As long as it takes to live one's vocation through? Time one can use to measure distances must be of the sort that schoolboy rulers are – straight, in one piece, with equidistant markings, made of tough and solid material. And such was, indeed, the time of modern living-towards-projects. It was like life itself – directional, continuous, and unbendable. Time that 'marches on' and 'passes'. Both life and time were made to the measure of pilgrimage.

For the pilgrim, for the modern man,[14] this meant in practical terms that he could/should/had to select his point of arrival fairly early in life with confidence, certain that the straight line of life-time ahead will not bend, twist or warp, come to a halt or turn backwards. Delay of gratification, much as the momentary frustration it begot, was an energizing factor and the source of identity-building zeal in as far as it was coupled with the trust in the linearity and cumulativeness of time. The foremost strategy of life as pilgrimage, of life as identity-building, was 'saving for the future', but saving for the future made sense as strategy only in as far as one could be sure that the future will reward the savings with interest and the bonus once accrued will not be withdrawn, that the savings will not be devalued before the bonus-distribution date or declared invalid currency; that what is seen today as 'capital' will be seen the same way tomorrow and the day after tomorrow. Pilgrims had a stake in the solidity of the world they walked; in a kind of world in which one can tell life as a continuous story, a 'sense-making' story, such a story as makes each event the effect of the event before and the cause of the event after, each age a station on the road pointing towards fulfilment. The world of pilgrims – of identity-builders – must be orderly, determined, predictable, insured; but above all, it must be a kind of world in which footprints are engraved for good, so that the trace and the record of past travels are kept and preserved. A world in which travelling may be indeed a pilgrimage. A world hospitable to the pilgrims.

[14] I have consistently spoken of the pilgrim as masculine. The choice has been deliberate. Whatever has been said thus far of the modern construction of life as pilgrimage has applied to males only. Women, together with other categories not thought of as capable of self-creation (or, rather, as called to transcend their present station and make themselves into something better than they are) were consigned to the background, to the landscape *through which* the itinerary of the pilgrim is to be plotted, were cast in perpetual 'here and now'; in a space without distance and time without future. Distance and linear time were masculine . . .

The world inhospitable to pilgrims

The world is not hospitable to pilgrims any more. The pilgrims lost their battle by winning it. They made the world into a desert, but then found out that the desert, though comfortingly featureless for those who seek to make their mark, does not hold features well. The easier it is to impress a footprint, the easier it is to efface it. A gust of wind will do. And deserts are windy places.

It soon transpired that the real problem is not how to build identity, but how to preserve it; whatever you may build in the sand, it is unlikely to be a castle. In a desert-like world it takes no great effort to blaze a trail – the difficulty is how to recognize it as a trail after a while. How to distinguish a forward march from going in circles, from eternal return? It becomes virtually impossible to patch the trodden stretches of sand into an itinerary – let alone into a plan for a life-long journey.

The meaning of identity, points out Christopher Lasch, 'refers both to persons and to things. Both have lost their solidity in modern society, their definiteness and continuity.' The world construed of durable objects has been replaced 'with disposable products designed for immediate obsolescence'. In such a world, 'identities can be adopted and discarded like a change of costume'.[15] The horror of the new situation is that all diligent work of construction may prove to be in vain; its allurement is the fact of not being bound by past trials, being never irrevocably defeated, always 'keeping the options open'. The horror and the allurement alike make life-as-pilgrimage hardly feasible as a strategy and unlikely to be chosen as one. Not by many, anyway. And not with great chance of success.

In the life-game of postmodern consumers the rules of the game keep changing in the course of playing. The sensible strategy is therefore to keep each game short – so that a sensibly played game of life calls for the splitting of one big all-embracing game with huge stakes into a series of brief and narrow games with small ones. 'Determination to live one day at a time', 'depicting daily life as a succession of minor emergencies'[16] become the guiding principles of all rational conduct.

To keep the game short means to beware of long-term commit-

[15]   Christopher Lasch, *The Minimal Self; Psychic Survival in Troubled Times* (London: Pan Books, 1985), pp. 32, 34, 38.
[16]   Lasch, *The Minimal Self*, pp. 57, 62.

ments. To refuse to be 'fixed' one way or the other. Not to get tied to one place, however pleasurable the present stopover may feel. Not to wed one's life to one vocation only. Not to swear consistency and loyalty to anything and anybody. Not to *control* the future, but to *refuse to mortgage* it: to take care that the consequences of the game do not outlive the game itself, and to renounce reponsibility for such consequences as do. To forbid the past to bear on the present. In short, to cut the present off at both ends, to sever the present from history. To abolish time in any other form but a collection or an arbitrary sequence of present moments; to flatten the flow of time into *a continuous present.*

Once dismantled and no more a vector, time no more structures the space. On the ground, there is no more 'forward' and 'backward'; it is just the ability not to stand still that counts. *Fitness* – the capacity to move swiftly where the action is and be ready to take in experiences as they come – takes precedence over *health*, that idea of the standard of normalcy and of keeping that standard stable and unscathed. All delay, also 'delay of gratification', loses its meaning: there is no arrow-like time left to measure it.

And so the snag is no more how to discover, invent, construct, assemble (even buy) an identity, but how to prevent it from being too tight – and from sticking to the body. Well constructed and durable identity turns from asset into liability. *The hub of postmodern life strategy is not identity building, but the avoidance of being fixed.*

What possible purpose could the strategy of pilgrim-style 'progress' serve in this world of ours? In this world, not only jobs-for-life have disappeared, but trades and professions which have acquired the confusing habit of appearing from nowhere and vanishing without notice can hardly be lived as Weberian 'vocations' (and as if to rub salt into the wound, the demand for the skills needed to practise such professions seldom lasts as long as the time needed to acquire them – as most students find out to their despair). Jobs are no more protected, and most certainly no better than the fragile and precarious places where they are practised; whenever the words 'rationalization' or 'investment' or 'technical progress' are pronounced, one knows for sure that the disappearance of further jobs and work-places is in the pipeline. The stability and trustworthiness of the network of human relations does not fare much better. Ours is the age of Anthony Giddens's 'pure relationship' which 'is entered for its own sake, for what can be derived by each person' and so 'it can be terminated, more or less at will, by either partner at any particular point'; of 'confluent love' which 'jars with the "for-ever", "one-and-only" qualities of the romantic love complex' so that 'romance can no longer be equated with permanence'; of 'plastic sexuality', that is sexual enjoyment 'severed from its age-old integration with reproduction, kinship and the generations'.[17] One can hardly 'hook on' an identity to relationships which themselves are irreparably 'unhooked'; and one is solemnly advised not to try – as the strong commitment, deep attachment (let alone loyalty – that tribute to the by now obsolete idea that attachment has consequences that bind, while commitments mean obligations) may wound and scar when the time to detach the self from the partner arrives, as it almost certainly will. Besides, all the forces of the world, including the most overwhelming among them, militate against stable partnership; and no wonder, since, as Dean MacCannell has pointed out,

> Families and stable adult couples, including homosexual arrangements that resemble the heterosexual set-up (namely, long-term stable couples as opposed to the 'Tea-Room Trade' model) are 'dysfunctional' within the framework of corporate capitalism. It is not that sexually paired couples are likely to spend their time together plotting the overthrow of the symbolic order. It is a simple matter that couples and family members have a demonstrated capacity to entertain each other almost endlessly using only their bodies, facial expressions, gift for language, and the simplest of technologies.[18]

The game of life is fast and all-engrossing and attention-consuming, leaving no time to pause and think and draw elaborate designs. But again, adding impotence to bafflement, the rules of the game keep changing long before the game is finished. Values to be cherished and actively pursued, rewards to be fought for and stratagems to be deployed to get them, are all calculated, in George Steiner's phrase, 'for maximal impact and instant obsolescence'. For *maximal impact*, since in the world over-saturated with information attention turns into the scarcest of resources and only a shocking message (a genuine Heideggerian *Stoß*), and one more shocking than the last, stands a chance of catching it (until the next shock, that is); and *instant obsolescence*, as the site of attention needs to be cleared as soon

---

[17]   Anthony Giddens, *The Transformation of Intimacy: Sexuality, Love and Eroticism in Modern Societies* (Cambridge: Polity Press, 1992), pp. 58, 137, 61, 52, 27.
[18]   Dean MacCannell, *Empty Meeting Grounds: The Tourist Papers* (London: Routledge, 1993), p. 60. One of the spectacular results of that pressure, MacCannell suggests, is that 'an emerging criterion for a certain kind of visible success, "star" status, for professional women, is a public declaration of homo- or bi-sexuality, or at least a denial of interest in heterosexual relations and their associated cultural baggage, the family, the "mommy track".'

as it is filled, to make room for new messages bursting through the gate.

The overall result is the *fragmentation* of time into *episodes*, each one cut from its past and from its future, each one self-enclosed and self-contained. Time is no more a river, but a collection of ponds and pools.

No consistent and cohesive life strategy emerges from the experience which can be gathered in such a world – none remotely reminiscent of the sense of purpose and the rugged determination of the pilgrimage. Nothing emerges from that experience but (mostly negative) rules of thumb: do not plan your trips too long – the shorter the trip, the greater the chance of completing it; do not get emotionally attached to people you meet at the stopover – the less you care about them, the less it will cost you to move on; do not commit yourself too strongly to people, places, causes – you cannot know how long they will last or how long you will count them worthy of your commitment; do not think of your current resources as capital – savings lose value fast, and the once vaunted 'cultural capital' tends to turn in no time into cultural *liability*. Above all, do not delay gratification, if you can help it. Whatever you are after, try to get it *now*; you cannot know whether the gratification you seek today will be still gratifying tomorrow.

I propose that in the same way as the pilgrim was the most fitting allegory of modern life strategy preoccupied with the daunting task of identity-building – the stroller, the vagabond, the tourist and the player offer jointly the metaphor for the postmodern strategy moved by the horror of being bound and fixed.

None of the listed types/styles are postmodern inventions – they were known well before the advent of postmodern times. And yet as much as the modern conditions reshaped the figure of pilgrim they inherited from Christianity, the postmodern context gives new quality to the types known to its predecessors – and it does it in two crucial respects. First, the styles once practised by marginal people in marginal time-stretches and marginal places are now practised by the majority in the prime time of their lives and in places central to their life-world; they have become now, fully and truly, *life-styles*. Second, though a foursome – the types are not a matter of choice, not either/or; postmodern life is too messy and incoherent to be grasped by any one cohesive model. Each type conveys but a part of the story which hardly ever integrates into a totality (its 'totality' *is nothing but* the sum of its parts). In the postmodern chorus, all four types sing – sometimes in harmony, though much more often with cacophony as the result.

The pilgrim's successors

The stroller

Charles Baudelaire baptized Constantin Guy 'the painter of modern life' because Guy painted city street scenes the way they were seen by the stroller (*flâneur*). Commenting on Baudelaire's observation, Walter Benjamin made *flâneur* into a household name of cultural analysis and the central symbolic figure of the modern city. All strands of modern life seemed to meet and be tied together in the pastime and the experience of the stroller: going for a stroll as one goes to a theatre, finding themselves among strangers and being a stranger to them (in the crowd but not of the crowd), taking in those strangers as 'surfaces' – so that 'what one sees' exhausts 'what they are', and above all seeing and knowing of them episodically. Psychically, strolling means rehearsing human reality as a series of episodes – that is, as events without a past and with no consequences. It also means rehearsing meetings as mis-meetings, as encounters without impact: the fleeting fragments of other persons' lives the stroller spun off into stories at will – it was his perception that made them into actors in the plays he scripted, without their knowing that they are actors, let alone the plot of the drama they play. The stroller was the past master of simulation – he imagined himself a scriptwriter and a director pulling the strings of other people's lives without damaging or distorting their fate. The stroller practised the 'as if' life and the 'as if' engagement with other people's lives; he put paid to the opposition between 'appearance' and 'reality'; he was the creator without penalties attached to creation, the master who need not fear the consequences of his deeds, the bold one never facing the bills of courage. The stroller had all the pleasures of modern life without the torments attached.

Life-as-strolling was a far cry from life-as-pilgrimage. What the pilgrim did in all seriousness, the stroller mocked playfully; in the process, he got rid of the costs and the effects alike. The stroller fitted ill the modern scene, but then he hid in its wings. He was the man of leisure and he did his strolling in his time of leisure. The stroller and the strolling waited in the periphery for their hour to arrive. And it did arrive – or rather it was brought about by the postmodern avatar of the heroic producer into playful consumer. Now the strolling, once the activity practised by marginal people on the margins of 'real life', came to be life itself, and the question of 'reality' need not be dealt with anymore.

'Malls' in their original meaning refer to the tracts for strolling.

Now most of the malls are *shopping* malls, tracts to stroll while you shop and shop while you stroll. The merchandisers sniffed out the attraction and seductive power of strollers' habits and set about moulding them into life. Parisian arcades have been promoted retrospectively to the bridge-heads of the times to come: the postmodern islands in the modern sea. Shopping malls make the world (or a carefully walled off, electronically monitored and closely guarded part of it) safe for life-as-strolling. Or, rather, shopping malls are the worlds made by the bespoke designers to the measure of the stroller. The sites of mis-meetings, of encounters guaranteed to be episodic, of the present prised off from the past and the future, of surfaces glossing over surfaces. In these worlds, every stroller may imagine himself to be a director, though all strollers are the objects of direction. That direction is, as their own used to be, unobtrusive and invisible (though, unlike theirs, seldom inconsequential), so that baits feel like desires, pressures like intentions, seduction like decision-making; in the shopping malls, in life as shopping-to-stroll and strolling-to-shop, dependence dissolves in freedom, and freedom seeks dependence.

The malls initiated the postmodern promotion of the stroller, but also prepared the ground for further elevation (or is it purification?) of the stroller's life-model. The latter has been achieved in the *telecity* (Henning Bech's felicitous term), the city-as-the-stroller-haunt, distilled to its pure essence, now entering the ultimate shelter of the totally private, secure, locked and burglar-proof world of the lonely monad, where the physical presence of strangers does not conceal or interfere with their psychical out-of-reach. In its telecity version, the streets and the shopping malls have been cleansed of all that from the stroller's point of view was sport-spoiling, an impurity, redundancy or waste – so that what has been retained can shine and be enjoyed in all its unsullied purity. In Bech's words,

> the screen mediated world of the telecity exists only by way of surfaces; and, tendentially, everything can and must be turned into an object for the gaze . . . [T]here is, by way of 'readings' of the surface signs, opportunity for a much more intense and changing empathy in and out of identities, because of the possibilities of uninterfered and continual watching . . . Television is totally non-committal.[19]

The ultimate freedom is screen-directed, lived in the company of surfaces, and called zapping.

[19] Henning Bech, 'Living Together in the (Post)Modern World', paper presented at the session on *Changing Family Structure and the New Forms of Living Together*, European Conference of Sociology, Vienna, 22–8 August 1992.

The vagabond
The vagabond was the bane of early modernity, the bugbear that spurred the rulers and philosophers into the ordering and legislating frenzy.[20] The vagabond was *masterless*, and being masterless (out of control, out of the frame, on the loose) was one condition modernity could not bear and thus spent the rest of its history fighting. Elizabethan legislators were obsessed with the need to rule the vagrants off the roads and back to the parishes 'where they belonged' (but which they left precisely because they *did not* belong there any more). The vagabonds were the advanced troops or guerilla units of post-traditional chaos (construed by the rulers, in the usual fashion of using a mirror to paint the image of the Other, as *anarchy*), and they had to go if order (that is, the space managed and monitored) was to be the rule. The free-roaming vagabonds made the search for new, state-managed, societal-level order imperative and urgent.

What made the vagabond so terrifying was his apparent freedom to move and so to escape the net of the previously locally based control. Worse than that, the movements of the vagabond were unpredictable; unlike the pilgrim or, for that matter, a nomad, the vagabond has no set destination. You do not know where he will move next, because he himself does not know or care much. Vagabondage has no advance itinerary – its trajectory is patched together bit by bit, one piece at a time. Each place is for the vagabond a stopover, but he never knows how long he will stay in any of them; this will depend on the generosity and patience of the residents, but also on news of other places arousing new hopes. (The vagabond is pushed from behind by hopes already frustrated, and pulled forward by hopes yet untested.) The vagabond decides where to turn when he comes to the crossroads; he chooses the next stay reading the names on the road signs. It is easy to control the pilgrim (or even a nomad), so utterly predictable thanks to the pilgrim's purpose-mindedness or the routine monotony of the nomadic cycle. To control the wayward and erratic vagabond is, on the contrary, a daunting task (though this proved to be at the end of the day one of the few problems modern ingenuity did resolve).

Wherever the vagabond goes, he is a stranger; he can never be 'the native', the 'settled one', one with 'roots with the soil' – and not for the lack of trying: whatever he may do to ingratiate himself in the eyes of the natives, too fresh is the memory of his arrival – that is,

---

[20]   See Zygmunt Bauman, *Legislators and Interpreters: On Modernity, Postmodernity and Intellectuals* (Cambridge: Polity Press, 1987), chap. 3.

of his being elsewhere before; he still smells of other places, of that beyond against which the homestead of the natives has been built. Entertaining a dream of going native can only end in mutual recrimination and bitterness. It is better for the vagrant, therefore, not to grow too accustomed to the place. Fortunately, other places beckon, not visited yet, perhaps less cruel or even more hospitable, certainly able to offer chances the present place has evidently denied. Cherishing one's 'out-of-placeness' is sensible strategy and the only chance of future reprieve. It gives present suffering an 'until-further-notice' flavour. It prevents the options from being cut out forever. If the natives turn unbearably nasty, one can always try to find more bearable ones.

The early modern vagabond wandered through the settled places; he was a vagabond because in no place could he be settled as the other people had been. The settled were many, the vagabonds few. Postmodernity reversed the ratio. Now there are few 'settled' places left. The 'forever settled' residents wake up to find the places (places in the land, places in society and places in life), to which they 'belong', non-existing or no more accommodating; streets neat today turn mean tomorrow, factories vanish together with jobs, skills find buyers no more, knowledge turns into ignorance, professional experience becomes liability, secure networks of relations fall apart and foul the place with putrid waste. Now the vagabond is a vagabond not for the reluctance or difficulty of settling down, but for the scarcity of settled places. Now the odds are that the people he meets in his travels are other vagabonds – vagabonds today or vagabonds tomorrow. The world is catching up with the vagabond, and catching up fast. The world is retailoring itself to the measure of the vagabond.

The tourist

Like the vagabond, the tourist used once to inhabit the margins of 'properly social' action (though the vagabond was marginal *man*, while the tourism was marginal *activity*), and has now moved to its centre (in both senses). Like the vagabond, the tourist is on the move. Like the vagabond, everywhere he goes he is *in*, but nowhere *of* the place. But there are as well differences, and they are seminal.

First, the balance between 'push' and 'pull' factors, in the case of the vagabond heavily weighed on the side of the 'push', in the case of the tourist shifts toward the 'pull' end. The tourist moves *on purpose* (or so s/he thinks). His/her movements are first of all 'in order to', and only secondarily (if at all) 'because of' (even if that 'in order to' happens to be but the goal of escaping the disappointment brought on by the last escapade; as Chris Rojek pointedly put it, the tourist streak in us is born of 'the restless dissatisfaction and desire for contrast

... We are never convinced that we have experienced things ... fully enough; we are always dully aware that our experiences could be better; no sooner do we enter "escape" activities than we feel nagging urges to escape from them'.[21] The purpose, then and now, is new experience; the tourist is a conscious and systematic seeker of experience, of a new and different experience, of the experience of difference and novelty – as the joys of the familiar wear off quickly and cease to allure. The tourists want to immerse themselves in the strange and bizarre element (a pleasant feeling, a tickling and rejuvenating feeling, one that blends vague danger with the sense of salvation – like letting oneself be buffeted by sea waves) – on condition, though, that it would not outlive its pleasure-giving facility and can be shaken off whenever they wish. They choose the elements to jump into according to how queer, but also how innocuous, they are; you recognize the favourite tourist haunts by their blatant, ostentatious (if painstakingly groomed) oddity, but also by a profusion of safety cushions and well marked escape routes. In the tourist's world, the strange is tame, domesticated, and no more frightens; shocks come in a package-deal with safety. This makes the world seem infinitely gentle, obedient to the tourist's wishes and whims, ready to oblige; but also a do-it-yourself world, pleasingly pliable, kneaded by the tourist's desire, made and remade with one purpose in mind – to excite, please and amuse. There is no other purpose to justify the presence of that world and the tourist's presence in it. The tourist's world is fully and exclusively structured by *aesthetic* criteria (ever more numerous writers who dwell on the 'aesthetization' of the postmodern world to the detriment of its other, also moral, dimensions, describe – even if unaware of it – the world as seen by the tourist; the 'aesthetized' world is the world inhabited by tourists). In contrast to the life of the vagabond, tough and harsh realities resistant to aesthetic sculpting do not interfere in the tourist's experience. One may say that what the tourist buys, what s/he pays for, what s/he demands to be delivered (and quits or calls the solicitors about if delivery is delayed) is precisely the right not to be bothered, freedom from any but the aesthetic spacing.

Second, unlike the vagabond, who has little choice but to be reconciled to the state of homelessness, the tourist has a home; or should have, at any rate. Having a home is a part of the safety package: for the pleasure to be unclouded and truly engrossing, there must be somewhere a homely and cosy place, indubitably one's own, to go

---

[21]   Chris Rojek, *Ways of Escape: Modern Transformations in Leisure and Travel* (London: Macmillan, 1993), p. 216.

to when the present adventure is over, or when the voyage proves to be not as adventurous as expected. 'The home' is the place to take off the armour and to unpack – the place where nothing needs to be proved and defended as everything is just there, obvious and familiar. It was the placidity of home that sent the tourist to seek new adventures, but it is the selfsame placidity that renders the search for adventures an uncloudedly pleasurable pastime: whatever has happened to my face here, in the tourist land, or whichever mask I don, my 'real face' is in safe keeping, pristinely clean, stain-resistant, unsullied. The problem, though, is that as the touristic escapades consume more and more of the lifetime, as life itself turns into an extended tourist escapade, as the tourist's conduct becomes the mode of life and the tourist's stance becomes the character – it is less and less clear which one of the visiting places is the home, and which but a tourist haunt. The opposition 'here I am but visiting, there is my home' stays clear-cut as before, but it is not easy to point out where the 'there' is. 'There' is increasingly stripped of all material features; the 'home' it contains is not even *imaginary* (any mental image would be too specific, too constraining) – but *postulated*; what is postulated is *having* a home, not a particular building, street, landscape or company of people. Jonathan Matthew Schwartz advises 'to distinguish the *homesick* searching from the nostalgic yearning'; the latter is, at least ostensibly, past-oriented, while the home in the homesickness is as a rule 'in the future perfect tense . . . It is an urge to feel at home, to recognize one's surroundings and belong there.'[22] Homesickness is a *dream of belonging* – of being, for once, *of* the place, not merely *in*. And yet if the present is notoriously the future plight of all future tense, the future tense of 'homesickness' is an exception. The value of 'home' in the homesickness lies precisely in its tendency to stay in the future tense forever. It cannot move to the present without being stripped of its charm and allure; when tourism becomes the mode of life, when the experiences ingested thus far whet the appetite for further excitement, when the threshold of excitement climbs relentlessly upwards and each new shock must be more shocking than the last one – the possibility of the home-dream ever coming true is as horrifying as the possibility of its never becoming real. Homesickness, as it were, is not the sole tourist's sentiment: the other is the fear of *home-boundedness*, of being tied to a place and barred from exit. 'Home' lingers at the horizon of the tourist life as an uncanny mix of shelter and prison. The tourist's favourite slogan

---

[22] Jonathan Matthew Schwartz, *In Defense of Homesickness: Nine Essays on Identity and Locality* (Copenhagen: Akademisk Forlag, 1989), pp. 15, 32.

is 'I need more space'. And space is the last thing one would look for at home.

The player

In play, there is neither inevitability, nor accident (there can be no accident in a world that knows no necessity or determination); nothing is fully predictable and controllable, but nothing is totally immutable and irrevocable either. The world of play is soft yet elusive; in it, the thing that matters most is how well one plays one's hand. Of course, there is such a thing as a 'stroke of luck' – when cards are stacked in one's favour or the wind helps the ball into the net. But the 'stroke of luck' (or a blow of misfortune, for that matter) does not lend the world the toughness it conspicuously lacks; it signals the limits of how far 'playing one's cards right' may go in making the win certain, while corroborating the no-necessity, no-accident status of the player's calculations.

In play, the world itself is a player, and luck and misfortune are but the moves of the world-as-player. In the confrontation between the player and the world there are neither laws nor lawlessness, neither order nor chaos. There are just the moves – more or less clever, shrewd or tricky, insightful or misguided. The point is to guess the moves of the adversary and anticipate them, prevent or pre-empt – to stay 'one ahead'. The rules the player may follow can be no more than rules of thumb; heuristic, not algorithmic instructions. The player's world is the world of *risks*, of intuition, of precaution-taking.

Time in the world-as-play divides into a succession of games. Each game is made of conventions of its own; each is a separate 'province of meaning' – a little universe of its own, self-enclosed and self-contained. Each demands that disbelief be suspended at the entry – though in each game a different disbelief is to be suspended. Those who refuse to obey the conventions do not rebel against the game; they only opt out and cease to be players. But 'the game goes on', and whatever the quitters say and do after that does not influence it a bit. The walls of the game are impenetrable, the voices outside reach the inside only as a muted, inarticulate noise.

Each game has its beginning and its end. The worry of the player is that each game should indeed start from the beginning, from 'square one', as if no games were played before and none of the players had amassed wins or losses which would make mockery of the 'zero-point' and transform what was to be a beginning into a precedent-bound continuation. For this reason, however, one must make sure that the game has also a clear, uncontested ending. It should not 'spill over' into the time after: as far as later games are concerned, no game played before must handicap, privilege or otherwise determine the players – *be of consequence*. Whoever does not like the outcome, must 'cut his losses' and start from scratch – and be able to do just that.

To make sure that no game leaves lasting consequences, the player must be aware (and so must his partners and adversaries) that 'this is *just* a game'. An important, though difficult to accept reminder, as the purpose of the game is to win and so the game allows no room for pity, commiseration, compassion or co-operation. The game is like war, yet that war which is a game must leave no mental scars and no nursed grudges: 'We are grown-up people. Let us behave like adults and part as friends', demands the partner-player opting out from the game of marriage, in the name of the gamesmanship of future, however serious or merciless, games. War that is a game absolves the conscience for its lack of scruples. *The mark of postmodern adulthood is the willingness to embrace the game whole-heartedly, as children do.*

What chance of morality? What chance of polity?

Each of the four types sketched above contains a solid dose of ambivalence of its own; in addition, they also differ from each other in a number of respects, and so blending them into one cohesive life-style is not an easy matter. No wonder there is quite a generous pinch of schizophrenia in each postmodern personality – which goes some way towards accounting for the notorious restlessness, fickleness and irresoluteness of practised life strategies.

There are, though, certain features which the four types share. The most seminal among them are their effects on popular moral and political attitudes, and indirectly on the status of morality and politics in a postmodern context.

Elsewhere I have suggested that modernity was prominent for the tendency to shift moral responsibilities away from the moral self either towards socially constructed and managed supra-individual agencies, or through floating responsibility inside a bureaucratic 'rule of nobody'.[23] The overall result was, on the one hand, the tendency to substitute ethics, that is a law-like code of rules and conventions, for moral sentiments, intuitions and urges of autonomous selves; and, on the other, the tendency towards 'adiaphorization' – that is, exemption of a considerable part of human action from moral

---

[23] See Zygmunt Bauman, *Modernity and the Holocaust* (Cambridge: Polity Press, 1989), chap. 7; Zygmunt Bauman, *Postmodern Ethics* (Oxford: Blackwell, 1993).

judgement and, indeed, moral significance. These processes are by no means a matter of the past – but it seems that their impact is somewhat less decisive than in the times of 'classic' modernity. I suggest that the context in which moral attitudes are forged (or not) is today that of *life-politics*, rather than social and systemic *structures*; that, in other words, postmodern life strategies, rather than the bureaucratic mode of management of social processes and co-ordinating action, are the most consequential among the factors shaping the moral situation of postmodern men and women.

All four intertwining and interpenetrating postmodern life strategies have that in common, that they tend to render human relations fragmentary (remember the 'purity' of relations reduced to a single function and service) and discontinuous; they are all up in arms against 'strings attached' and long-lasting consequences, and militate against the construction of lasting networks of mutual duties and obligations. They all favour and promote a *distance* between the individual and the Other and cast the Other primarily as the object of aesthetic, not moral evaluation; as a matter of taste, not responsibility. In effect, they cast individual autonomy in opposition to moral (as well as all the other) responsibilities and remove a huge area of human inter-action, even the most intimate among them, from moral judgement (a process remarkably similar in its consequences to bureaucratically promoted adiaphorization). Following the moral impulse means as-suming *responsibility* for the Other, which in turn leads to the *en-gagement* in the fate of the Other and *commitment* to her/his welfare. The disengagement and commitment-avoidance favoured by all four postmodern strategies has a backlash effect in the shape of the sup-pression of the moral impulse as well as disavowal and denigration of moral sentiments.

What has been said above may well seem jarringly at odds with the cult of interpersonal intimacy, also a prominent feature of postmodern consciousness. There is no contradiction here, though. The cult is no more than a psychological (illusory and anxiety-generating) com-pensation for the loneliness that inevitably envelops the aesthetically oriented subjects of desire; and it is, moreover, self-defeating, as the consequence-proof interpersonality reduced to 'pure relationships' can generate little intimacy and sustains no trustworthy bridges over the sandpit of estrangement. As Christopher Lasch noted a decade and a half ago, 'the cult of personal relations . . . conceals a thoroughgoing disenchantment with personal relations, just as the cult of sensuality implies a repudiation of sensuality in all but its most primitive forms.' Our society 'has made deep and lasting friendships, love affairs and marriages increasingly difficult to achieve'.[24]

Political disablement of postmodern men and women arrives from the same source as the moral one. Aesthetic spacing, preferred by and dominant in all listed postmodern strategies, differs from other kinds of social spacing (like moral or cognitive) in that it does not choose as its points of reference and orientation the traits and qualities possessed by or ascribed to the objects of spacing, but the attributes of the spacing subject (like interest, excitement, satisfaction or pleasure). As Jean-François Lyotard recently observed, 'the objects and the contents have become indifferent. The only question is whether they are "interesting".'[25] The world turns into a pool of potentially interesting objects, and the task is to squeeze out of them as much interest as they may yield. The task and its successful accomplishment stand and fall, however, by the effort and ingenuity of the interest-seeker. There is little or nothing that can be done by, and about the objects themselves.[26] Focusing on the interest-seeking subject blurs the contours of the world in which the interest is to be sought. Met (mis-met?) only perfunctorily, in passing, surface-deep, the objects do not come into vision as entities in their own right, such as may need more vigour, improvement, or a different shape altogether; we do not ruminate on how to rectify commodities displayed on the supermarket shelves – if we find them unsatisfactory, we pass them by, with our trust in the supermarket system unscathed, in the hope that products answering our interests will be found on the next shelf or in the next shop. Emancipation, says Lyotard, 'is no more situated as an alternative to reality, as an ideal set to conquer and force itself upon reality from outside'; in consequence, the militant practice has been replaced by a defensive one, one that is easily assimilated by the 'system' since it is now assumed that the latter contains all the bits and pieces from which the 'emancipated self' will be eventually assembled.[27] The 'system' has done what it possibly can. The rest is up to those who 'play it'.

---

[24] Christopher Lasch, *Culture of Narcissism: American Life in an Age of Diminishing Expectations* (New York: Warner Books, 1979), pp. 102, 69.

[25] Jean-François Lyotard, *Moralités postmodernes* (Paris: Galilée, 1993), pp. 32–3.

[26] Says Lasch: 'Having no hope of improving their lives in any of the ways that matter, people have convinced themselves that what matters is psychic self-improvement: getting in touch with their feelings, eating health food, taking lessons in ballet or belly-dancing, immersing themselves in the wisdom of the East, jogging, learning how to "relate", overcoming the "fear of pleasure".' (*Culture of Narcissism*, p. 29) Let us add that the diffuse, unfocused feeling that not all is well with the programme tends to be articulated as an issue of therapy aimed at the hapless or inept self-improver – but is channelled away from the programme itself; if anything, the programme emerges from the test with reinforced authority.

[27] Lyotard, *Moralités postmodernes*, pp. 66–8.

This spells trouble – condemnation, derision, banishment – to the poor, to those unable to lead the life of the stroller, tourist or player, to the 'spoil-sports' who refuse to play the game and thus add nothing to the joys of those who do play it, even if they do not poison the pleasure of playing it. As Jean Baudrillard put it,

> This easy life knows no pity. Its logic is a pitiless one. If utopia has already been achieved, then unhappiness does not exist, the poor are no longer credible . . . While frequenting the rich ranchers or manufacturers of the West, Reagan has never had the faintest inkling of the poor and their existence, nor the slightest contact with them . . . The have-nots will be condemned to oblivion, to abandonment, to disappearance pure and simple. This is 'must exit' logic: 'poor people must exit'. The ultimatum issued in the name of wealth and efficiency wipes them off the map. And rightly so, since they show such bad taste as to deviate from the general consensus.[28]

Again, let us not be fooled by media-promoted bouts of collective charity frenzy, which end as soon as attention (and fashionable table-talk) moves to new and greener, media-promoted pastures. These are Bakhtin's carnival events, intervals in the continuous drama of quotidianity, serving mostly to underline and emphasize the daily and the normal – their better entrenched and far more important opposite. As Stjepan G. Meštrović aptly put it,

> genuine morality, the habits of self-abnegation and love of neighbour, diminish in intensity . . . Meanwhile, the poor have become poorer, and the rich have become richer, while the media refer to 'compassion fatigue' in order to explain why hardly anyone really cares about starvation and other suffering in the world.[29]

---

[28] Jean Baudrillard, *America*, trans. Chris Turner (London: Verso, 1988), p. 111.

[29] Stjepan G. Meštrović, *The Barbarian Temperament: Toward a Postmodern Critical Theory* (London: Routledge, 1993), p. 5. All statistics show unanimously the steady fall of the poor's share in national wealth and the steady growth of the share of the rich. (In the last thirty years, as computed by Ignacio Ramenet, the distance between well-off and poor countries increased fivefold. About a billion men and women exist now on roughly 40 pence a day) – see *Le Mode Diplomatique* October 1994). Just how difficult it is to stop that trend, when the stroller-tourist-player mentality dominates political life, has been put poignantly by Richard Alcock: 'The Duke of Westminster and his ilk, who pay in more than they get out, would have to be persuaded that they were getting something from the system, not in terms of a state pension and £50-odd a week dole when needed, but in the indirect benefits of living in society in which the poor are reasonably well fed and healthy, and are not hanging around street corners for

Overdrawing the picture, but only slightly, one may say that in the popular perception the foremost, perhaps the sole duty of the postmodern citizen (much like the duty of the inmates of Rabelais's Abbey of Télème) is to lead an enjoyable life. To treat the subjects as citizens, the state is obliged to supply the facilities deemed necessary for such a life, and not to give occasion for doubt whether the performance of the duty is feasible. This does not necessarily mean that the life of a so-reduced citizen must be an unmitigated bliss. Discontent does arise, sometimes so acute as to prompt action reaching beyond the ordinary preoccupation with self-care. This happens time and again, even regularly, whenever the non-individual limits of the individual pursuit of 'the interesting' are brought into relief; whenever factors evidently beyond individual control (like, for instance, planning decisions about a new bypass, motorway, residential developments likely to attract 'outsiders', a factory suspected in advance of polluting an 'area of natural beauty', a travellers' camp spoiling an 'area of acute scientific significance') interfere with the interest-content of the environment. And yet the momentary explosions of solidary action which may result do not alter the essential traits of postmodern relationships: their fragmentariness and discontinuity, narrowness of focus and purpose, surface-deep shallowness of contact. Joint engagements come and go, and in each case, indeed, the emergent 'totality' is no more than 'the sum of its parts'. Besides, however numerous and multi-sided they are, the diffuse grudges and grievances, as a rule spawning one-issue campaigns, do not add up, condense or show a propensity for reinforcing each other. On the contrary, vying with each other for the scarce resource of public attention, they divide as much as they unite. One may say that the fragmented bones of postmodern contention do not fit together to form a skeleton around which a non-fragmentary and continuous, shared engagement could be wrapped.

Stuart Hall has pithily summarized the resulting condition and the prospects it may or may not hold:

> We don't have alternative means by which adults can benefit from the ways in which people have released themselves from the bonds of traditionalist forms of living and thinking, and still exert responsibilities for others in a free and open way. We have no notion of democratic citizenship in this sense.[30]

---

nefarious purposes.' ('New Poverty Overtakes Beveridge's Welfare State', in *The Guardian*, 6 September 1993)

[30]   Stuart Hall, 'Thatcherism Today', *New Statesman and Society*, 26 November 1993, p. 16.

Or perhaps we may have – imagine – such a notion; what we truly cannot imagine, having no time left for exercising imagination, is a network of relationships that would accommodate and sustain such a notion. It is, in the end, the old truth all over again: each society sets limits to the life strategies that can be imagined, and certainly to those which can be practised. But the kind of society we live in leaves off-limits such strategies as may critically and militantly question its principles and thus open the way to new strategies, currently excluded for the reason of their non-viability . . . *This chapter is based in part on a seminar prepared for the Open University.

4

A Catalogue of Postmodern Fears

In human life, fear is no news. Humanity knew it from its inception; fear would find a place close to the top in any imaginable shortlist of humanity's most conspicuous characteristics. Each era of history had its own fears which set it apart from other epochs; or, rather, each gave the fears known to all epochs names of its own creation. These names were concealed interpretations; they informed of where the roots of the feared threats lay, what one could do to keep the threats away, or why one could do nothing to ward them off. After all, another of humanity's most conspicuous traits is that cognitive and conative faculties intertwine so closely that only people called philosophers, well trained in the art of separation, can take them apart and imagine one without the other.

The threats themselves seem to have been always, stubbornly, the same. Sigmund Freud classified them once for all time:

> We are threatened with suffering from three directions: from our own body, which is doomed to decay and dissolution and which cannot even do without pain and anxiety as warning signals; from the external world, which may rage against us with overwhelming and merciless forces of destruction; and finally from our relations to other men.[1]

One may see that these 'directions' are already interpretations, though perhaps the most constant and resilient among them – to the

---

[1] Sigmund Freud, *Civilization and its Discontents*, trans. Joan Rivière (London: Hogarth Press, 1973), p. 14.

point of being 'self-evident' and not taken as interpretations at all. Looming large behind all three is just one 'mother of all threats', the threat that daily begets all other threats and never lets them toddle out of reach: the threat of the end, of an abrupt end and an endmost end, the one end beyond which there is no beginning. Death is the archetype of such an end, the only end that may appear in no other but a singular form. It so happened that to be human means simultaneously to be time-binding and time-bound; the time-binding mind has all the reasons to experience itself as eternal, yet it dwells in a blatantly and incurably transient casing. The transience of the latter dwarfs and cramps and humiliates the eternity of the first; eventually it will cut short that eternity the first is capable of, but long before that it boils down the cloudless 'forever' to the worrisome 'as long as'. To be human means to know this and to be unable to do anything about it and to know of this inability. This is why *to be human means also to experience fear*.

The constant principle of all strategies that had been deployed through history to make life with fear liveable was that of shifting the attention from things one can do nothing about, to things one can tinker with; and to make the tinkering energy- and time-consuming enough to leave little room (better still none at all) for the worry about things no tinkering could change. A pocketful of small coins with which to buy little graces allowed the putting off of the moment of confrontation with existential insolvency. Each era minted its own coins, as each era made different graces worth seeking or imperative to seek.

Fears of Panopticon

Certainty and transparency are often presented as the 'project' of modernity. Under closer scrutiny, though, they look more like unanticipated products of crisis-management than preconceived tenets. Modernity itself looks more like an enforced adjustment to a novel and unforeseen condition, than a contrived 'project'. Modernity emerged as an involuntary, no-choice response to the collapse of the *ancien regime* – a type of order which did not, need not think of itself as an 'order', let alone as a 'project'. It can be narrated as a story of long and inconclusive escape from the great terror which that collapse brought in its wake.

The name of the terror was *uncertainty*, lack of understanding, not knowing *how to go on*. The tight mesh of communal surveillance was torn up, and fear of the unknown hovered among the shreds. No one tore the mesh up deliberately; it just gave up under the pressure of lengthening chains of human interactions and frantic restlessness of 'unencumbered' individuals which it could neither contain nor accommodate. The so-called 'project' of modernity was not much more than making a virtue out of necessity. According to the principle 'If you cannot join them, beat them', the things whose demise led to the present turmoil and its fears, stood accused of horrors most horrid and were given names meant to alert and repel. When war was declared, the tradition, custom, or communal particularism against which it was waged already swayed on its last legs, consumed by terminal disease.

The concentric propaganda assault against the last shreds of diffuse and already blatantly ineffective *mini*-orders was an apologia-by-proxy for the concentric material efforts to install a new *global* order. The latter task called for 're-encumbering' of the 'unencumbered', 're-embedding' of the 'disembedded'; a made-to-order certainty of power-assisted monotony had to fill the gap left by unreflexive, spontaneously formed and self-reproducing certainties of communally assisted custom. 'Order' moved now from the beginning to the end of action: what used to be achieved matter-of-factly (and was seen only now, when it was no more, as an achievement), was to be a product of *regimentation*. The diffuse and mutual surveillance that sustained the integrity of mini-orders was to be made uni-directional, and concentrated in the central tower of modern Panopticon.

Following Jeremy Bentham's insight, Michel Foucault pointed out that this streamlining of surveillance from top to bottom, the asymmetry of gaze, setting out the surveillance as a professional and skilful function, was the common feature of modern inventions as otherwise functionally diverse as schools, military barracks, hospitals, psychiatric clinics, workhouses, industrial plants and prisons. All these institutions were factories of order; like all factories, they were sites of purposeful activity calculated to result in a product conceived in advance, in their case in restoring certainty, eliminating randomness, making the conduct of the inmates regular and predictable – certain – once more. This new order, Bentham shrewdly observed, needed but 'safe custody, confinement, solitude, forced labour, and instruction' – a range of factors sufficient to serve 'punishing the incorrigible, guarding the insane, reforming the vicious, confining the suspected, employing the idle, maintaining the helpless, curing the sick, instructing the willing in any branch of industry or training the rising race in the path of education' alike. The vision of Panopticon was not spun of malice, spite or misanthropy; nor was it knowingly cruel. A genuine reformer intoxicated by the shining vision of human progress and spurred into action by the urge to speed it up, Bentham sought after all, in everything he thought of, the 'happiness of the greatest number'. He believed that the side-product of the panoptical factory of order would be the happiness of the inmates: 'Call them soldiers, call them monks, call them machines; do they were but happy ones, I should not care.' The inmates are bound to be happy, it seems, because the deepest source of their unhappiness was uncertainty; regiment uncertainty out of existence, put in its place certainty of necessity, however sad and sorrowful, and you are almost there: in the happy world of born-again order.

The spectre of uncertainty is thus exorcized through regimentation. Certainty is restored by forces external to the individual – from *outside*. In the last account, the modern cure for uncertainty boiled down to curtailing the realm of choice. Not the theoretical, abstract realm of choice, which modernity kept widening, thereby expanding the volume of anxiety and fear, but a practical, pragmatically sensible realm, a realm of 'realistic' and not-too-costly choices – and so the realm of choices likely to be seen as being 'in the best interest' of the chooser, and thus the most probable to be chosen. (Bentham again: 'If a man won't work nothing has he to do, from morning to night, but to eat his bad bread and drink his water, without a soul to speak to.'[2] Theoretical realm of choice is for the Panopticon's inmates as ample as for anybody, yet the practical realm shrinks to the choice between stultifying and shabby idleness and stultifying and shabbily paid work; the latter is therefore likely to be chosen, and certainty rules again – or almost.)

Re-establishing order (that is, a setting which in subjective perception rebounds, reassuringly, as certainty) through the force of regimentation was a viable idea only on condition that anyone to be regimented was placed under the influence of one, or several, panoptical institutions. This, indeed, the modern legislation tried to achieve, by relentlessly extending the compulsory schooling period, by making military service universal and compulsory, and above all by linking livelihood to 'employment' – to being under someone's supervision, to having a boss. (If 'regular' employment was absent, and livelihood was derived from state or communal benefits, the boss was to be replaced by public inspectors with roughly the same, if not wider, supervisory prerogatives.) Between themselves, the surveilling-drilling-disciplining factories of order and certainty super-

[2]   *The Works of Jeremy Bentham*, vol. 4 (Edinburgh: William Tait, 1843), pp. 40, 64, 54.

vised the whole length of *man's* life, except the small stretches at the beginning and the end – where whatever uncertainty might be experienced was not seen as a 'social problem'. (The other half of the population – *women* – were to be placed under the surveillance of male 'heads of the family', expected to perform the boss's role; it was presumably the deployment of the family as a complementary surveillance agency which prompted Foucault to describe the panoptical power as 'capillary', penetrating in the likeness of the blood veins every tissue and cell of society at large.)

With panoptical institutions firmly established as the principal in-dustrial plants of new certainty, individuals were construed as, first and foremost, the actual or prospective inmates of such institutions. For the great majority of the male population, that meant above all factories and military barracks. In order to be subjected to the cer-tainty-yielding procedure, men had to be able to pass the entry tests set for inclusion in factory work or soldierly pursuits. Their 'social fitness' was measured by their ability to perform industrial work and military activities. At the time, both types of activity required appli-cation of physical force and skills located in limbs and muscles; they required, in other words, *strong bodies*. The kind of bodily exercise required by the factory and the army defined what the 'strong body' meant; it set the standard for strength and infirmity, health and illness. At all times, says Bryan S. Turner, the pioneer and founder of the sociology of the body, there is 'a potentiality which is elaborated by culture and developed in social relations.'[3] Modern culture and the modern web of social relations developed the potentiality into a body – primarily, of the industrial worker and the soldier. 'To be healthy' – bodily 'normal' – meant to be fit for factory work and/or military service. The well documented panics among the politicians, medics, educators and philosophers of the nineteenth century at the sight of the genuine or alleged 'physical deterioration' of the population, and particularly of its lower classes, was argued in terms of the worry about the economic and military potential of the nation. Yet under-neath this argument it is easy to discern another, more fundamental worry about the preservation of the very fabric of society, the rule of law and order – which under modern conditions was maintained with the help of industrial and military drill. A man incapable of employment or enlisting was a man essentially outside the net of social control – much like that bugbear of the seventeenth-century law-and-order panic, the 'vagrant', eluding the surveillance capacity

---

[3] Bryan S. Turner, *Regulating Bodies: Essays in Medical Sociology* (London: Routledge, 1992), p. 16.

of the village community and the parish, the sole vehicles of law-and-order of that era.

The most spectacular and far-reverberating splashes of 'bodily inadequacy' panic were caused by wars, which by their dramatic nature tended to condense and raise to high pitch concerns diffuse and low-key at normal times. In his classic study of the eugenics movement J. R. Searle documented the 'Boer War panic about the possible deterioration' and the ensuing intense 'preoccupation with "National Efficiency", and despondency about the apparent failure of "environmental" social policies'. But the eruption of war and the frantic effort to recruit soldiers fit for the strenuous life of warfare only ignited into a flame the constantly smouldering anxiety about the frailty of law-and-order, insufficiently supported by the modern drilling arrangements:

> Middle class commentators on the 'social question' from the 1870s onwards viewed with fear the casual labourers and the inhabitants of the slum areas of the big cities; they noted with both disappointments and apprehension that these people had not 'responded' to attempts by legislators and charitable organizations to raise them to a higher national and moral plane, and some were tempted to explain this by the hypothesis of urban degeneration.[4]

Indeed, as Daniel Pick has shown in his seminal study, virtually all the most prominent thinkers of the second half of the nineteenth century expressed in one form or another their fear of 'degeneration' which threatens civilized nations if not attended to in time. The 'strong body' stayed at the focus of these concerns; 'degeneration', a notoriously vague and ill-defined concept[5] (more a catching-all

---

[4] J. R. Searle, *Eugenics and Politics in Britain, 1900–1914* (Leyden: Noordhoff, 1976), pp. 9, 20. As shown by Chris Shilling (*The Body and Social Theory* (London: Sage, 1993)) an outcry about the 'deterioration of the body' accompanied as a rule the eruption of major wars. An outcry was the national reaction to the statistics of American youths' bodily qualities published on the occasion of a recruitment drive during the First World War. 'A professor of physiology at Cornell estimated that New Yorkers alone carried ten million pounds of excess fat that would have been better used as rations for soldiers.' (p. 30)

[5] As J. Edward Chamberlain and Sander J. Gilman put it in their introduction to the book of essays they commissioned and edited (*Degeneration, the Dark Side of Progress* (Columbia University Press, 1985)), 'degeneration was one of the most uncertain of notions, and – like some viruses – one of the most difficult to isolate. The idea of degeneration could comfortably be caught up in the tapestry of ambivalence, to be sure, and whether it was conceived as warp or woof could be a matter of taste.' (p. xiii) Indeed, the irreparable ambivalence was an asset

expression of diffuse feelings than a scientific term referring to a definite set of phenomena), was wrapped nevertheless around the vision of 'energy loss', bodily softness, limpness and flaccidity. 'How few thoroughly strong people we meet' was for Herbert Spencer the principal item in his long inventory of the looming dangers. The newly noticed and allegedly unprecedented flabbiness of the human body, which rendered it unsuitable for the taxing rhythm of industrial and military pursuits, meant, in Spencer's view, 'a deliberate storing up of miseries for future generations. There is no greater curse to posterity than that of bequeathing them an increasing population of imbeciles and idlers and criminals.'[6]

The ostensibly growing numbers of the 'unemployable' and the 'unfit for military service' triggered an intellectual and legislative panic by being read (not at all wrongly) as signals of failure in the most decisive of modern undertakings. Those temporarily out of work or out of active service were still to be measured by the standard of the tasks from which they were currently excluded – tasks whose prospect nevertheless gave shape and purpose to their temporary idleness; this assumption was pointedly conveyed by their description as 'reserve army of labour' or 'soldiers in reserve'.

From purveyors of goods to sensations-gatherers

Neither labour nor soldiering are today much in demand. 'Technical progress' has come to mean not creation of new jobs and depleting the 'reserve army of labour', but – on the contrary – making massive employment increasingly irrelevant from the point of view of the volume of production. Investment came to mean shedding jobs, and industrial labour seems to perform in the twentieth century a 'disappearing act' strikingly similar to the one that agricultural labour in Western Europe went through one century before. Temporary, part-time, flexible, mostly female and poorly anchored service jobs which came to (partly, and imperfectly) replace the life-long, long-hours, clock-in-clock-out, mostly male and solidly grounded industrial jobs,

rather than a handicap in the case of a notion which deserved its tremendous popularity and central place in public debate to the (1) feat of tying together the otherwise disparate fears of relapse into chaos, (2) making the ineffable amenable to articulate expression, and (3) masking the dangers one could not stave off with practical tasks one could apparently perform; a notion which could be of pragmatic value only on the condition of dissimulating its genuine referents.
[6]   See Herbert Spencer, *The Study of Sociology* (New York: Appleton, 1874), pp. 342–5.

are woefully unsuitable to render the social order the same drilling-disciplining service their predecessors were expected to deliver. Quite a similar change happened to the military pursuits. There is little that contemporary high-tech warfare could conceivably gain from the mobilization of mass armies. As in industry, so in the army technical progress means cutting down personnel – both in active service and reserves. As fear-dispersing, surveilling, drilling and disciplining factories of certainty, industry and the army have definitely outlived their usefulness. (No wonder one hears no more of the 'moral mission' of the employers, such a recurrent motif in the self-consciousness of the nineteenth century – see my *Memories of Class* 1983, Routledge.)

The 'regime of regimentation', of which the factory and the army were principal tools and institutional models, replaced the original modern fear of uncertainty with the fear of falling out with norms – fear of deviation and the ensuing punishment. Sociology, the self-consciousness of modern society as codified by the turn of the century, generalized from the modern experience and presented society 'as such' as normatively regulated, held together by punitive sanctions; as a setting in which the conduct of the individuals was made uniform by the pressure of externally applied forces (though, like in so many other cases, the owl of Minerva spread its wings at dusk, and the story of the day was told in full only when the day was already disappearing into night). Uniformity of behaviour, replicated by conformity of attitudes ('socialization' was explicated as educating people in such a way that they *want* to do what they *must* do), was the most central of societal concerns and the yardstick with which to measure functions of most, perhaps all, social institutions. If there was an element of voluntarity left in the individual actors exposed to external drill, it expressed itself in actively seeking norm and instruction; in the overwhelming desire to *conform*, to be like others and to do what others do.

No more prospective workers and/or soldiers, men (and women, who are no more regimented by the factory/army-regimented paterfamilias), have been freed from panoptical pressures to conform. With those pressures out of the way, however, the fear of uncertainty could no longer be dealt with by replacing it with the concern to avoid deviation – as it was since the inception of modern society. The fear itself remained, though – if anything, growing deeper and more awesome for being confronted point-blank. The individual's identity remains as under-defined, floating and 'disembedded' as it has been throughout modern times, yet seems more virulent and nerve-racking, with the powerful 're-embedding' mechanisms losing their normative potency or simply no more there.

The reproduction of the conditions of social life is now performed other than by collectivized, societal means; it has been to a large extent privatized – removed from the realm of state politics and, indeed, of public decision-making. 'Privatization' means here, however, not just a shedding of the responsibility by the sites of concentrated societal power and leaving the matters of social integration and systemic reproduction to the free play of private initiative – it goes further than that. Processes are now by and large *de-institutionalized*, building up from the grass-roots level out of the individual, DIY efforts at self-formation. No more state-managed and institutionally supplied services for those who seek escape from the under-determination, unclarity and uncertainty of being; not assuaged any more by the regimen of necessities making up for the absent inevitability, fear of uncertainty now confronts its victims in all its pristine severity. All its enormous pressure falls upon the individual virtually unmediated, and needs to be repelled or neutralized by individual action.

Instead of stimulating the administrative bustle on high, fear of under-determination whips up the individual into a frenzy of self-forming and self-asserting efforts. Uncertainty must now be overcome by one's own means; the scarcity of *because-ofs* must be compensated for by home-made *in-order-tos*. Defeat or inconclusiveness of victory in the never-ending battle of self-formation rebounds as the pain of *inadequacy* – now replacing deviation as the most feared penalty for individual failure. Not the old-style inadequacy measured by too large a distance from a clear-cut and solid standard to which one was bullied or exhorted to conform, but new and improved, postmodern inadequacy in the sense of failing to acquire the shape and form one wished to acquire, whatever that form might have been; failing to stay on the move but also to stop at the spot of one's choice, to stay flexible and ready to assume shapes at will, to be simultaneously pliable clay and accomplished sculptor.

Chisels, spatulas and other modelling tools are supplied socially (more precisely, purchasable in the shops), together with the cut-out patterns to guide the modelling. But the responsibility for undertaking and seeing through the sculpting job lies now squarely on the clay-sculptor's shoulders (much as in Kafka's *Trial*, where the law court kept a bland face and never sent a summons, and it was up to the accused to write down the charges and seek the hearing and the verdict). The supervisor, the foreman, the teacher all vanish – together with their powers to coerce, yet also to release from responsibility. It is now a matter of self-supervising, self-scrutinizing and self-teaching. The individual is his/her own guard and teacher;

to reverse Maurice Blanchot's phrase – everyone is now free, but everyone is free inside their own prison, the prison s/he freely builds.

So it is no more the task to conform that spurs the individual's life efforts, but a sort of meta-effort, *the effort to stay fit to make efforts*. The effort not to grow rusty, stale, jaded; not to get stuck at any stopover for too long; not to mortgage the future; not to prejudice court verdicts in case the court decides to speak, not to be bound by verdicts of one court only, to pick jurisdiction according to one's own liking; to keep wide the 'space' in which to move.

There is an evident selective affinity between the privatization of the uncertainty-handling function and the market catering for private consumption. Once the fear of uncertainty has been reforged into the fear of personal self-forming ineptitude, the offer of the consumer market is irresistible; it needs no coercion and no indoctrination to be taken up; it will be freely chosen. The reward which the regimen of surveillance and coercion offered in exchange for conformity was freedom from the torments of choice and responsibility. Such freedom is not on offer under the regime of self-formation serviced by market commodities. But the prizes which this new regime offers are glittering enough to dazzle out of existence the sombre spectre of responsibility; it is the freedom not to think of responsibility – not to be burdened by the worry about the consequences, to split life into episodes which are not outlived by their outcomes and do not prejudice episodes still to come – which the market offers. Instead of the enforced, imposed irresponsibility of the prisoner (which weighs down heavily as deprivation and slavery), the irresponsibility of a butterfly (which is worn lightly and joyously as gift and freedom). Light is now where darkness was; passage into new dependence feels like liberation, like 'getting out'.

As always in the case of selective affinities, there would not be much use in trying to set apart the cause and the effect; is the fear of inadequacy the cause of consumerist enthusiasm, or was it rather the clever stratagem or an unanticipated consequence of the expanding consumer market that replaced the fear of deviation with the fear of inadequacy as the popular translation of the fear of uncertainty? Arguments may be easily advanced for either one of the alternative answers, yet it does not matter much anyway since – much as in the case of capitalism in Weber's rendition – the light cloak has long turned into an iron cage from which there is no visible escape. Fear of inadequacy and consumer frenzy beef up each other, draw their energy from each other and see to it that the 'other' is alive and well.

Whichever way this came to be, the modern individual evicted from the position of Panopticon-inmate, the position lived as the role of *goods-purveyor* (a role no longer in ample supply), has found him/herself in the position of goods-consumer, lived as the role of a *pleasures-collector* – or, more exactly, a *sensations-gatherer*. The two positions point to two different, collective and privatized, methods of tackling the fear of uncertainty gestated by the great 'disencumbering' process called modernity. The two roles point to two different – collective and privatized – agencies charged with the task of applying these methods. The only thing which emerged intact, nay unscathed, from the change of guard is the fear of uncertainty itself – though now dressed as the fear of inadequacy rather than deviation.

Fear of *deviation* is a closely condensed kind of anxiety. It is relatively easy to discern a common content behind the variety of forms; Horkheimer and Adorno could unerringly pinpoint the 'fear of void', experienced as the fear of being different and thus lonely, as the hard core of modern anxieties. The task is less straightforward in the case of the postmodern fear of *inadequacy*. Partly, because the world itself in which it operates is – unlike the 'classic' modern world – fragmentary, and because the postmodern time, in stark opposition to the linear and continuous modern time, is 'flattened' and episodic. In such a world and in such a time categories refer more to 'family resemblances' than to 'hard cores' or even 'common denominators'. In the rich pool of postmodern anxieties hardly a single trait could be found which would appear in every specimen. 'Inadequacy' serves here as a label to file together a great variety of fears – differently oriented, differently experienced, differently tackled. No one of the many fears can be easily pinpointed as the 'main link' in the chain of anxieties, let alone the 'primal cause' of the whole lot. Instead of chasing a postmodern 'mother of all fears', it is prudent to settle for an inventory of postmodern anxieties. This, and no more than this, the rest of the chapter attempts to do.

From health to fitness

The modern body, the producer/soldier body, was regimented – buffeted into shape by shrewdly manipulated environmental forces, and triggered into regular motions, like on Taylor's assembly line, by ingeniously designed surroundings. The sole contribution required of the body itself was that it would be capable of mustering the inner strength needed to respond to stimuli promptly and with the required vigour. That capacity was called 'health'; obversely, 'illness' stood for incapacitation. For all practical intents and purposes, the consumption deemed necessary to secure health so understood and to stave off incapacitation boiled down to nutrition, and food needed to be ingested in quantities required to keep the supply of muscle energy up to the work/soldiering standards. Everything above that quantity was classified as luxury; it was the sign of profligacy if consumed, of prudence and morality if saved or invested. At the dawn of our century the first 'minimum standard of living' calculated by Seebohm Rowntree for British workers did not include tea, their favourite drink and the indispensable element of their socializing rituals – for the then obvious reason of being devoid of nutritional value. Note that thinking has not changed much in our times as far as the poor, the flawed consumers, those refused entry to postmodern society, are concerned; for many years now Peter Townsend has conducted a heroic yet inconclusive battle to include, say, the absence of money for Christmas cards among the indicators of a life below the poverty level. Beverages continue to be particularly frowned upon; their consumption is caustically remarked upon as the sign of indulgence and excess. Above the poverty line, though, bodily needs are seen today in an entirely different light. They are, first and foremost, *consuming* bodies, and the measure of their proper condition is the capacity to consume what the consumer society has to offer.

The postmodern body is first and foremost a receiver of *sensations*; it imbibes and digests *experiences*; the capacity of being stimulated renders it an instrument of *pleasure*. That capacity is called fitness; obversely, the 'state of unfitness' stands for languor, apathy, listlessness, dejection, a lackadaisical response to stimuli; for a shrinking or just 'below average' capacity for, and interest in, new sensations and experiences. 'To be depressed' means to be unwilling to 'go out and enjoy oneself', to 'have fun'. The most popular and frightening 'disorders' are, one way or the other, *consumption* disorders . . . To keep the body fit means to keep it ready to absorb and to be stimulated. A fit body is a highly sensitive, finely tuned instrument of pleasure, any pleasure, whether sexual, gastronomical, or derived from mere physical exercise and demonstration of fitness. It is not so much the performance of the body that counts, as the sensations the body receives in the course of the performance; those sensations must be deep and deeply gratifying – 'thrilling', 'ravishing', 'enrapturing', 'ecstatic'.

Since the depth of 'sensation' is much less amenable to exact measurement and target-setting than 'performance', assessed in terms of its tangible products and 'objective' results, the side-effect of the shifting emphasis is the devaluation of the once central notion of 'normality' (and, by the same token, of 'abnormality'). Modern medicine struggled to draw a clear and visible line between health and illness, and thus made the distinction between the normal and the abnormal into its major concern; the distinction was to be, ideally, defined in empirically testable and quantifiable terms and then measured precisely – much like the 'normal temperature' of the body is measured with a medical thermometer. This is hardly a viable prospect in the case of sensation, always a subjectively lived-through event, impossible to articulate in intersubjectively communicable terms and so to convey, put alongside somebody else's sensation and be 'objectively' compared. One is condemned to live forever in doubt as to whether one's own sensations 'match the standard', and – more poignantly still – whether they reach the peak that other people are capable of climbing. However deeply experienced, sensations can always be deeper and are thus never deep enough; whatever happens can be bettered – in every ointment of achievement there is a fly of suspicion that the actually felt experience was but a pale shadow of what the 'real' experience could be (and if it *could*, it *should*). The idea of 'normality' does not make sense under this condition. There is a sliding and ascending and infinite scale of rapture which, when applied to the actually experienced, casts on every experience a deep shadow of 'malfunction'. The sliding scale of pleasure turns into a sliding scale of dysfunction, and spells endless disaffection and restlessness forever.

Every exercise of fitness, however spectacular and satisfying, is thus poisoned by a bitter taste of foreshadowed unfitness; and unfitness portends losing out on the chances of foretold pleasure. The search for the 'truly fit' body is plagued by anxiety which is unlikely ever to be dispelled. The body's capacity for vivid sensation and ecstasy is doomed to be forever short of the elusive ideal – hence no amount of care or drilling of the body is ever likely to put paid to the gnawing suspicion of malfunctioning. No remedy is likely to emerge victorious from the test; remedies keep their authority as long as they are dreamed of and feverishly sought, but are disqualified almost at the moment of their application. One follows the recipe of 'sensual enhancement' diligently and arduously, yet whatever improvement follows is bound to stop short of the promised and expected. Remedies are fast discarded, new and improved ones must replace them at an ever increasing pace; fitness of the body is not an end that can be reached, and there is no moment in sight when one can say with unclouded conviction: I've got it. Impatience climbs the ceaselessly rising pile of successive disappointments, spurred by suspicion of inadequacy.

All this, let us remember, happens to a body no longer regimented

– at least not in the way the producing/soldiering body once was. The other side of external coercion and surveillance was collective dissent and protest; political oppression always tends to rebound in political opposition. But the sensations-gathering body is a DIY creation, and its dysfunctions are self-inflicted mishaps. Failures do not add up to the vision of collective deprivation, and complaints do not congeal into collective vindications; redress, whatever its substance, must be individually sought, obtained and applied. The drilling of the producer/soldier body unites; the self-drill of the sensations-gatherer body divides and separates. The National Health Service is a natural outgrowth of the way the concept of health is socially constructed: national services are by their very nature made to deal with norm and abnormality – with such human aspects that are common to all, that can be statistically averaged and proclaimed a norm which casts all peculiarity as abnormality. But a 'National Fitness Service' would be a contradiction in terms. And at the times when concerns with fitness gain priority over the worry about health (societal institutions being no more interested in the norm-enforcement or in the supply of producers and soldiers), the National Health Service also seems less 'natural' and 'obvious' than before. Its bequeathed concept, entrenched and institutionalized in its traditional structure, is ill prepared to render the kind of services that the shift of emphasis from health to fitness prompts its clients to seek.

The body is now an uncontestedly *private property*, and it is up to the owner to cultivate it; s/he has no one to blame for the weeds overgrowing the garden or the watering sprinklers going bust. This casts the owner in an eerie, untenable position. S/he must be in control, but it is s/he that must be controlled; the body must float in the stream of sensations, fit to abandon itself to the unthinking pleasures of experience – yet the 'owner' (and the trainer) of the body, who 'sits inside' the body at the time of the experience and can only by the force of imagination be 'detached' from it, must monitor that floating and that self-abandonment, assess and measure it, compare, pronounce on its quality . . . André Béjin offers the clinical diagnosis of such an aporetic condition in the case of the pursuit of orgasmic sensations, now the widely acknowledged 'sense' of sexual performance:

> One must . . . abandon oneself to sensation without ceasing to submit one's action to a rational calculation of 'sexual expedience'. The pleasure should be at one and the same time an absolutely spontaneous happening and a theatrical performance stage-managed by the brain . . . So one finds oneself instructed to distance oneself from one's body by means of the mind,

the better to coincide with the sensations that arise spontaneously in it, to be a spectator of the sexual act without ceasing to take part in it, to be overwhelmed by stimuli while at the same time activating them through fantasies one has evoked oneself and mastered, expressing oneself 'spontaneously' in the course of actions which have to be programmed . . .[7]

A truly schizophrenia-prone situation; one needs to *learn* how to expose oneself to *what precedes and surpasses all learning*; one needs to apply the *brain* to stimulate and stretch the *visceral*; one needs to train and drill and otherwise *coerce* the body in order to let it go, to set it free from control, to make it fit for *unhampered* enjoyment . . . One needs to be in and out at the same time: staying out is the indispensable prerequisite of being truly in, while incurably contaminating the 'innateness' of the 'in'. The switch from societally administered surveillance and drill to self-monitoring and self-drilling cancels the distinction between the subject and the object, between the actor and the object of action; cancels even the distinction between doing and suffering, between action and its products. What once used to be a contradiction becomes an aporia: the confused state of a quicksand-style ambivalence never to be resolved, as each attempt to get out results only in sinking deeper into the mire.

Bodily fitness as the supreme goal, meant to be pursued, yet never reached, by means of self-coercion, is bound to be forever shot through with anxiety vainly seeking an outlet, but generating a constantly growing demand for ever new yet untested outlets. I propose that this product of the 'privatization' of the body and of the agencies of social production of the body is the 'primal scene' of postmodern ambivalence. It lends postmodern culture its unheard-of energy, an inner compulsion to be on the move. It is also a crucial cause, perhaps the prime cause, of its in-built tendency to instant ageing – the neurotic, 'rhyzomic', random, chaotic, confused, compulsive restlessness of postmodern culture with its breathtaking succession of fads and foibles, ephemeral desires, short-lived hopes and horrid fears devoured by fears yet more horrid. Postmodern cultural inventiveness may be compared to a pencil with an eraser attached; it wipes out what it writes and thus cannot stop moving over the dazzling blankness of paper.

The primal ambivalence spills into many moulds, takes up many shapes and is given many names. One of the seminal forms it takes

---

[7] André Béjin, 'The Influence of the Sexologists and Sexual Democracy', in *Western Sexuality: Practice and Precept in Past and Present Times*, ed. Philippe Ariès and André Béjin, trans. Anthony Foster (Oxford: Blackwell, 1985), p. 211.

is the aporetic ambiguity of *proteophobia* and *fixeophobia* – of the fear of never reaching the peak (and never knowing the road that leads to it), and the fear of reaching it (and knowing for sure that it has been reached). The target of genuine fitness may forever elude the seeker; but it may also be hit, and one does not know – one cannot know – one does not wish to know – which eventuality to consider more sinister. From the peak, there is nowhere to climb, after all – all roads lead down the slope . . . One cannot stop hoping that the ultimate sensation can be attained; but attaining it will be *the end* – a death by proxy, letting in that most heinous fiend whom all the labours one went through were meant to keep out.

Proteophobia and fixeophobia feed and support each other. Together, they see to it that on the way to the fulfilment of the 'project Body' – an infinitely sensitive, experience-attuned body, there be no limit to self-flagellation; that no rapture be ever recognized as the ultimate and never to be bettered, no sensation as leaving-nothing-to-be-desired, no stretch of the road already passed as absolving from further explorations.

The body under siege

The anxiety-generating and incurable ambivalence of the 'project Body' makes the task of circumscribing and guarding the boundaries of the body (a task which Mary Douglas had shown long ago to be strewn with nerve-rending ambiguities at all times and in all cultures) particularly daunting and thus a particularly fertile ground for multiple fears. Most sensations that the pleasures-collector's body may experience need stimuli coming from the outside world; the consumerist condition makes it imperative that the body opens up as widely as possible to the potential of rich and ever richer experiences contained in such stimuli, and the fitness of the body is measured by its ability to absorb them. Yet the same exchange with the outside world compromises the individual's control over bodily fitness; the intense border traffic, the unavoidable condition of sensations-gathering, is at the same time a potential threat to fitness, which in its turn is the condition of the body's capacity for gathering sensations. That capacity may be diminished if immigration control is not vigilant enough; admission must be selective at all times – but would not all selectivity impoverish the pool of potential sensations, and prevent the body from experiencing who knows how many yet unknown ones?

The contents of the top twenty bestselling books, like all notoriously short-lived fashions, change kaleidoscopically from one week to another, yet two types of books are assured pride of place on each list – cookbooks and dieting/slimming books. Not just ordinary cookbooks – but collections of ever more refined, exotic, out-of-this-world, exclusive, fastidious and finical recipes; promises of taste-bud delights never experienced before and of new heights of ecstasy for the eyes, nose and palate. Side by side with the cookbooks, as their undetachable shadow, the dieting/slimming books, the no-nonsense recipes for self-drill and self-immolation, instructions how to heal what the other books might have damaged and purge what the other books might have left behind: the capacity to live through wondrous sensations, which made the self-flagellation imperative in the first place.

The perfection of the *modern* body was visualized in the likeness of Renaissance-style harmony, guided by the principle of moderation and temperance, tranquillity and stability. The social sciences, accordingly, defined human needs as the urge to placate and remove tensions and needs-satisfaction as the state of no-tension; perfection was seen as a condition in which all movement grinds to a halt, as no further improvement is possible. The postmodern practice of body training results, on the contrary, in a Gothic-style construction, composed of excesses alone and held together solely through finely balancing the tensions that tear it apart. Select your tensions wisely, so that you may squeeze their exhilarating potential to the full, and taste of ever new 'ultimate experiences' while remaining open to future, yet more 'ultimate' ones. The no-tension state is a nightmare; the question is not how to avoid tensions, but how to compensate for one tension with another, matching one. One needs a tasty way to intoxicate, and a tasty way of sobering up.

Over all this the individual, the private owner of the body, is in charge. The protection of the boundary and the administration of the territory inside the boundary is her/his responsibility. The enormity of the task, further aggravated by its intrinsic ambivalence, breeds a siege mentality: the body, and particularly its fitness, is threatened from all sides. And yet one cannot securely fortify oneself against the threats, as the border traffic is not merely unavoidable, but positively desired: its intensity is, after all, the ultimate purpose of 'keeping fit'. This is therefore a siege that will be never raised – a permanent siege, a life-long siege.

Given the ambiguity of the fitness ideal and the ambivalence of the means that serve it, it is hardly a wonder that from time to time, and ever more frequently, the siege mentality condenses into brief yet violent explosions of body-panic. At all times poison is sniffed in every morsel of food and pathogenic side-effects in every bodily activity; yet refusing food as such and halting all bodily activity is not a viable proposition, let alone a solution reconcilable with the life of the sensations-gatherer. One can only let off the relentlessly accumulating steam of suspicion and frustration in sporadic campaigns against specific brands of food or particular kinds of bodily actions (or in expunging their poisonous impact by ingesting other substances or straining the body in other types of motions). The energy invested in the campaign rebounds in the comforting and temporarily reassuring feeling that the 'enemy at the gate' has been defeated and need not be feared any more. As the self-contradictory ideal of fitness can, however, never be reached (not to mention the non-feasibility of the death-avoidance dream, for which 'keeping the body fit' is the postmodern replacement, or rather cover-up), no successive campaign can attain conclusive results. A particular food has been anathematized, a particular bodily exercise condemned and avoided, yet the plight remains as fraught with contradictions as before and the goal stays as distant as ever.

And so the demand for new, preferably more spectacular body panics continues. The only lasting result of past campaigns is the increased speed with which the wheels of the poison/antipoison factories rotate and the new feats of ingenuity of the commercial suppliers of anti-poisons yet to be unmasked as poisons-in-disguise . . .

From handling to tasting

Every ego conjures up the Other and is itself conjured up in the course of that conjuring – but each ego has an Other cut to the measure of its own concerns and desires, and thus the Other of the pleasures-collector's ego is unlike the Other of the goods-purveyor's ego.

The goods-purveyor's Other has all the solid, corporeal materiality of nature, of things 'natural'. It extends in space, it has weight, it is impenetrable and cannot be wished away – an object of *handling*. It enters the world of the ego as, interchangeably, raw stuff for processing or resistance to action. It lends itself to ego's will and sets the limits to ego's willing. It is the expanse of ego's freedom and constraints on that freedom. Consequently, it is an object of absorption and assimilation, or of the struggle.

The sensations-gatherer's Other is made of the rarefied and ethereal substance of impressions. It is a surface, rough or smooth, to be stroked or licked – an object of *tasting*. It can be passed by or turned away from, and then it drops out of interested attention, and so ceases to exist, its existence being the interest it excites. It enters the world of the ego as an anticipated source of pleasure, it leaves that world as the anticipation unfulfilled or pleasure used up. It is, interchangeably, raw stuff for experience or disappointment for the senses. Consequently, it is a terrain for exploration and adventure, or a disused and barren field drained of excitement.

At all times, the Other is the unmastered and unruly future, the seat of perpetual uncertainty – and, as such, a focus of attraction and fear. The Other of the goods-purveyor attracts as a chance for *action*; the Other of the pleasures-collector attracts as a promise of *sensations*. The fear which emanates from the first Other is that of resistance to action, of the threat to reaching the goal. The fear which the second Other exudes is that of insipidity of experience, frustration of the search for stimulation. The first Other may prove to be a *trouble*; the second, a displeasure, or a lack of pleasure, or pleasure short-of-the-expected – a *disappointment*.

The world of the goods-purveyor, of the producer/soldier tends to be spaced *cognitively*. Its charting is the play of ends-and-means relevances, of matching means against appointed ends and ends against available means. The cognitively spaced world is the yield of goal-pursuit and attendant calculation, but it is also, though secondarily, the testing ground of the limits of the capacity to act, and to act effectively. The world of the sensations-gatherer, of the consumer, tends to be spaced *aesthetically*. Its charting is the play of sensation-arousal relevances, of matching objects against the sensations sought, or matching the search against the available objects' sensation-generating capacities. The aesthetically spaced world is the yield of the pursuit of experience, of novel experience, and experience more intense than the experience before – but it is also, and in the first place, the sediment of the ongoing testing of the experiencing capacity of the body and the ongoing effort to expand it.

The goods-purveyor's being-in-the-world, and thus her/his engagement with the Other, is *outward-looking*; it is structured and moved by the interest in what can be done with, and to the world, and the Other in that world. It is monitored and assessed by the depth of the traces it left on that world, by the change it made to that world's corporeal condition. The sensations-gatherer's being-in-the-world, and thus her/his engagement with the Other, is *inward-looking*; it is structured and moved by the interest in what can be experienced by immersing oneself in that world and rubbing oneself against the Other. It is monitored and assessed by the depth of sensations it stimulates, by the change it makes to the subject's sensual condition. For the goods-purveyor, the world is an instrument to be played on. The pleasures-collector is herself/himself the instrument from which the pleasing tune is to flow.

Neither the goods-purveyor nor the sensations-gatherer are by the nature of their being-in-the-world prompted to engage in *moral* spacing. It can be shown that for both moral spacing is in principle counter-productive. Neither of the two may gain from *being-for* the Other – while both are likely to lose. The Other of the producer/ soldier is part of the job to be performed; its relevance – and thus its treatment – is defined beforehand by the end to be reached and the means needed to reach it. Assigning to such an Other any other significance would detract from the resilience with which the end is pursued and the precision with which the end and the means are matched. The Other of the consumer is the pool of sensations; its relevance – and thus its treatment – is defined and redefined in the course of the encounter by the quality of experience received or hoped to be received. Assigning to such an Other any other significance would diminish the concentration, weaken the stimulation and eventually dilute the experience itself.

At the first glance, neither of the two castings spells much hope for the moral relationship, for the being-for. If anything, they both proclaim the irrelevance of moral-type togetherness and struggle to emancipate from moral constraints. One casting demands that the identity of the Other is disregarded or violated, changed beyond recognition or dissolved. The other casting posits the Other as a balloon full of potential sensations whose skin may only be discarded once drained of contents, shrivelled and limp. Not much chance for the Other in either case. Or so it seems.

And yet . . . There is a measure of ambiguity in the sensations-gatherer's being-in-the-world which does not appear as much in the goods-purveyor's straightforward, goal-oriented existence. Ambiguity lodged in the nature of sensations-gathering pursuits, or rather in the way in which those pursuits dovetail with the world in which they are carried on. Lest her/his hopes of fulfilment should be dashed, the pleasure-collector cannot afford that annihilation of the Other's identity, of the otherness of the Other, which for the goods-purveyor is the mark of the trade and comes matter-of-factly. The pleasures-collector may approach the Other as supplier of sensations, and treat the relations asymmetrically, yet the fact remains that the Other is capable of performing the assigned task only in as far as s/he remains an Other, and her/his otherness (that impenetrable and unpredictable, absolute, future-like alterity) is preserved. While seeking to slake her/his own thirst for exciting experience, the pleasures-collector develops willy-nilly vested interests in keeping the otherness of the Other – and the Other's right to her/his otherness – intact and unscathed; indeed, it has interests in fomenting the Other's autonomy, prodding it and nurturing it. There is, to be sure, always a distance between having interests, knowing them, and acting upon them. One may be unaware of having interests, and when aware one may still refrain from pursuing them, having weighed the problems in which their pursuit may embroil them. (And the problems of attending to the Other's otherness, as I tried to show in chapter 4 of *Postmodern Ethics*, are enormous and promise no easy solution.) Assuming responsibility for the alterity, the identity, the autonomy of the Other is in no way a transcendental necessity for the pleasures-collector's life. But it is, undoubtedly, a crucial condition of success; an indispensable part, one may say, of any sound description of the 'pragmatics of the trade'.

Admittedly, this is a shaky and precarious base for the hope of moral engagement of the postmodern consumer; even wobblier and less reliable as a foundation of the engagement itself. It cannot be otherwise – as we have seen in the first chapter, there are reasons to suspect that morality can dream of unshakeable foundations only to its own detriment . . . One would be ill advised, though, to dismiss that base as it is just on the ground of its unsafeness. As far as the hope of moral engagement goes, 'tasting' the world seems to offer a considerable advance on 'handling' it. S/he who handles is oblivious to, often angered by, the shapes of things as they are – as s/he knows what shape (or shapelessness) s/he wants them to have. S/he who tastes, wants things to have flavour, and an original flavour, and a flavour of their own. And s/he may – just may – acquire taste in *helping* things develop fully the taste they, and only they, can offer. And the taste, the charm, of the thing called 'the Other' is its own, unrepeatable, unique, autonomous alterity. The same force that sets the sensations-seekers-and-gatherers apart may also bring them together; not just render them tolerant of each other's uniqueness, but solidary: finding the pleasure precisely in each other's autonomy and assuming the responsibility for each other's uniqueness.

5

The Stranger Revisited –
and Revisiting

Not all city life is modern; but all modern life is city life. For life to turn modern means to become more like life in the city. That is:

- Having more than one destination for every itinerary to choose from and needing to reflect upon, to navigate and to monitor one's movements to reach the destination chosen.
- Receiving on one's way signals in excess of one's need of orientation, and thus needing to select the relevant sensations from noise and/or to insert meaning into the senseless.
- Moving through a space populated by others who are guided by similar needs, and thus needing to calculate their movements while navigating one's own itinerary.
- The movements of the others being not fully predictable and thus not entirely calculable – navigating contains always an element of risk and adventure and is always plagued by the paucity of reliable signposts and in need of more routine.

The gap between what one needs to know in order to navigate and what one knows or thinks one knows about actual and possible moves of the others is perceived as the element of 'strangeness' in the others; this gap constitutes them as *strangers*. City life is carried on by strangers among strangers. In the words of Michael Schluter and David Lee, the stranger is 'everyone of us going out'.[1]

[1] Michael Schluter and David Lee, *The R Factor* (London: Hodder & Stoughton, 1993), p. 15.

The gap is an utterly ambivalent territory – the site of danger as well as freedom. The ambivalence of prospects rebounds in a similarly ambivalent sentiment of exhilarating adventure and becrippling confusion. The gap allures as much as it repels – its attraction and its loathsomeness pegged to each other, feeding each other, wedded to each other for better or worse; forever.

The secret of city happiness is knowing how to enhance the adventure brought about by that under-determination of one's own destination and itinerary, while at the same time confining, or making innocuous, the threat arising from the similar under-determination of other strangers; the two objectives clearly at odds with each other, since everyone in the city is a stranger and all constraint imposed on the status of the stranger must limit the threat one abhors together with the freedom one desires.

What the ideal of a happy city demands is the striking of a compromise, steering towards a subtle balance between opportunities and dangers, making a 'settlement' (in Lars-Henrik Schmidt's felicitous phrase)[2] between conflicting demands – not radical 'solutions'. The quandary is how to sacrifice of freedom only that little, and no more, that is necessary to render the anguish of uncertainty bearable – liveable with. Throughout modern history, however, most fantasies and planning blueprints of the happy city have veered toward the ultimate showdown between the oppositions which can stay alive only together, none being able to survive the demise of the other. They resoned with the most profound and least curable affliction of modern men and women, bound (in Alf Hornborg's words) to 'oscillate between a longing for *communitas*, a desire to be a part of something greater than the bounded Self, and the fear of self-dissolution'[3] – only to find out over and over again that freedom without community means madness, while community without freedom means serfdom.

Two strategies of living with strangers

Theoretically speaking, one could pursue 'radical solutions' of city life ambivalence following one of the two 'rational' (though equally

---

[2] See Lars-Henrik Schmidt, *Settling the Values* (Aarhus: Center for Kulturforskning, 1993), pp. 1–8.
[3] Alf Hornborg, 'Anthropology as Vantage-Point and Revolution', in *Anthropological Visions: Essays on the Meaning of Anthropology*, edited (in Swedish) by Kaj Århem; here quoted from the author's English translation.

self-defeating) strategies. One is to drastically reduce, or eliminate altogether, the element of surprise, and thus unpredictability, in the conduct of strangers. The other is to devise ways and means to render that element of contingency irrelevant; to blend the movements of strangers into the background one need neither notice nor care about. Both strategies aim at transforming the city into what Lyn Lofland described as the '*routine* world of strangers'[4] (a 'routine' world being a world of repetitive events and learnable patterns; a world free of contingency). The two strategies, however common, did not exclude other strategies, also ineffective but in addition denied a strong claim to rationality. Most prominent among the latter have been the recurrent attempts to burn out the uncertainty in effigy – to focus the abhorrence of indetermination on a selected category of strangers (immigrants, the ethnically different, vagrants, travellers or the homeless, devotees of bizarre and thus conspicuous subcultures) while hoping against hope that their elimination or confinement would provide the sought-after solution to the problem of contingency as such and install the dreamt of routine.

All utopias, these crystallized precipitations of diffuse longings and scattered hopes of the modern mind, followed the first of the two 'rational' strategies: they were utopias of an orderly, transparent and predictable, 'user-friendly' world. And they were all architectural and 'urban-planning' utopias. (The very word 'order' made its way into modern thought from architecture, where it was first deployed to denote a whole in which all parts fit each other and none could be replaced without destroying the harmony, and a situation that no change could improve.) Readers of utopias are invariably struck by the meticulous attention the authors paid to the layout of streets and public squares, the designs of homes, the specifications of the numbers of inhabitants and their movements through public spaces; also by the inordinately large proportion of text devoted to those concerns – such concerns as we used to associate with city planning. What directed the gaze of the dreamers of order to architecture and kept it there was the belief – tacit or explicit – that men and women behave as prompted by the world they inhabit: make that world regular, and you will make regular their cravings and their actions. Eliminate from that world everything accidental and unplanned – and you will cut away the roots of all waywardness and erratic conduct. In this sense, city planning was a war declared on strangers – on that underdetermination, that puzzling idiosyncrasy, which makes strangers

---

[4]   See Lyn Lofland, *A World of Strangers: Order and Action in Urban Public Space* (New York: Basic Books, 1973), pp. 176ff.

out of the others; not a war aimed at a conquest (a forceful conversion of the multitude of strangers into so many individual ac-
quaintances, tamed and domesticated) – but at the excision and burning
out of the 'strange' (that is, of everything unique, surprising, baffling
in them, through reducing the strangers to categories in which all
members are *the same*). The stranger was the enemy of uniformity
and monotony, and the city planning guided by urban utopia (the
utopia of perfect society achieved through city planning) was about
exterminating whatever there was strange in the strangers and, if
needed, the strangers themselves.

In *The Conscience of the Eye*, the most perceptive analysis of the
ideas that guided modern city planning and the realities that resulted
from them, Richard Sennett finds the grid (a city of streets intersect-
ing under right angles, a city composed of a vertical and lateral series
of identically shaped and sized blocks) to be the fullest and most
fitting expression of the dream of the city as uniform, impersonal,
cool, neutral setting for life. Grids substituted faceless, anonymous
'nodes' and crossings for self-imposing and meaning-enforcing, dictatorial centres – with a hope to impose an artificially and artfully
designed, homogeneous, uniform space upon the chaos of nature and
historical contingencies.

> The grid can be understood as a weapon to be used against environmental
> character – beginning with the character of geography. In cities like Chicago
> the grids were laid over irregular terrain . . . The natural features that
> could be leveled or drained, were; the insurmountable obstacles that
> nature put against the grid, the irregular course of rivers or lakes, were
> ignored by these frontier city planners, as if what could not be harnessed
> to this mechanical, tyrannical geometry did not exist . . . The farms and
> hamlets dotting nineteenth-century Manhattan were expected to be engulfed
> rather than incorporated as the grid on paper became building in fact.[5]

As it happened, stifling or ignoring the careless eccentricity of nature
and the capriciousness of historical accidents proved neither easy nor
devoid of problems of its own; much more off-putting, though, was
the abysmal failure to achieve what the geometric elegance of the
grid was hoped to attain. The grid did not make urban space uniform, easy to read and safe to move through. It soon turned into a
matrix for a new heterogeneity, a canvas on which a variety of city
dwellers was yet to embroider its own, unplanned and erratic designs.
To their bafflement and despair, in order to convey the realities of

[5] Richard Sennett, *The Conscience of the Eye: The Design and Social Life of Cities*
(London: Faber & Faber, 1993), p. 52.

city life the pioneers of urban sociology had to draw on the map of Chicago convoluted, uneven, geometrically inelegant figures which in their turn ignored the geometric harmony of the grid determined to ignore the inherent anarchy of nature and history.

The city that emerged at the far end of modern development is anything but a homogeneous space. It is rather an aggregate of qualitatively distinct areas of highly selective attraction, each distinguished not only by the type of its permanent dwellers but also by the type of incidental strangers likely to visit it or pass through it. The borderlines between the areas are sometimes clearly drawn and guarded, more often blurred or poorly signposted, and in most cases contested and in need of constant realignment through borderline skirmishes and reconnaissance forays. Under these circumstances, the 'strangehood' of strangers has become a matter of degree; it changes as one passes from one area to another, and the rhythm of the shift differs between various categories of strangers. One person's home ground is another person's hostile environment. Freedom of movement within the city has become, one may say, the principal *stratifying* factor. The elevated position in the social hierarchy of the city may be best measured by the degree to which the confinement to one area only may be avoided and the 'no-go' areas may be ignored or securely bypassed, so that all desirable sites in the city remain accessible.

In other words, city dwellers are stratified according to the degree to which they can behave as if the second strategy of 'life among strangers' could be successfully deployed; the degree to which they can *ignore* the presence of strangers and defuse the dangers it augurs. The point is that the resources which are necessary to behave in such a way are unevenly distributed among the city dwellers, and thus the chances to act in the spirit of the second strategy are anything but equal. Many residents of the contemporary city are left without a feasible strategy and, more often than not, must confine their chart of liveable (and, indeed, 'public' – freely accessible) space to the strictly circumscribed 'ghettoized' area, able at best to try to keep the rest of the city inhabitants off limits. (Imprinting the stamp of ownership and the 'No Entry' sign on the claimed area is achieved, to invoke Dick Hebdidge's list, through 'rituals, dressing strangely, striking bizarre attitudes, breaking rules, breaking bottles, windows, heads, issuing rhetorical challenges to the law'.[6] The famous 'no go areas' look different, depending from which side one looks at them: for those lucky enough to circulate outside they are 'no *go in* areas', but

6   Dick Hebdidge, *Hiding in the Light* (London: Routledge, 1988), p. 18.

for the insiders 'no go' means 'no *going out'*.) For the 'rest of the city dwellers', who enjoy the freedom to span the areas of the sprawl-ing city on their journeys – the consequence of the stratification is the ability to eliminate the ghetto-dwellers from the inventory of strangers they are likely to encounter. The network of inner-city motorways, thoroughfares and throughways, and of course the secure fortresses of burglar-proof private cars with reinforced glass and anti-theft locks allow them to bypass the spaces where such strangers are likely to be met without actually entering or visiting them. The inherent variety of city habitats has been, if anything, reinforced; but they may ignore at least the most unprepossessing and threatening of its fragments. Most of that variety remains for them invisible and need not be calculated when one's own actions are plotted. Freedom depends on how much of that variety can be treated as non-existent, or intermittently kept at arm's length when cumbersome and exploited when enjoyable.

To sum up: city life has different meanings for different people – and so does the figure of the stranger and the set of entities to which it refers. This trivial truth needs to be reiterated because of the pro-nounced tendency (broken only by the researchers who focus closely on 'subcultures' – ethnic, class, generational, gender-related) to de-scribe the experience of postmodern city life from one perspective only: that of the postmodern, 'democratized' yet commercially regi-mented, version of *flânerisme*, once a pastime confined to a narrow stratum of affluent men of leisure, today much more widespread, but still mostly a middle-class preoccupation (or at least the life-style of fully fledged consumers). Whenever that experience is interpreted, one should keep in mind that the double freedom to move every-where and to ignore selectively is its baseline condition.

The stranger, as seen by the *flâneur*

In his series of remarkable studies of contemporary city life, most notably in *Citysex*,[7] Henning Bech spells out the constitutive features of contemporary city life as experienced by the stroller. In a frag-ment Bech used as the motto for his *Living Together* essay, Charlotte

[7] Henning Bech, 'Citisex', revised paper from the International Conference on *Geographies of Desire: Sexual Preferences, Spatial Differences*, University of Am-sterdam, 19–19 June 1993; see also 'Living Together in the (Post)modern World', paper presented at the session on *Changing Family Structures and New Forms of Living Together*, European Conference of Sociology, Vienna, 26–28 August 1992.

Brontë reports the 'elation and pleasure', 'ecstasy of freedom and enjoyment' she felt during her walk in London thanks to 'wandering whither chance might lead' and having 'mixed with the life passing along'. Following the chance, yet encountering life everywhere the chance may lead, and everywhere encountering life that *passes along* (stays within the sight long enough to be grasped by wandering attention, yet not long enough for the attention to feel tied down, coerced to stop, compromised in its freedom to follow the chance; long enough to set the imagination free, but not long enough to challenge whatever has been imagined with obstinate, hard counter-truth) is the source of elation and ecstasy, an experience akin to erotic, orgasmic pleasure; this is, in a nutshell, the lesson derived by Bech from his vivisection of urban experience.

And this is the case not *in spite of* but *thanks to* the 'universal otherhood' that rules city life; not because of some magic transformation of distance into proximity, of the cancelling out of the mutual estrangement of the strangers, but on the contrary: if in the city experience pleasure took (or, rather, takes – sometimes) the better of its other concomitant – fear – it is thanks to the preservation of the strangehood of the strangers, freezing the distance, preventing proximity; pleasure is drawn precisely from mutual estrangement, that is from the absence of responsibility and the assurance that, whatever may happen between the strangers, it will not burden them with lasting obligations, will not leave in its wake consequences (notoriously difficult to determine) likely to outlast the enjoyment of the moment (deceptively easy to control).

Trying to grasp the nature of city encounters which do not cancel, but protect and reinvigorate the estrangement of strangers, Erich Fromm used the metaphor of the snapshot:

> Taking pictures becomes a substitute for seeing. Of course, you have to look in order to direct your lens to the desired object . . . But *looking* is not *seeing*. Seeing is a human function, one of the greatest gifts with which man is endowed; it requires activity, inner openness, interests, patience, concentration. Today a *snapshot* (the aggressive expression is significant) means essentially to transform the act of seeing into an object . . .[8]

In the idea of the 'snapshot', both parts of the word are important: what matters, is that this is a *shot*, which hits where I direct the barrel; that the impact falls upon the object while leaving me, who holds the

[8]   Erich Fromm, *The Anatomy of Human Destructiveness* (London: Jonathan Cape, 1974), p. 343.

gun, unaffected; and that it is a *snap* shot, a momentary link between the shooter and the hit, one lasting no longer than it takes to discharge the gun. The 'snapshot' kind of looking – looking without really seeing – is a *momentary* event (thus not mortgaging the onlooker's future freedom of target-selecting) and an *episode* (that is, a self-enclosed event, untied to the events before and untying the episodes after; it frees the present from the constraints of the past and of the burden of the future).

Superficiality, emotional and temporal flatness, splicing of the time flow into unconnected fragments used to be the pleasures of the lonely *flâneur*, the pioneer onlooker, the first practitioner of looking without seeing, of skin-deep encounters, of creaming off the enticements of the other without committing oneself to give anything in exchange; that flatness and superficiality is now within reach of most (though not all!) urban dwellers, and those who set the scene for urban strolls or otherwise cater to the cravings and the moods of the actual and would-be strollers know it and make the best of the infinite commercial opportunities this condition opens. One of the great number of glossy magazines that represent (and set the standards for) the world-made-to-the-measure-of-strollers, *The Face*, subjected to close and remarkably insightful scrutiny by Dick Hebdidge,[9] may serve as a paragon of new urban reality: 'Looking takes precedence over seeing ("seeing " over "knowing") . . . Reality is as thin as the paper it is printed on. There is nothing underneath or behind the image and hence there is no hidden truth to be revealed . . .'

> *The Face* is not read so much as wandered through; 'cruised'. The 'reader' is licensed to use whatever has been appropriated in whatever way and in whatever combination proves most useful and most satisfying. (There can be no 'promiscuity' in a world without monogamy/monotheism/monadic subjects; there can be no 'perversion' in a world without norms . . .) By cruising, the 'reader' can take pleasure in a text without being obliged at the same time to take marriage vows and a mortgage on a house.

The message is as simple as it is unqualified and overwhelming: the 'separation of pleasure/use value from any pledge/commitment to "love, honour and obey" '. Elsewhere, I have pointed to that separation as the primary mechanism of the postmodern version of *adiaphorization* – the stripping of human relationships of their moral significance, exempting them from moral evaluation, rendering them 'morally irrelevant'. Adiaphorization is set in motion whenever the relationship involves less than the total person, whenever the object

---

[9] See Hebdidge, *Hiding in the Light*, p. 159ff.

of the relationship is a selected aspect – a 'pertinent', 'useful' or 'interesting' facet of the Other – since it is only the *full* relationship, a relationship between spatially and temporarilly *whole* selves, that may be 'moral', that is embrace the issue of responsibility for the other. Preventing the looking from turning into seeing – an effect which the organization of modern city life works to achieve – is, alongside modern bureaucracy with its 'floating of responsibility' and modern business with its spatial and temporal limitation of human contact through contract and formal pledge, a major mechanism of adiaphorization. City life is a life morally impoverished and thus free to be subjected to unchallenged rule of other than moral criteria – an ideal haunt for the pleasurable-sensations seekers guided in their pursuits solely by aesthetic interest.

According to Henning Bech's analysis, the exhilarating sensation of opportunity and freedom associated with city life comes not only from the abundance of impressions on offer, but also – perhaps mainly – from the 'liberation from oneself', the suspension of the total, and therefore morally self-conscious and self-limiting self; by necessity – perpetually reinforced through joyously embraced choice – urban relations are anonymous and non-committal. They are also saturated with the spirit of consumerism: they are entered only to be dissolved again, they last as long as the pleasure they bring, and fall apart once a greater pleasure, from a different source, begins to beckon: human encounters, just like the appropriation of supermarket commodities, are picked up and discarded with ease, motivated and sustained as they are solely by shifting attention and desire.

Drifting, non-committal relationships between strangers seem to be oriented by the search for, primarily, *tactile* pleasures. (This is, one may guess, what suggested to Bech the mainly sexual nature of city pleasures.) Looking without seeing stops, after all, at the surface, and surfaces present themselves to the senses as potential objects of, above all, tactile sensations: the non-seeing gaze is a substitute for, or a premonition of, touching without holding, stroking without arresting. The 'presentation of self' in city life is first and foremost, perhaps exclusively, the presentation of surfaces – the visuality of presentation is shot through with the anticipation of tactility; it is the potential tactile pleasures that are put on display, given commanding and obtrusive presence – made *visually* salient.

In the street life of the city, people are to each other surfaces; every stroller moves through a constant display of surfaces, and every stroller is constantly on display as s/he moves. Exposure entails allurement (that all too easily can be read out as invitation), but no promise and no commitment; it contains therefore a huge load of risk. Possibilities of sweet success and humiliating defeat are finely balanced and hardly ever separable. The city street is simultaneously exciting and frightening; apparently, through reducing the self to a surface, to something one can control and arrange at will, it offers the self security against intruders; in fact, because of semantic confusion the surfaces cannot but emanate, one needs to remain constantly on guard, yet, even with all the care one takes to calculate one's moves, every step taken is pregnant with risk. In the long run, the gamble one cannot avoid is exhausting, and the thought of a refuge – a *home* – grows into a temptation ever more difficult to resist.

The stranger *ante portas*

In his seminal study of contemporary chauvinism and racism,[10] Phil Cohen suggests that all xenophobia ethnic or racist, all positing of the stranger as an enemy and, unambiguously, as the outer boundary and limit to one's individual or collective sovereignty, has the idealized conception of the secure home as its sense-giving metaphor. The image of the secure home transforms the 'outside of home' into a terrain fraught with danger; the inhabitants of that outside turn into the carriers of threat – they need to be contained, chased away and kept away:

> the external environment can come to be seen as uniformly undesirable and dangerous, whilst behind the symbolic lace curtains, 'personal standards can be maintained.' The sense of home shrinks to that space where some sense of inherent 'order and decency' can be imposed on that small part of a chaotic world which the subject can directly own and control.

It is the dream of 'defensible space', a place with secure and effectively guarded borders, a territory semantically transparent and semiotically legible, a site cleansed of risk, and particularly of the incalculable risks – which transforms merely 'unfamiliar people' (those, under normal circumstances of the city stroll, obscure objects of desire) into downright enemies. And city life, with all the intricate skills, taxing efforts and strenuous vigilance it calls for, cannot but render those dreams of home ever more intense.

The 'home' of that dream derives its meaning from the oppositions between risk and control, danger and security, combat and peace,

[10] See Phil Cohen, *Home Rules: Some Reflections on Racism and Nationalism in Everyday Life* (University of East London, The New Ethnicities Unit, 1993).

episode and perpetuity, fragmentation and the whole. That home, in other words, is the craved-for remedy for pains and distress of city life, that life of strangers among strangers. The trouble is, though, that the remedy can only be imagined and postulated; in its craved-for shape it is as unachievable as the vexing features of city life, and their ubiquitousness, are unavoidable. It is the irreality of the postulated remedy, the yawning gap between the dreamt-of home and every construction of brick and mortar, every 'watched neighbourhood', that makes territorial warfare into the only modality of home, and border skirmishes into the only practical means of rendering the borders, and the home itself, 'real'. The stranger is constantly *ante portas*, but it is the declared presence of the stranger, of a stranger conspiring to trespass, to break in and invade, that makes the gate tangible.

The stranger *ante portas* (at the gate – this is the only place where such a stranger can be found) is not that stranger we have just visited in the preceding section: not the stranger melting into, or solidifying from, the backcloth of the city stroll: all similarity, one may say, is here purely accidental. The shared name is a prolific source of theoretical, and often also practical, confusion. Perhaps the two strangers ought to be given different names. Short of that, they need to be conceptually separated. The stranger *ante portas* is stripped of that ambiguity which makes the population of the city street the source of unremitting, though often costly, pleasure. If the intermittently pleasurable/risk-emanating stranger is the construction of the stroller on his/her sensation-seeking expeditions, the stranger *ante portas* is the construction of homesick wanderers overwhelmed by sensations while not able any more to escape being bombarded by them. It is at the moments of homesickness that the stroller reconstructs the stranger from temptation into threat, from the source of fleeting pleasure into the omen of *ubi leones*. One is prompted to say that the stranger of the city stroller is the sedimentation of *proteophilia*, while the stranger of the home-defender is the precipitate of *proteophobia*. And the incurably protean world of contemporary cities breeds philic and phobic reactions in equal measure.

In contemporary cities, *identity* is forever, and incurably, divorced from *natality*. Surfaces into which the strangers turned for each other have no 'natural' behind or beneath, no obvious depth to which they belong and which belongs to them. To quote Sennett again, the narrative of surface-like life is non-sequential, the experience of differences non-linear. (We may say: sights of surfaces do not accumulate; or, in other words, one cannot reconstitute the self out of surfaces, however many.) 'A man or woman can become in the course of a lifetime like a foreigner to him or herself, by doing things or entering into feelings that do not fit the familiar framework of identity, the seemingly social fixities of race, class, age, gender, or ethnicity.'[11] No identity is fixed, each one needs to be construed – and, moreover, without any guarantee that the construction will ever be finished and the roof will be laid over the completed edifice. There is no 'return' to natality – the past has not been stored in a warehouse until such time as it may be taken out, dusted and restored to its former beauty, it needs to be sewn anew, from the selfsame tokens of meaning encountered – always fleetingly – in the city street. In this respect there is no status difference between back and forward, past and future, 'glorious heritage' and daring project. Whether the sought-after home is imagined in the past or knowingly located in the future – it is always a *postulated* home, and it takes incessant labour and intense emotional dedication to prevent the hope that feeds the postulated target from drying up.

The stranger, Janus-faced

The city is the site of pleasure and danger, of opportunity and threat. It attracts and repels, and cannot do one thing without doing the other. The city breeds excitement and fatigue, offering on one tray tidbits of freedom and enemas of disempowerment. The modern promise to purify the crystal of pleasure and drain off the contaminating impurities failed to materialize, while the zealous attempts to act on that promise through forcing urban life into a reason-dictated frame, and prohibiting everything that the design had not made obligatory, only added new, artificially produced malfunctions to the old, spontaneously emerging blights. It seems that the ambiguity of city life is here to stay. As Jonathan Friedman commented, the invasion of variegated, often contradictory, cultural offers

> that are usually held at a distance by modernist identity appears to pervade every aspect of the contemporary condition. This invasion combines a certain exhilaration, the exhilaration of new found meaning, and fear, the fear of the outsider, of treachery and violence. The invasion is not merely geographic, the implosion of 'the others', but internal as well, the implosion of formerly repressed psychic desires, the surfacing of the other within.[12]

[11] Sennett, *The Conscience of the Eye*, p. 148.
[12] Jonathan Friedman, 'The Implosion of Modernity', quoted from the manuscript.

Nowhere is that invasion felt so acutely and poignantly as on city strolls (and that includes, to an ever growing degree, the strolls accomplished daily through the medium of what Bech called the 'telecity', the medium which accentuated and brought to the radical extreme the 'surface-producing' inclination of the urban space). And nowhere is the mixture of exhilaration and fear experienced more intensely. It is here, in the city, that the enjoyment of protean, unbound identity and the desire for 'home', for a 'community' that binds and puts an end to the perpetual exile of postmodern Proteus, are born – as twins, perhaps as Siamese twins. In the words of Dean MacCannell,

> the central problem of postmodernity will be to create ersatz 'communities' to manufacture or even sell a 'sense' of community . . . The complexity of this feat of social engineering – that is, the construction of a believable symbol of community where no community exists – should not be underestimated, nor should the drive to accomplish this feat be underestimated.[13]

The experiential ambiguity of the postmodern city rebounds in the postmodern ambivalence of the stranger. He has two faces. One is enticing because it is mysterious (sexy, as Bech would say), inviting, promising joy to come while demanding no oath of loyalty; the face of infinite opportunity, yet untried pleasure and ever new adventure. The other face is also mysterious – but it is a sinister, menacing and intimidating mystery that is written all over it. Both faces are but half-visible and blurred. It takes an effort to read clear features into the place where the face should be – an interpretative effort, a meaning-awarding effort. It is left to the interpreter to fix the meaning, to recast the fluid impressions into sensations of pleasure or fear. These sensations are then solidified into the figure of the stranger – as contradictory and ambiguous as the sensations themselves. Mixophilia and mixophobia vie with each other, locked in a competition neither can win.

[13]   Dean MacCannell, *Empty Meeting Grounds: The Tourist Papers* (London: Routledge, 1992), p. 89.

6

Violence, Postmodern

We can now do what we want, and the only question is what do we want?
At the end of our progress we stand where Adam and Eve stood: all we are
faced with now is the moral question.

Max Frisch

Virtually all writers attempting to come to grips with the phenomenon of violence find the concept either under-, or over-defined,
or both. They also report in other writers (if they not display it themselves) an amazing reluctance, or ineptitude, to resolve the confusion
and put things straight. Above all, they find in the texts they read
plenty of understatements and half-truths, a lot of embarrassed silence, and other signs of shamefacedness. There must be something
about violence that makes it elude all conceptual nets, however
skilfully knit. And there is. Namely, our modern ambivalence about
might, force and coercion.

From the start, modernity was about forcing things to be different
from what they are. About amassing more power-generating energy
and drawing on its supplies more lavishly and more often in order
to shuffle things around, giving more room to some and less to
others. And about being always one step ahead of reality: having
always more means of acting than the ends of the present action
require, having always more energy than what the already recognized
needs present as necessary. (Energy is after all a pure *pouvoir*, ability
to do things, whatever those things may yet turn out to be.) Modernity can live without coercion about as well as fish can live without
water. The perceptive Polish-French historian Krzysztof Pomian called
Europe a civilization of *transgression*, marked by 'diminishing respect
for barriers, obstacles, prohibitions', a civilization which thinks that
'borders are there solely in order to be transgressed', and one which
'does not just tolerate transgressions as far as they remain marginal;

it provokes them.'[1] A lot of power is needed in order to bend and twist things behind the frontier, so that they acquire a shape deemed better, and to push the frontier further back, so that an ever larger territory contains things of the right shape only. Without, there would be no *ordering activity*, and modernity can ill afford to live without it, once the automatic mechanisms of reproducing social life have gone bankrupt, have been disallowed or been taken apart.

Modernity, as John Law recently remarked, has

> spawned a monster: the hope or the expectation that everything can be pure; the expectation that if everything were pure it would be better than it actually is; and we have concealed the reality that what is better for some is almost certainly worse for others; that what is better, simpler, purer, for a few rests precariously and uncertainly upon the work and, very often, the pain and misery of others.[2]

Ordering makes protruding the difference previously unnoticed and creates a difference where there was none; it splits the set of objects within the field about to be ordered into such as fit the order and such as do not. The latter must be *coerced* to change themselves or to change their places. 'In the case of the modern European', observed Michael Winter wittily, 'the finger on the outstretched arm pointed not upwards or downwards, as in medieval times, but straight toward the horizon.'[3] And the chance was, let us add, that the space between the pointing finger and the horizon was densely populated by people who ill-advisedly deemed that space to be their home and farm and did not expect other people's fingers to decree otherwise.

Modernity is by its nature a frontier civilization, which re-creates itself and rejuvenates through a constant supply of lands to conquer and ever new invitations to, or pretexts for, transgression. Since ordering activity never leads to one, single, finite order, and cannot help generating rubbish alongside cleanliness, ugliness alongside beauty, ambivalence alongside clarity, and areas of confusion alongside orderly ones – there is little chance that the supply of rejuvenating challenges will ever run short. Thus, energy has been the most overwhelming, guiding obsession of modern civilization – and energy means the ability to act, the capacity for doing and redoing,

[1] Krzysztof Pomian, 'L'Europe et ses frontières', in *Le Débat*, no. 68 (1992), p. 30ff.
[2] John Law, *Organizing Modernity*, (Oxford: Blackwell, 1994), pp. 6–7.
[3] Michael Winter, *Ende eine Traumas: Blick zurück auf das utopische Zeitalter Europas* (Stuttgart: J. B. Matzler, 1993), p. 330.

making things change, coercing things into becoming different from what they are or to leave the stage.

This is why modern consciousness is and must be double-faced about the use of force, coercion, violence. Modernity legitimizes itself as a 'civilizing process' – as an ongoing process of making the coarse gentle, the cruel benign, the uncouth refined. Like most legitimations, however, this one is more an advertising copy than an account of reality. At any rate, it hides as much as it reveals. And what it hides is that only through the coercion they perpetrate can the agencies of modernity keep out of bounds the coercion they swore to annihilate; that one person's civilizing process is another person's forceful incapacitation. The civilizing process is not about the uprooting, but about the *redistribution* of violence.

'Force is a means specific to the state', concluded Weber, and we all repeat after him. 'In the past, the most varied institutions . . . have known the use of physical force as quite normal. Today, however, we have to say that a state is a human community which (successfully) claims *the monopoly of the legitimate use of physical force* within a given territory.'[4] Thanks to the state monopoly, coercion gets split into two sharply distinguished kinds, respectively characterized as legitimate and illegitimate, necessary and gratuitous, desirable and undesirable, useful and harmful. By the look of them, the two now separate categories have nothing to distinguish them from each other except the – always partisan – justification given to one but refused to another. True, they have now been given different names: one category of coercion is called 'enforcement of law and order', while the nasty word 'violence' is reserved only for the second. What the verbal distinction hides, though, is that the condemned 'violence' is also about certain ordering, certain laws to be enforced – only those are not the order and the laws which the makers of the distinction had in mind. As Hélé Béji observed, there is one thing which justice shares with injustice: 'it needs, to be effective, all the authority of force.'[5]

So what is the actual meaning of the distinction? What does it

---

[4] From *Wirtschaft und Gesellschaft*; quoted after *From Max Weber*, ed. H. H. Gertz and C. Wright Mills (London: Routledge, 1970), p. 78.

[5] Hélé Béji, 'Le Patrimoine de la cruauté', in *Le Débat*, no. 73 (1993), p. 167. Béji goes on to demonstrate that the renegotiation of the apportionment of justice and injustice, vice and merit, 's'est accompagnée d'une manifestation de la puissance'. 'Legitimate coercion' is redubbed as violence only when its perpetrators are defeated and its victims sit in court. Otherwise, without such (again violent!) redealing of cards, 'la mémoire transforme la cruauté en histoire, elle lui donne un sens, un statut, elle l'intègre pieusement au patrimoine . . .' (p. 163)

convey? Like most oppositions which the practice of modernity generated, and the modernity-legitimating discourse reforged into categories of reason (categories as messy as the practices they processed),[6] this one stands for *the distinction between the designed order and all the rest*; between the controlled and the uncontrolled, the regular and the erratic, the predictable and the unpredictable, the foreseeable and the unexpected, the grounded and the contingent, the monotonous and the spontaneous. (One is tempted to borrow Youri Lotman's striking metaphor of, on the one hand, a powerful river that sweeps away or devours everything obstructing its flow, but whose direction is strictly determined by the riverbed and thus steady and known in advance; and, on the other, a minefield, in which locally condensed explosions will surely occur, but no one really knows when and where.)[7]

The notion of *Irritationserfahrungen*, coined by Jan Philipp Reemtsma, splendidly captures the real meaning of 'violence', as construed in modern discourse (and first in modern practice). Another of Reemtsma's concepts, is that of the *shock*: 'reaction to the unexpected, unheard of events which reveal the habitual forms of truth and information-processing as inadequate.'[8] Violence is the productive waste of the order-factory; something that cannot be recycled into something useful, handled with available tools – and something that has not been calculated into the costs of the productive process. If order-making means coercing things into *regularity*, 'violence' stands for *irregular* coercion, such as saps regularity here and now, that regularity which is synonymical with order. Such coercion is *violence*.[9] Since no order is ever exactly like it wants itself to be, and since one

[6] Helmut König writes: 'Often is the road from the concept of civilization meant to be descriptive-analytical, to a concept which is normative and prescriptive, very short' (*Mittelweg*, vol. 36 no. 6 (1993), p. 50). The road is indeed short, but contrary to König, it is trodden, as a rule, in the opposite direction.

[7] See Y. M. Lotman, *Kul'tura i vzrȳv* [Culture and Explosion] (Moscow: Gnosis, 1992), p. 9. In the minefield, Lotman emphasizes, the choice of the location where the explosion occurs 'is not defined by either causal laws or probabilities – in the moment of explosion those two mechanisms are switched off.' The choice is *accidental*.

[8] See Jan Philipp Reemtsma, 'Die "Signatur des Jahrhunderts" – ein kataleptischer Irrtum?', in *Mittelweg*, vol. 36, no. 5 (1993), p. 9.

[9] What follows is that Ulrich Bielefeld's observation that 'unexpected violence is possible at any time' ('Die Folgen der Gewalt', in *Mittelweg*, vol. 36 no. 6 (1993), p. 82) is as correct as it is tautological. 'Violence', by the definition coined by the theory and praxis of the modern ordering bustle, is precisely what is 'unexpected'. Any planned, designed, legitimized, 'official' application of force would be found another name.

man's order is another man's disorder, and since the visions of order keep changing, as the order-keepers themselves – the borderlines between the opposed categories tend to be blurred; but more importantly yet, the distinction between order-keeping and violence is endemically a contested one. It is never conclusively drawn: the borderline barriers stay effective only as long as there are heavily armed men to guard them.

The drifting frontier

The opposition 'order-keeping versus violence' is but one of the many by-and-large overlapping oppositions (like those between reason and passion, rationality and affectivity), superimposed over one central modern opposition between the controlled and the uncontrolled, regular and irregular, predictable and unpredictable. The ordering activity, the major pastime of modern institutions, is mostly about the imposition of monotony, repeatability and determination; whatever resists this imposition is the wilderness behind the frontier, a hostile land still to be conquered or at least pacified. The difference between the controlled and the uncontrolled space is that between *civility* and *barbarity*. In the land of civility, no coercion (ideally) comes by surprise and from unexpected quarters; it can be rationally calculated, become the 'known necessity' which one can even, following Hegel,[10] celebrate as freedom . . . In the land of barbarity, coercion (here called violence) is diffuse, dispersed, erratic – and thus unpredictable and incapacitating. But in the land of barbarity the rules of civility do not bind. It is a catch-as-catch-can, all-allowed-if-it-works territory; since they are by definition violent, barbarians are legitimate objects of violence. Civility is for the civil, barbarity for the barbaric.

In his perceptive study of the intimate link between modern civility and modern philosophy, Howard Caygill points out that:

---

[10]   Or, indeed, with Norbert Elias, according to whom the concentration of force in the hands of the state and state-authorized institutions, together with the 'civilizing change of behaviour' ('The moderation of spontaneous emotions, the tempering of affects') led to a situation when physical violence 'is no longer a perpetual insecurity . . . but a peculiar form of security'. A 'continuous, uniform pressure is exerted on individual life by the physical violence stored behind the scenes of everyday life.' (*The Civilising Process: State Formation and Civilisations*, trans. Edmund Jephcott (Oxford: Blackwell, 1982), pp. 236, 238).

the rational management of violence within the nation state was only possible when potential and actual violence had been displaced to the border, whether through the export of refractory elements of the population or the import of plundered wealth to support the welfare institutions of the metropolis.

That condition, though, is no more met today:

> With the limits for territorial expansion themselves reaching the limit . . . reasoned civility and sovereign violence threaten to collapse into each other . . . [T]he potential for violence displaced to the periphery returns to the centre with increasing speed . . .
> The border between civility and violence is no longer to be found at the limit of a sovereign, territorial space, but now traverses that space.[11]

This is undoubtedly a seminal observation – but two qualifications are needed before it is accepted and before its consequences are traced.

First, throughout the history of modernity, the frontier between civility and barbarity never coincided with the borders of the nation state, and even less with the shared circumference of the 'civilized part of the world' as a whole. Hiroshima got rid of the barbarians 'out there', but Auschwitz and the Gulag of the barbarians 'in here'. At no moment of modern history were the barbarians allowed to confine themselves to 'standing at the gate' – they were sniffed at and spied on and dug up all over the place, in a most capricious manner resonant with their own definitional capriciousness. For the ancients who invented the word to denote all non-Greeks (and later those beyond the reach of Roman Law), barbarians aroused fear only when they came too close for comfort and themselves stood *ante portas;* they were not the objects of missionary activity nor wardenship. Modernity from the start *historicized* and *internalized* the status of barbarians. Barbarity was now not just a different form of life, but a form left behind, doomed to extinction – barbarians were living fossils, or beings who decisively outlived their time and should make themselves absent as soon as possible. Equally seminally, barbarians were now viewed as something of a 'fifth column', sitting in ambush inside the fortress of the civilized world and waiting for their moment to take revenge for the blows inflicted upon them by the civilizing process. Barbarians served as a major instrument in the modern

---

[11]　Howard Caygill, 'Violence, Civility, and the Predicament of Philosophy', in *The Political Subject of Violence*, ed. David Campbell and Michael Dillon (Manchester University Press, 1993), pp. 51–2.

'implantation of fear' (Reemtsma), the emotion modernity was keen to propagate as it added urgency, even an apparent sense, to the ever new transgressions 'modernization' set out to accomplish. They also served as an instrument of stratification and reproduction of cultural hegemony. More than a pinch of 'barbarity' was sprinkled into the official identity kits of the indolent, improvident, fickle and irresponsible poor, of the passion-ridden, thoughtless and frivolous female, of awkward and assimilaton-resistant cultural/ethnic minorities, and of any other category presumed too obstreperous and wayward to be safely kept at bay by the ordinary measure of daily coercion – be they criminals (subjects of the extra coercion of penology), mentally deficient (subjects of the extra coercion of psychiatry), or countless other degenerates. (In Daniel Pick's pithy conclusion, in nineteenth-century Europe degeneration 'became indeed the condition of conditions, the ultimate signifier of pathology'; it was at once universalized as the potential fate of all and . . . particularized as the condition of the others.')[12]

Finally, and perhaps most seminally, there was always a wild man lying in trap inside every civilized one. 'The barbarian' was intuited and intimated as sleeping inside every sane and healthy modern man, ready to wake up and run berserk at the first moment of inattention. Fighting, chaining and keeping chained the 'wild man within' was arguably the most widely engaging and the most news-covered battle-front of the always belligerent civilization of modernity. To serve this battle-front the most ingenious weapons kept being invented throughout modern history, and to serve on this front every modern man was enlisted to be a soldier; there was no lull in the combat. Each modern body was a jail, each modern man was a jailer guarding the dangerous psychopath inside, and the duty of jailers was to keep the bars locked and the alarms working. The vigilance never seemed to be sufficient, as misdeeds of the 'wild man within' were sniffed in every passion, any outburst of emotion, any break of etiquette, any show of affection. The bugbear of the barbarian in all of us was the most powerful weapon deployed in the modern battle to impose the designed order and a network of routine convention upon the contingent and obstreperous world of daily life; the fact that the barbarian

[12] Daniel Pick, *Faces of Degeneration: A European Disorder, c. 1848–c. 1918* (Cambridge University Press, 1989), pp. 8, 42–3. By the end of the nineteenth century a prestigious periodical of the British intellectual elite wrote that 'barbarism, cupidity and ruffianism' among the 'lower stratum' are 'as rife now as they were in the days of Sir Robert Walpole and Lord George Gordon. We see by what a thin and precarious partition after all are we divided from the elements of violence which underlie all civilized sanctions.' ('Mobs', in *Blackwoods* (1893), p. 123)

was so ubiquitous helped tremendously, by supplementing the state-administered big prisons with countless DIY little ones. To sum up, one may say that civility – that cultural crusade of modern elites and the armed campaign of the modern state – set, so to speak, its own rules of the game and reserved to itself the right to decide who is the barbarian. The border between the civil and the barbaric was never just one line and always 'traversed the space'.

Second, neither is it exactly true that the 'border between civility and violence is no longer to be found at the limit of the sovereign territorial space'. The orthodox, old-fashioned wars 'between us and them' are waged and will go on being waged for some time yet under the banners of the holy crusade of civilization against barbarism, peace against violence. The punitive expedition to the Gulf was but a most spectacular recent example – but the odds are that it is not going to be the last. In keeping with Ulrich Beck's vision of the world managed by man-made yet man-uncontrolled forces, the wheels of the arms-industry churn up ever more sophisticated and destructive weapons which, like all technological means that precede their objectives, feverishly seek the battlefields which might give them meaning. ('Our time thinks in terms of "knowing how to do it", even where there is nothing to be done', wrote Karl Jaspers already in 1958,[13] and subsequent history gave more weight still to his observation.) It is now the pacified 'sovereign territory' of civilization which keeps creating and re-creating objects to be stigmatized later as violent, and therefore legitimate targets of pacifying missions. It is now the civilized world with its overstocked military warehouses and myriads of military research-and-development staff eager to have its latest inventions tested 'in action', that keeps the supplies of the 'barbarism outside' constant and plentiful. Besides, there are powerful mechanisms in motion which may survive only if they pump ever more ingenious means of violence onto the other side of 'the limit of the sovereign territorial space', as if to plant ever new fresh targets for the war against violence. As in the poet's commentary on the duel between western technology sold and western technology unsold during the Gulf campaign:

> Our smiling erstwhile customer
> Is now the Prince of Lies.
> Committing vile atrocities,
> Surprise, surprise, surprise . . .

---

[13] Karl Jaspers, *The Future of Mankind*, trans. E. B. Ashton (University of Chicago Press, 1961), p. viii.

The question is, then, to what extent is the civilized part of the world capable of exercising the 'civilizing', pacifying influence on the 'less civilized', or 'under-civilized' periphery, fraught with violence, plagued as it is by multiple and unending tribal wars and ever too eager to resort to massacre and the rule of terror. In the times of the Great Divide the 'civilized' countries on both sides of the ideological rift were by and large in agreement (in practice, if not in theory), that political loyalty of the local leaders in peripheral countries should take precedence over their attachment to the principles of civilized rule; if anything, 'strong' (merciless, tyrannical) rulers were preferred for reasons of their reliability. On the other hand, with the collapse of the Berlin Wall, and with it the power-politics motivations for global policing, there is little left to spur the 'civilized centre' into a remedial, let alone preventive, action – apart from its desire to stem the tide of possible refugees (and, most crucially, a new wave of would-be immigrants knocking at the door of the affluent nations; the latter was the outspoken motive for intervention in the former Yugoslavia, spelled out by the American Secretary of State during a brief moment when America seemed to be willing to engage its troops in order-installing activity).

It may be said, though, that the political and particularly economic pressure which the governments of the 'civilized centre' exert to sponsor democratic rule and respect for human rights is perhaps a less radical and slow-acting, yet nevertheless potent method of civilizing influence and gradual elimination of barbaric forms of violence. This would be the case, if not for the fact that governmental spokesmen are not the sole 'interface' between the 'civilized' and 'less civilized' parts of the globe – and, in the wake of the disbanding of power-blocs and overall slackening of governmental interest in global politics, not at all the most seminal of the interfaces. If in the power-blocs era it was the political/military competition between the hostile blocs that saturated the periphery with weapons of mass annihilation (weapons creating a truly explosive mixture when combined with local dictatorial powers and festering tribal conflicts), the same effect is achieved today, and possibly to a degree higher than ever before, by the cut-throat competition between non-national arms-producers and traders, sometimes aided and abetted by local politicians eager to gain votes through 'saving jobs', but in most cases 'deregulated' (in practice, if not in theory, since supra-national) – and thus freed from pernickety governmental supervision and able to go where profits beckon. The combination of pre-modern animosities (and most of all the pre-modern inability to cohabit peacefully with difference) with most advanced modern weapons and techniques of mass destruction more than balances the possible 'civilizing' impact of preaching democracy and the promotion of human rights.

All this said, we must agree that the overall tendency has been grasped by Caygill correctly – the 'potential for violence' – once promised to be, and sometimes even declared to be, exiled forever – is fast 'returning to the centre'. But in what form?

The ways and means of separating deeds and morals

Whether in the form officially stigmatized as violence, or disguised as 'promotion of law and order' (or, indeed, as the 'civilizing process'), coercion is always, at least from the point of view of the coerced, *cruel*. To coerce means to be cruel. (As the two last British prime ministers like to repeat whenever they visit new pains on their subjects, 'If the medicine is not bitter, it does not work.') Not only the inventors and designers of coercive measures must be cruel or insensitive to other people's pain, but also the countless 'mediating agents' who implement their designs. If one agrees with Emmanuel Lévinas, as I do, that 'the justification of the neighbour's pain is certainly the source of all immorality',[14] then one would have to accept as well that there is more than a casual connection between the ability to commit cruel deeds and moral insensitivity.[15] To make massive participation in cruel deeds possible, the link between moral guilt and the acts which the participation entails must be severed. Modern

[14]   See Emmannel Lévinas, 'Useless Suffering', in *The Provocation of Lévinas: Rethinking the Other*, ed. Robert Nernesconi and David Wood (London: Routledge, 1988), p. 163.
[15]   In his remarkable study of the role played by sentiments in moral behaviour, Arne Johan Vetlesen opposes Hannah Arendt's interpretation of Eichmann's capacity for evil as arising from his 'thoughtlessness': 'Eichmann was *not* merely thoughtless, but first of all *insensitive* . . . Insofar as he adopts an objectifying attitude toward his fellows, as opposed to participatory-empathic one, Eichmann for all practical purposes *prevents the domain of moral phenomena to be disclosed to him.*' *(Perception, Empathy and Judgment: An Inquiry into the Preconditions of Moral Performance* (Pennsylvania State University Press, 1994), p. 305) Expectedly, Vetlesen takes exception also to Hans-Otto Apel's appeal to the 'responsibility of reason, which must take the place of a consciousness of sin based to some extent on instinct' (*Diskurs und Verantwortung* (Frankfurt: Suhrkamp, 1988), pp. 17–18) as misguided; whatever hope there is for morality, it must be related to the preservation of the instictive repulsion to gratuitous cruelty. Modern reason, on the contrary, has been known for the ingenuity with which such repulsion is suppressed or made irrelevant.

organization, with its scientific management and co-ordination of human actions, achieves just that; I have described in detail the way it does it in *Modernity and the Holocaust* and in *Modernity and Ambivalence*. What I suggested there was that the principal tool of that severance was and remains *adiaphorization*: making certain actions, or certain objects of action, morally neutral or irrelevant – exempt from the category of phenomena suitable for moral evaluation. The effect of adiaphorization is achieved by exluding some categories of people from the realm of moral subjects, or through covering up the link between partial action and the ultimate effect of co-ordinated moves, or through enthroning procedural discipline and personal loyalty in the role of the all-overriding criterion of moral performance.

Adiaphorization was throughout the modern era, and increasingly so, the accomplishment of modern bureaucracy aided and abetted by modern technology – and this, I suggest, still remains the case today to a large, perhaps even growing, extent. At least two new developments have added new power to the typically modern, yet by now traditional, methods of adiaphorization.

The first is the overall effect of 'insensitivitization' to cruelty which may arise out of the unprecedentedly huge volume of exposure to the images of human suffering. (There is hardly a day without dozens of corpses and killings being brought into our view on the television screen, whether in the time-slots described as 'the news', or such as are classified as drama or comedy or police series, feature films or children's programmes.) Norbert Elias saw in the end of public executions the sign of the civilizing progress; yet hangings in public, alongside so-called blood sports, were rare, festive and party-like occasions, belonging to what Mikhail Bakhtin described as the 'carnival culture' – the periodical spectacular reversals of the daily norms in order better to underline the binding routine of quotidianity; carnival culture was an emphatic statement about the unusuality and exceptionality of whatever happened during the 'breaks' in normal life – and, obliquely, about the validity of the prohibition which disallowed the mixing of carnival-type conduct with the daily routine. Today we live in a constant carnival of cruelty; obviously, 'constant carnival' is a *contradictio in adiecto*, a carnival that is constant is no more a carnival – which means, in fact, that sightings of cruelty spilled over from the separated and isolated reserve into the mainstream of daily experience. One outcome is that the sheer numbers and monotony of images may have a 'wearing off' impact; to stave off the 'viewing fatigue', they must be increasingly gory, shocking and otherwise 'inventive' to arouse any sentiments at all or indeed draw attention. The level of 'familiar' violence, below which the cruelty of cruel acts escapes attention, is constantly rising.

Even more important yet is the way the sights of violence are composed and enter daily life. By the nature of the media, 'made up', simulated and directed images of cruelty are much more vivid, gripping, and indeed 'dramatic', than ostensibly straightforward records of 'what actually happened'. 'Reality' seems impoverished, 'technically imperfect', and, indeed, 'less interesting'. Real cruelty seems inferior, toned down, pale, not really up to the standards of the 'genuine stuff' – of what the incapacitating, maiming, mental and physical torture and refined killing 'may be' if approached in high-tech and expertly designed manner. The staged cruelty now sets the standard for what 'merely happens with the cameraman around'; the 'reality' tends to be evaluated according to how closely it comes to the dramatic ingenuity and precision of a crime or disaster movie or to the productivity of an arcade game with its thousands of 'aliens' 'terminated' every minute.

On the other hand, the electronic mediation of the 'real war' can make the lot of the squeamish much easier. One can easily forget what this shooting and bombing is all about; after all, one is not really shooting or bombing, but moving the joystick and pressing the buttons. Himmler could worry about the mental sanity of his *Einsatzgruppen* charged with the killing of the Bolsheviks and the Jews point-blank. General Schwarzkopf did not have to worry about the integrity of his mass-killers. They never looked their victims in the eyes; they counted the dots on the screens, not corpses. His pilots returned from their bombing sorties in a state of excitement and elation: 'It was just like in a movie', 'Just like a computer game', they reported. And his world-wide admirers watched with bated breath on their TV screens pictures they knew well from the amusement arcades: dots converging on crosses. What they saw was a game well played.

This is it: the dividing lines between the 'news', the drama and the game grow increasingly tenuous, reality becoming in the process but one of many images, and not a particularly clear or interesting ('amusing') one at that. All images vie with each other for attention in the same universe of meaning, that of amusement – inside the aesthetically spaced world, structured by the relevances of attractiveness, pleasure-potential, interest-arousal. As Jean Baudrillard does not tire of repeating, this is a world of simulacra, where images are more real than reality, where everything is a representation and thus the difference between representation and what is represented can no more be made; while all those so 'palpably realistic', vivid images serve but as a cover-up for the absence of such reality as could conceivably hold authority over them. With realities 'melting' into their ostensible representations, the adiaphorization of life may be well-nigh complete; as the 'not for real' becomes fast the standard for the 'for real' (and the dividing line between them is ever more difficult to spot), the aesthetic criteria proper for the world of play and amusement may well displace the now irrelevant moral criteria, at home in the world of human interaction.

The second new development that considerably enhanced the orthodox modern mechanisms of adiaphorization is an entirely new quality of the distance between the perpetrators of cruelty and their victims. Half a century ago Max Frisch noted in his diary that 'we are not all of us cut out to be slaughterers. But almost all of us can become soldiers, can stand behind a gun, consult a watch, and pull a cord.'[16] He spoke of guns and cords. Whatever has replaced them has now added a totally new dimension to his observation. In the words of Michael J. Shapiro, with most updated weapons of mass murder the 'enemies' 'had become wholly and continuously invisible to those who, relying on electronic identification systems, had to strike at what can be seen only as symbols rather than discernible bodies'. Note: the electronics do not just mediate the action, taking upon themselves the task of delivering the ultimate killing blow, but they also take over the responsibility for 'identifying' (choosing!) the victims. Responsibility, which according to Hannah Arendt tended to float in all bureaucracies, is now 'floating' as never before. The so-called 'innocent' victims (that fraudulent expression conveying mostly the message that most, or 'normal', victims are not innocent and deserve their lot) can be now easily explained away as '*computer mistakes*'.

> [The] objects of violence in the Gulf War were obscure and remote, both in that they were removed from sight and other human senses and that they emerged as appropriate targets through a tortuous signifying chain. More generally, they were remote in terms of the *meanings* they had for their attackers and the attackers' legitimating and logistical supporters.[17]

Splitting the action from its moral significance was never easier and never more complete.

But the new weapons augur another breakthrough as well: as one

---

[16] Max Frisch, *Sketchbook 1946–1949*, trans. Geoffrey Skelton (New York: Harcourt Brace Jovanovich, 1977), p. 34.

[17] Michael J. Shapiro, 'That Obscure Object of Violence: Logistics and Desire in the Gulf War', in *The Political Subject of Violence*, pp. 118, 126.

of the Gulf pilots summed up his 'combat' experience, 'we could reach out and touch him, but he could not touch us'. On this view, war, once properly described as a 'combat', is now more akin to what one used to associate with executions, punitive expeditions, or police sweeps: the objects of action are not expected to answer back, all the action is one-way, all the initiative is on one side only. Nothing is expected to be proved in the course of combat, the roles and the rights are divided and settled before the first shot will have been fired. The perpetrators can be pretty sure that their actions will remain unpunished and their right to engage in them uncontested. The generals and the mass media popularizers of their thoughts kept repeating, with the listeners nodding their approval, that the main strategic principle is 'to save lives'. The phrase tacitly assumed that certain types of lives only are to be saved – are worthy of saving. The one way of saving them was to destroy as many other, unworthy lives as possible, in a manner which pre-empts their attempts to respond in kind before they meet their fate. The most updated weapons and most updated strategies are those of massacre and slaughter, not of combat. Thanks to that, few if any occasions are left to doubt that even the violence of war abroad can be subsumed under the home category of 'defending law and order', that destruction is a 'creative destruction', that the sufferings of the few are a low price to be paid for the happiness of the many.

In short, one may say that the orthodox bureaucratic mechanisms of adiaphorization are alive and well; if anything, they have been reinforced, thanks to the influx of new technologies of informatics and weaponry. And yet it may be argued that the principal adiaphorizing mechanisms, and thus also the 'enabling' factors of violence, shift today, under postmodern conditions, away from the world of bureaucratic organization and toward the world of daily life.

Adiaphorization, the postmodern version

Heide Gerstenberger pointed out the close connection between the forms of violence (also the most extreme among them) of modernity and the modern forms of daily life: 'The process of destruction, set in motion in the time of National Socialism, was entwined in the form of the daily praxis of the modern world . . .'[18] I suggest that a

[18] Heide Gerstenberger, 'Vernichtung und Alltag: Anmerkungen zur Erforschung des Alltags in Nationalsozialismus', in *Mittelweg*, vol. 36 no. 3 (1992), p. 41.

similarly close link can be traced between the relatively novel forms of violence, which hit the headlines today, and the postmodern phenomena with which daily life in Europe is now increasingly saturated. In particular, that aside from the characteristically modern mechanisms of adiaphorization, the relatively new, postmodern mechanisms are built into the structure of daily life, rebounding in characteristically postmodern modes of violent actions.

The most seminal change underlying the passage into the postmodern phase of modernity can be found in the profound modification of the way in which individuality is socially constructed and of the fashion in which the bulk of the population is socially integrated and riveted into the process of systemic reproduction.

Under modern conditions human individuals were constructed mainly as *producers/soldiers*; that is, the roles of producers and soldiers, which all or most were meant to perform and for which they were groomed, supplied between themselves the main patterns and the criteria of evaluation serving the formation of individuals. The emerging individuality was therefore marked by the following features: (1) Individuals were first and foremost carriers of kinetic force, which could be turned into the creative or destructive labour of producer or soldier; as such, they had to be capable of generating such force in a steady manner and, as far as possible, be immune to fatigue. (2) Individuals were 'disciplined' actors, that is actors whose behaviour was by and large regular and above all amenable to regulation, actors who responded in a repetitive and predictable manner to stimuli, and were capable of monotonous conduct if subjected to steady and co-ordinated pressure. (3) In the fashion of Lego or Meccano assembly pieces the individuals were incomplete when alone, meant to be combined with other units to form meaningful totalities; the individual's boundaries were first and foremost interfaces, designed not so much to circumscribe as to fit and adhere. (4) The major model of propriety – that is, of the harmony between what the individual ought to be like and what s/he was – was *health*, the idea closely related to the capacity of performing well in the above three areas. 'Health' stood for bodily strength and energy, as well as the ability to behave in a disciplined, regular and required fashion and to fit the co-ordinated activities of larger groups. Conversely, bodily weakness or insufficient ability to submit and to fit were seen as symptoms of ill health, and as such medicalized or articulated as cases for psychiatric treatment.

Under postmodern conditions human individuals are constructed mainly as *consumers/players*; that is, the roles of consumers and players, which all or most of them are meant to perform and for which they are groomed, supply between themselves the main patterns and the criteria of evaluation serving the formation of individuals. The emerging individuality is therefore marked by the following features: (1) Individuals are first and foremost 'experiencing organisms', seeking new experience (in both *Erfahrung* and *Erleben* sense of 'experience') and immune to saturation effect – that is, capable of absorbing, and of responding to, a steady and preferably growing flow of stimuli. (2) Individuals are 'originative' actors, that is actors characterized above all by spontaneous and easily triggered motility and pliability of behaviour, only to a minimal degree tied by previous learning and acquired habits. (3) Though never fully balanced, individuals tend to self-equilibrate as nearly self-contained and self-propelling units; such 'inner regulation' is retained also in the course of sociation, of which it is simultaneously the purpose and the motive. (4) The major model of propriety is therefore *fitness* rather than health. 'Fitness' stands for the individual's bodily and spiritual capacity to absorb, and creatively respond to, a growing volume of new experience, ability to withstand a fast pace of change, and ability to 'keep on course' through self-monitoring and correcting the inadequacies of performance. Conversely, bodily flaccidity and spiritual *ennui* (diminished absorptive capacity and insensitivity to stimuli), as well as a higher-than-average level of disturbance in the ongoing processes of self-equilibration, are symptoms of 'unfitness' – medicalized or articulated as cases for psychological counselling or psychiatric treatment.[19]

It can be shown that there is an intimate causal/functional bond

[19] As a paradigm for the discussed change we can take the case convincingly presented by André Béjin of the progressive replacement of 'psychotherapy' with 'sexual therapy' (or, more precisely, 'orgasmology') – for which the 'perisexual matters', 'contraception, pregnancy, abortion, venereal disease – are only of secondary interest'. ('The Decline of the Psycho-analyst and the Rise of the Sexologist', in *Western Sexuality: Practice and Precept in Past and Present Times*, ed. Philippe Ariès and André Béjin, trans. Anthony Forster (Oxford: Blackwell, 1985), p. 183ff.) The emphasis has shifted, in a decisive and radical manner, from 'how to do things' to 'how to experience them'. What is, furthermore, articulated as a 'therapeutical problem' is no more *deviation* (the typically modern nightmare), but *dysfunction* (understood as an inability to 'live through' the experience in appropriately intense fashion and to draw from it the sensations it is capable of generating). According to the model of fitness underlying the practices of orgasmology, one must 'abandon oneself to sensation without ceasing to submit one's actions to a rational calculation of "sexual expedience". The pleasure should be at one and the same time an abolutely spontaneous happening and a theatrical performance stage-managed by the brain.' ('The Influence of Sexologists and Sexual Democracy', in *Western Sexuality*, pp. 211ff.)

between the shift under discussion and the fast-falling demand for producing and soldiering performances of humans. Production and war can now be conducted to great effect while engaging but a minute (and rapidly shrinking) fraction of the population; though by no means marginal in *systemic* survival and reproduction, the 'productively engaged' individuals are increasingly marginalized in the *societal* division of labour. Claus Offe was the first to articulate this process in his concept of the 'de-centring of work'. De-centring of work, however, means also the fall in importance of panoptical and legitimizing strategies (of systematic coercion and ideological mobilization), crucial at the time when the productive/soldiering capacities remained central at all – systemic, societal and motivational – levels; contrary to Habermas, there is no 'legitimation crisis' in the postmodern state – it is just that postmodern conditions have made legitimation redundant.

What cannot be done today without active involvement of all or a great majority of the population, is the dispensation of the products ('clearing demand') and thus reproduction of the need to restock, the reproduction of the productive conditions – implemented in contemporary society through the mechanism of the market. The market engages men and women in the capacity of consumers. The 'postmodern individuality formation' sketched above is aimed at the shaping of a perfect consumer.

In my study *From Pilgrim to Tourist*[20] (further elaborated in chapter 3 above), I suggested that if the figure of the pilgrim was the apt metaphor for the type of individuality modernity favoured and promoted, there is no one pattern that could serve as a metaphor for the individual shaped under postmodern conditions. Instead, one needs a mixture of metaphors; I proposed that the figures of the stroller (*flâneur*), the vagabond, the tourist and the player, between themselves and only together, convey the complexity and inner aporia of the postmodern identity-process. However different they may be from each other, all four intertwined and interpenetrating postmodern life-models have this in common, that they aim at splicing the life-process into a series of (ideally) self-contained and self-enclosed episodes without past and without consequences, and as a result tend to render human relations fragmentary and discontinuous; they bar the construction of lasting networks of mutual duties and obligations. They all cast the Other primarily as the object of *aesthetic*, not *moral* evaluation; as a source of *sensations*, not *responsibility*. They therefore

---

[20] In *Questions of Cultural Identity*, ed. Stuart Hall and Paul du Gay (forthcoming).

tend to remove a huge area of human interactions, even the most intimate among them, from moral judgement. They, one may say, now do the job which in the heyday of modernity was performed by bureaucracy with its institutional 'rule of nobody'; they are the new, postmodern factors of adiaphorization. Following the moral impulse means assuming the responsibility for the Other, which in turn leads to the engagement in the fate of the Other and commitment to her/ his welfare. Disengagement and commitment-avoidance favoured by all four postmodern strategies have a backlash effect in the shape of the suppression of moral impulse and disavowal and denigration of moral sentiments.

Alongside the traditional tranquillizers of moral emotions, there are thus new and improved ones, and this time available without prescription issued by authorized state agencies. Thanks to the new adiaphorizing concoctions, violence may return to the sites from which the 'civilizing process' promised to evict it forever: to the neighbour-hood, to the family, to the couple partnerships – the traditional sites of moral proximity and face-to-face encounter. A widely publicized symptom of that return is the growing difficulty – indeed, confusion – in setting apart stern parental guidance and the abuse of children, flirting and harassment, sexual advance and violent assault. As the institutional frames within which the entered obligations were forcefully held and in the virtual absence of uncontested, universally agreed (or enforced) standards, an admixture of violence is now suspected and expected to appear in the most intimate of human relationships, where love and mutual well-wishing were supposed to rule supreme; meanwhile, the once tolerated degree of compromise involved in all negotiated togetherness tends to be more and more often recast as undue and unendurable violence performed upon the self-assertive rights of the self.

One consequence of the passage from the producer/soldier society to that of the sensation-gathering consumers was the gradual dissipation of the capillary vessels of the panoptical system of order-maintenance. Marriages, families, parenthood, neighbourhoods, work places have lost much of their role of the frontier outposts of the societally managed factory of order. Coercion applied there daily and matter-of-factly lost its function as the vehicle of 'law and order', and so can be challenged as gratuitous violence and unforgivable cruelty. The once uncontested hierarchies can be challenged anew, habitual patterns of relations renegotiated, old rights to coerce and demand discipline vociferously questioned and violently resisted – so that the overall impression is created that the sum total of violence is on the increase while the previously complied with or just unnoticed exercise of superior power is being reclassified as illegitimate violence. The notorious ambivalence of 'order keeping' and 'violence' is being once more laid bare by the new contest of meanings.

The characteristically postmodern stocks of violence are 'privatized' – dispersed, diffuse and unfocused. They are also 'capillary', penetrating the most minute cells of social tissue. Their ubiquitous presence has a double, ambivalent effect of the exhilarating experience of ultimate emancipation (eulogized by some authors as the gateway into the '*post-devoir*' era) on the one hand, and gnawing fear of a totally deregulated and uncontrollable, Hobbesian world on the other. That fear, in its turn, is the pool from which energy of another postmodern development, that of neo-tribalism, is drawn (though, let us note, in social movements, as in cars, the kind of fuel used by the engine does not determine the direction in which the vehicle is moving). With the state ceding the integrative function to intrinsically deregulating and privatizing market forces, the field is left to the not so much 'imagined', as *postulated* 'communities' to pick up the orphaned task of supplying the collective guarantees of privatized identities. Postmodern thinking is awash with dreams of communal and local truths and certainties hoping to do the civilizing job that the big truths and certainties of nation-states, posing as spokesmen of universality, failed to perform; to supply such a unity of thought, feeling, will and action as would render any but gratuitous violence unthinkable. But the neo-tribal, postulated communities are bound to belie such hopes. Neo-tribalism is bad news for all wishing to see the discourse and argument replacing knives and bombs as tools of self-assertion.

There are two major reasons for the close partnership between neo-tribal postulated communities and violence.

The first is the postmodern cultural context of information overflow, in which public attention is the scarcest of resources and in which Descartes' cogito has been rephrased as 'I am noticed, therefore I exist', (and for practical purposes unpacked as 'I shout, therefore I exist'). The louder the shouting, the better noticed, hence more solid, is the existence. With public attention dulled and made *blasé* by diversions ever more plentiful and lurid, only shocks stronger than yesterday's shocks stand a chance of capturing it. There is therefore an upward trend in the shocking power of shocks, with the ingenuity and malice and gratuity and senselessness of violent acts rightly seen as the best strategy. 'Escalation of violence' is an outcome of the fast wearing off of even the most spine-chilling and nerve-rending shocks. As Lewis Carroll put it, here it takes all the running you can do to keep in the same place . . . In our sensation-addicted world, ever stronger stimuli are needed to keep the attention awake for longer than a fleeting moment.

The second is the existential modality of neo-tribes themselves – as *postulated* communities, communities which, unlike the tribes of yore, have no established institutions, no 'dead hand of tradition', to keep them in shape, to perpetuate and reproduce. Postulated communities are *noch–nicht–geworden* entities – they 'exist' only in the future tense; in other words, their existence is but a hope of coming into being, never guaranteed and devoid of self-confidence. Hence endemic nervousness, irritability and bad temper; such communities, after all, can secure a presence, however brief, in the world only on condition of beefing up and then harnessing the most intense loyalties of their would-be members. And the tested method to reach this purpose is, once more, violence – both outwardly and inwardly targeted. The intended members of the neo-tribal group must be made, as Ferenc Feher and Agnes Heller recently put it, into 'both malleable puppets in the hands of the gurus and, simultaneously, aggressive stormtroopers toward the outgroup . . .'[21] The most awesome tyranny is practised under the mask of martyrdom. As E. M. Cioran warned, 'fiery eyes presage slaughter', while 'no protection is adequate against the claws of a prophet.'[22] The more nebulous the prophecy, the more fiery the eyes and the more gory the slaughter.

Violence, do-it-yourself style

The recollectivization of violence in the service of neo-tribal self-assertion is just one outcome of the postmodern privatization of identity problems. The other is the tendency to deploy gradually 'normalized', legally allowed and culturally approved forms of violence in the service of individual self-assertion, now increasingly guided by the pursuit of flexibility and perpetual openness of options, by the wish to avoid 'future-mortgaging' commitments, by resentment of being bound by the needs of others and reluctance to accept

[21] Ferenc Feher and Agnes Heller, *Biopolitics* (Vienna: European Centre, 1994), p. 28. And this could be done only through 'practising brain-washing under the name of "raising consciousness" or (better still) "sensitivity training", branding as traitors those who maintain amicable relations with the outgroup or express doubts about the ingroup's strategy or choice of methods' (p. 31).

[22] E. M. Cioran, *A Short History of Decay*, trans. Richard Howard (London: Quartet Books, 1990), p. 4. Cioran also warns that, more often than not, the martyr proves to be a 'tyrant manqué', and that 'the great persecutors are recruited among the martyrs not quite beheaded'. What violence can be performed by the oppressed community under the slogan of salvaging it from violence done to it, was explained admirably by Geoff Dench in *Minorities in the Open Society: Prisoners of Ambivalence* (London: Routledge, 1986).

inconvenience that carries no visible benefit to one's own consumer gratification.

Most vexing are the bounds which can be avoided, inconveniences which can be escaped from. As a matter of fact, duties or commitments begin to feel vexing, become 'problems', only when means appear to avoid them; once means are available, it feels both stupid and criminal not to use them, and the suppliers of tools see to it that it feels that way and that the compulsion sets in to use the tools just for the reason for which Sir Edmund Hillary climbed Mt Everest: because they are there . . . And we know that the invention and the production of new tools long ago gained independence from the logic of tasks to be performed, that 'technology develops because it develops', that ever new means are developed following solely their own momentum (more precisely, the momentum of research laboratories and marketing profits), and that in its market rendition instrumental rationality expresses itself in the means seeking goals, rather than goals setting the criteria for means-choice. On the occasion of the international conference called at Bonn in May 1994 to consider a bio-ethical convention, the participants reflected sadly on the limited impact such a convention can exert on practice, given that 'whatever is technically possible, is right to do', while one of them, Hiltrud Breyer, predicted that the research of the 'retarded' and 'retardation' pursued by genetic engineers 'will reopen the back door' for disqualifying ever new categories of humans as 'inferior' and 'backward'.[23] For the prospects of coercion in the service of individual self-assertion, this general rule spells a constant widening of the horizons and a constantly growing range of tasks entailed in the overall principle of 'being in control' (that is, of *not* being constrained by commitments or obligations towards others).

The German psychiatrist Klaus Dörner, together with the team gathered around the Gutersloh clinical centre he leads, has analysed for many years now the consequences of the described trend. His conclusions are devastating: the same modern frame of thinking in which was formed the Nazi vision of cleaning the world of useless or poisonous or morbid categories of humans is still shaping our own view of the individual and shared life-tasks; we may now be entering the era of a 'continuous and silent holocaust' – a holocaust which, as for the Nazi perpetrators before they had been 'proved to be wrong' by military rout, seems to be an act of 'emancipation' (*Befreiung*). The Nazis, Dörner points out, were also *Bürger*, who like

---

[23] See 'Eine Biotechnik für ganz Europa', in *Die Tageszeitung*, 2 May 1994, p. 13.

all ordinary folk before and after sought answers to whatever irritated them as their 'social problems'. And the more instruments to tinker with realities of life we have, the more aspects of the social setting in which we live look like 'problems' – unbearable problems, problems we *must* 'do something about'. As we move with increasing speed towards the 'one-third society', ever more people become 'problems', and since means are available to remove them, and thus get rid of the problems, there seems to be no reason at all why their presence – constraining presence, offending presence, oppressive presence – should be tolerated and borne.

There are, accoding to Dörner, ample prodromal symptoms of such 'holocaust new style' – of the piecemeal, surreptitious variety. One is the sudden explosion of interest in *Sterbenhilfe*, and public sympathy shifting perceptibly, and with the active assistance of expert opinion, towards the acceptability of 'death on demand' in the case of men and women who, by the rising standards of our society, are incapable of carrying on a 'meaningful' or 'satisfying' life. Another is the already well-nigh universal support for abortion on demand, equally represented in public consciousness (and before that, in market publicity and expert counselling, in that order) as a condition of freedom; woman's ownership of her body, the refusal to be burdened with the consequences of one's action (and with the fast progress of genetic engineering, also dislike of certain traits of another being who may claim care and thus constrain freedom of choice or cause inconvenience) being considered as good enough reasons for refusing another human being the right to live. What unites the two symptoms is that they spell trouble for the weak, indolent and defenceless in the name of untying the hands of the strong. Freedom now, as always, tends to be defined in terms of the rights of the high and mighty.[24] As always, it includes the right to decide monologically what is 'in the best interest' of the other and, obviously, whose interests are to be sacrificed for the sake of common welfare and *impartial* reason.

In no way does it imply that issues are straightforward and ethical solutions can be proclaimed loud and clear. The present plight would be much easier than it is if only one could say with any degree of conviction that the evil lies squarely on the side of the self-assertive drives and the good may be served by putting a brake on what is perceived as the individual's emancipation. This is, however, not the

---

[24] See Klaus Dörner, *Tödliche Mitleid: Zur Frage der Uneträglichkeit des Lebens. oder: Die Soziale Frage: Entstehung, Medizinisierung, NS-Endlösung – heute und morgen* (Gütersloh: Jakob van Hoddis, 1993), pp. 128ff.

case. The difficulty of combating the 'silent', 'crawling', or 'piece-meal' holocaust rests in the ineradicable ambivalence of virtually every issue at stake. The rights and wrongs are more often than not evenly or almost evenly balanced. Arguments on both sides of the conten-tion have valid moral reasons to appeal to – and few, if any, may be dismissed off-hand as unwarranted or confused. As in all but the most extreme cases of moral choices, any line drawn between 'still right' and 'already wrong' is tenuous and almost certain to be con-tested. The point is that – as the fast-multiplying 'means' transform ever more areas of life into 'problems' clamouring for solution and frontierlands to be conquered by advancing individual liberty prodded by the self-assertion drive – the more there are of the grey areas, ambivalent situations, and moral dilemmas of no unambigously right solution. Also, the more occasions there are for cruelty masquerading as care and for violence that thinks of itself as kindness.

An inconclusive conclusion

I propose that *the specifically postmodern form of violence arises from the privatization, deregulation and de-centralization of identity problems.* The dismantling of the collective, institutionalized and centralized frames of identity-building, whether accomplished by design or by default, whether welcomed or bewailed, has had this effect, that – as Peter Wagner recently pointed out – the site from which an intervention on behalf of common interests capable of overriding localized animo-sities 'could be undertaken, previously held by the state, is seen as non-existent or empty'. What is needed is a 'communicative process about what it is that various social groups . . . have in common under current social practices, and to find out whether they have to commonly regulate the impacts of these practices'. This need, how-ever, is seeking anchorage in vain, because of – as Hannah Arendt put it – 'the emptiness of political space'.[25] The void is filled by neo-tribal would-be communities, and if it is not filled by them, then it stays wide open, densely populated by the individuals lost in the hubbub of conflicting noises, with a lot of opportunity for violence and little, perhaps none at all, for argument.

Theoretically, one cannot refuse Wagner's conception its reason. Since the dawn of modernity 'pacification' always consisted in in-ternalizing the previously external violence – through conquest and

[25] See Peter Wagner, *Sociology of Modernity: Liberty and Discipline* (London: Routledge, 1994), pp. 176, 190.

incorporation, through recasting what used to be diffuse and erratic violence into the steady pressure of regular coercion. 'A world-wide state-like institution' of one sort or another, but always armed with a policing force and preferably monopolizing the use of coercion, leaps to mind automatically whenever we think of the ways to pacify the presently dispersed, 'uncoordinated' use of force. One should be grateful, under the circumstances, to Jeffrey Weeks for his salutary reminder that 'humanity is not an essence to be realised, but a pragmatic construction, a perspective, to be developed through the articulation of the variety of individual projects, of differences, which constitute our humanity in the broadest sense.'[26] 'Humanity' enjoys no status advantages over neo-tribes. Like them, it is but 'postulated'; like them, it exists but in the future tense; like them, it has but human affection and dedication for its bricks and mortar. And like them, it needs to have its hands carefully watched – so that those around the table are not cheated, as they used to be so many times before, into mistaking the *ad hoc* interest of the bank-holder for the sought-after universal rules. Finally, like them, it faces the task of finding *unity in diversity*. Such an attempt is known to have been undertaken many times before, but has always been stronger in its declaration of intent than reliable for its delivery. Up until now, either unity or diversity had to give. And there is no guarantee of any kind that history will not repeat itself this time. As before, we need to act without victory being assured in advance. This was, by the way, always the case. Only now we know that it was, and that it is.

[26] Jeffrey Weeks, 'Rediscovering Values', in *Principled Positions: Postmodernism and the Rediscovery of Value*, ed. Judith Squires (London: Lawrence & Wishart, 1993), p. 200. Weeks charges the exclusive-loyalty-demanding communities with promoting 'ethnocentrism while claiming a universal validity' (p. 202), which means revisiting the roads trodden by all modern formations with integrative ambitions, and may also lead to the reiteration of their crimes. 'The challenge', says Weeks, 'is to construct that unity [of humanity] in a way which achieves ("invents" or "imagines") a sense of "universal human values" while respecting human variety and difference' (p. 199). Indeed.

7

Tribal Moralities

7.1 The Body as Task

Two closely related features more than any other marked the modern spirit: the urge to *transcend* – to *make* things different from what they are – and the concern with the *ability* to act – the *ability to make* things different. It was making things different, and the power always to act in excess of the task at hand, that was represented throughout modern history as the liberation of mankind, the freedom of the human species, which the Enlightenment promised to bring about and modernity boasted of installing.

It was not so much that transcendence makes things better; it was, rather, that things as they are are not good enough. Happiness is an escape from disaffection. The Angel of History, as Walter Benjamin observed, is always about to move away 'with his face turned toward the past'.[1] Fortunately for someone blessed with a tankful of fuel, 'things as they are' can be moved away from: they do not have enough pulling power. They are devoid of authority, of good enough reason to be what they are, unless shaped and reshaped on purpose, to the measure of the current human capacity to shape. The easier we can move away from things, the less authority we are inclined to allow them; *our* ability to move away is the measure of *their* arbitrariness, and so – in a world governed by reason – of their *unbearability*. The need to change and the ability to change prompt and define each other.

[1] Walter Benjamin, *Illuminations: Essays and Reflections*, trans. Harry Zohn (New York: Schocken Books, 1968), p. 257.

'Science teaches the elites that frontiers exist solely to be trans-gressed',[2] wrote Krzysztof Pomian. The aquired habit soon turned into compulsion, into the sole acceptable way of life; European civilization set out to invent frontiers with the sole purpose of transcending them ... If it is the available energy which decides the volume of the required action, everything tends to turn into a frontier; the very possession of the capacity to transcend made the transgression imperative. The ability of transgressing 'delegitimizes' the frontiers about to be transgressed.

In the words of Patrice Rolland, the world left behind in the act of modern transgression 'is a genuine state of nature, that is one which legitimizes the absolute power of the founder; as to the latter, he is not bound by any norm, since he starts from a void, a political and juridical nothingness'.[3] As Edward Craig put it, the property which humans were credited as possessing 'to the highest possible degree' was a 'total freedom from external determinants of choice'.[4] Certainly the things about to be transgressed – animate or inanimate, non-human or human – have no power to set the norms or to draw the limits to transgression; their effort to do so, or mere listless resistance, could only be perceived as a constraint on liberty – the most heinous of crimes and the least bearable of conditions. 'The foundation cannot be completed except through ... the destruction of all enemies so that society may consist solely of the friends of freedom.'[5]

Having thus divided the world into actors and their objects, and its forces into the will to move and obstacles to the movement, the modern spirit falls into 'abstract intoxication, the delirium of the clean slate'. It is only the available resources and know-how that draw the line between the desirable and the impossible – with nothing left in between. The actual daring and the scope of transcendence depend solely on the technology one can master. Through the use of the guillotine, wrote Jean-Marie Benoist, the French Revolution

> married mechanization to political death ... we have passed from the artisan stage (Damien, the noose, the axe) to one of manufacture, that is of an industrial decapitation. The carts carrying the condemned to the

[2]   Krzysztof Pomian, 'L'Europe et ses frontières', in *Le Débat*, no. 68 (1992), pp. 42, 45.
[3]   Patrice Rolland, 'Robespierre, ou La Fondation impossible', in *Le Débat*, no. 68 (1992), p. 50.
[4]   Edward Craig, *The Mind of God and the Works of Man* (Oxford: Clarendon Press, 1987), p. 28.
[5]   Patrice Rolland, 'Robespierre ...', p. 57.

guillotine prefigured the modern slaughterhouses: Dachau, Katyń, Lubianka.[6]

If the means to overcome resistance are there, what reason can one think of to refrain from crushing it? Turgot advised the French king: nothing 'need prevent you from altering the laws . . . once you accept that such a change is just, beneficial and feasible'.[7] 'Is it not evident that by management the human species may be moulded into any conceivable shape?' – asked in passing, as one asks an evidently rhetorical question, another thinker imbued with the modern spirit.[8] But 'Fear, force, and coercion is a tactic entirely appropriate to the management of brutes'[9] – and brutes, only brutes, are those who by fear, force and coercion may be – must be (but, above all, *allow themselves to be*) pushed or goaded or bullied into a shape different from the present one . . . Ultimately, 'when objects stand in the way of the shakers and doers of the world, they are removed' – observes the shrewd analyst of power as shape-management, Yi-Fu Tan.[10] Removal – incarceration, banishment, destruction – is the form that transcendence takes when applied to those who refuse (or are refused the permission) to partake.

At the threshold of the triumphant and self-celebratory implementation of that principle, Auguste Comte coined his famed justification for the unstoppable growth of human knowledge: 'Savoir pour prévoir, prévoir pour pouvoir.' The meaning of knowledge is in *what you can do with it*: the more you can do, the better the knowledge. Note that *pouvoir* – 'being able' – lacks the object, and so the substance. It does not matter *what we do*, providing *we are able to do it*; or, rather, being able to do it is all the reason we need for doing it. What counts is the amplitude, the excess of means – free means waiting to be applied; it will be decided later what objectives one can put them to. Technology develops because it develops – Jacques Ellul concluded. 'There is no call towards a goal; there is constraint by an engine placed in the back and not tolerating any halt for the machine'. Means *precede* the goals; it is the availability of means

[6]   Jean-Marie Benoist, 'Au nom des Lumières', in *Le Monde*, 6 January 1989, p. 2.
[7]   Quoted after *Enlightened Absolutism (1760–1790)*, ed. A. Lentin (Newcastle: Avero, 1985), p. 15.
[8]   J. Burgh, *Political Disquisitions* (London: Dilly, 1775), vol. 3, p. 176.
[9]   Andrew Scull, 'Moral Treatment Reconsidered', in *Mad-Houses, Mad-Doctors, and Madmen*, ed. Andrew Scull (London: Athlone Press, 1981), pp. 109–10.
[10]   Yi-Fu Tan, *Dominance and Affection: The Making of Pets* (New Haven: Yale University Press, 1984), p. 2.

that triggers the ferocious search for ends. 'When technicians came to a certain degree of technicity in radio, fuel, metals, electronics, cybernetics etc., all those things combined and made it obvious that we could fly into the cosmos, etc. It was done because it could be done. That is all.' Only then does one remember the 'what for' question: 'Given that we can fly to the moon, what can be done *on it* and *with it?*' Well, we can always ask schoolchildren to set experiments for the astronauts to fill cosmic time . . .[11]

It is in this context that one needs to assess and evaluate the role which biology – the exploration of the 'natural state' of living organisms – and medicine – the practical, applied side of biology, the strategy and the technology of changing and transcending that natural state – have played within modern civilization.

In that modern civilization, human beings were from the start the prime targets of transcendence. True – the better order, meant to replace the wasteful and chaotic work of blind and uncontrolled forces, was to give justice to genuine human potential; to allow humans to live 'according to their nature'. But the true nature of the humans was not what they were, tangibly and concretely, but precisely what they *were not* and could not become without push and pull; the 'true nature' was *noch nicht geworden*, unfulfilled, still waiting to be let out. Real, empirical men and women were but crude mutilations of what they could be and what they were called to be, pale reflections of their true potential. In order to acquire their genuine essence, to become what nature predestined them to be, they had first to be transformed, and that gigantic task of transformation needed the guidance of those who knew what human nature was meant to be and knew how to lift the empirical men and women to that high standing which their *true nature* decreed.

The great transformation needed first and foremost a spiritual uplifting: refinement, culture, *Bildung*. Modernity was the time of cultural crusades, of merciless war against prejudice and superstition, parochialism and the 'dead hand' of tradition; of disqualifying and uprooting *particularizing* authorities seen to be standing in the way of human homogeneity hoped to be reached once life had been subjected solely to the dictate of Reason; of training and drilling, cultivating, 'civilizing', educating, converting. Through the conversion and assimilation of the different, the present heterogeneity was to be replaced with the *Neue Ordnung* populated by uniformly perfect beings.

As far as its human targets were concerned, modernity was, first

---

[11] Jacques Ellul, *Technological Society*, trans. Joachim Neugroschel (New York: Continuum, 1980), pp. 273, 280.

and foremost, the work of *culture*. The very idea of culture implies that by themselves human beings are not fit to give justice to their potential; they must be helped, prompted by heteronomous agents and stimuli, forced if necessary. Thus, to be complete, the work of culture must make use of diverse yet mutually complementary resources and strategies. Schooling, therapy, jailing and universal surveillance were all indispensable parts of the job. People were to be educated into a new, orderly world; some of them, who were diagnosed *incapable* of absorbing such patterns of conduct as their education was to install, were classified as pathological cases and had to be cured if possible; some others were visibly *unwilling* to surrender to such patterns and – as deviants or criminals – had to be reformed by severe punishment; finally, those *immune* to treatment and chastening had to be separated from the 'healthy' and 'normal', and incarcerated or otherwise 'eliminated'. To be sure, the borderline between the last two categories (and primarily between two methods of 'handling' them – since 'categories' were but projections of the intended method of action) was always dim; medics, psychiatrists and jailers constantly quarrelled about who among them was best qualified to deal with what – as they all agreed – was *abnormal* behaviour; whether a particular abnormality was a 'medical', 'mental', or 'penal' case was, all along, the issue most hotly disputed.

Guarding the frontiers of civilization

In the early years of great transformation, biology stood for the limits to realistic efforts; once a case was described as *biologically* determined, it was deemed to stay – perhaps forever, but certainly for a long while – beyond human reformatory powers. 'Biologically determined' meant 'immune to reforms pursued through education and persuasion'; having a defect which prevents its carrier from being assimilated into healthy and normal society – at least in his/her present state. If treatment for the defect is not known, the only 'solution' is strict separation of the defective from the healthy. To quote just one yet characteristic voice, 'the impotent, the mad, criminals and decadents of every form, must be considered as the waste-matter of adaptation, the invalids of civilization . . . It is impossible to accept social solidarity without reservation in a society where a certain number of members are unproductive and destructive.'[12] Biological argument occupied the opposite pole to that of

---

[12] Charles Féré, quoted after Daniel Pick, *Faces of Degeneration: A European Disorder, c. 1848–c. 1918* (Cambridge University Press, 1989), p. 32.

Helvétius's confident 'l'éducation peut tout'; and to the sanguine hope/ promise of liberalism to assimilate everyone and everybody into one united company of rational human beings by the simple expedient of re-education.

Biology occupied therefore from the start a hotly contested spot, pregnant with profound political and *weltanschauliche* controversies. Anxieties born of rapid change, uncertainties brought about by the uprootedness and fluidity of modern existence, fears fed by living towards a never fully achieved and forever elusive future – all focused on the territory where the experts and the politicians promised to discover and to protect the dividing line between reliable and un-reliable, the trustworthy and the deceitful, certainty and the vagaries of unruly fate. This circumstance assured a special status to biology and related technosciences: this was the status of an *alter ego* of the cultural transformation standing at the heart of the modern project, the site of extreme ambivalence and a magnet for extreme emotions.

That was, however, only one among the causes of biology's 'special status'. Another was the unceasing modern efforts to *deconstruct mortality*. Death was 'the scandal of modernity', as it was bound to remain the epitome and archetype of the limits to human potential; the ultimate challenge to the modern ambition to transcend all limits and open up human potential to its alleged infinity.[13] The modern response to the challenge was to decompose death, which one could do nothing about, into a multitude of diseases, pathological muta-tions and ailments – which one could, in principle at least, correct or rectify. The result was the fragmentation of the one, unique (as well as distant) event of death into a host of death-preventing and death-postponing acts filling the whole of life. Death, so to speak, colonized life, and *fighting death* – survival, self-preservation – turned into *the meaning of life*. The *Angst* bred by the inevitability of death was spread all over the life-process, transformed by the same token into a sequence of 'death-preventing' actions and lived in the state of constant vigil-ance against everything faintly smacking of 'abnormality'. This vast area of modern anxiety has been, again, taken over and administered by biology and associated technosciences – mainly medicine and psychiatry.

As mentioned before, Daniel Pick has suggested that the develop-ment of the nineteenth-century medical sciences and practices can be best understood against the background of that century's 'degeneration panic'. Modern life brought new or previously unnoticed threats and

---

[13] I have analysed this issue fully in my *Mortality, Immortality, and Other Life Strategies* (Cambridge: Polity Press, 1992), chap. 4.

worries, too numerous and too baffling for the feeling of security to take root. The area of 'normality' and 'health' seemed thin and fragile, open on all sides to the invasion of not fully understood and feebly controlled forces; a situation propitious to constant, never allayed anxiety, one that fostered a feverish search for protective measures. The perception of threats as infinite and fuzzy was itself a reflection or the projection of the boundlessness and haziness of indecision and uncertainty. This is why the ubiquitous yet elusive idea of *dégénérescence*

> was never successfully reduced to a fixed axiom or theory . . . Rather it was a shifting term produced, inflated, refined and re-constituted in the movement between human sciences, fictional narratives and socio-political commentaries . . .
> Crucially, there was no one stable referent to which degeneration applied; instead a fantastic kaleidoscope of concerns and objects . . . from cretinism to alcoholism to syphilis, from peasantry to urban working class, bourgeoisie to aristocracy, madness to theft, individual to crowd, anarchism to feminism, population decline to population increase . . .
> [Degeneration] connoted invisibility and ubiquity . . . It was a process which would usurp all boundaries of discernible identity, threatening the very overthrow of civilization and progress.[14]

The two related, yet different discourses and fields of practice in which biological sciences and technologies were fixed joined forces in giving weight to two mutually complementary strategies which those sciences and technologies originated, promoted and monitored. The first was the enhancement of *health*. The other was the elimination of *disease*.

The protection of 'normality', of good health, has become everybody's concern and has turned into everybody's task. Health was not 'just there' – it had to be constructed and daily reproduced according to strict rules and with the help of the right equipment. The life choices – at least for the resourceful who could choose – were medicalized, pre-selected and monitored by medical expertise. Shutting down and sealing the numerous apertures through which death seeped into the living organism was conceived as a personal duty, a duty to be performed daily and through the duration of personal life. The fulfilment of the duty took the form of a strictly observed bodily regime – of regular exercise, a balanced diet, a carefully structured daily and annual rhythm of activities, a consistently growing list of avoidances and self-denials.

[14] Pick, *Faces of Degeneration*, pp. 7, 15, 10.

The body itself turned into an object for technology; the owner of the body was now a manager, a supervisor and an operator rolled into one, and the medical profession supplied him or her with ever more complex technological products to perform these functions. Lion Tiger dubbed the whole process as one of the 'industrialization of the body', offering as an example data obtained for the USA in a study conducted by the Alan Gutmacher Institute: among 36.5 million fertile women, 11.6 million have been sterilized, 10 million used birth-control pills, 2.3 million used the intra-uterine devices, about 5 million relied on the partner's use of a condom, 1.9 million employed diaphragms, 1.5 million used spermicidal chemicals.[15] Freedom to control one's own body and manipulate its actions came hand in hand with the growing dependence on technology and its offers; individual power was closely intertwined with submission to expert guidance and the necessity to consume technology products. More and more the owner of the body came to think and live as a foreman appointed by medical authorities to invigilate and supervise the piece of machinery assigned to his or her care. Health concerns manifested the ambivalent mixture of self-confidence and the acute sense of deficit and insufficiency. Scientists, says Tiger, 'have broadly speaking seen humans as relatively passive pieces of physiology . . .'[16] By a curious paradox, human individuals who accepted and internalized this view of themselves took that acceptance for the sign of their emancipation as active controllers of their own fate.

War against disease, or against that elusive, diffuse ill-health given the all-embracing and frightening name of 'degeneration', was an indispensable complement of health-building and health protection. The many and ever more numerous diseases which the medical profession separated, named and classified were the preliminary forays of the advancing army of death; once that invincible army had been split into smaller units, one could fight the enemy troops unit by unit, as they came. They always came from the outside – outside of the affected organism, or outside of the 'normal state' of that organism. The medical profession was determined to find out and demonstrate that each disease has its *cause*, so that each disease could be fought (and, hopefully, defeated) by singling out and eliminating that single and eliminable cause.

Against a threat so depicted, the proper strategy was evidently the one well known and tried in endless struggle against an external

---

[15]   Lion Tiger, *The Manufacture of Evil: Ethics, Evolution and the Industrial System* (New York: Harper & Row, 1987), p. 219.
[16]   Tiger, *The Manufacture of Evil*, p. 10.

enemy: a strategy of forceful separation, keeping the enemy at a distance, digging moats, erecting walls and turrets, fortifying the borders with guns and manning them with watchful guards. What was needed for such a strategy to be applied was to identify the enemy, to describe it in detail or to brand it, so that it will be easily recognizable; and then to segregate, to prevent contact, and, best of all, to remove the enemy altogether beyond reach. Once followed, that strategy had to lead, gradually and in often imperceptible little steps, to the identifying and marking of the 'carriers of disease', and particularly the carriers of non-curable diseases. The Other, as Sander Gilman put it, was 'both ill and infectious, both damaged and damaging.'[17] And, as Stephan L. Chorover put it at the end of a long and thorough investigation of the inner logic of that strategy, this was the 'sociobiological framework' on which 'the justifications for genocide were ultimately built'. This framework 'has been erected in the name of science long before National Socialism became a reality'. 'The Nazi extermination programme was a logical extension of sociobiological ideas and eugenics doctrines which had nothing specifically to do with Jews and which flourished widely in Germany well before the era of the Third Reich' – much as they thrived in the USA, England and all parts of the modern world.[18]

The carriers of disease; the incurable; the defective; the incarnation, the embodiment of death, the hurdle on the road to rational order, the smudge which needs to be erased from the face of the world for the perfect harmony to shine through. *Unwertes Leben* – lives of no visible use for a society struggling for self-improvement and perfection. Eliminating them was a redeeming experience – not a destructive, but a *constructive* act, a service rendered to the holy cause of the

---

[17] Sander L. Gilman, *Difference and Pathology: Stereotypes of Sexuality, Race and Madness* (Ithaca: Cornell University Press, 1985), p. 130.

[18] Stephan L. Chorover, *From Genesis to Genocide: The Meaning of Human Nature and the Power of Behaviour Control* (Cambridge, Mass.: MIT Press, 1979), pp. 109, 80–1. In his eye-opening study *Tödliche Mitleid: zur Frage der Uneträglichkeit des Lebens. oder: Die Soziale Frage: Entstehung, Medizinisierung, NS-Endlösung – heute und morgen* (Gütersloh: Jakob van Hoddis, 1993), Klaus Dörner points out that in its wish to shed the ballast of imperfection and underperformance modern society continually divides and redivides itself into 'die Tüchtigen und die Minderwertigen', the latter – the underperforming and retarded, having no obvious function to play and thus entering the totality solely in the form of a 'social problem' to be resolved. The Nazis, says Dörner, were also *Bürger*, who 'like other citizens before and after sought an answer to their social problems' (p. 13). When cast on the carriers of the 'social problem', the eyes acquired the 'Pannwitz look' so vividly described by Primo Levi – 'this thing out there belongs to a species the destruction of which makes obviously good sense' (p. 9).

nation's health and fitness. Destroying the carriers of disease was like destroying death itself – in effigy. Raoul Hilberg's famous logical sequence which ended with the Holocaust, but which started from definition and proceeded through segregation, isolation and deportation – was it not the sequence tried and pursued many times over in the ritual of fighting against death in its many disguises of bacteria, viruses, polluting substances? One should steer clear of 'filthy places' and 'unsavoury substances'. The contagious magic of avoiding bodily contact with danger is the main concern of the hygiene-conscious. Hygiene is served by tools of separation: brooms, brushes, scrapers, soaps, cleaning sprays, washing powders; also by barbed wire or walls of camps and reservations and ghettos (and, indeed, Cyclon gas) for the unclean and the polluting. As Robert Proctor found out,

> it was largely medical scientists who *invented* racial hygiene in the first place. Many of the leading institutes and courses on *Rassenhygiene* and *Rassenkunde* were established at German Universities long before the Nazi rise to power. And by 1932 it is fair to say that racial hygiene had become a scientific orthodoxy in the German medical community.[19]

For obvious reasons the German case has been widely publicized and studied with more zeal and dedication than the developments which paralleled it closely in other European countries and wherever those countries set their outposts in far-away places, among the races earmarked for elimination, and hence unclean and polluting. As Daniel Pick has warned, this politically dictated imbalance in research interests 'can have an unwarrantedly reassuring, or even anaesthetizing effect on our perception of the rest of Europe'; in fact, in France or England things did not look much different. Having done his best to redress the balance, Pick came to the conclusion that the events of 1939–45 may appear 'as the realization, the crystallized evidence, of all that had been sinister in the Victorian and Edwardian literature on progress and decay, crime and social pathology'.[20]

The role in which biology and the technoscience it spawned had been cast in the overall project of modernity might or might not lead to a genocide perpetrated as a pragmatically praiseworthy, morally neutral and creative step on the road of societal self-improvement. But the possibility of such a consequence was rooted in that role, as

---

[19]   Robert Proctor, *Racial Hygiene: Medicine under Nazis* (Cambridge, Mass.: Harvard University Press, 1988), p. 38.
[20]   Pick, *Faces of Degeneration*, pp. 31, 239.

defined (and spurred on to be performed) by modern mentality and the modern pattern of human existence. Among the distinctive features of modernity largely responsible for that possibility was the urge to construct a perfect, harmonious world for humans (that is, such humans as are fit to enter the kingdom of harmony), and the confidence that this can be done – given time, resources and will. It was within the context of that dream and that conviction that biology, particularly in its biotechnological extension, was called to offer its contribution to societal efforts of self-transcendence and self-perfection; and in that context its sinister potency has surfaced.

Border control privatized

Today, in the world which some observers call 'postmodern' and some others 'late modern', dreams of a rationally flawless and aesthetically perfect order are no more in fashion; the powers eager and resourceful enough to bring it about are nowhere in sight; and the confidence that the objective can be reached has few preachers, while the belief that reaching it would have beneficial consequences has all but evaporated. Does this mean that the lethal sting has been pulled out from biological technoscience? Can we now revel in its generous gifts without fearing the poison? Are we now safe in the hands of medical expertise however firm and at times hurting their hold upon our lives feels? I suggest that the way in which biological technosciences are located within the context of the postmodern world is no more reassuring than the old, modern context. It offers little reason for comfort. Some old dangers are gone, or at least have become more remote. But new dangers have come to replace them.

The oppressive, omniscient and ubiquitous State may be disappearing, yet the oppression itself does not share its lot. Modern obsessions have only dispersed; one may say, they have been 'privatized', while coping with the tensions they breed has been ceded to the DIY devices. At the top, where the powers that be reside, the modern spirit of transcendence has all but evaporated, replaced by worried, backward-looking crisis-management and gap-filling; instead, men and women as individuals have been left with the necessity to self-construct and self-reconstruct, to patch together their identities through transcending today whatever they managed to put together yesterday. The huge State-wide garden has been split into innumerable small allotments. What used to be done in a condensed and concentrated fashion, through universal laws instilled thanks to the State's normative fervour and guarded by the state police, is now done in an uncoordinated way by commercial companies, quasi-tribal groups, or the individuals themselves. We are, as before, striving for rationality, but this is now micro-rationality (or, rather, micro-rationalities – as a rule acting at cross-purposes, clashing with each other, refusing to merge or so much as compromise), which cannot but 'produce irrationality at the level of the whole'.[21] We are, as before, deeply concerned with hygiene – that is, with locating 'harmful substances', their segregation and separation – but our zealous efforts are now aimed in dispersed and contradictory directions, so that hygienic achievements of some cannot but be seen by others as production of new poisons and dangers. In our postmodern world, modern mentality has been prised away from the coordinates supplied by the authoritatively promoted target of universally accepted and universally founded truth; it is now a mentality unsure of its foundations, legitimacy or purpose. A kind of mentality that can only prompt quirky, freak, erratic actions, adding to the already ample pool of uncertainty it originally intended to conquer.

Hans Jonas, one of the greatest moral philosophers of our century, put it the following way:

> The very same movement which put us in possession of the powers that have now to be regulated by norms . . . has by a necessary complementarity eroded the foundations from which norms could be derived . . . Now we shiver in the nakedness of a nihilism in which near-omnipotence is paired with near-emptiness, greatest capacity with knowing least what for.[22]

While Ulrich Beck expressed the same predicament with vividness all the more dramatic for its laconic brevity: 'Wir sind die Zeit mit der kleinstmöglichen Ursache und der größtmöglichen Zerstörung.'[23] 'We' are not a collectivity, which the ambitions of the orthodox modern state strove to recast into a totality, but a collection of individuals who have been abandoned, each one on her or his own, to

---

[21] Willem H. Vanderburg, 'Political Imagination in a Technological Age', in *Democratic Theory and Technological Society*, ed. Richard B. Day, Ronald Beiner and Joseph Masciulli (Armonk, NY: M. E. Sharpe, 1988), p. 9.
   As John Law perceptively observes, 'the problem of the social order is replaced by a concern with the plural processes of socio-technical ordering' – but the 'modern reflexive project of monitoring, sense making and control' remains very much in force (*Organizing Modernity* (Oxford: Blackwell, 1994), p. 2).
[22] Hans Jonas, *Philosophical Essays: From Ancient Creed to Technological Man* (Englewood Cliffs: Prentice Hall, 1974), p. 19.
[23] Ulrich Beck, *Gegengifte: die organisierte Unverantwortlichkeit* (Frankfurt on Main: Suhrkamp, 1988), p. 14.

the care of purchasable expert services and expertly produced self-help books. 'In an analogue of capitalist investment, the individual is seen as a *sui generis* enterprise, the value of which is improvable by investments of money and time'[24] in expert-guided therapy or self-therapy.

From the start modernity meant an excess of means over ends, abilities and resources always rushing ahead of objectives and feverishly seeking their own uses. But in our postmodern times the means are about the only powers left in the field vacated by the goals. Liberated at last from the constraints of the authoritatively set tasks, they may now grow without end – subject solely to the momentum gestated in the network of competing laboratories, seats of expertise, research teams and knowledge merchants.

> The best image [writes Cornelius Castoriadis] is that of a World-War-I-style trench warfare against Mother Nature. Machine guns are constantly being fired across the entire front, but huge battalions are sent into action whenever a breach seems to open up; one takes advantage of every breakthrough that may result, but does so without any overall strategy . . . [Indeed,] if you do not know where you want to go, how could you choose one road rather than another, and for what reason would you do so? Who among the proponents of technoscience today really knows where they want to go?

And so we are lumbered with 'a hammer without a hand guiding it, its mass constantly increasing, its pace ever swifter'.[25]

'We', let me repeat, are the loose medley of men and women told to look after themselves (each one for him/herself), take good care of their bodies, mould their own unique personalities, given full vent to the unique 'genuine potential' always sticking out from what they

---

[24]   Tiger, *The Manufacture of Evil*, p. 137.
[25]   Cornelius Castoriadis, *Philosophy, Politics, Autonomy: Essays in Political Philosophy*, ed. David Ames Curtis (Oxford University Press, 1991), pp. 250, 249, 259. In the comments added to the third (1993) edition of *Tödliche Mitleid* (p. 129ff.), Klaus Dörner presents the 'Bioethical Movement' in Germany as well as the 'Deutscher Gesellschaft für humanes Sterben' as attempts to translate the visions once pursued by the oppressive state into the tasks voluntarily, and joyfully, undertaken by individuals and performed (with the experts' help, of course) in a DIY fashion. Getting rid of 'social problems' like senile infirmity or unwanted children or less-than-the-preferred human traits through 'death on demand' or 'abortion on demand' tends to be portrayed as 'liberation of the individual', and, simultaneously, the individual's duty. W. Wolfensberger coined the phrase – in a book under that name – *Das neue Genozid an den Alten, Benachteiligen und Behinderten* (Gütersloh: Jakob van Hoddis, 1991).

have already become – and desperately seeking someone with a trust-inspiring authority to tell them how to go about all these baffling duties, none of which they can acquit themselves on their own. The potentials today are *global* as never before, yet their realization is left to *individual* initiative; means of species-wide consequences (anthrax, as Castoriadis remarked, 'is to genetic engineering as gunpowder is to the H-bomb') are to be used according to privately set ends.

Nothing has deprived the essential tenets of the modern project of their centuries-old authority. As before, we are hostages to the imagery of 'rational mastery' over human nature, identity and fate, and of the artificial, designed, monitored and reflexively improved rationality of life. Now, however, the awesome dream of the species has crumbled into little private nightmares, and the promise of human happiness in the wholly rationalized world has disintegrated into the lonely, but dutiful chase of happiness through the little 'rationalizations' of individual life. As the happiness is slow to come, and since once it comes one can be never sure how long it will stay – the chase can never stop, and needs ever new moving targets to pursue. It is the function of supplying such targets in ever larger quantities and ever new alluring forms that provides today the setting for biologically inspired technosciences.

To quote from Jonathan Raban's shrewdly perceptive and haunting exploration of contemporary urban life:

> In this search for the disappearing self, the physical body becomes a central symbol; the stomach, intestines, and organs of reproduction are solemnly attended to, as vessels in which the precious self is contained.
> [Raban found the following instruction in one of the bestselling bibles of 'macrobiotics': 'The kitchen is the studio where life is created . . . Only you are the artist who draws the painting of your life'.] Its readers 'create themselves over gas rings, feeding their immaculate insides on harmoniously balanced amounts of yin and yang foods . . . Serious, narcissistic, terrifyingly provident, like all fanatics they brim with latent violence; when they exclude and condemn, they do so with a ringing stridency . . . They are miniaturists in their talented cultivation of themselves.[26]

As indicated earlier, two types of books can be found in large quantity on each American list of current bestsellers – cookbooks and diet books. And one type of activity is constantly high up on every successive list of fashions: bodily exercise, be it jogging or aerobics, yoga or marathon running. Attention to the body has turned into a supreme preoccupation and the most coveted pastime of our

---

[26] Jonathan Raban, *Soft City* (London: Collins Harvill, 1988), pp. 174–5.

times. Mind-boggling fortunes are made on health-foods and drugs, exercise gadgets and 'teach yourself' books on family medicine and fitness. Following the latest fashion in body care and escaping the latest scare of health hazards is the prime criterion of high culture and good taste, and the prime 'must' in the unceasing work of self-construction. Freedom merges here with dependence, liberation with slavery. We are all today addicts of biotechnoscience. The few of us who are not, run a dire risk of being ostracized, decried for our ignorance, and stigmatized as deviants – if not as the postmodern equivalents of Typhoid Mary.

This is not, however, the sole change in the social role and impact of biology and related technosciences. Their impact did not stop at the colonization of private life; much of politics today is but an extension of bodily obsession – a 'body care by other means'; a sort of attempted recollectivization of the privatized health concerns. If individuals scared of the innumerable threats to life and health unite forces for common action, it is more often than not in order to chase away or trample down a danger which they see as threatening each of them individually, but too resilient or powerful to be defeated by individual efforts. Joint action is, then, a struggle against 'health hazards consolidated'. As a rule, the consolidation means tracing the 'rational causes' of the diffuse and all-penetrating *Deathfright* to ostensible culprits – for instance, to a company accused of adding more than other companies to the water or air pollution, to throwing the climate out of balance or otherwise damaging benevolent Mother Nature. Or to a category of people in the neighbourhood, who thanks to their strange look or bizarre habits have been made to measure for the sought-after signified for the 'Danger, beware' signifier. These may be foreigners, 'alien bodies' exactly like the assumed causes of death, or travellers – vagabonds without a permanent abode, constantly on the move, precisely like the evasive causes of death they came to symbolize; most of all, those who happened to be foreign *and* vagrant at the same time. Gypsies stand out as the favoured focus for popular scares about dirt, putrefaction, pollution. As the gypsies cross all national borders, popular resentments cross-fertilize and self-reinforce; the ubiquitousness of the gypsies resonates with the universality of the *Deathfright* . . .

To define, to separate, to banish (that is, deport or destroy); the classic sequence frames the strategy of virtually all health-scare-fomented politics. Around the struggle against 'health hazard consolidated' spring political movements, highly strung and militant, jittery and pugnacious, all the more tense and agitated for the feebleness of their foundations; they have nothing but their own collective fear-fed zeal to stand on, nothing but spectacular mischief to make their imprint on reality look real. For these reasons they would attract to the ranks of the activists the most volatile, mainly marginal and unattached elements within society at large – those already threatened, so to speak, by *social* death, those most overwhelmed by the craving for an identity which they otherwise have been denied. But however small their ranks, they act as an avant-garde for a much larger body of troops; it is to unload the shared burden of death-scare, to pierce a hole through which the steam accumulated in all sections of society may be let off, that they perform their spectacles of ritual debasement, murder or humiliation of the fears embodied in the appointed carriers of death.

And then there are the wondrous means of shaping and kneading and moulding other people's bodies which contemporary biotechnoscience puts in the hands of the individuals. It is an assumption seldom questioned in our part of the world that in their mothers' wombs, children are extensions of maternal bodies, and as bodies with all their parts and attachments are private possessions. The mother, we believe, has the right to decide whether she does or does not want that particular bodily extension. (Much as she is free to diet away the 'fatty bits' or let them be sucked out.) Parents are also within their rights when they want to decide what kind of children they wish (or, for that matter, *do not* wish) to bring into the world – and now genetic engineering technics give them an entirely new, unprecedented opportunity to act on their preferences.

At least theoretically, this new situation creates two complementary possibilities. One is open to the minority that can afford to 'customize' their offspring. They will soon be able to select the concoction of their own choice from the long and varied menu of genes, and the doctors will see to it that the children are made exactly to order – in a test tube, if necessary.

The other possibility is open to the majority who lack the means and resources to avail themselves individually of the jet-set medicine offers. As in other cases, the individual achievements of the elite will be replicated – dissolved, diluted – in the collective impersonality of mass politics. (Just like the elitist bid for individual immortality is reflected in the distorting mirror of mass jingoism and flag-waving calculated to secure the immortality of the nation.) One can expect the temptation to exert political pressure in order to oblige national health institutions to purify the future nation of all accidental pollutions, and political parties lining up to legislate what the nation demands.

Since we now have the means to prevent the unplanned – also of the kind previously described as biological, in the sense of remaining 'off-limits' and being unpreventable – whatever is defined today as bodily deformity or mere abnormality may well be criminalized, while the list of deformities and abnormalities will be growing unstoppably as the mapping of chromosomes, and expanding the inventory of available tinkering practices proceeds at an accelerating pace. Whatever can be defined, can be changed. What used to be the result of fate will become a choice; and what is, admittedly, a matter of choice is bound to turn, sooner rather than later, into an obligation. In the present multi-cultural world, we now face for the first time the genuine chance of the 'race' turning from a political myth or cultural construct into biological reality – which it claimed to be all along yet never was . . . For the first time we now have the means to 'naturalize' cultural differences, something which in the past, as Roland Barthes discovered, we could do only in the realm of mythology.

The dissipation of the socio-political frame which gave biotechno-science its by now well known, sinister genocidal twist has removed certain dangers from the agenda, or at least made their repetition unlikely in the time of postmodernity. But new times, new socio-political frames, bring new – yet unexplored, only intuited – dangers. These new dangers, all the more sinister for our ignorance about their nature, deserve to be counted among the foremost risks of Ulrich Beck's *Risikogesellschaft*. The question of how to prevent them from becoming a reality will probably shape the political agenda of the future. If it does not shape that agenda, there may be no future to be shaped; or, rather, no humans of the sort capable of shaping it.

7.2   Racism, Anti-racism and Moral Progress

In *Tristes tropiques*,[1] one of the most hauntingly beautiful and thoughtful works of anthropology ever written, Claude Lévi-Strauss suggested that 'primitive' societies deal with their danger-carrying strangers with the help of a strategy different (though not necessarily inferior) from the one that we practise and consider normal and 'civilized'. Theirs is the *anthropophagic* strategy: they eat up, devour and digest (*biologically* incorporate and assimilate) the strangers who carry powerful, mysterious forces – perhaps hoping to avail themselves in this way of those forces, absorb them, make them their

---

[1]   Paris: Plon, 1955; see chap. 38; English translation by John Russell published as *A World on the Wane* (London: Hutchinson, 1961).

own. Ours on the contrary is an *anthropoemic* strategy (from Greek εμειν, 'to vomit'). We throw the carriers of danger up – and away from where the orderly life is conducted; we keep them out of society's bounds – either in exile or in guarded enclaves where they can be safely incarcerated without hope of escaping.

Thus far Lévi-Strauss. I propose, though, that the strategic alternative he describes is endemic to every society, including our own, rather than marking the distinction between historically successive types of societies. *Phagic* and *emic* strategies are applied in parallel, in each society and on every level of social organization. They are both indispensable mechanisms of social spacing, but they are effective precisely because of their co-presence – only as a pair. Alone, each strategy would spawn too much waste to be able to secure a more or less stable social space. Together, however, the two strategies may tackle each other's waste, each making the costs and inadequacies of the other somewhat less unbearable.

The phagic strategy is *inclusivist*, the emic strategy is *exclusivist*. The first 'assimilates' the strangers to the neighbours, the second merges them with the aliens. Together, they polarize the strangers and attempt to clear up the most vexing and disturbing middle-ground between the poles of neighbourhood and alienness – between 'home' and 'abroad', 'us' and 'them'. To the strangers whose life conditions and choices they define, they posit a genuine 'either–or': conform or be damned, be like us or do not overstay your visit, play the game by our rules or be prepared to be kicked out from the game altogether. Only as such an 'either–or' the two strategies offer a serious chance of controlling the social space. Both are therefore included in the tool-bag of every social domination.

The administration of strangers

Rules of admission are effective only in as far as they are complemented by the sanctions of expulsion, banishment, cashiering, blackballing, sending down – but the latter series may inspire conformity only as long as the hope of admission is kept alive. Uniform education is supplemented by 'corrective institutions' awaiting the failures and the recalcitrant, cultural ostracism and denigration of 'alien customs' are supplemented by the allure of cultural assimilation, nationalistic proselytism is supplemented by the prospect of 'repatriation' and 'ethnic cleansing', legally proclaimed equality of citizenship is supplemented by immigration control and deportation rules. The meaning of domination, of control over social spacing, is to be able to alternate phagic and emic strategies and to decide when one or the other is to be put in operation, as well as to adjudicate on which of the strategies is 'appropriate' for the case in question.

In the modern world, strangers are ubiquitous and irremovable; simultaneously an indispensable condition of life (for modern life to be possible, the majority of human beings in whose company it is lived must be cast as strangers, allowing for no more than Goffman's 'civil inattention') and the most painful of that life's congenital ailments. The two strategies are in no way 'solutions' to the 'problem' of strangers – neither to the anxiety they generate nor to the endemic ambivalence of their status and role; they are but ways of 'controlling' the 'problem', 'settling' the matters as they come. Whoever is in control (in charge of social spacing), reforges the aporetic phenomenon of strangehood into social domination; the level and scale of domination reflect the level and the scale of control.

The confused, ambivalent sentiments aroused by the presence of strangers – those under-defined, under-determined others, neither neighbours nor aliens, yet potentially (incongruously) both – I propose to describe as *proteophobia*. The term refers to the apprehension aroused by the presence of multiform, allotropic phenomena which stubbornly elide assignment and sap the familiar classificatory grids. This apprehension is akin to the anxiety of misunderstanding, which – after Wittgenstein – can be explicated as 'not knowing how to go on'. Proteophobia refers therefore to the dislike of situations in which one feels lost, confused, disempowered. Obviously, such situations are the productive waste of social spacing: we do not know how to go on in certain situations because the rules of conduct that define for us the meaning of '*knowing* how to go on' do not cover them. We set apart such anxiety-arousing situations, therefore, precisely because there has already been some social spacing done, and so we have mastered some rules which regiment conduct within the ordered space – and yet in some cases it is not clear which of these rules apply. Encounter with strangers is by far the most blatant and harrowing (though also the most common) of such cases. From the point of view of those in charge of order, strangers are the solid leftovers of the productive process called 'social spacing'; they posit perennial problems of recycling and waste-disposal. Only the domination-induced and -sponsored myopia casts, however, the last two activities on a different level than the 'positive' effects of social spacing.

The administration of social space does not eliminate proteophobia; neither is it meant to. It *uses* proteophobia as its main resource, and willingly or inadvertently, but constantly, *replenishes* its stocks. To control the processes of social spacing means more often than not to shift the foci of proteophobia, to select the objects on which proteophobic sentiments are targeted, and then to expose such objects to the alternation of phagic and emic strategies.

Moral progress?

One needs to be defeated first to be accused of immorality, and for the charge to stick. The leaders of Nazi Germany who ordered extermination have been judged, sentenced and hanged – and their deeds, which would have gone down in history textbooks as the story of human ascent if Germany had emerged victorious, have been classified as crimes against humanity. The verdict is safe – as much as the victory which rendered its passing possible. It will stand until the cards are reshuffled and so is historical memory reshuffled to suit new hands. Unless the victors are defeated in turn, their own cruelty, or the cruelty of their acolytes and protegés, will not be committed to trial. Justice is visited upon the defeated – but since the story of justice cannot be told by anyone except by today's victors, it presents the world each time as one in which immorality and punishability are synonymical, and justice is done.

The modern era had been founded on genocide, and proceeded through more genocide. Somehow, the shame of yesterday's massacres proved a poor safeguard against the slaughters of today, and the wondrous sense-making faculties of progressive reason helped to keep it weak. As Hélé Béji recently observed, 'the deep malaise in the wake of the Vietnam war was not a remorse for victimizing the people, but the singeing contrition of defeat'. There was no malaise if the victimization did not end in defeat. (As Hannah Arendt pointed out, one had not heard much breast-beating in the aftermath of the extermination of the Hottentots by the Boers, savageries committed by Carl Peters in German South Africa, or the reduction of the population of the Congo from 20 to 8 million under the auspices of King Leopold II of Belgium.)[2] If there is a malaise, as after the ignominious intervention in Vietnam, the lesson absorbed and memorized by the defeated is the need for more force and more effective force, not

---

[2]   See Hélé Béji, 'Le Patrimoine de la cruauté', *Le Débat*, no. 73 (1993), pp. 164–5. (Béji here quotes Hannah Arendt's study of imperialism.) 'There is one thing', says Béji, 'which justice shares with injustice; both need, to be exercised, all the authority of force.' (p. 167) The very notion of the 'crime against humanity' would have never taken root in modern consciousness had it not been accompanied by a convincing demonstration of might.

more ethical conscience. In America, the shame of Vietnam boosted high-tech warfare much more than it did moral self-scrutiny. With electronic surveillance and smart missiles, people can now be killed before they have a chance to respond; killed at a distance at which the killer does not see the victims and no more has to (or, indeed, could if wished) count the bodies.

Victors, triumphant or frustrated, do not emerge morally enno-bled (whatever magnanimity they display is due to the redundancy of cruelty, rather than to a sudden surge of moral sentiments); but neither do (at least not necessarily) their victims. Victims are not always ethically superior to their oppressors; what makes them look morally better, and makes credible their claim to this effect, is the fact that – being weaker – they have had less opportunity to be cruel. But there is no reason why they should derive from their defeat lessons different from those drawn by their frustrated oppressors: namely, that the safeguard against future calamity is not ethical pos-turing, but plentiful and powerful weaponry (though the second in no way excludes the first: the first being a useful tool to obtain the second, and the second an infallible support for the first). When their turn had arrived and they conquered Laos and Cambodia, the Viet-namese troops showed that there was little they failed to learn from their American tormentors. The genocide perpetuated by the Croat *ustashi* and their Muslim volunteer helpers during the Nazi rule made the descendants of the Serbian victims all the more eager to kill and rape and ethnically cleanse.[3] The memories of the Holocaust firmed the hand of the Israeli occupiers of the Arab lands: mass deportations, roundings-up, hostage-taking and concentration camps are well re-membered as cost-effective. As history progresses, injustice tends to

---

[3] The term 'ethnic cleansing' was first used in a decree issued by the *ustashi* minister Milan Zanić on 2 May 1941, to 'ethnically cleanse' the newly born Croatia of Serbs, Jews and Gypsies. (Another minister of the same government, Andrij Artukovic, forbade the Serbs, Jews, Gypsies and dogs to enter restau-rants, parks and means of public transport.) The words became flesh – genocide of Serbs, Jews and Gypsies followed, perpetrated by *ustashi* troops eagerly as-sisted by Bosnian Muslim SS units. This *ustashi* tradition is today openly re-ferred to by the stormtroopers led by Dobroslav Paraga, the leader of the 'Croatian Law Party' (HOS), which include quite a large group of mercenaries, ordered not to take prisoners alive . . . The Serbs responded in kind: a similar tactic has been adopted by Vejislav Ěeljow's (the leader of the 'Radical Serb Party') and Zeljko Raznjatović's 'White Eagles', who resurrect in their turn the tradition of Mihajlovic's *chetniks*. Both sides accept (each invoking the 'lessons of history') that 'only *faits accomplis* count' (Andrzej Grajewski, 'Trzecia Wojna Bałkańska', in *Przegląd Polityczny*, no. 21/22 (1993), pp. 54–66).

be compensated for by injustice-with-role-reversal. It is only the victors, as long as their victory stays unchallenged, who mistake, or misrepresent, that compensation as the triumph of justice. Superior morality is all too often the morality of the superior.

No victory over inhumanity seems to have made the world safer for humanity. Moral triumphs, apparently, do not accumulate; in spite of the narratives of progress, movement is not linear – yesterday's gains are not reinvested, nor are the bonuses once awarded irreversible. Ever anew, with each shift in the balance of power, the spectre of inhumanity returns from its exile. Moral shocks, however devastating they might have seemed at the time, gradually lose their grip until they are forgotten. All their long history notwithstanding, moral choices seem to always start from square one.

No wonder there are powerful reasons to doubt the reality of moral progress, and in particular the moral progress of the kind that modernity claims to promote. Moral progress seems to be threatened at the core – by the very fashion in which it is promoted. The intimate affinity between the moral superiority of order and the all-too-material superiority of its guardians renders every order endemically precarious and a standing invitation to trouble: it makes the guardians nervous, and their wards envious. The first would not hesitate to coerce the recalcitrant into obedience, absolving the coercion they commit as moral benevolence or an act of justice. The second would not shirk violence, to gain for themselves the right of granting, or refusing, absolution.

The new world disorder, or respacing the world

The experience of insecurity is at its most acute whenever the sediment of socialization loses its solidity – and therefore the extant social space loses its transparency together with its constraining and enabling powers. The spontaneous reaction to such experience is a magnified intensity of spacing efforts. Whatever stable co-ordination/separation between social, aesthetic and moral spacing has been reached in the past, now collapses. The terms of armistice and *modus vivendi* between the three spacings are to be renegotiated, and more probably fought for and won anew. The potential for clash and discord between the spacings, never fully dormant, now erupts and comes into the open.

There is no effective centralized policing which could offer the precarious, continuously re-produced space an appearance of naturalness. The feebleness of convention in which apparently tough and solid space used to be grounded is laid bare, and so the power struggle and perpetual tug-of-war are revealed as the sole reliable grounds of orderly habitat. The task of constructing a new meaningful social space is undertaken singly, severally and collectively; at all levels, the absence of a co-ordinating/policing agency keen and resourceful enough to arbitrate and in the end impose peace terms (that is, an *order* and binding *law* that set the standards against which all attempts at shifting the social, aesthetic and moral boundaries may be cast as deviant or subversive, and effectively marginalized) leads to the endless multiplication of scattered grass-roots initiatives, adds fierceness and determination to each and renders any agreed solution a remote prospect.

Bouts of such insecurity are in no sense novel; neither are the typical responses to them. Both are known to appear throughout history in the aftermath of wars, violent revolutions, collapse of empires, or as concomitants of social departures too vast or too fast to be assimilated by the extant policing agencies. The present explosion of respacing efforts throughout Europe (and the never fully extinguished smouldering of such efforts in the post-colonial world) can be accounted for by the same orthodox reasons. The foundering of the Pax Sovietica, of the Pax Titoica, of the Berlin Wall, and the respacing frenzy that followed, are but the most recent cases of a recurrent phenomenon whose most vivid and best remembered pattern had been set by the Dark Ages in the wake of the collapse of Pax Romana.

If the resurrection of tribalism and parochialism after the demise of the tightly policed Soviet empire, inside which pernickety oppression co-operated with insidious indoctrination in prolonging the artificial life of the moribund order, was something to be expected – the resurgence of essentially similar tendencies in the 'thoroughly modern' countries of the West took many an observer by surprise. And yet, paradoxically, the bipartite division of the world, widely and rightly viewed as the source of global insecurity, appears in retrospect as a perhaps macabre, but effective warrant of stability on *both sides* of the barricade. The broad outlines of global space were drawn with a power immune to challenge and questioning – a circumstance which even the most perceptive minds obliquely endorsed through their astonishing failure to visualize the possibility of change. With the disappearance of barbed wire and tank columns that marked such outlines, unthought-of possibilities have been thrown wide open. The world chart, and the local charts that drew their derivative authority from it, have become fluid again: not a source of grim reassurance any more, a call to arms instead.

Insecurity and cruelty

The paradox of the man-made collective identities of the nation-state era – the kind of identities which might hold fast only when perceived as 'given' and thus cast beyond human power of manipulation – has not gone away; if anything, it has become sharper than at any previous stage of the modern era. Its solution, on the other hand, has become more difficult than ever. Identities may be safe and 'unproblematic' only inside a secure social space: spacing and identity-production are two facets of the same process. But it is precisely the great modern project of a unified, managed and controlled space which has today come under pressure and faces its critical challenge.

Ever since, with the dawn of the modern era, it had become a conscious, purposeful activity – identity-building has always contained a mix of 'restorative' and 'productive' objectives (the first category expressed in the invocation of *Blut und Boden, la terre et les morts*; the second in the requirement of patriotism, denunciation of lukewarmness as treachery, and demand for vigilance against turncoats). Today, however, productive aspects come clearly to the fore – as the ostensibly firmest foundations of identity (such as territory or racial stock) have been exposed by current practice (at least in that part of the world already close to the postmodern condition) as irreparably fluid, ambivalent and otherwise unreliable. There is, therefore, a sort of 'social demand' for such 'objective' foundations of collective identities which openly admit of their historicity and human-made origins, yet nevertheless may be ascribed a supra-individual authority and a value that the carriers of identity can disregard only at their peril. Concerns with identity (that is, the uncontentious social space), complete with the xenophobia they gestate in volumes inversely proportional to the self-confidence of its carriers, will in all probability seek anchor in the territory classified as 'culture', which, indeed, is virtually tailor-made to meet the intrinsically contradictory demand. The phenomenon described by Simmel as the 'tragedy of culture' (the contradiction between the modality of culture as a product of the human spirit, and the awesome, massive 'objectivity' of created culture as experienced by individuals no more able to assimilate it) has become a hundred years later the last straw of hope for the seekers of solid identities in the postmodern world of contingency and mass migration.

The focus of, simultaneously, contentious social spacing and identity-building is now the contrived, made-up community masquerading as a Tönnies-style inherited *Gemeinschaft*, but in fact much more akin to Kant's aesthetic communities, brought into being and kept in existence mostly, perhaps solely, by the intensity of their members' dedication. Features properly belonging to aesthetic space tend to submerge and colonize social space and drift into the role of the principal tools of social spacing. The community produced with such tools never ceases to be produced; it 'exists' solely in the process of production. It is not even 'imagined' – but *postulated*; its location is in the future, and it is brought from there into the present forcefully, though always ephemerally, through the combined force of individual loyalty acts. Because of in-built uncertainty, such a community lives under the condition of constant anxiety and thus shows a sinister and but thinly masked tendency to aggression and intolerance. This is a community that has no other ground but the individual decisions to identify with it – yet one that needs, in order to muster loyalty, to impress itself upon the minds of decision-makers as *superior to*, and *preceding*, any individual decision; a community which has to be built year by year, day by day, hour by hour, having the liquid fuel of popular emotions as its only life-blood. A community, therefore, which is bound to remain endemically precarious and hence bellicose and intolerant, neurotic about matters of security and paranoiac about the hostility and ill intentions of its environment. Such new-style communities are Michel Maffesoli's *neo-tribes*, all the more hypochondriac and quarrelsome for being deprived of what the old-style tribes derived their security from: the effective powers to 'objectify' their ascendancy and monopolistic claims to devotion and obedience.

These 'neo-tribes' lead in principle an episodic, sometimes ephemeral, life; they come into being in a moment of instant condensation – but then face daily the danger of evaporating, together with that energy of self-dedication which lent them for a time the appearance of solidity. However brief their ascendancy, it would not be possible at all were the brevity of commitment acknowledged and conceded, let alone endorsed, in advance. Production must be narrated as restoration or restitution; building new ground must be thought of as the mapping of extant continents. The counter-factuality of self-image is the prime condition of success, even such fragile and elusive success as there is. Hence the concepts drawn from cultural discourse come in handy: concepts like forms of life, tradition, community. The rejection of strangers may shy away from expressing itself in racial terms, but it cannot afford admitting being arbitrary lest it should abandon all hope of success; it verbalizes itself therefore in terms of the incompatibility or unmixability of *cultures*, or of the self-defence of a form of life bequeathed by tradition. The horror of ambivalence sediments in consciousness as the value of communal cohesion and consensus that only shared understanding can bring. Arguments that wish to be as firm and solid as those once anchored in the images of soil and blood now have to dress themselves in the rhetoric of human-made culture and its values.

Thus, paradoxically, the ideologies that currently accompany the strategy of communal identity-building and the associated policies of *exclusion* deploy the kind of language that was traditionally appropriated by *inclusivist* cultural discourse. It is culture itself, rather than a hereditary collection of genes, that is represented by these ideologies as immutable: as a unique entity which *should be* preserved intact, and a reality which *cannot* be significantly modified by any method of cultural provenance. Cultures, we are told, precede, form and define (each one in its own *unique* way) the selfsame Reason that previously was hoped to serve as the main weapon of cultural homogeneity. Much like the castes or estates of the past, cultures may at best communicate within the framework of the functional division of labour, but they can never mix; and they should not mix lest the precious identity of each should be compromised and eroded. In a grotesque reversal of culture's history, it is not cultural *pluralism* and separatism, but cultural *proselytism* and the drive towards cultural unification that are now conceived of as 'unnatural' – as an abnormality to be actively resisted and defied.

No wonder contemporary preachers of exclusivist ideology disdainfully reject the racist label. Indeed, they neither need nor deploy the arguments of the genetic determination of human differences and the biological grounds of their hereditary continuity. And so their adversaries do not often advance the contrary case, the case of cohabitation and mutual tolerance, when they insist that the racist label fits. The true complexity of the adversaries' task derives from the fact that the cultural discourse, once the domain of the liberal, assimilationist, *inclusivist* strategy, has been 'colonized' by the *exclusivist* ideology, and so the use of traditional 'culturalist' vocabulary no more guarantees the subversion of exclusivist strategy. The root of the present weakness of the so-called 'anti-racist' cause so poignantly felt throughout Europe lies in the profound transformation of the cultural discourse itself. Within the framework of that discourse, it has become exceedingly difficult to advance without contradiction (and without the risk of criminal charges) an argument against the permanence of human differentiation and the practice of categorial separation. This difficulty has prompted many authors, worried by the apparent inability of the 'multiculturalist' argument to challenge, let alone to arrest, the advance of pugnacious tribalism, to double their efforts in the refurbishing of the 'unfinished modern project' as the only rampart still capable, perhaps, of stemming the tide. Some, like Paul Yonnet,[4] go as far as to suggest that the anti-racist forces, preaching as they are mutual tolerance and peaceful cohabitation of diverse cultures and tribes, are to blame for the growing militancy of the exclusivist tendency – merely a 'natural' response to the 'unnatural' regime of perpetual uncertainty which the preachers of tolerance purport to install. With all its self-confessed artificiality – so Yonnet suggests – the original Enlightenment-inspired project of homogeneous order, with its promotion of universal values, uncompromising stance toward difference and relentless cultural crusades, stood a better chance (perhaps the only chance there ever was and could be) to replace mutual extermination with peaceful coexistence.

The 'Other', as we have seen before, is a by-product of social spacing; a left-over of spacing, which guarantees the usability and trustworthiness of the cut-out, properly spaced habitable enclave; the *ubi leones* of the ancient maps signifying the outer frontiers of the human *habitat*. The *otherness* of the Other and the security of the social space (also, therefore, of the security of one's own identity) are intimately related and support each other. The truth is, however, that neither of the two has an objective, real, or rational 'foundation'; the sole foundation of both, as Cornelius Castoriadis put it,

> being belief in it and, more specifically, its claim to render the world and life coherent (sensible), it finds itself in mortal danger as soon as proof is produced that other ways of rendering life and the world coherent and sensible exist . . .
>
> Can the existence of the other as such place *me* in danger? . . . It can, under one condition: that in the deepest recesses of one's egocentric fortress a voice softly but tirelessly repeats 'our walls are made of plastic, our acropolis of papier-mâché'.[5]

The voice may be soft, but it takes a lot of shouting to stifle it, particularly since the inner voice is but an echo of loud voices all around – each peddling an altogether different recipe for a world both meaningful and secure. And, since shouting is the only thing one can do to promote one's cause, each voice is a voice of reason, each recipe is rational: it is always one rationality against the other, and reasoned argument would help little. Each recipe has good reasons to be accepted, and so at the end of the day only the pitch of

[4] See Paul Yonnet, *Voyage au centre du malaise français* (Paris: Gallimard, 1993).
[5] Cornelius Castoriadis, 'Reflections on Racism', trans. David Ames Curtis, in *Thesis Eleven*, no. 31 (1992), pp. 6, 9.

voice and the size of chorus offer a guarantee of being in the right. I shout, therefore I am – is the neotribal version of the *cogito*.

Postmodern tribes are brought into their ephemeral being by explosive sociality. Joint action does not follow shared interests; it creates them. Or, rather, joining the action is all there is to the sharing. Joint action deputizes for the absent force of law-supported socialization; it may rely on its own force alone, and on its own it must accomplish the daunting task of structuration – that means to assert simultaneously its own identity and the strangehood of the strangers. What used to surface on carnival occasions, to be a momentary rupture of continuity, a festive suspension of disbelief – becomes the mode of life.

Postmodernity has two faces: the 'dissolution of the obligatory in the optional'[6] has two apparently opposite, yet closely related effects. On the one hand, the sectarian fury of neotribal self-assertion, the resurgence of violence as the principal instrument of order-building, the feverish search for home truths hoped to fill the void of the deserted *agora*. On the other, the refusal by yesterday's rhetors of the *agora* to judge, discriminate, choose between choices: every choice goes, providing it is a choice, and each order is good, providing it is one of many and does not exclude other orders. The tolerance of the rhetors feeds on the intolerance of the tribes. The intolerance of the tribes draws confidence from the tolerance of the rhetors.

There are, of course, good reasons for the present reticence of the rhetors, once only too eager to discriminate and legislate. The modern dream of happiness-legislating Reason has brought bitter fruits. The greatest crimes *against* humanity (and *by* humanity) have been perpetrated in the name of the rule of Reason, of better order and greater happiness. A mind-numbing devastation proved to be the issue of the marriage between philosophical certitude and the arrogant self-confidence of the powers-that-be. The modern romance with universal Reason and perfection proved to be a costly affair; it also proved to be abortive, as the great factory of order went on producing more disorder while the holy war against ambivalence spawned more ambivalence. There are reasons to be wary of modern promises, and of the tools alleged to make them true. There are

---

[6] Alain Finkielkraut, *Le Mécontemporain: Péguy, lecteur du monde moderne* (Paris: Gallimard, 1991), p. 174. Finkielkraut continues: 'Désormais *post*-moderne, l'homme contemporain proclame l'égalité de l'ancien et du nouveau, du majeur et du mineur, des goûts et de cultures. Au lieu de concevoir le présent comme un champ de bataille, il l'ouvre sans préjugé et sans exclusive à toutes les combinaisons.'

reasons to be chary and heedful of philosophical certitude; and there are reasons to consider such caution prudent and realistic, since the appointed marriage partner of universal certitude – the powers boasting universalizing ambitions and resources to support them – is nowhere to be seen.

But the reticence itself is costly. Just as the modern romance with transparency and *Eindeutigkeit* bred opacity and ambivalence, postmodern tolerance breeds intolerance. Modern etatization of social space spawned oppression massive and condensed; the postmodern privatization of social spacing spawns oppression scattered and small-scale, but manifold and ubiquitous. Coercion is no more the State's monopoly, but this is not necessarily unambiguously good news, as it does not mean less coercion. The grand certitude has dissipated, but, in the process, has split into a multitude of little certainties, clung to all the more ferociously for their puniness. One wonders what sort of service is offered to the uncertainty-stricken world by (to quote Castoriadis's pithy characterization) 'the intellectual boy-scouts of the past few decades, who preach both the rights of man and the idea that there is a radical difference between cultures that forbids us from making any value judgments about other cultures'[7] – though many such cultures, having avidly and joyfully embraced Western guns and video-recorders, show amazing reserve when it comes to the borrowing of such Western inventions as habeas corpus or citizenship.

There is no easy exit from the quandary. We have learned the hard way that while universal values offer a reasonable medicine against the oppresive obtrusiveness of parochial backwaters, and communal autonomy offers an emotionally gratifying tonic against the stand-offish callousness of the universalists, each drug when taken regularly turns into poison. Indeed, as long as the choice is but between the two medicines, the chance of health must be meagre and remote.

One may say, however, that both corrective therapies tend to become pathogenic for the same reason. They both accept and tolerate their objects – be they 'bearers of the rights of man' or 'faithful sons of the people' – in any capacity but one: that of the moral selves. Autonomy of the moral self is one capacity that neither of the two would admit gladly, since both encounter it as an obstacle to any certainty, including the kind of certainty they are bent on securing or protecting. If either had things its own way, the outcome would be strikingly similar: disqualification and then gradual extinction of moral impulses and moral responsibility. It is precisely this effect

---

[7] Castoriadis, 'Reflections on Racism', p. 10.

that debilitates and incapacitates in advance the only forces that would stand a chance of arresting the treatment at the point where it turns murderous. Once expropriated or excused from moral responsibility, subjects know no more (as Bertrand Russell put it) when to start screaming.

As far as the prospects of safeguarding human lives against cruelty (something which both the modern project and its postmodern rejection promised, though each sniffed the roots of cruelty under a different tree) are concerned, it does not matter much who is in charge of social spacing and whose charts are proclaimed obligatory; it does not matter either whether it is the social, or the aesthetic spacing which structures human habitat. If anything does matter, it is the redemption of moral capacity and, in effect, the re-moralization of human space. To the likely objection 'This proposition is unrealistic', the proper response is: 'It had *better* be realistic'.

7.3   A Century of Camps?

By common consent, the seventeenth century figures in history books under the name of the Age of Reason. Its immediate successor, predictably, is described as the Age of 'reason speaking' – of Enlightenment. Quite often one hears the nineteenth century being called the Age of Revolutions, thus suggesting the word becoming flesh. We are now in the last decade of the twentieth century and in the *fin-de-siècle* atmosphere the temptations to draw the line and compute the balance are rampant and overwhelming. (This is precisely why Jean Baudrillard, only half jokingly, advised us to skip the last decade, bound to be wasted on obituary-writing, and go straight to the next century.) How will our century go down in history? Will it be under the name of the 'Age of the Camps', of flesh turning cancerous?

This, of course, is not for us to decide – the coming generations are not bound by our opinions, just like us feeling free to overturn the views the ancestors held of themselves. By their fruits thou shalt know them, and we do not know, and cannot know, what the lasting legacy of our trials and tribulations will prove to be, and in what way our children and the children of our children would sort out the seminal from the freak, the durable from the episodic, the memorable from the forgettable, in that stretch of history filled and made by our biographies. We can hardly anticipate, let alone pre-empt, their verdict; after all, the contemporaries of the Inquisition, witchhunts, gory peasant rebellions and the vagrancy scare could be excused for

having no inkling that long after their deaths their times would be
called the Age of Reason.

We can hardly refrain from doing our own thinking nevertheless;
we cannot neglect our human, all-too-human need to reflect, to 'make
sense', to perceive a form in the formless, to divine order in chaos,
to guess a method in what otherwise would feel like unadulterated
madness. Aware as we are that all verdicts are bound to be only
until-further-notice, that our present is the future's past and that the
future is bound to reshuffle and reorder its past many times over, we
still cannot help doing our own accounts and passing our own verdicts. And when we do this in the last decade of the twentieth century, the shadows cast by Auschwitz and the Gulag seem by far the
longest and likely to dominate any picture we may paint. Many
things happened in this century of ours, and all significant and truly
consequential things tend to happen unannounced, without warning
and audible notice. None of the things that happened in this century
were, however, more unexpected than Auschwitz and the Gulag,
and none could be more bewildering, shocking and traumatic to the
people trained, as we all have been, to see their past as the relentless
and exhilarating progression of the ages of reason, enlightenment
and emancipatory, liberating revolutions.

It is not just the name of our own century that is at stake. How
are we to see the progression that brought us here – when we are
here already and know what that 'here' is like and what it is capable
of? Coming after that progression, as its culmination and legitimate
issue, our century – if it is to be recorded as the 'Age of the Camps'
– must be also, cannot but be, the *age of revaluation*: revaluation of the
past, of its inherent tendency and hidden potential, of the meaning
of the last few centuries of our joint history, of the 'modernity'
which that history spawned and left in its wake.

What we learned in this century is that modernity is not only
about producing more and travelling faster, getting richer and moving around more freely. *It is also about – it has been about – fast and
efficient killing, scientifically designed and administered genocide.*

As human history goes, cruelty and mass murder is not exactly
news, and modernity could be exonerated for not quite succeeding,
in the short time-span of a mere three hundred years, to eradicate
hatred and aggression with thousands-of-years-old roots and to quell
the passions precipitated by the millions of years of species' evolution. Some of us, indeed, console ourselves in precisely this way:
we, the modern and the civilized. have not done *enough*, but what we
have done was the *right* thing to do; we have not progressed far
enough, but we have been moving all along in the right direction.

What we need is more of the same, done with greater vigour and determination. There is nothing wrong with our civilization; its only – temporary – failure is that the snuffing out of the animal in the human, the barbarian in the civilized man, which it promised and did its best to achieve, took longer than expected. This is a pleasant, comforting thought. If only it were credible as well.

The problem, however, is that it is not all that credible. Even a massive outburst of evil instincts, always a flickering and brief event, would not sustain the long-term *institution* of the camps and all that huge network of co-ordinated activities which were necessary for their operation. Three days after *Kristallnacht*, the most spectacular of the street-violence explosions ignited by the Nazi regime in Germany, Hermann Göring gathered one hundred of the most prominent members of the German elite to proclaim: 'Meine Herren, diese Demonstrationen habe ich satt . . . The problem, in the nutshell, is unambiguously an economic one.' Sporadic explosions of spontaneous or contrived hatred would not suffice; only thoroughly modern instrumental reason, cool and unemotional, making the conduct of the operation *independent* from the feelings and ideals of its perpetrators, could do the trick. The camps were not just the old human cruelty escaping the dungeon to which it had been confined or returning from the exile where it was meant to stay till the end of time. The camps are a modern invention; an invention possible only thanks to the accomplishments modernity is proud of more than of anything else – to rationality, technology, science, its favourite and favoured children; an invention which derives its need and usefulness and functionality from the declared ambitions of modern society, a society that views having such ambitions as the foremost mark of its superiority.

I propose that the most bewildering, and indeed terrifying, lesson of the specifically twentieth-century kind of genocide is that it is not possible to surmise or anticipate (let alone to predict with any degree of confidence) the massive collapse of humanity by measuring the intensity of evil streaks in individual characters, the proportion of individuals with sociopathic dispositions, or the frequency of heterophobic beliefs. Even the most scrupulous scrutiny of the daily civility of human conduct may be of little help. The most prestigious and respectable press of the civilized world, the acknowledged voice of enlightened opinion, was full of praise and admiration when reporting the daily life of Germany under Nazi rule: *The Times*, the *New York Times* and *Le Figaro* alike were waxing lyrical when they wrote of it: of the streets shining with cleanliness and with law and order – no strife, no mass demonstrations, no protest marches, no terrorist acts, just peaceful, hospitable, well fed and smiling people. And a famous American sociologist 'proved scientifically' and beyond reasonable doubt and to wide public acclaim that under the Soviet regime the youth was more socially minded and better behaving than in the West, better protected against the notorious pathology haunting Western adolescence, less prone to addictions and deliquency. But it was these law-abiding, peaceful people, disciplined workers, exemplary husbands and family fathers, who were about to commit jointly, or to allow to be permitted, a crime without equal in human history. And it was those disciplined and well behaving youngsters who were about to stand guard on the watch-towers of the Gulag Archipelago.

I propose that whoever asks her/himself how the camps were possible must not look into the statistics of overt or crypto-sadists, psychopaths and perverts – but elsewhere: to that curious and terrifying socially invented modern contraption which permits the separation of action and ethics, of what people do from what people feel or believe, of the nature of collective deed from the motives of individual actors.

Modernizing cruelty

Such conditions – conditions without which there would be no camps and no genocide, conditions which turned the unthinkable into reality – are accomplishments of our modern civilization, and in particular of three features which underlie, simultaneously, its glory and its misery: *the ability to act at a distance, the neutralization of the moral constraints of action*, and its 'gardening posture' – *the pursuit of artificial, rationally designed order.*

That one can kill today without ever looking the victim in the face, is a banal observation. Once sinking a knife into the body, or strangling, or shooting at close distance have been replaced with moving dots over a computer screen – just like one does in amusement arcade games or on the screen of portable Nintendo – the killer does not need to be pitiless; he does not have *the occasion* to feel pity. This is, however, the most obvious and trivial, even if the most dramatic, aspect of 'action at a distance'. The less dramatic and spectacular manifestations of our new, modern, skills of distant action are more consequential yet – all the more so for not being so evident. They consist in creating what may be called a *social and psychological*, rather than a merely *physical and optical*, distance between actors and the targets of their actions. Such social/psychological distance is

produced and reproduced daily, and ubiquitously, and on a massive
scale, by the modern management of action, with its three different,
yet complementary aspects.

First, in a modern organization every personally performed action
is a mediated action, and every actor is cast in what Stanley Milgram
called the 'agentic state': almost no actor ever has a chance to develop
the 'authorship' attitude towards the final outcome of the operation,
since each actor is but an executor of a command and giver of another; not a writer, but a translator of someone else's intentions.
Between the idea which triggers the operation and its ultimate effect
there is a long chain of performers, none of whom may be unambiguously pinpointed as a sufficient, decisive link between the design
and its product.

Second, there is the horizontal, functional division of the overall
task: each actor has but a specific, self-contained job to perform and
produces an object with no written-in destination, no information on
its future uses; no contribution seems to 'determine' the final outcome
of the operation, and most retain but a tenuous logical link with the
ultimate effect – a link which the participants may in good conscience claim to be visible only in retrospect.

Third, the 'targets' of the operation, the people who by design or
by default are affected by it, hardly ever appear to the actors as 'total
human beings', objects of moral responsibility and ethical subjects
themselves. As Michael Schluter and David Lee wittily yet aptly
observed, 'in order to be seen at the higher levels you have to be
broken up into bits and most of you thrown away'. And again,
about the *Gleichschaltung* tendency that inevitably follows such fragmentation: 'the institutions of the mega community deal more read-
ily with the capacities in which people are all the same than those
marking each of them out as individual and unique.'[1] As a result, most
actors in organizations deal not with human beings, but with facets,
features, statistically represented traits; while only total human persons can be bearers of moral significance.

The global impact of all these aspects of modern organization is
what I have called (borrowing the term from the vocabulary of the
medieval Church) – the moral *adiaphorization* of action: for all practical purposes, the moral significance of the ultimate and combined
effect of individual actions is excluded from the criteria by which
individual actions are measured, and so the latter are perceived and
experienced as *morally neutral* (more exactly, but with the same effect, moral significance is shifted from the impact of action on its

---

[1]   Michael Schluter and David Lee, *The R Factor* (London: Hodder & Stoughton,
1993), pp. 22–3.

appointed targets, to motives such as loyalty to the organization, collegial solidarity, the well-being of subordinates, or procedural discipline).

The fragmentation of the objects of action is replicated by the fragmentation of actors. The vertical and horizontal division of the global operation into partial jobs makes every actor into a *role-performer*. Unlike 'the person', the role-performer is an eminently replaceable and *exchangeable* incumbent of a site in the complex network of tasks – there is always a certain impersonality, a distance, a less-than-authorship relationship between the role-performer and the role performed. In none of the roles is the role-performer a whole person, as each role's performance engages but a selection of the actor's skills and personality features, and in principle should neither engage the remaining parts nor spill over and affect the rest of the actor's personality. This again makes the role-performance ethically adiaphoric: only *total* persons, only *unique* persons ('unique' in the sense of being irreplaceable in the sense that the deed would remain undone without them) can be moral subjects, bearers of moral responsibility – but modern organization derives its strength from its uncanny capacity for splitting and fragmentation, while on the other hand providing occasions for the fragments to come together again has never been modern organization's *forte*. Modern organization is *the rule of nobody*. It is, we may say, a contraption to *float responsibility* – most conspicuously, moral responsibility.

Thanks to all these inventions, often discussed under the name of 'scientific management', modern action has been liberated from the limitations imposed by ethical sentiments. *The modern way of doing things does not call for the mobilization of sentiments and beliefs.* On the contrary, the silencing and cooling off of the sentiments is its prerequisite and the paramount condition of its astounding effectiveness. Moral impulses and constraints have not been so much extinguished, as neutralized and *made irrelevant*. Men and women have been given the opportunity to commit inhuman deeds without feeling in the least inhuman themselves. It is only when (to quote Hannah Arendt again) 'the old spontaneous bestiality gave way to an absolutely cold and systematic destruction of human bodies', that 'the average German whom the Nazis notwithstanding years of the most furious propaganda could not induce to kill a Jew on his own account (not even when they made it quite clear that such a murder would go unpunished)' served 'the machine of destruction without opposition'.[2] *Modernity did not make people more cruel; it only invented a way in which*

---

[2] See Hannah Arendt, *The Origins of Totalitarianism* (London: André Deutsch, 1986), part 3.

cruel things could be done by non-cruel people. Under the sign of modernity, evil does not need any more evil people. Rational people, men and women well riveted into the impersonal, adiaphorized network of modern organization, will do perfectly.

Unlike so many other acts of mass cruelty which mark human history, the camps were cruelty *with a purpose*. A means to an end. Of the Jewish holocaust, Cynthia Ozick's wrote that it was a gesture of an artist removing a smudge from an otherwise perfect picture. That smudge happened to be certain people who did not fit the model of a perfect universe. Their destruction was a *creative* destruction, much as the destruction of weeds is a creative act in pursuit of a designed garden beauty. In the case of Hitler, the design was a race-clean society. In the case of Lenin, the design was a class-clean society. In both cases, at stake was an aesthetically satisfying, transparent, homogeneous universe free from agonizing uncertainties, ambivalence, contingency – and therefore, from the carries of lesser value, the backward, the unteachable and the untouchable. But this was, was it not, precisely the kind of universe dreamed up and promised by the philosophers of Enlightenment, to be pursued by the despots whom they sought to enlighten. A kingdom of reason, the ultimate exercise in human power over nature, the ultimate display of the infinite human potential . . .

As Götz Aly and Susanne Heim have shown in their most scrupulous and penetrating study, the murder of European Jews can be fully understood only as an integral part of an overall attempt to create a New Europe, better structured and better organized than before; this vision required a massive translocation of population, which always happened to dwell where it should not and where it was *unerwünscht* since there was no use for it . . . This was, the authors point out emphatically, a thoroughly *modernizing* effort, since its ultimate purpose was 'to destroy the pre-modern diversity and to introduce the "new order"' – a task which called in equal measure for *Umsiedlung*, *Homogenisierung* and *Mobilisierung*. It is easy, yet unforgivable, to forget that the famous Desk IVD4 headed by Eichmann was established in December 1939 to deal not only with the 'Umsiedlung' of the Jews, but also of Poles, French, Luxemburgers, Serbs, Croats and Slovenes.

The modern spirit's dream is one of a perfect society, a society purified of extant human weaknesses – and foremost among those weaknesses are weak humans, humans not up to scratch when measured by the standard of human potential as revealed and articulated by Reason and its spokesmen. (The mass destruction of Jews and gypsies followed the scientifically conceived strategy elaborated by, as Aly and Heim describe them, 'expertocracy', including first and foremost elites of science, and tried first on the mentally ill and other 'misfits' in the ill-famed campaign of *Gnadentodt*). And the *ambition* is to make this dream real through the continuous, determined and radical effort of 'problem-solving', through removing one by one all the hurdles standing on the road to the dream – and that includes the men and women who make problems, who *are* the problem. The modern mind treats the human habitat as a garden, whose ideal shape is to be predetermined by carefully blueprinted and meticulously followed-up design, and implemented through encouraging the growth of bushes and flowers envisaged by the plan – and poisoning or uprooting all the rest, the undesirable and the unplanned, the weeds. Eastern Europe, say Aly and Heim, appeared to the 'New Order' builders as 'one great waste land, waiting to be cleaned up for a new building site'.

The most extreme and well documented cases of 'social engi-neering' in modern history (those presided over by Hitler and Stalin), all their attendant atrocities notwithstanding, were neither outbursts of pre-modern barbarism not yet fully extinguished by the new ra-tional, civilized order, nor the price paid for utopias alien to the spirit of modernity; nor were they even, contrary to frequently voiced opinions, another chapter in the long and not at all finished history of 'heterophobia' – that spontaneous and irrational resentment of everything strange, alien, unfamiliar and thus frightening. On the contrary, they were legitimate offspring of the modern spirit, of that urge to assist and speed up the progress of mankind toward perfection that was the most prominent hallmark of the modern age; of the optimistic view that scientific and industrial progress removes in principle all restrictions on the possible applications of planning, education and social reform in everyday life, of that confidence that all social problems can be finally solved and the world can be remade to the measure of human reason. The Nazi and Communist promot-ers of the orderly, accident-free and deviation-free society deemed themselves the scions and knights of modern science and the true soldiers of progress; their breathtaking visions drew legitimacy (and – let us never forget – an embarrassingly large degree of intellectual sympathy among the most prominent members of the 'enlightened classes' of Europe) from such views and beliefs already firmly en-trenched in the public mind through the century and a half of post-Enlightenment history, filled with scientistic propaganda and the visual display of the wondrous potency of modern technology. To quote Aly and Heim again, 'in their abstraction these thought-models stood in a jarring opposition to the sergeant's ire'. They needed 'scrupulously elaborated theory, which required that entire classes, minorities and peoples be displaced and decimated'.[3]

Neither the Nazi nor the Communist vision jarred with the audacious self-confidence and hubris of modernity; they merely offered to do better, and more ruthlessly (but more speedily in its result), what other modern powers dreamed of, perhaps even tried, but failed or did not have the guts to accomplish:

> What should not be forgotten is that fascist racism provided a model for a new order in society, a new internal alignment. Its basis was the racialist elimination of all elements that deviated from the norm: refractory youth, 'idlers', the 'asocial', prostitutes, homosexuals, the disabled, people who were incompetents or failures in their work. Nazi eugenics – that is, the classification and selection of people on the basis of supposed genetic 'value' – was not confined only to sterilization and euthanasia for the 'valueless' and the encouragement of fertility for the 'valuable'; it laid down criteria of assessment, categories of classification and norms of efficiency that were applicable to the population as a whole.[4]

Indeed, one must agree not only with this observation of Detlev Peukert, but also with his conclusion: that National Socialism merely 'pushed the utopian belief in all-embracing "scientific" final solutions of social problems to the ultimate logical extreme'. The determination and the freedom to go 'all the way' and reach the ultimate was Hitler's or Stalin's, yet the logic was construed, legitimized and supplied by the spirit and practice of modernity.

The most atrocious and revolting crimes of our century have been committed in the name of human mastery over nature, and so also over *human* nature, human needs, cravings, dreams. When the task of mastery is given uncontested priority over all other considerations, human beings themselves become superfluous – and the totalitarian states which gave that task such a priority strove to *make* human beings superfluous. In this context, the camps – senseless in every

---

[3]   See Götz Aly and Susanne Heim, *Vordenker der Vernichtung: Auschwitz und die deutschen Pläne für eine neue europäische Ordnung* (Hamburg: Hiffman & Campe, 1991), pp. 14–15, 10; Götz Aly, 'Erwiderung auf Dan Diner', in *Vierteljahrshefte für Zeitgeschichte*, vol. 4 (1993). An originally small office established on 6 October 1939 to supervise the 'transfer of nationalities' in Europe (Reichskommissar für die Festigung deutschen Volkstums) soon developed into a widely ramified, mighty institution employing, as well as 'office workers', thousands of economists, architects, agronomists, accountants and all sorts of scientific experts (*Vordenker* . . ., pp. 125–6).

[4]   D. K. Peukert, *Inside Nazi Germany*, trans. Richard Deveson (New Haven: Yale University Press, 1987), p. 208.

other respect – had their own, sinister *rationality*. The camps were the tools in that task, the wholesome means to the fulsome end, meant to perform three vital jobs. They were laboratories where the new unheard-of volumes of domination and control were explored and tested. They were schools in which the unheard-of readiness to commit cruelty in formerly ordinary human beings was trained. And they were swords held over the heads of those remaining on the other side of the barbed-wire fence, so that they would learn not only that their dissent would not be tolerated but also that their consent was not called for, and that pretty little depends on their choice between protest and acclaim. The camps were distillations of an essence diluted elsewhere, condensations of totalitarian domination and its corollary, the superfluity of man, in a pure form difficult or impossible to achieve elsewhere. The camps were patterns and blueprints for the totalitarian society, that modern dream of total order, domination and mastery run wild, cleansed of the last vestiges of that wayward and unpredictable human freedom, spontaneity and unpredictability that held it back. The camps were testing grounds for societies run as concentration camps.

This is how Ryszard Kapuściński, the most indefatigable and observant among the war-correspondents reporting from contemporary battlefields of oppression and freedom, described in his latest book, *Imperium* (Warsaw, 1993), his experience of entering the Soviet Union through the Trans-Siberian railway:

> Barbed wire, Barbed wire – this is what one sees first . . .
> At the first glance, this barbed, rapacious barrier looks senseless and surreal; who will try to cross it, if snowy desert spreads as far as eye can reach, no tracks, no people, snow lies two metres thick, one cannot make a step – and yet this wire wants to tell you something, give you a message. It says: take note, you are crossing the border into another world. From here, you won't escape. This is a world of deadly seriousness, command and obedience. Learn how to listen, learn humility, learn how to occupy as little room as possible. Best of all do what is for you to do. Best of all keep quiet. Best of all do not ask questions.

That particular barbed wire Kapuścinski wrote about has by now been dismantled – as has been the totalitarian state that built it. But it speaks still, it keeps sending a message to all who want to listen. And the message is: there is no orderly society without fear and humiliation, there is no human mastery over the world without trampling on human dignity and exterminating human freedom, there is no fight against the obstreperous contingency of the human condition that does not in the end make humans superfluous. In the camps, it was not just human endurability that had been put to the test. It was also the feasibility of the great modern project of ultimate human order, which the test has shown to be, inevitably, an *inhuman* order. In the camps, that project found its *reductio ad absurdum*, but also its *experimentum crucis*.

To be sure, the transparent, orderly, controlled world cleansed of surprises and contingency was but one of modern dreams. Another was the dream of human freedom – not the freedom of the human species, which permits scoffing at nature with its constraints and individual humans with their wants, but the freedom of men and women as they are and desire to be and would become if given the chance. What many have *suspected* all along but most of us *know* today is that there is no way to make both dreams come true together. And today there are not many enthusiasts around impressed by the dream of engineered, State-administered order. We seem to be reconciled to the incurable messiness of the world; or are too busy chasing the seductive baits of the consumer society and thus have no time to ponder its dangers; or would have no guts or stamina to fight it, were we willing or able to pay attention.

This does not mean necessarily that the age of the camps and of genocide has drawn to its close. In 1975 the Indonesian army occupied the neighbouring territory of East Timor. Since then, 'a third of the population has been slaughtered. Whole villages have been massacred by troops given to raping, torturing and mutilating indiscriminately.' The response of the Western, civilized world? *Our* response?

> The US condoned the invasion, asking only that it should wait until after President Ford's official visit, Australia has signed trade deals with the Jakarta regime to exploit East Timor's oilfields, and Britain has supplied Indonesia's military dictatorship with large quantities of arms, including planes needed to bomb civilian communities. Asked about the British position, former Defence Minister Alan Clark replies: 'I do not really fill my mind much with what one set of foreigners is doing to another.'

This much we can read in *The Guardian* of 22 February 1994 – twenty years after the genocide of the East Timor population started. We do not know whether the troops who tortured and mutilated and killed did what they did out of a deep hatred they felt for the conquered people, or just because that was what the commanders' command and the soldiers' soldiering was about. What we do know is that the minister of the country which sold the troops the planes to do the job of extermination felt no emotions of any kind, except, perhaps, the satisfaction of a business deal well done. And since the minister in question belonged to a party which British electors voted back into power three times since the planes had been delivered and used, we may surmise that the voters, much like the minister they voted for, did not fill their minds much with what one set of foreigners did to another. We may also safely bet that it is true that the East Timorians were exterminated because the world the rulers of Indonesia wished to build had no room for them, and thus it could be created only if East Timorians were destroyed; we may say that the destruction of East Timorians was – for Indonesian rulers – an act of creation.

'Between 1960 and 1979', says Helen Fein in her comprehensive study of contemporary genocide, 'there were probably at least a dozen genocides and genocidal massacres – cases include the Kurds in Iraq, southerners in the Sudan, Tutsi in Rwanda, Hutus in Burundi, Chinese . . . in Indonesia, Hindus and other Bengalis in East Pakistan, the Ache in Paraguay, many peoples in Uganda . . .'[5] Some of us heard of some of these cases, some of us never heard of any. Few of us had done anything to stop them from happening or to bring those who made them happen to court. What all of us can be pretty sure of, if we put our minds to it, is that our governments, for our sake – to keep our factories open and to save *our jobs* – supplied the guns and the bullets and the poison gas to enable the murderers do *their jobs*.

In every genocide, the victims are killed not for what they have done, but for what they are; more precisely still, for what they, being what they are, may yet become; or for what they, being what they are, may not become. Nothing the appointed victims may or may not do would affect the sentence of death – and that includes their choice between submissiveness or militancy, surrender or resistance. Who is the victim and what the victims are is a matter for their executioners to decide. In a succinct definition by Chalk and Jonassohn, 'genocide is a form of one-sided mass killing in which a state or other authority intends to destroy a group, as that group and membership in it are defined by the perpetrators.'[6] Before the perpetrators of genocide acquire the power over their victims' *life*, they must have acquired the power over their *definition*. It is that first, essential power that makes *a priori* irrelevant everything the victims already defined as unworthy of life may do or refrain from doing. Genocide starts with *classification* and fulfils itself as a *categorial killing*. Unlike enemies in war, the victims of genocide have no selves and

[5] Helen Fein, *Genocide: A Sociological Perspective* (Sage, 1993), p. 6.
[6] Frank Chalk and Kurt Jonassohn, *The History and Sociology of Genocide: Analyses and Case Studies* (New Haven: Yale University Press, 1990), p. 23.

so are the kind of subjects who may not be judged by their deeds. They are not selves even in the sense of being bearers of guilt or sin. Their only, and sufficient, crime is having been classified into a category defined as criminal or hopelessly diseased. In the ultimate account, they are guilty of being accused.

This stoutly monological character of genocide, this resolute pre-emption of all dialogue, this prefabricated asymmetry of relation-ship, this one-sidedness of authorship and actorship alike, is – I propose – the most decisive constitutive feature of all genocide. And, ob-versely, genocide can not be conceived of, let alone enacted, if the structure of relationship is in one way or another prevented from being monologic.

Yet states, even in our relatively small, postmodern part of the globe, where states stop well short of their past totalitarian visions and abandoned or were forced to abandon the hopes of resorting once more to a monologic stance, where the order-making and order-keeping efforts and the coercion that goes with them – once con-densed and monopolized by the the sovereign state and its appointed agents – are now increasingly deregulated, privatized, dispersed, reduced in scale 'totalitarian solutions' – so Hannah Arendt warned us – 'may well survive the fall of totalitarian regimes in the form of strong temptations which will come up whenever it seems impos-sible to alleviate political, social, or economic misery in a manner worthy of man.' And there is plenty of misery around, and more is to come in the ever more overpopulated and polluted world running short of resources and of demand for the hands and the minds of men and women as producers. At least every tenth adult all over the wealthy part of the world (as some observers say, every third; we live, they say, already in a 'two-thirds society', and given the present pattern of change, will reach a 'one-third society' in thirty years or so) is currently superfluous – neither the bearer of potentially useful labour nor a potential client of the shopping malls. If the classic nation-state used to polarize society into fully fledged members of national/political community and aliens deprived of citizen rights, the market which takes over the task of integration polarizes society into fully fledged consumers, amenable to its seductive powers, and into flawed consumers, or non-consumers, unable to respond to the bait and thus from the viewpoint of the market totally useless and redundant. To put it bluntly, yesterday's underdogs were non-producers, while today's underdogs are non-consumers. The 'under-class' which replaced the 'reserve army of labour', the unemployed and the poor of yesterday, is not marginalized through its handicapped position among the producers, but through its exile from the category of consumers. Unable to respond to market stimuli in the way such stimuli are meant to elicit, such people cannot be kept at bay through the methods deployed by market forces. To such people, the old-fashioned tested methods of coercive policing and criminalization are applied by the state in its continuing capacity of the guardian of 'law and order'.

It would be silly and irresponsible to play down, under the circumstances, the temptations of 'totalitarian solutions', always strong when certain humans are declared redundant or forced into a superfluous condition – though in all probability the totalitarian-style solutions will presently hide under other, more palatable names. And it would be naive to suppose that the democratic rule of the majority provides, of itself, a sufficient guarantee that the temptation of totalitarian solutions will be rejected.

In times when large majorities of men and women of the affluent countries are integrated through seduction, public relations exercises and advertising, rather than by enforced norms, surveillance and drilling, the repression of the marginals who escape the net of allurements or are unable to climb into it becomes an inevitable complement of seduction: as the tested way of dealing with those who cannot be dealt with through seduction, and as a stern reminder to all those put off by the vagaries of the consumer game that the price to be paid for not paying the price of market-life anguish is the surrender of personal freedom.

In a recent study significantly subtitled 'Towards Gulags, Western Style?'[7] the Norwegian criminologist Nils Christie has convincingly demonstrated 'the capacity for modern industrial society to institutionalize large segments of the population', manifested, among other ways, in the steady rise of the population of prisons. In the USA in 1986, 26 per cent of black male school drop-outs were in jail; the numbers have risen since then, and are still growing fast. Obviously, the prisons of liberal-democratic societies are not the camps of totalitarian states. But the tendency to criminalize whatever is defined as 'social disorders' or 'social pathologies', with its attendant separation, incarceration, political and social incapacitation and disfranchisement of the genuine or putative carriers of pathology, is to a large extent a 'totalitarian solution without a totalitarian state' – and the style of 'problem solving' it promotes has more to do than we would wish to admit with the 'totalitarian bent', or the totalitarian temptations apparently endemic in modernity.

---

[7] See Nils Christie, *Crime Control as Industry: Towards Gulags, Western Style?* (London: Routledge, 1993).

But let us repeat that it would be premature to write obituaries of the 'classic', Hitler- and Stalin-style camps. Those camps were a modern invention, even when used in the service of anti-modern movements. The camps, together with electronically guided weaponry, petrol-guzzling cars and video cameras and recorders will in all probability remain among the modern paraphernalia most vociferously demanded and most avidly snatched by societies exposed to the modernizing pressures – even such among them as are up in arms against other modern inventions, like *habeas corpus*, freedom of speech, or parliamentary rule, and deride individual liberties and the tolerance of otherness as symptoms of godlessness and degeneration. All our postmodern retrospective wisdom notwithstanding, we live and will be living for some time yet in an essentially modern and modernizing world, whose awesome and often sinister capacities have perhaps become more visible and better understood, but have not vanished for that reason. The camps are part of that modern world. It still remains to be proved that they are not its integral and irremovable part.

Is therefore our century to be branded by historians as the 'Age of the Camps'? Time will tell what the most lasting consequence of Auschwitz and the Gulag will be. Will it be the temptation to resort to their experience whenever it is impossible to alleviate accumulated human misery, or whenever the picture of future bliss is so tempting that disregard for those living in the present seems a reasonable price to pay? Or, on the contrary, will it be the role which that experience played in our sobering up to the murky side of modern progress, in our discovery of the congenital malaise of the modern spirit, in our new readiness to reflect on the human costs of social improvement? If the first possibility prevails, then indeed the Age of the Camps will be the true and legitimate heir to the ages of Reason, of Enlightenment and of Revolutions. If the second possibility comes out on top, our century may still go down in history as the Age of Awakening. We cannot be sure that the choice is ours. But we cannot say that we did not know there was a choice.

7.4 *'Antisemitism' Reassessed*

In the neo-tribal world new fault-lines appear by the hour, long-healed ones re-emerge and old but persistent ones are redrawn and re-armed. In all cases, the neo-tribal context invests the divisions and the battles with new meanings – the easier to overlook the firmer the grip of interpretive tradition entrenched in historical memory. Not only the new context gives specific colouring to the new and original phenomena which it spawns, but it also re-evaluates the old conceptual stocks and thus offers the chance of revising once-trusted orthodox models. The phenomenon described under the sometimes too generic, sometimes insufficiently generic name of 'antisemitism' is (not the only, but particularly conspicuously) a case in point. It is against this phenomenon, and the many narratives spun around it, that one can see clearly just how misleading a guide that unreflected-upon historical memory may be to the proper understanding of the world one inhabits.

Historical memory needs to be frequently revisited and reassessed, lest it should prevent instead of empower such understanding. In this chapter I shall attempt, tentatively, such a reassessment, and for this purpose I shall articulate and briefly discuss the following three propositions:

1. The area delineated and separated by the notion of 'antisemitism' (the cutting criteria being *hostility* to the Jews and hostility to *the Jews*) is too narrow to account fully for the phenomenon the notion intends to grasp; it leaves aside quite a few socio-psychological realities without which understanding must remain inconclusive if not faulty. I propose that what must be explained first – what indeed must stand in the focus of the explanatory effort, is rather the phenomenon of *allosemitism*, of which *anti*-semitism (alongside *philo*-semitism, as it were) is but an offshoot or a variety.

'Allosemitism' is a term coined by the Polish literary historian and critic, Artur Sandauer.[1] 'Allus' is the Latin word for *otherness*, and 'allosemitism' refers to the practice of setting the Jews apart as people radically different from all the others, needing separate concepts to describe and comprehend them, and special treatment in all or most social intercourse – since the concepts and treatments usefully deployed when facing or dealing with other people or peoples, simply would not do. 'Allosemitism' is essentially noncommital, just like the above practice is; it does not unambiguously determine either

---

[1] See Artur Sandauer, 'O sytuacji pisarza polskiego pochodzenia żydowskiego w XX wieku (Rzecz, którą nie ja powinienem był napisać)' ['On the plight of the Polish writer of Jewish origin in the 20th century: an essay which not I should have written'], in *Pisma Zebrane*, vol. 3 (Warsaw: Czytelnik, 1985). The only direct reference to Sandauer's concept in English writings I found in the seminal study of Bryan Cheyette (see his *Constructions of 'the Jew' in English Literature and Society: Racial Representations, 1875–1945* (Cambridge University Press, 1993), p. 8). Cheyette's book is a shining example of the cognitively revealing and illuminating use to which the selection of *allo-* rather than *anti*-semitism as the field of study may be put.

hatred or love of the Jews, but contains the seeds of both, and assures that whichever of the two appears is intense and extreme. The original noncommitment (that is, the fact that allosemitism is, and perhaps must be, already in place for anti- or philo-semitism to be conceivable) makes allosemitism a radically *ambivalent* attitude. There is therefore a sort of resonance (in semiotic terms, isomorphism) between the intellectual and emotional ambivalence of allosemitism and the endemic ambivalence of the Other, the Stranger – and consequently the Jew, as (at least inside the European *oikoumene*) a most radical embodiment, the epitome, of the latter.

2. The common habit of considering animosity toward the Jews as a case of heterophobia – the resentment of the different – is again both constraining and diluting, and thus thwarting rather than assisting comprehension. I propose that the generic phenomenon of which resentfulness of the Jews is a part is *proteophobia*, not *hetero*-phobia; the apprehension and vexation related not to something or someone disquieting through otherness and unfamiliarity, but to something or someone that does not fit the structure of the orderly world, does not fall easily into any of the established categories, emits therefore contradictory signals as to proper conduct and is behaviourally confusing; something or someone that in the result of all these foibles blurs borderlines that ought to be kept watertight and undermines the reassuringly monotonous, repetitive and predictable nature of the life-world. If all activity of spacing, ordering and structuring is aimed at making some sequences of events more probable and reducing the probability of others, so that the business of anticipation and choice be made somewhat less risky – then the stubborn presence of things or persons resistant to such manipulation uncovers the limit to those ordering intentions or hopes, thus revealing the feebleness of such ordering efforts; the 'un-fitting' become a fissure in the world-order through which ultimately invincible chaos is, reluctantly and depressingly, sighted.

Again, there is a certain correspondence, a certain affinity between the endemic under-determination, under-definition of the protean phenomena (one may say that they are undefinable by definition – since they explode the very categories meant to service the defining business), the vagueness and diffuseness of the proteophobic anxiety, and the categorial elusiveness of the Jews who for an important part of European history tended to sit astride all the usual divides and elide all the criteria normally deployed to draw them.

3. The third impediment to the comprehension of Judeophobia is the widespread tendency to consider antisemitism as cut of one block, as a well-nigh timeless accompaniment of history, itself rooted in a

virtually exterritorial and extemporal prejudice. Elsewhere I have argued that exiling the Jewish fate to a specialist branch of history and eliminating it from the mainstream historical narrative (particularly the narrative of modern civilization) diminishes the interpretive potential of the latter. But it must be stressed that the charge is valid both ways; namely, that cutting off the study of antisemitism from the flow of universal history and confining it to the exploration of the internal history of the Jews and their relations with their immediate neighbours (brought within the narrative solely in the role of the Jews' neighbours, considered solely from the point of view of what they did or did not do to the Jews) impoverishes, perhaps even bars, the understanding of Judeophobia.

True, the history of animosity and persecution inside our civilizational orbit is by now two millennia long – and the very persistence of the 'Jewish problem', of the Jews 'being a problem', suggests the continuity and enduring presence of certain constant generating factors. Longevity of historical phenomena always tends to encourage non-historical explanations. But already the thoroughly modern origin of the very term 'antisemitism', which recast the object of hostility as 'Jewishness' instead of 'Judaism', should alert us to the fact that using the same name to denote phenomena separated by centuries hides as much as it reveals. Like all other histories, so the history of the Jews is a subtle interplay of continuity and numerous discontinuities; and like all other 'special' histories, it is at each stage part and parcel of the currently prevailing type of society. I propose that factors generating apparently similar attitudes and practices of resentment changed and keep changing following the social and cultural transformations of society at large, and therefore they ought to be analysed separately for each successive socio-cultural formation.

In this chapter, I shall consider the distinctive shapes and causes of pre-modern, modern and postmodern allosemitism as a case of proteophobia.

Jews are unlike the others

In 1816, when all over Western Europe the visible and the invisible walls of Jewish ghettos were crumbling and Jews were shaving their beards and hiring gentile tailors, Friedrich Rühs noted that whatever they do, the Jews possess their own inimitable *Volkseigentümlichkeit* of such a kind that 'they should be proud of their distinctions, and even wear a special ribbon to distinguish themselves – as a sign of honour.'[2] Was Rühs a Jew-hater, or a Jew-lover? Was his admiration of Jewish distinction genuine, or just a clever mask? We cannot be sure, and I daresay it does not much matter. What does matter is that Rühs could not bear the thought of Jews melting inconspicuously into the crowd, as they were about to do in those early years of emancipation, so that the Jew-hater and the Jew-lover alike would no longer tell them from the next person. Rühs felt that the Jews were different, and that that difference mattered, and that it mattered so much that everyone everywhere should be warned: here he comes, the bearer of the difference, be on the alert, the habitual ways of thinking and acting won't do, a special attitude and treatment are in order. The special ribbon could indeed be a badge of distinction, like the Legion of Honour. But then it could be a sign of stigma and shame like the pointed hats the Jews were required to don when still confined to the ghetto. What is important is that it had to be a sign, and a visible one, and one visible at a distance. Jews were not like other people and other people should know that they were Jews.

A century and a half later, Witold Gombrowicz, the great Polish émigré writer, noted in his diary:

> Hearing from these people that the Jewish nation is like other nations, feels like hearing that Michelangelo is not different from other men . . . Unfortunately, those who received the right to superiority, have no right to equality . . . The Jewish genius is obvious in its structure – that is in being tied, like all individual genius, to the disease, fall, humiliation. One is a genius because one is ill. Superior, because humbled. Creative, because abnormal . . . The history of the Jews is a secret provocation, like the biographies of great men – provoking fate, inviting all disasters which may help to fulfil the mission of the chosen nation . . . You will not get rid of this horror imagining yourselves being 'ordinary' and feeding on the idyllic pap of humanitarianism.[3]

The perceptive, yet not perceptive enough non-Jewish eye traced the Jewish unnerving uniqueness back to their ambivalence. What it missed was seeing through that ambivalence further still, to its roots, deeply sunk in the gentile stereotyping of the one group in their midst they could not come to terms with and make up their minds about. It was another eye, that of the French-Romanian philosopher E. M. Cioran, that saw what Gombrowicz failed to see:

---

[2]   Quoted after Michael A. Mayer, *The Origins of the Modern Jew: Jewish Identity and European Culture in Germany, 1749–1824* (Detroit: Wayne State University Press, 1979), p. 140.
[3]   Witold Gombrowicz, *Dzienniki, 1953–1955* (Paris: Instytut Kultury, 1957), p. 121.

To be a man is a drama; to be a Jew is another. Hence the Jew has the privilege of living our condition *twice over*. He represents the alienated existence *par excellence* or, to utilize an expression by which the theologians describe God, the *wholly other* . . . Emancipated from the tyranny of local commitment, from the stupidities of *enracinement*, without attachments, acosmic, he is the man who will never be *from here*, the man from somewhere else, the stranger *as such* who cannot unambiguously speak in the name of the natives, of *all* . . .

Exodus is his seat, his certainty, his *chez soi*. Better and worse than us, he embodies the extremes to which we aspire without achieving them: he is *us* when we are beyond ourselves . . .[4]

Cioran concludes with a quotation: 'The nations feel toward the Jews the same animosity the flour must feel toward the yeast that keeps it from resting.' True – for all flour that dreams of resting. Less true for flour which dreams itself a scone. It all depends on what the flour is after. But whether the yeast is liked or disliked, it is always 'a problem' for the same reason: for its restlessness, for portending the end of tranquillity, for demonstrating the non-finality of what is. This is what ambivalence, that sworn enemy of the law of contradiction and the law of the excluded middle, those twin pillars of all order, does. The Jew is ambivalence incarnate. And ambivalence is ambivalence mostly because it cannot be contemplated without ambivalent feeling: it is simultaneously attractive and repelling, it reminds one of what one would like to be but is afraid of being, it dangles before one's eyes what one would rather not see – that the settled accounts are still open and the lost possibilities are still alive. It is an insight into the truth of being which all ordering bustle is trying hard, though in vain, to shut off.

How did the Jews become ambivalence incarnate? There was, from the start, from the times of antiquity, an incongruous, in a way an absurd feature in the Jewish mode of existence which must have made the neighbours pause and wonder: a numerically tiny nation, negligible as a military power, one of the many petty pawns the ancient empires handed over from one to the other as they rose and fell in rapid succession – and yet a nation imbued with a sense of grandeur, of being chosen, of being the hard centre of the world and of history; indeed, so convinced of its centrality that it looked at the rest of the universe, natural and human, as a pool of resources God draws upon in His special relationship with His chosen people to reward them for piety or punish for misdeeds. As David Biale suggested,

---

[4] E. M. Cioran, *The Temptation to Exist*, trans. Richard Howard (London: Quartet Books, 1987), pp. 80–1.

if the Jews survived the trials and tribulations of the ancient Middle
East it was above all thanks to that ambiguity:

> If they had possessed real power on the scale of the ancient empires, they
> probably would have gone the way of the Assyrians and Babylonians. But
> if the Jews had not developed a myth of their centrality, they would likely
> have vanished like other small nations . . . Relative lack of power com-
> bined with a myth of power was perhaps one of the keys to Jewish sur-
> vival in antiquity.[5]

Perhaps the Jews emerged from the ancient era as Jews thanks to that
ambiguity entrenched in the very mode of being Jewish; but most
certainly they have been admitted into the post-ancient, Christian-
dominated world in the capacity of that ambivalence which was to
serve as that world's *alter ego*, marking the spatial and temporal
boundaries of Christian civilization.

Indeed, in the course of its self-definition and boundary-drawing,
Christianity marked the Jews as, above all, an oddity – the uncanny,
mind-boggling and spine-chilling incongruity that rebelled against
the divine order of the universe. Many varieties of logical incoherence – indeed, all the unresolved contradictions swept under the car-
pet in the orderly home of the Christian Church – converged in the
image of the Jew laboriously construed by Christian thought and
practice in the process of their self-assertion. There were in the image
of the Jews the mutually exclusive, though already loaded with the
most awesome ambivalence, motifs of parricide and infanticide: the
Jews were the venerable ancestors of Christianity, who, however,
refused to withdraw and to pass away once Christianity was born
and took over, and having overstayed their time and outlived their
divine mission continued to haunt the world as living fossils; and the
Jews gave birth to Jesus only to reject, denigrate and disown Him.
The Jews were guilty of blurring the most vital boundary separating
believers from non-believers, the true faith from paganism: the Jews
were *not heathens* – there was a sense in which they were more un-
pagan-like than the Christians themselves – and yet they were simultaneously *more pagan* than the 'ordinary' heathens (they rejected Christ
knowingly). The other non-Christians around were the ignoramuses
waiting to be enlightened, to receive the Good News and be converted into Christians – but Jews were *infidels*, who from the beginning stared the truth in the face and yet refused to admit it and

---

[5]   David Biale, *Power and Powerlessness in Jewish History* (New York: Schocken
Books, 1986), p. 28.

embrace it. Ordinary heathens paved the road to Christianity's future; the Jews challenged its past and clouded its present. One may
say that the Jews served as the waste-yard onto which all the ambivalence squeezed out of the universe could be dumped, so that the self-
identity of the Christian world could be of one block and at peace
with itself.

I suggest that the allosemitism endemic to Western civilization is
to a decisive extent the legacy of Christendom. The Christian Church's
struggle with the inassimilable, yet indispensable, precisely for its
inassimilability, modality of the Jews bequeathed to later ages two
factors crucial to the emergence and self-perpetuation of allosemitism.
The first factor was the casting of Jews as the *embodiment of ambivalence*, that is of dis-order; once cast in this mould, Jews could serve
as a dumping ground for all new varieties of ambivalence which later
times were still to produce. And the second was the *abstract* Jew, the
Jew as a concept located in a different discourse from practical
knowledge of 'empirical' Jews, and hence located at a secure distance
from experience and immune to whatever information may be supplied by that experience and whatever emotions may be aroused
by daily intercourse. The unbridgeable divide between 'the Jew as
such' and 'the Jew next door' was already firmly established when,
at the dawn of the modern era, the Jews turned into the next-door
neighbours.

Jews mean the impossibility of order

Ambivalence is what all ordering activity is sworn and set and hoped
to eliminate. Ambivalence is the *cause* of all ordering concerns: life-
business needs clarity about the situation and certainty about the
choices and their consequences, and it is precisely the absence of that
clarity and that certainty which rebounds as ambivalence, triggering
an effort to introduce order – that is, to clear the mess: to confine
every object and every situation to a category of its own and *only*
the category of its own – and so to make the obscure transparent and
the confused straightforward. But ambivalence is also the *effect* of ordering bustle. The production of order has its toxic waste, a vain
attempt to impose discrete classes upon non-discrete time/space.
Inevitably, therefore, all classification must have its leftovers which
span the sacrosanct divide between the classes; no filing is neat and
complete enough to do without cross-references and a thick file
labelled 'miscellaneous' that pokes fun at the serious business of filing;
and no garden design, however shrewd, can avoid recasting some

plants as weeds. There is hardly a couple as divorce-proof as that of order and ambivalence. Ambivalence is one enemy without which order cannot live.

The outcasts of any society, so the great Norwegian ethnographer Fredrik Barth sums up his studies,[6] are those who 'break the taboo'; those who break what cannot be broken if the group at large is to keep its identity. The *destruction* of such outcasts, whether physical or symbolic, is a *creative* act; their extinction (short of extinction, expulsion; short of expulsion, confinement; short of confinement, branding) is the construction of order.

And there was a lot of taboo-breaking at the dawn of modernity and has been ever after. Walter Benjamin once said that modernity was born under the sign of suicide. There must have been a suicidal tendency built into the modern urge to melt all solids and profane everything sacred, considering that modern battles are waged in the name of the new and improved order. And it all started with the original sin of breaking down the ascriptive castes in which belonging preceded life and everyone was born into his rightful place to live among others born into their rightful places. Now, among the broken ramparts and shattered walls, everyone was free, but freedom meant searching for a home which was not yet: a lifetime of homesickness. The new times were exhilarating, but frightening. It was no fun to be locked in one shelter. It was no fun not to have shelter that one could lock oneself in.

Early and classic modernity was the time of *les classes dangereux, mobile vulgus*, mean-streets and rough-districts panics; the time of revulsion against the *parvenu* and against the *pariah* masquerading as a parvenu; the time of crowd scare. The anonymous stranger in the street was modernity's invention, and also its most horrifying bane. As Jonathan Raban pithily put it, 'in rural areas the majority of the victims of violent crimes know their assailants . . . In cities, the killer and the mugger come out of the anonymous dark, their faces unrecognizable, their motives obscure.' And even if you have been spared the fate of the victim, 'you have to act on hints and fancies' 'which resist all your attempts to unravel their meaning . . . So much takes place . . . , so little is known and fixed.'[7] The great fear of modern

[6] See Fredrik Barth, *Ethnic Groups and Boundaries: The Social Organization of Cultural Difference* (Bergen: Universitets Forlaget, 1969), pp. 30ff.

[7] Jonathan Raban, *Soft City* (London: Collins, 1988), pp. 13, 15. Raban sums up: 'the very plastic qualities which make the city the great liberator of human identity also cause it to be especially vulnerable to psychosis and totalitarian nightmare.' (p. 18)

life is that of under-determination, unclarity, uncertainty – in other words, of ambivalence. It is difficult to fight ambivalence, and quite impossible to win the war; one faces evasive and slippery guerilla units instead of a front line along which one could deploy one's own forces, or enemy concentrations one could bomb out of existence. And so one tries to reforge the diffuse anxiety into a concrete fear; one cannot do much about anxiety, but one can do something – one can *think* that one did something – about the causes of fear. And so the temptation is to 'de-ambivalentize' the ambivalence, by condensing it or focusing it onto one obvious and tangible object – and then burn ambivalence down in this effigy.

As we have seen before, the Jews had entered modern times already cast in the role of ambivalence incarnate. What happened inside the modern world only corroborated the received wisdom. In the mobile world the Jews were the most mobile of all; in the world of boundary-breaking, they broke most boundaries; in the world of melting solids, they made everything, including themselves, into a formless plasma in which any form could be born only to dissolve again. As the eponymical ghetto dwellers, the Jews were walking reminders of the still fresh and vivid memories of stable, transparent caste society; among the first to be released from special laws and statutes, they were walking alarms alerting one to the arrival of the strange new world of the free-for-all. Not only did they stand for the endemic ambivalence of the new universal otherhood, but in their plight they brought together what cannot be logically reconciled: the status of *pariah*, that creature of the caste society, and the status of the *parvenu*, that invention of the modern freedom of movement. They embodied incongruence, artificiality, sham and the frailty of the social order and the most earnestly drawn boundaries. As Shulamit Volkov found out, 'antimodernism tended to flourish where a modern pattern of social stratification did not neatly unseat the traditional one, but tended to coexist with it.'[8] But the Jews were the most conspicuous and ubiquitous carriers of that forbidden coexistence. In the words of Jacob Katz, the outcome of Jewish emancipation was the pariah's successful assault on the highly prestigious professions and cleansing of Jewish money from the stigma of low and despicable rank it bore.[9] The Jews were the low moving up, and thus instilled in the high the fear of going down; they epitomized the world

---

[8] Shulamit Volkov, *The Rise of Popular Antimodernism in Germany: The Urban Master Artisans, 1873–1896* (Princeton University Press, 1978), pp. 329–30.
[9] See Jacob Katz, *From Prejudice to Destruction: Anti-Semitism, 1700–1933* (Cambridge, Mass.: Harvard University Press, 1980), pp. 81ff.

not just *turned*, but keeping on *turning* upside down – the world in which nothing stands still and can be relied upon. This is what Éduard Dumont, the great law-giver of modern antisemitism, shrewdly picked up in his long litany of Jewish sins: 'In which old parish registers will you find the names of these newcomers, who still a century ago did not even have the right to dwell on the land from which they now chase us away?'[10] More poetically but no less on target, Ezra Pound likened the Jews to 'slime', 'morass', 'pea-soup' and 'fungus'.

The modern hatred of the Jews was a case of *proteo*-phobia; there were many strangers around, the world was bristling with them ('Seldom in the West is the stranger another person coming in; rather he is every one of us going out'),[11] and the modern man and woman is well trained by now in the complex art of living a stranger's life among strangers. Judeophobia meant making the Jews into an effigy not just of otherhood, but of that ambivalence with which the ubiquitous presence of the notoriously under-defined and thus unreliable (and probably guileful) strangers stains the otherwise transparent world. Jews were to bear the brunt of the notorious *Haßliebe*, the mixture of attraction and repulsion, of admiration and fear, (or – in technical terms coined by Miller and Dollard – of adience and abience), with which people tend to react to phenomena that sit astride the barricade or cross closely guarded frontiers; such phenomena are threatening, but they also surely contain some awesome, formidable, enviable powers. Doing something about the Jews was not just an effort to make the world pleasingly uniform again, but an effort to fight the world's contingency, opacity, uncontrollability. In other words, an effort to fight ambivalence.

Changing times, changing places

Frames may be put together solidly enough to survive the change of social formations and cultures – but it is social formation and culture that each time paints the picture inside the frame. Even if allosemitism may be rightly seen as a durable, perhaps permanent ingredient of Western/Christian civilization, successive social and cultural formations decided each time, and each time anew, its meaning and consequences.

[10] Éduard Dumont, *La France juive: essai d'histoire contemporaine*, 8th edn (Paris: Flammarion, n.d.), vol. 1, p. 29.
[11] Michael Schluter and David Lee, *The R Factor* (London: Hodder & Stoughton, 1993), p. 15.

In the pre-modern world, the Jews were an estate among the estates, a caste among the castes. Like other castes, they were more or less barred from (and barring) *conubium, commensality* and *commercium* with other castes; like other castes, they were relatively self-contained, autonomous and self-perpetuating. What set the Jews apart from other castes like them was the already formed aura of ambivalence.

One aspect of that ambivalence, arising from the role allotted to the Jews in the ongoing process of the self-assertion of Church rule, I have already discussed. (Let me repeat that what the Christian discourse produced was the ambivalence of the *abstract* Jew, the notional Jew, the Jew as a mythical genus which cast its shadow on 'empirical' Jews, but could not be reduced to what the 'empirical' Jews were or did.) Yet there was also another, more mundane aspect of Jewish ambivalence, closely related to the role caste-ascribed to them in pre-modern society. Throughout Europe, the Jews were deployed as *mediators* between high and lowly, in the service of princes or lords of the manor. For those on high they were servants – a prism through which the lower classes were sighted; for those at the bottom they were powerful oppressors – a prism through which the ruling and exploiting classes were gleaned. As Anna Żuk found out in her pattern-setting study of pre-modern Poland, 'the nobility and gentry bestowed on the Jews emotions reserved for the lower classes, treating them with disrespect, patronizingly, fully confident of their own superiority . . .' The lower classes, on the other hand, 'exhibited a tendency to include Jews in the same subjective category as the privileged classes on the evidence of the service function performed by certain Jews for these classes.'[12] This co-presence of two mutually incompatible diffractions of the same mediating, 'prismatic' category was potentially an explosive mixture, but for a time, thanks to an only rudimentary cultural exchange between the top and the bottom of society, kept inside a delayed-action bomb which was to explode with all its devastating force only later, during the Great Modern War against ambivalence.

Relations between estates or castes of pre-modern society were hardly ever sweet and friendly. Neither were the attitudes taken to the Jews by those with whom (due to their caste-ascribed functions) the Jews interacted. No wonder that, as Jacob Katz pointed out, 'the Jew whose work took him out of the ghetto and among Gentiles for the day or the week felt as if he were leaving his natural environment

---

[12] Anna Żuk, 'A Mobile Class. The subjective element in the social perception of Jews: The example of eighteenth-century Poland', in: *Polin*, vol. 2 (1987), p. 169.

and entering a strange world. Only on returning home in the evening, or at least for the Sabbath, did he find any satisfaction beyond the goal of earning a living.'[13] With all this, the Jews, their unique casting notwithstanding, were perceived by the pre-modern mind as perhaps awkward and unpleasant, yet an indispensable part of the Divine Chain of Being – as necessary and meaningful a part of the Creation as anything else in the world. According to Alina Cała's pioneering study of popular images of the Jews, Jewish caste 'could be distinguished by ambivalently viewed traits and felt as threatening, but its existence was necessary'; for the pre-modern mind, 'the world and life exist thanks to a certain harmony of cosmic conflicts';[14] we may say that the pre-modern mind held a truly 'gothic' view of the way the world was built and functioned, and disappearance of any tensions that held that world together, if at all imaginable, would be seen as the end of the world. As Norman Cohn summed up his own findings: 'pogroms as spontaneous outbreaks of popular fury are a myth, and there is in fact no established case where the inhabitants of a town or village have simply fallen upon their Jewish neighbours and slaughtered them.'[15] Pre-modern men committed acts of violence when things were not like they were *yesterday* – and not because they were not like they could – should – be *tomorrow*. In times when things were getting worse the accumulated popular fury was often channelled against the Jews – but this was the work of skilful operators, seldom or never on the initiative of the *populus*.

It all changed with the advent of the Modern Age. Now it was living-towards-a-project, tearing up the imperfect present in the name of the perfect tomorrow – and not, as we know from Barrington Moore Jr., the defence of yesterday's injustice taken for the standard of justice. Now the Divine Chain of Being needed urgent repair, as many of its links had no visible use or were not polished enough to enter the world of perfection. The Modern Age, as I suggested in my previous work, is the Age of Gardening – the time when society is treated as a garden needing design and cultivation; and as every gardener knows, an indispensable part of cultivation is weeding – the protection of plants which fit the design against the voraciousness and poisonous impact of such as do not. When *society* is turned into

---

[13] Jacob Katz, *Exclusiveness and Tolerance: Studies in Jewish–Gentile Relations in Mediaeval and Modern Times* (Oxford University Press, 1961), p. 133.
[14] See Alina Cała, *Wizerunek Żyda w polskiej kulturze ludowej* (Uniwersytet Warszawski, 1992), pp. 119, 139.
[15] Norman Cohn, *Warrant for Genocide* (London: Eyre & Spottiswoode, 1967), pp. 264–5.

a garden, the idea of *unwertes Leben* is bound to occupy in every blueprint of a better society just as central a place as the need to fight weeds and parasites is allotted in every good gardening handbook.

The Jews, already inherited by modernity in their capacity of ambivalence incarnate, were predestined for the role of the eponymical weed – indeed, of the generic appellation and a prototype of all 'social weediness'. Modern practice stands out from other practices for its obsessive preoccupation with ordering, and all ordering is about neat divisions and clear-cut categories, casting all ambivalence, automatically, as the prime and the most awesome of weeds. Making order is a synonym for the fight against ambiguity. Making modern Europe was synonymical with allosemitism veering towards its antisemitic pole.

As I proposed in *Modernity and the Holocaust*, there was no door shut on the way to modernity in which the Jews did not put their fingers. The order modern Europe was to build was to be the state-national order, and that involved political powers waging cultural crusades against ethnic minorities, regional customs and local dialects, so that the myth of national self-sameness could be made into the legitimizing formula of political powers. Into this Europe of nations, states, and nation-states, the Jews were almost the only category that did not fit, having gypsies for their sole company. Jews were not an ethnic minority in any one of the nation-states, but scattered all over the place. Neither were they the locally residing members of a neighbouring nation. They were the epitome of incongruity: a non-national nation – and so cast a shadow on the fundamental principle of modern European order: that nationhood is the essence of human destiny. Hannah Arendt saw Jewish exiles from Germany at their first meeting on the French side of the border. The chairman said: 'We have been exemplary Germans; there is no reason why we could not be exemplary Frenchmen.' No one laughed, Arendt noted.

The sacrosanct borders between the nations were not the only ones the Jews sat awkwardly across. In 1882 Leo Pinsker noted down: 'For the living, the Jew is a dead man; for the natives an alien and a vagrant; for the poor and exploited a millionaire; for patriots a man without country; for all classes, a hated rival.'[16] And unlike in premodern times, the images begotten in socially remote places did meet and communicate; in the case of Jews, the mutually inconsistent and jointly incongruous images mixed without blending into the

---

[16] Quoted after George L. Mosse, *Toward the Final Solution: A History of European Racism* (London: J. M. Dent & Sons, 1978), p. 188.

most fantastic and mind-boggling combinations, into the very epitome
of incoherence. The resulting composite image of the Jew made light
of all social, political and cultural distinctions crucial to life-orienta-
tion and, indeed, of the idea of the world as essentially an orderly
place.

To summarize, modern antisemitism was a constant yield of the
modern ordering flurry. Accordingly, the Jews were the most obvious disposal site for the otherwise disparate class-bound and nation-
bound anxieties, the most convenient buckle with which to pin such
anxieties, hold them together and harness to the state-initiated ideological mobilization, and the most obvious effigy in which to burn
them. The Holocaust was but the most extreme, wanton and unbridled – indeed, the most literal – expression of that tendency to burn
ambivalence and uncertainty in effigy; one reached by a state bent on
a total order of a made-to-measure society (note how only the death
of Stalin prevented Jews from being destroyed Hitler-style in another
state bent on total order); the extreme which many would wish to
reach but not all dared and fewer still had the chance to.

In these postmodern times of ours the ordering obsession is still
very much the mark of thinking and action. What are now absent are
models of global order, the will to pursue such models at the expense
of the present, and powerful institutions, most notably nation-states,
able and willing to serve as a vehicle of such pursuit and for that
purpose condensing and tying together the diverse ordering impulses.
The concentrated coercion of the modern state is once more par-
celled out into decentralized, diffuse and localized violence, now
deployed mostly as a tool of collective self-assertion and identity-
building.

The large identities which modern nation-states painstakingly built
are crumbling, notwithstanding the half-hearted and doomed attempts
to revive them through bouts of state-sponsored anti-immigration
legislation. (Though spurred by partisan calculations of political
profits, such a legislative flurry is bound to remain lackadaisical and
ineffective, unable as they are to outweigh the overwhelming contrary pressures of an increasingly global economy and the supra-state
integration which comes in its wake.) Identity-building, and even
more identity-holding, has become under the circumstances a DIY
job, without obvious workshops and factory managers. One may
say that identity-production, much like all the rest of industry, has
been deregulated and privatized, with the State ever more often
declaring it not its business and not its responsibility and leaving it
to the putative wisdom of market forces.

Without clear institutional anchorage and guarantees, concerns with identity are fraught with anxiety rebounding as aggression. Collective identities can only be born – and survive, however briefly – through acts of self-assertion; the louder, the more attention-drawing and shocking, the better. As no act is powerful enough to lay future uncertainties to rest, identity-seeking is an intensely emotional process, punctuated by explosions of collective frenzy. Identities are made almost entirely of emphatic, possibly violent, acts of self-separation, which always involve naming and assaulting a selected, concrete Other. The Jews come in handy here, long established as they are in European culture as the eponymical Other against whom group identities are articulated. More often than not, however, they are neither the most convenient nor the most obvious target for self-assertion actions; other groups, more conspicuous and closer to home, serve the purpose better. Postmodernity makes remote the prospects of antisemitism as state policy; but it also reduces the grass-root, DIY antisemitic posturing to but *one among many* battlegrounds on which the would-be collective identities undergo their baptism by fire.

Under postmodern conditions, where politics is wrapped increasingly around identity-conflicts rather than around orthodox national, class or status contradictions, allosemitism is likely to lose the unique position it occupied in pre-modern times and throughout modern history. Unlike in the modern era with its ambitions of homogeneity, differences are no more seen as a temporary nuisance bound to be got rid of tomorrow; variety and plurality of the forms of life are here to stay, and the human essence seems to consist in the universally shared ability to establish and protect what Paul Ricoeur called *l'ipséité* – the identity distinctive from other identities. The postmodern taste for *mixophilia* is constantly buffeted by the opposite tendency of *mixophobia*; it would be vain to predict which of the two opposite currents will eventually prevail; most probably, they would need to coexist, uneasily, for quite a long time to come.

The pressure to social separation, superimposing militant pluralism upon cultural plurality and steering towards updated versions of the *Volksgeist* cult, purification rites, ritual border-skirmishes, and a lot of ever more imaginative symbolic violence is likely to persist, perhaps even gather in force. In his seminal, eye-opening study of contemporary intolerance,[17] Phil Cohen suggests in fact that the roots of

---

[17] Phil Cohen, *Home Rules: Some Reflections on Racism and Nationalism in Everyday Life* (University of East London, 1994). Among many seminal observations with which Cohen's study is fraught, one should point out particularly the warnings that 'the more powerless or marginal the individual or group, the greater

the exclusivist tendency, being extemporal, are by and large immune
to changing social and cultural settings: they are deeply sunk in the
probably universal and eternal craving for 'home' – for the comfort
of homeliness, cosiness, being *chez soi* – and racist or chauvinis-
tic ideological formulae are as a rule metaphorical transmutations
of 'the elision between hearth and heath'. This may be true or not,
yet whatever is the case the future of judeophobia, exactly like the
future of all other hetero- and proteo-phobic responses to ambivalence, is tied to the current struggle between tolerance and intolerance gestated in equal measures by the postmodern collapse of
modern certainties and modern forms of oppressive regulation. As I
tried to reason in *Modernity and Ambivalence*, tolerance stands a chance
of resisting the adversary of intolerance only if it succeeds in elevat-
ing itself to the level of solidarity.

But this is another story – and one we will have to live through
first to narrate it later.

---

the pressures to adopt imaginary positions of omnipotence from which to
broadcast one's political or personal centrality, to cast out the taint of exclusion
through the counter assertion of moral superiority . . .'; that 'victims can also
turn executioners'; that 'the project of turning defensible spaces into training
grounds for more collective and political ambitions becomes too easily displaced
into local demarcation disputes over spheres of influence'; and that 'ideologies
continually fabricate their own procedures of empirical validation, their own
rationalities' and thus, when it comes to the pragmatics of self-assertion, rational
dialogue falls apart into monologues that are mutually incommunicado.

8

Morality and Politics

8.1 Intellectuals in the Postmodern World

The word 'intellectuals' first appeared in the language of public debate in France – after the publication of Émile Zola's open letter to Felix Faure, the President of the Republic (in *L'Aurore litéraire* of 13 January 1898), protesting in the name of superior values of truth and justice against the mistrial of Dreyfus. In the weeks following the publication of Zola's letter, the paper went on publishing, in two dozens of issues, *protestations* signed by hundreds of distinguished publicly known names. These were, above all, the names of prominent university teachers of various areas, each followed by a string of academic titles and honorary distinctions; but among the academics, there was also a generous sprinkling of artists, architects, lawyers, surgeons, writers, musicians. Already in the 23 January issue the editor, Georges Clemenceau, could announce that a new, powerful political force has been born, and that rallying around a political idea was the act of its birth. He gave this new force the name of the intellectuals: 'Is not this a sign, all these intellectuals arriving from all corners on the horizon, which unite around an idea?'

Clemenceau referred to high-class specialists, each a luminary of his or her respective profession, who thought it his or her right and duty to rally to the defence of important values once they found them not sufficiently protected, or indeed threatened, by the actions of state authorities. By taking that step, the signatories of the letters gave expression to two tacit assumptions.

First, despite all the differences of expertise and professional function, there is an important attribute shared by the academics, artists, lawyers, writers or musicians of distinction: thanks to the exceptional knowledge not available to ordinary people, knowledge which they have acquired and which they have demonstrated in their respective professional practices, they are all particularly close to the central values that sustain and determine the quality of society as a whole: they are, so to speak, the guardians of truth and objectivity, the circumstance which raises their sights above the level of narrow group interests and partisan prejudices. By being the foremost practitioners of their own specialisms, by carrying exceptional public trust and esteem due to their specialist excellence, they are also experts in the general cultural values which transcend any single specialism and any particular social function. They have the *right*, therefore, to bring the enormous public deference in which they are held on account of their professional achievements to bear on their standing in public matters of general interest and concern: they have the right to speak with authority on questions not directly entailed in their specialist credentials. They are Régis Debray's *haute intelligentsia* – 'collectivity of persons, socially founded in making public their individual opinions concerning public affairs, independently of the regular civic procedures to which ordinary citizens are confined'.[1] Collectively, they hold power which, though coming from different sources, can be put aside (and if need be against) that of elected politicians.

Second, taking a stance in matters of public policy, particularly in matters of ethical significance, becomes a *duty* of such persons whenever the politicians, the professional managers of the public arena, fail in their care. As a group, the intellectuals hold a *responsibility* for monitoring and scrutinizing the actions of the appointed wardens of public values; and an *obligation* to intervene if they find those actions below standard. In doing so, the intellectuals transcend their own group or work-related interests; they are, at least in their own understanding, one 'non-selfish' category within society – and for this reason non-partisan, objective in their opinions, and entitled to speak on behalf of society as a whole. In Lucien Herr's poignant articulation, only the intellectuals are people 'who know how to put the law and the ideal of justice above their personal interests, natural instincts and group egoism'.[2]

In other words, as this particular story goes, 'intellectuals' are those

---

[1] Régis Debray, *Le Pouvoir intellectuel en France* (Paris: Ramsay, 1979), pp. 43–4.
[2] P. Ory and J. -F Sirinelli, *Les Intellectuels en France, de l'affaire Dreyfus à nos jours* (Paris, 1986), p. 18.

who possess (or claim to possess) both the ability and the *duty* to act as the 'collective conscience' of the nation and thus to transcend both the specialist divisions in their own ranks and the sectional, interest-bound divisions inside the nation whose supreme values they protect and promote. They are defined by what they do *over and above* their professional duties. Being an intellectual means *performing a peculiar role* in the life of society *as a whole*. It is this performance that makes one an intellectual, not just the fact of rendering specialized, however refined and intricate, services; not just the fact of being a member of the 'knowledge class', having obtained formal credentials in the process of education or the membership of a specific professional group (the latter being a necessary but not a sufficient condition of joining the category of the intellectuals).

Once coined by Clemenceau, the concept of the intellectuals functioned throughout this century more as a postulate, a project, a mobilizing call, than an empirical, 'objective' definition of a particular category of the population. Though it assumed a descriptive form, its true meaning was an open invitation, to be responded to by personal choice of engagement: an *appeal* to certain prestigious groups of society to admit having special global responsibility – and to take it up and exercise it in the service of the society as a whole. At the same time, it was a legitimizing device, justifying political intervention once it has been undertaken. Starting from Jules Benda's highly influential manifesto of 1927, this understanding of a special political responsibility and social mission of intellectuals was to dominate – even if through objections voiced against it – the self-consciousness of the educated classes.

From the very start, therefore, the concept of the intellectuals was a militant, mobilizing concept, with its fighting edge turned against two adversary tendencies: the growing fragmentation of the knowledge class caused by the occupational specialization, and the declining political significance of the learned professions (and of the 'public' in general) at a time when politics was itself becoming a separate, full-time occupation confined to its own full-time practitioners. Though ostensibly forward-looking, the concept bore therefore a nostalgic flavour; it was a call to reassert and restore the unity and high public authority of men of knowledge, once (truly or allegedly) enjoyed, but now assumed to be being eroded and about to be lost.

Modern origins of the intellectuals

According to Robert Muchembled, the 'civilizing process', the principal cultural factor in the emergence of modernity, consisted above all in a 'cultural desynchronization' between the elites and the masses. More precisely, from the sixteenth century on, Western Europe was the scene of a cultural self-separation of the elites: of an acutely self-conscious drive, which congealed the rest of society into a 'mass' – defined mostly in terms of its ignorance, irrationality, 'vulgarity', brutality, impaired humanity, insufficient emancipation from animal nature, and being in the grips of passions that needed either domestication or taming.[3]

Though birth and wealth had deeply split European society for centuries before, it was only at the threshold of modern times that the dominant and the dominated had become *culturally* estranged, with the dominant defining their own way of life as 'cultured' (refined, polished, civilized) and thereby proper or superior. They now ruled in the name of promoting superior values; either guarding them from contamination and abasement, or spreading them among the inferior (uncouth, unrefined, uncivilized) part of the population, thus merging the role of the supervisor with that of the teacher. Such a self-definition reforged the actual *domination* – political, economic and social – into a project of cultural *hegemony*. This in turn constituted the dominated *mass* (and a mass it was in as far as the shared feature of 'unrefinedness', waiting to be 'cultured', overrode and effaced whatever might have differentiated the dominated population) as a prospective object of either a protracted civilizing crusade or close surveillance, monitoring and control. Whichever strategy would be chosen, the humanity of the 'masses' was conceived of as in some important respects incomplete, and the masses themselves as incapable of completing it by their own efforts. Thus, the self-separation of the elite had split society into three, rather than two, social groupings: the elite, serving as a self-appointed model of *l'honnête homme*, *l'homme civilisé*, or *l'homme de lumières*; the *masses* ('the Other' of the elite), accordingly raw, uncivilized and unenlightened; and a third category – the missionaries, *trainers* or teachers meant to refine, civilize and enlighten the masses. (This third category came, after some delay, to complement the guardians of order appointed to disarm, police and neutralize the 'unrefined', and thus unpredictable, 'dangerous classes'.)

The teaching profession was destined to become the major vehicle of the new order; an order unlike any other known in the past. Modern order was unique in the sense that from the start it was conscious of itself as a human product; as an artificial form to be moulded in the raw, pliable, yet awkward stuff of society. It was a self-reflecting and self-monitoring order, viewing blind and meaningless nature as

---

[3] Roger Muchembled, *Culture populaire et culture des élites en France* (Paris: Fayard, 1978), pp. 13, 220ff.

its only alternative, and itself as the only – forever precarious – protection against chaos. Such an order was unsure of itself, mindful that any lapse of vigilance might restore natural anarchy. Refining the potential 'human beast', keeping human passions in check and cultivating rational faculties instead, was the principal remedy against chaos and *bellum omnium contra omnes*.

It was the last precept that opened a functionally significant social space for the producers and distributors of ideas. On their part, the latter did their best to assure that the precept was assigned the most crucial strategic role in the order-building and order-servicing processes. Culture as a theory of social *order* and as a social practice of *cultivation* was a product of that mutual reinforcement. The *theory* assumed that men and women by themselves were unfit to coexist peacefully and unprepared to face the complex and constraining demands of social life; that they would not overcome that handicap without qualified help; and that they must therefore be assisted by 'people in the know'; they must be educated, and educated so that they embraced the ideas and skills that the knowledgeable people guarantee to be right and proper. The *practice*, on the other hand, was to establish the rule of the *men of ideas*; to elevate the indoctrination to the position of the decisive mechanism of production and sustenance of social order. Once theory is accepted and put into practice, one may repeat after Ernest Gellner: 'at the base of the modern social order stands not the executioner but the professor. Not the guillotine, but the (aptly named) *doctorat d'état* is the main tool and symbol of state power. The monopoly of legitimate education is now more important, more central than is the monopoly of legitimate violence.'[4]

Thus the stage was set for a mutually gratifying co-operation between the 'professors' and their employer, the State. They needed each other, as long as power without knowledge was by definition headless; knowledge without power toothless. The rulers and the teachers saw the world from the same, managerial vantage point: as the shapeless, virgin expanse to be cultivated and given form. They perceived themselves in similar terms: as form-givers, designers, architects, legislators, gardeners. Each was incomplete without the other; only together might they view themselves as spokesmen and guardians of society as a whole, as carriers/practitioners of society's supreme values and destiny. There was little room for friction. And if there is no friction, one would expect little chance for either side to stand aside and 'objectify' itself as a separate entity.

Under such circumstances, and as long as they lasted, the performers

---

[4] Ernest Gellner, *Nations and Nationalism* (Oxford: Blackwell, 1983), p. 134.

of the intellectual task would not set themselves apart from the fabric of social order. They would not set themselves off as *'intellectuals', distinct from, not to say antagonistic to, the rulers endowed with the right and duty to command the life and progress of society*. Neither would they claim to be a cohesive group annointed with a joint mission and burdened with shared, group-related grievances. Most certainly, it would not occur to them to say what Valéry was to say a century or so later: 'the sting of all intellectual life is the conviction of failure, of abortive character, of insufficiency of past intellectual lives.'[5] To say that, they must have first become *critical* of the current managers of social order from whom they felt estranged. They must have conceived of themselves as solely responsible for the promotion of values which the managers of society either cannot or would not instil or protect. They could constitute themselves as intellectuals (a separate group, with qualities, credentials, responsibilities and tasks all of its own) only in the activity of *critique* (that is, an activity perceived and classified as critique because turned against the *officially sanctioned* order, or against the official management of *existing* order – not merely the order which the official authorities of society were themselves up against, wishing to dismantle and replace it).

The 'intelligentsia' of the civilizational periphery

The conditions for the estrangement and antagonism between the political rulers and the educated classes, and thus for the self-assertion of intellectuals as the bearers of socio-cultural critique, appeared first at the periphery of the modernized section of the world. For the peripheral countries, which had not yet entered the path of profound social transformations, but were already made aware of their effects by the enviable experience of the already 'modern' nucleus of the contemporary world, modernity was not an unplanned outcome of social change: it was conceived of *before* it became a reality, and thus could only be thought of as a deliberately embraced *project*, a consciously pursued goal. Being 'peripheral', such countries were cast by the centre as 'uncivilized', 'relatively backward', 'late developing', 'lagging behind'. Once this classification, backed by the authority of undoubtedly 'advanced' and evidently 'superior' states (since they were politically and militarily dominant), was conceded by

---

[5] Paul Valéry, *Mauvaises pensées et autres* (Paris: Gallimard, 1943), p. 9.

'weaker', peripheral societies – their own conditions, yesterday still seen as normal (or too normal and familiar to be 'seen' at all) had been suddenly redefined as aberrant, or retarded, or 'in the grip of obsolete tradition', or otherwise shameful, contemptible, humiliating and in the end unbearable. The reality, or putative reality (always in a somewhat beautified and sanitized rendition) of the 'developed' centre became the utopia of the 'undeveloped' periphery.

The newly conceived handicap set off the process that anthropologists call 'stimulus diffusion': a process in which an *idea* of a 'superior' social form travels on its own, unaccompanied by the socioeconomic conditions that gave it birth, having thus acquired the status of *millennial urge* – of a dream to be reforged into reality by conscious human effort. If in the case of 'leading' countries, where the stimulus originated, the man-made character of the new pattern could sometimes pass unnoticed (as indeed it did in the beginning), or be theorized retrospectively as an outcome of a nature-like process, no room was left for ambiguity as far as the 'led' countries were concerned. There, the process could not be conceived in any but a blatantly *cultural* form: as a product of radical and revolutionary, but carefully designed legislation, of vigorous and purposeful human activity, of 'breaking' old forms and 'building' new ones – all leading to, and depending on, the construction of the 'New Man' fit to sustain, and to live in, the 'New Order'.

The act of embracing foreign patterns by which from now on the local conditions were to be measured and evaluated (only to stand condemned as a consequence) made those who embraced them into critics of their own society. They positioned themselves, at least mentally, outside the native reality, and that mental distance condensed both the 'reality' and their own condition into 'objective' entities sharply opposed to, and at war with, each other. In this opposition, native reality was constituted as an object of thorough and deliberate transformation, and/or as an obstacle to such a transformation which needs to be broken if the desired transformation is to take place; their own condition, on the other hand, was constituted as that of the carrier of transformation – a civilizing agent, cultivator, legislator. Reality was wanting, imperfect, devoid of authority; mere raw material, on which future action was yet to impress a form.

Historically, the travelling stimulus originated in the Western European centre of the modernizing/civilizing process reached first Eastern Europe – geographically closest to the birthplace of modernity. No wonder that it was in that part of the world that the concept and the practice of the *intelligentsia* were first coined and tried (the word itself entered the international vocabulary in its Russian form) – thus setting a pattern to be endlessly rehearsed later in countless, less or more distant places of the globe affected by the missionary zeal of a civilization confident of its universality. Ostensibly, the term was but a technical one: it denoted a thin stratum of people with educational credentials, people who deployed mental rather than physical skills in their work. The true meaning of the new concept (one determinant to large extent of the ensuing practice) can be best gleaned however from the semantic *opposition* in which the idea appeared from its conception – an opposition between 'intelligentsia' and 'the people'. The 'intelligentsia' was, so to speak, the defining agent in the opposition; the image of 'the people' was construed as the Other of the intelligentsia. 'The people' were inert clay to the intelligentsia's creative zeal; they stood against the 'intelligentsia' as the slothful against the energetic, superstitious against the educated, benighted against the enlightened, ignorant against the knowledgeable; in short, backward against progressive. The people were a mass as-yet-formless, ready to receive any shape which the well-informed, skilful action of the intelligentsia might bestow; and they would never be trusted to reach such a shape were the intelligentsia lacking in zeal and resolution.

Arnold J. Toynbee[6] suggested that the intelligentsia, as a 'class of liaison-officers', and by the same token 'a transformer class', was 'born to be unhappy'. It was bound to be viewed in its own country as a 'bastard and hybrid', 'hated and despised by its own people', while 'no honours' were paid to it 'in the country whose manners and customs and tricks' it had mastered and was 'whole-heartedly devoted to'. Such a sad fate was inescapable, as the intelligentsia inhabited a no-man's land between its own society, from which it had decided to alienate itself, and the 'pattern society', of which it had chosen to act as a keen spokesman, but which would never agree to accept it as an equal partner. The intelligentsia of the peripheral societies found itself in a virtual double-bind: viewed suspiciously, often derided by 'the people' whom it had chosen to make happy, while at best condescendingly tolerated by the elite whose authority it helped to build up and believed to be unquestionable – it might well end up wishing a plague on both their houses. Its critical stance was, so to speak, over-determined; and so was its acute awareness of its own uniqueness and solitude. Above all, its members felt themselves to be indeed the *transformer* class: a class burdened with the responsibility for remaking the society into something else than

[6] Arnold J. Toynbee, *A Study of History*, vol. 5 (Oxford University Press, 1939), pp. 154–5).

it was thus far, transforming the course of its history, forcing it 'onto the right path'.

Estrangement and engagement

It was this peripheral consciousness of the 'mission to transform', coupled with the poignant experience of solitude and alienation, that served as a pattern after which the twentieth-century discussion of the social placement, identity and role of the intellectuals was shaped and developed. Arguably, no other author influenced the course of this discussion more than Karl Mannheim, who linked the social 'uprootedness' of the knowledge class, its apparent estrangement from all established classes – with their unique potential to stand in judgement of all sections of society, including the class of political rulers. According to Maurice Natanson's commentary on Mannheim's *freischwebende Intelligenz* – it is because he is 'bound by no formal commitments' and 'can move lightly through traditional formulations of social causation, control, and prediction', that the intellectual becomes an 'unmasker, penetrator of lies and ideologies, relativizer and devaluator of immanent thought, disintegrator of *Weltanschauungen*'.[7] The unique insight and perceptiveness of the unattached intellectuals, which give them the clarity, truthfulness and authority of judgement the more 'settled' classes can never possess, derives, according to Mannheim, precisely from the freedom with which members of the knowledge class may move between sections of society: 'it is clearly impossible to obtain an inclusive insight into problems if the observer or thinker is confined to a given place in society.' 'The formation of a decision is truly possible only under conditions of freedom based on the possibility of choice which continues to exist even after the decision has been made.'[8] The fact that intellectuals do not quite belong to any of the classes locked in a mutual conflict of interests, that they are rejected by each one of these classes while refusing to commit themselves fully to any of them, is the guarantee of impartiality, and therefore the truth, of intellectual judgement. A society which desires a genuinely 'scientific' politics, which wishes to legislate its affairs according to trustworthy knowledge and demands of reason, ought to admit this fact and thus entrust the task of decision-making to its intellectuals.

[7] Maurice Natanson, *Literature, Philosophy and the Social Sciences* (The Hague: Martinus Nijhoff, 1962), p. 170.
[8] Karl Mannheim, *Ideology and Utopia* (London: Routledge, 1968), pp. 72, 143.

Mannheim's formulations were in their essence a bid for power, made on behalf of the knowledge class; or, at least, a bid for the role of the authoritative counsellors and controllers of the power-holders and 'public assessors' of the rationality of their decisions. The bid was expressed in a typically twentieth-century idiom, invoking the accepted authority of the 'exact sciences' to make the case for the political wisdom of men of knowledge. In its substance, however, Mannheim's bid restated the self-understanding of intellectual potential and mission going back at least to Francis Bacon's vision of the 'House of Solomon' as the site from which laws of society are pronounced, and fully articulated in the philosophy of the Enlightenment. According to that self-understanding, no other class in society, because of its innate limitations, is truly in a position to decide what is right and proper for the society as a whole. Introducing to his English readers the Enlightenment view of the task the intellectual carriers of culture are called to perform, Matthew Arnold decried all other classes as incapable of promoting the 'sweetness and light' culture may offer: the aristocracy, because they are 'barbarians' (caring solely about external polish and etiquette), the bourgeoisie, because they are 'philistines' (pretending to possess understanding they do not have), the working classes, because they are a mere 'populace' (buffeted by instincts and wants and rejecting all standards). Only the few self-chosen individuals who detach themselves from the habitat of the classes they have been born into, and devote themselves fully to the promotion of culture, can secure the ultimate triumph of harmony where now class egoism and inter-class conflict rule. And they must be ready to struggle against the sloth and inertia that make all the classes reluctant or unable to accept and deploy the values they promote: 'Culture indefatigably tries not to make what each raw person may like, the rule by which he fashions himself; but to draw ever nearer to a sense of what is indeed beautiful, graceful, and becoming, and to get the raw person to like it'.[9]

The bid for the supreme competence in matters related to legislating the best organization of society and selecting the contents of universal education puts the intellectuals in competition with the political classes while making ambivalent their relationship with the 'masses'. The latter is, so to speak, the *raison d'être* of intellectuals and the elevated social position they claim; in Pierre Bourdieu's words, 'in the mythology of artists and intellectuals, whose outflanking and double-negating strategies sometimes lead them back to "popular" tastes and

[9] Matthew Arnold, *Culture and Anarchy* (Cambridge University Press, 1963), pp. 105, 50.

opinions, the "people" so often play a role not unlike that of the peasantry in the conservative ideologies of the declining aristocracy'.[10] The 'people' are the natural ally of the intellectuals in their competition with the power-holders, whom the intellectuals accuse of neglecting their duties toward their wards. On the other hand, however, all too often the intellectuals find the 'people' slow or altogether reluctant to accept their judgements in matters of propriety and taste – an attitude which the intellectuals are prompt to bewail and condemn to the point where their own posture *vis-à-vis* the 'people' becomes a mixture of fear and contempt.

John Carey's *The Intellectuals and the Masses* has been the latest in a not too long list of studies in the convoluted story of the romance between the self-appointed spiritual shepherds and their intended flock. Carey's book was received by the critics with a venom and malice rarely encountered even in a realm of academic criticism not particularly notorious for its civilized manners; and no wonder, since the evidence accumulated by Carey brings into the open some of the most vehemently denied and concealed (because the most painful) of the guilty feelings haunting the intellectual profession. That evidence shows that Nietzsche's contemptuous opinion of 'the great majority of men' who 'have no right to existence, but are a misfortune to higher men', so that breeding a better race would require the 'annihilation of millions of failures', far from being a one-off and freak slip-of-the-tongue of a man known to be carried away by his own eloquence on more than one occasion, struck a deep chord in many a man of letters and was replicated far and wide: 'Dreaming of the extermination or sterilization of the mass, or denying that the masses were real people, was . . . an imaginative refuge for early twentieth-century intellectuals.'[11] The most virulent aversion thrives among the ruins of unrequited love.

Intellectuals seldom find themselves capable of overcoming the inertia or resistance of the 'people' without access to the means of coercion and persuasion administered by the political class; this is another powerful source of ambivalence that marks the turbulent relationship between the intellectuals and the masses. As Theodor Adorno put it,

> culture suffers damage when it is planned and administered; when it is left to itself, however, everything cultural threatens not only to lose its

---

[10]   Pierre Bourdieu, *Distinction: A Social Critique of the Judgement of Taste* (London: Routledge, 1984), p. 62.
[11]   See John Carey, *The Intellectuals and the Masses: Pride and Prejudice among the Literary Intelligentsia, 1880–1939* (London: Faber & Faber, 1992), p. 15.

possibility of effect, but its very existence as well ... The spirit in its autonomous form is no less alienated from the manipulated and by now firmly-fixed needs of consumers than it is from administration.[12]

Hence the frequently noted ambiguity demonstrated by intellectuals towards the form the guidance of the 'people' should take. Strong powers pursuing a vision of an 'ideal society' against the wishes of a population still too 'immature' to appreciate its virtues attracted intellectual enthusiasm as often as did the demands of democratic autonomy and freedom from state interference in the choices made by its subjects; neither totalitarian nor democratic regimes needed to complain of the shortage of intellectuals ready to support and promote their cause.

According to the recent study of English professional life by Harold Perkin, the transformation of the educated elite into experts/professionals has had a profound effect on their attitude toward their 'human objects', now perceived as passive recipients of their expert skills; the present attitude is one of arrogance and disdain. There seems to be no visible intention to 'converse' with the lay public, now treated solely as a collection of 'objects' to 'act upon'. Only 'colleagues', or other experts/professionals are seen as potential partners of conversation – yet the relations between the spokesmen of diverse fields of expertise (and diverse institutional settings) express themselves first and foremost in the competition for public funds and professional jealousy. Hence 'one professional cannot open his mouth without being despised by another one'; discreditation of other experts is seen as the surest way to elevate one's own prestige, the collegial critique is on the whole soaked with malice and envy, and the prospects of professions uniting to assume collectively the responsibility of the 'intellectuals' are slim and remote.[13]

The general opinion expressed in contemporary analyses is distinctly pessimistic regarding the prospects of resurrecting the public prominence of intellectuals as the 'collective conscience of society' reminiscent of the pre-war and immediately post-war years. The time of glory and political influence of intellectuals as a group jointly responsible for the culture and ethical standards of nations, as a collective bearer of universal human values is seen as past and unlikely to return.

[12] Theodore Adorno, 'Culture and Administration', *Telos*, no. 37 (1978).
[13] Harold Perkin, *The Rise of Professional Society* (London: Routledge, 1989), pp. 390–8.

The social dislocation of intellectuals

Modern states in Europe were *nation-states*, with the ostensibly 'natural' boundaries of nations replacing the pre-modern 'hereditary rights' of ruling dynasties. The pretence of representing the allegedly ancient and by now fully formed national units masked the intense effort of nation-building, the essence of the early modern state's struggle for authority. The nineteenth century was the time of widespread cultural crusades aimed at making the assumed, but in fact non-existent national unity into reality. Diverse languages spoken by the population inhabiting national territory were declared 'local dialects' which needed to be replaced by the unified, 'standard' version of national language through educational effort and the enforcement of 'correct' language in public places and on public occasions. Diverse communally sustained group memories were suppressed and supplanted by a unified historical curriculum, aimed at the preservation of the 'shared national heritage'. Communal traditions, customs, festivals, rituals were redefined as residues of ignorance and prejudice and replaced with a uniform calendar of national festivities and authoritatively set 'national usages', or wrenched from communal administration and then adapted and invested with new global-national meaning. Above all, nation-building called for a condensed and protracted effort to develop and instil a supra-local, supra-class and supra-ethnic vision of 'national consciousness', coinciding in scope with the actual or intended domain of the nation-state. In the process, competitive claims of other would-be nations, vying to appropriate and assimilate the same local histories, languages and cultures, were to be fought and defeated. All this put the educated elite, recast as the 'spiritual leaders of the nation' or the 'guardians of national heritage', at the very heart of the process of the 'primitive accumulation of authority' of the modern state.

This centrality ceased to be evident, however, once the authority of the nation-states had been firmly established and the reproduction of 'law and order' routinely secured through means other than ideological mobilization. With growing affluence and the rise of consumer-, rather than producer-oriented society, social integration came to be reproduced primarily through the seductive impact of the commodity market, while simultaneously the intensity of the political engagement of the citizenship by the state diminished. Cultural uniformity gradually lost much of its political importance, and the state lost much of its original interest in cultural choice and in promotion of a particular cultural entity; political domination was secure even without the support of cultural hegemony. This led to the gradual curtailment (mostly self-curtailment) of political supervision over the realm of culture. Even in countries where, as in France, the state agencies remain active in subsidizing and promoting cultural creativity and disseminating cultural products, the state's artistic patronage carefully avoids taking a partisan stance and favouring one rather than another cultural alternative: 'The word "culture" entails now an enormous aggregate of "cultures", each equal to all the others ... The cultural state, wishing to be a national one, wants also to be pluralistic and even cameleon-like, following changes in fashions and generations.'[14]

The cultural neutrality of the state meant the emancipation of the culture-creating intellectual elite from the resented, often pernickety interference of politics; it was hoped to elevate still further the public standing and influence of intellectuals by putting them firmly in sole control of culture, which they always claimed as their proper and natural domain. This, however, did not happen – or, for at least two reasons, was not seen as happening by the intellectuals themselves.

First, the separation between state and culture and abandonment of state-enforced cultural politics deprived cultural activity of previously enjoyed political significance and thus also of public relevance; cultural creation, choice and consumption were all now privatized – relegated to the private sphere. The joy of the unprecedented freedom of creation, acquired thanks to the official recognition of the political neutrality of culture, was soured by the feeling that artistic or literary choices matter little, if at all, for anybody else than the artists and writers themselves: freedom of culture came together with the gnawing suspicion of irrelevance.

Second, the control-desk of culture unmanned in the wake of the state's withdrawal did not become the property of the intellectuals. It has instead been captured by market forces. If the grip of political supervision has been radically relaxed, the hold of the marketing criterion of profitability proved to be no less – perhaps even more – constraining than political control used to be; it was also blatantly out of tune with the traditional ideology of the intellectuals. With the former managers of culture – the political elite of the nation-state – the intellectuals shared the belief in the 'objective hierarchy' of cultural values, the conviction that some cultural choices are better than others, and the determination to assist the 'better' choices to be made

---

[14] Michel Fumaroli, *L'État culturel: essai sur la religion moderne* (Paris: Gallimard, 1992), p. 30.

while warding off the danger of inferior preferences. Neither this belief nor that determination can be found in the cultural *market* which supplanted cultural *policies* of the state; indeed, cultural favouritism of any kind goes against the grain of market philosophy and practice. The market recognizes no cultural hierarchy except the one of sellability; best-seller lists are the only recognized orders of cultural preference – and, indeed, the only criteria of excellence.

Market choices are not necessarily the ones intellectuals would have made according to their own strict and sophisticated standards; this in itself would be a sufficient reason for alarm, but an insult has been added to the injury by the market's denial – in practice, if not in theory – that *any* hard-and-fast, previously worked-out standards, apart from the estimation of the probable merchandising potential, are either conceivable or called for. With such an attitude from the new managers of cultural distribution, the very foundation of the intellectuals' social significance has been sapped. Under the new conditions, 'the philosophical desire to be able to decide definitely between art and non-art cannot be satisfied'; but throughout intellectuals did not 'simply intend to classify things into useful categories . . . but rather to separate the deserving from the undeserving, and to do it definitely'.[15] It is this right that has been now denied – and even if not denied explicitly, made ineffective in practice.

The advent of market domination over culture has been thus perceived far and wide by the intellectual milieu as expropriation; the outright condemnation of commercialized culture, as expressed in the 'mass culture' theory dominating the social sciences from the 1950s for three decades, was the initial intellectual response. In that theory, market forces and profit-seeking traders of cultural goods were accused of causing cultural uniformity, the 'homogenization' of distinct cultural products – and by so doing promoting a new sort of insipid and faceless 'middle-brow' culture mostly at the expense of quality, 'high culture' and cultural creativity in general.

That homogenization, by the prospect of which the intellectuals were so alarmed forty or so years ago, did not occur, though. On the contrary, the cultural market seems to thrive on cultural diversity and rapid succession of cultural fashions. The cultural scene as set by market forces is reminiscent more of a whirlpool of variegated, often mutually opposite, products and patterns, than of a stultifying, standard-enforced uniformity. It is this absence of privileged standards, and not the dull 'middle-brow' monotony, that proved to be the

[15] Howard Becker, *Art Worlds* (Berkeley: University of California Press, 1982), pp. 151, 137.

most serious challenge to the orthodox role of the intellectuals and their once unquestioned authority in the matters of taste and of cultural as well as ethical choice. Choice has been *privatized* – made into an attribute of individual freedom and identity-building. The promotion of any particular cultural pattern as essentially better than, or in any way 'superior' to, other available or conceivable choices, has been widely castigated and disdainfully rejected as an act of oppression. In an unexpected twist, virtually reversing the original responses of intellectuals, the market has been promoted to the rank of the principal mainstay of freedom. The modern foundation of the collective power of the intellectuals has been eroded: there is little demand left for the skills they prided themselves on throughout modern history – those of the ethical and cultural *legislators*, the designers and guardians of proper cultural standards.

The substitution of a string of consumer choices for unified 'life-projects' has one more adverse impact on the traditional intellectual function. In the wake of the privatization and fragmentation of identity-construction the frustration which follows the failure of efforts and the resulting disaffection tend to be 'privatized'; they become diffuse and not adding up, non-cumulative, resistant to all attempts to condense them into a unifying 'public cause', and even more to gathering them around an alternative social vision. Persons attempting to go on playing the traditional intellectualist role are split between countless parties, causes, religious sects etc. to whom they offer their service or guidance. Diverse and dispersed single-issue grievances have no 'common denominator': no single conflict can be charged with the causal responsibility for the whole panoply of complaints and postulates. Political programmes aimed at majority support may only be composed as 'rainbow coalitions', unlikely to survive the issue that for a fleeting moment brought them together. Most importantly, market-caused grievances when processed through the channels of privatized lives rebound in still more demand for market services and so strengthen, rather than undermine, the market's grip over the social and cultural spheres. Another pillar of intellectual social importance – their role of spokesmen for common causes, theorists of 'good society' and designers of alternative social arrangements – has been all but dismantled.

The market, moreover, promotes a culture of 'maximal impact and instant obsolescence.'[16] The market cannot prosper without a constantly accelerating succession of fashions and public moods (as a French critic observed caustically – were Émile Zola given access to television, he would at best be allowed enough time to shout *J'accuse*

---

[16]   George Steiner, *Extraterritorial* (Harmondsworth: Penguin, 1975), p. 174.

. . .); public attention, bombarded with contradictory offers, has itself become the major stake of the market game – the most coveted, and the most scarce of commodities. Shifting attention replaces a sense of historical process with that of a collection of unconnected and inconsequential episodes; it flattens historical time into a 'perpetual present' (the experience which has been reflected, perversely, in recent announcements of the 'end of history'). In George Steiner's pithy summary, we are in a 'cosmic casino'. Only rhetorical games are played; sometimes they happen to be profound, but in order to be played in public view, with at least an appearance of an impact, they must always be amusing – have 'an entertainment value' – so that they can capture, if only for a brief moment, public attention. 'One exists only in as far as others speak of him – praise him, quote, criticize, slander, deride etc.'[17]

Fame has been replaced by *notoriety*: not a considered reward for achievement, a repayment of public debt for individual service to public cause, but just the artefact of 'forcing one's way through', with any available means, into public attention, brandishing the entertainment or the shock value of the message and/or of the message delivery as credits. If intellectuals counted themselves among the chosen minority who could claim special entitlements to *fame*, they have no privileged claim to *notoriety*. On the contrary, the traditional intellectual pursuits, the major cause of their past fame, are not fit to be conducted under public gaze and are not calculated for instant applause. When notoriety rather than fame is the measure of public significance, the intellectuals find themselves in competition with sportsmen, pop stars, lottery winners, as well as terrorists and serial killers. In this competition they have no great hope of winning; but to compete they must play the game of notoriety according to its rules – that is, adjust their own activity to the principle of 'maximal impact and instant obsolescence'. The justice or truth of intellectual ideas is increasingly irrelevant to the allocation of public attention; what count are their repercussions, the amount of media time and space devoted to them – and this depends first and foremost on their selling/rating potential.

It may well be that the historical glory of intellectuals was tied closely to other, now largely extinct, factors of the modern age – great utopias of perfect society, projects of global social engineering, the search for universal standards of truth, justice and beauty, and institutional powers with ecumenical ambitions willing and able to act upon them. The elevated rank of intellectuals as agents and arbiters of historical progress and the guardians of the collective conscience

---

17   Debray, *Le Pouvoir intellectuel en France*, p. 168.

of the self-improving society could not outlive the belief in progress and survive the privatization of self-improvement ideals. (This is, for some authors, the reason why the intellectuals never enjoyed a European-style social prestige in the atmosphere of the 'American Dream', which represented the improvement as mainly a private, rather than social, accomplishment.) Intellectuals have little to offer to the privatized lives of the 'contented majority' of affluent countries, unless they merge into the commercialized 'cultural scene', offering their ideas as merely another commodity in the overcrowded superstore of self-assembly identity kits. Most certainly, they have lost their role as cultural *legislators*, hoping at best to make indispensable their new function of cultural *interpreters* – translators in the ongoing exchange between autonomous, diverse but equivalent cultural styles. The collapse of the Communist alternative to the consumer-market society has delivered an additional blow to the standing of intellectuals as the arbiters of real and tangible choice between alternative social arrangements. There are no more 'genuine' alternatives – that is, in political language, power-assisted, armed-to-the-teeth alternatives – to adjudicate between.

Towards a recomposition?

What has been said here, cannot be summarized better than by quoting some recent words of Georges Balandier (*Le Monde*, 22 October 1993):

> Great public debates lost their vigour, the traditional institutions (notably the university) lost power to the benefit of the news broadcasters and the media, and that 'city of the intellectuals', the publishing houses and the press, opened up to multifarious competitive influences . . .
> The passions weakened as the certainties have been lost, pluralism of ideas comes together with the 'compromise with the market', the 'logic of the spectacular' gets the upper hand, but [and here comes the surprise! – Z. B.] the intellectual configuration recomposes itself and the decline may be reversed.

But how is that 'recomposition' possible? Does it stand any chance of success when a return to the old nostalgically remembered role of the 'natural' (and seen as natural, and enthroned as natural) legislators of public mores is by common admission out of the question?[18] And

---

[18] Though some intellectual spokesmen, notably Pierre Bourdieu (see his 'L'intellectuel dans la cité' in *Le Monde*, 5 November 1993) want us to believe that business being as usual, such a return is exactly what needs to be done and *can* be done, and depends on nothing but the intellectuals' own decision.

the return is indeed out of the question in view of the inner split – professional as well as political, inside the learned classes themselves; in view of the only too obvious zeal of many intellectuals of the retribalized world to exchange the universal sun for the homely glow of the family lamp and to serve as enlighteners of petty local despots;[19] in view of the evident absence of earthly powers which could absorb and be interested in absorbing the message of universality that made the hum of the legislative function of the intellectuals of yore . . .

And so, how? Jean-François Lyotard seemed to have taken a full stock of the present plight and come up with the answer (see his 'La Ligne de résistance' in the same issue of *Le Monde*): in our post-legitimation era whatever we do cannot count on the comfort of supra-human truth which would release us from the responsibility for doing what we do and convince us and everyone else that we have the right to do it and that what we do is right. In the post-legitimation era, we can only 'advance without authority'. . .

> Writing is a feeble attempt to respond to a demand; an effort, necessarily flawed, to match the obligation that does not emanate from an Other (one does not know what it is that Other demands, nor whether he demands anything) – but which resides secretly inside the one who sets out to write, and resides there in a non-prescriptive mode . . .
>
> The 'writer' writes to learn what the Other demands – assuming He demands something – or to learn why He does not demand anything . . . That demand, which may well express itself in silence, to make audible, in words, something that has not been said, something that He did not know how to say.

Writing is a duty, suggests Lyotard, not the right – birthright, right of anointment, or usurped right – of the intellectuals. The duty to express what otherwise would remain silent; and there in the

---

[19]   There exist more than isolated instances of intellectuals offering their services to emerging (or aspiring) tribalisms of the postmodern era. For reasons explained before, intellectuals were always fascinated with power, and with the prospects of ecumenical authority falling apart, the widespread intellectual bewitchment by the resurrection of 'communities' looks dangerously like a postmodern version of the old romance. What the outcome of such flirting may be, one can learn from a historical precedent: as Hannah Arendt warned, there was once among the intellectual elite, and not that long ago, 'the terrible, demoralizing fascination in the possibility' that 'man may be free to change his own past at will, and that the difference between truth and falsehood may cease to be objective' and that 'the old truth had become pious banalities, precisely because nobody could be expected to take the absurdities seriously' (*The Origins of Totalitarianism* (London: André Deutsch, 1986), pp. 333–4.)

twenty-four-hour-a-day din and commotion of electronic highways, among would-be, have-been and virtual realities that outshout each other in the vain struggle to document their own reality and out-real other realities, most of the voices stay silent permanently and without hope of ever being heard. The duty to make them audible is, though, a duty without authority, and without even the hope that sometime, somewhere, the unshakable foundation of that duty will be found, or built, to retrospectively release the doers from the responsibility (or is it guilt?) for what they have done. The assumption of such a duty means moving in the dark, taking risks – taking *responsibility* for the audibility of the numb.

In their recent study of the 'reinventing partisanship' in America of the 1950s after long years of intellectual absence (or exile) from the public scene, Andrew Jamison and Ron Eyerman surveyed life and work of fifteen thinkers whose importance only later years were to recognize in full. What united these thinkers, otherwise widely different in beliefs and style, was, in the authors' view, a common understanding of their own social role:

> Making partisanship personal and potentially meaningful once again is what united the people discussed in this book. What made them special and worthy of remembrance is that they consciously sought to preserve their autonomy and freedom of expression even while they took political stands and spoke out on the issues of their day. They refused to accept the main drift of the times. But their partisanship was of a new type. Their commitment was not to any one idea or ideology, or even to a political party or party program . . .
>
> These radical witnesses were rather partisans of critical process, seeing their task, indeed, the main task of the intellectuals, not to formulate truths but to help others to share in the collective construction of truth. Their ambition was to catalyze dialogic understanding in the general public . . . Theirs was a commitment to arguing in public, to opening up and keeping open spaces for what has been called 'critical discourse'.[20]

'Such spaces seemed to be threatened in the mass society of the 1950s', conclude the authors, 'and their preservation had to be fought for.' Spaces for critical discourse, we may add, are now threatened once more, and the threats are deeper than ever before. They emanate from a time/space in which information no more informs and the craving for orientation generates more disorientation, while the clash

---

[20]   Andrew Jamison and Ron Eyerman, *Seeds of the Sixties* (Berkeley: University of California Press, 1994), p. 210.

of efforts to obtain clarity and promises to deliver it result in more *mistification* (in the etymological sense of mist-making, covering in mist). In the deafening tumult of public spaces, dialogue is still-born or ages before maturing. To make the dialogue possible is one public service no high technology and none of the countless branches of refined expertise seem to offer.

Lyotard's proposition does not bring strategic certainty nor guarantee success, nor any assurance of support from history, to those who would wish to follow it. It demands courage and perhaps sacrifice without promising reward other than the feeling that the duty has been done. It is not, therefore, a pragmatically felicitous proposition, not a particularly tempting one, not one likely to be welcomed with open arms as the long dreamed-of solution to the intellectualist quandary. But, it seems, this is the only feasible, sensible, and, indeed (whatever its practical worth) *realistic* programme that the intellectuals of the postmodern era have and are likely to have for some time to come.

That is, if Balandier's 'recomposition' is not to turn out to be another still-born dream and false start.

8.2   *Europe of Nations, Europe of Tribes*

Fifty years ago – after more than a century spent on disputing and contesting inter-state frontiers, a century which culminated in the thirty-years long, bloodiest war in human memory, the unity of Europe – even the civilizational unity, not to mention the economic or political one – must have seemed a remote prospect, if not a downright fantasy. In the last half century, though, that unity proved (or at least seemed to be proved) remarkably easy to achieve, prodded and propped by what was commonly perceived as the greatest danger visited upon the continent since the Islamic invasion. Europe asserted itself as a self-conscious entity in response to the perceived threat of the all-out assault or a piecemeal absorption by the expanding Communist empire. That danger made the boundary of Europe easy to draw; it had been marked in an unmistakable fashion by the thousands of miles long stretch of barbed wire, backed by dozens of nuclear launching pads and thousands-strong tank columns. Thanks to that wire and those tanks, the boundary was also indisputably real and the politicians who negotiated the principles of peaceful and friendly cohabitation of the diverse residents of 'our common European home' could in all honesty take its shape for granted.

One is tempted to say that the post-war creation (or, rather, re-creation) of Europe proved to be perhaps the most seminal, and thus far the most lasting consequence of the Communist totalitarian episode. After many false starts before, this time the new European self-identity re-emerged, in an almost textbook fashion, as a *derivative of the boundary*. Before it has acquired any *positive* unified substance – economic, political, social or cultural – Europe has already been 'integrated' *negatively*, by the jointly perceived need to contain the common enemy on the other side of the border; one may say, indeed, that all the positive substance that eventually came to be construed has been an upshot of the boundary-drawing and boundary-defending urge.

And yet – however European identity was articulated or theorized by its prophets, aspiring managers or court poets, it owed most of the solidity and security it enjoyed over the post-war years to the political and military threat to which the co-ordination of western-European economic, political and military resources was but a response. With that threat gone, European identity is currently facing a double jeopardy. First, it has no evident, powerful and wilful enemy against whom all its members feel the duty to defend themselves, overriding their traditional divisions and animosities. Second, it faces the prospect of diluting itself (and thus losing some of its hard-gained cohesion) by being stretched beyond the reach of the economic/political network it has thus far been painstakingly constructing. It may not be that clear, moreover, why the unfinished construction of the network should go on pushing aside the thus far played-down or disparaged tribal/national loyalties.

As to the first challenge – it is just possible, though by no means certain, that the enemy against whom European identity was formed remained an enemy long enough to fulfil its 'midwife' role; that the all-European institutions nurtured by that conflict pushed the integration of national economies and legislatures to the point of no return; that, more importantly still, this integration has acquired by now its own momentum and may go on developing solely under the impact of its inner institutional – bureaucratic or financial – logic, no more dependent on a shared perception of a joint enemy nor, more generally, on the force of popular mobilization or consent. Even in this case, however, it may be that further progress of economic and political unification will not be followed by a parallel reinforcement of the sense of European identity; that the *systemic* and the *social* integrations will part ways. Lacking in urgency once supplied by the common threat, the sense of European identity may not be a strong enough factor to survive 'second thoughts', to counteract the 'falling back' tendency – the retrenchment of old localized loyalties and the birth of new particularistic identities and allegiances.

The second challenge – incorporation of new areas into the realm of 'greater Europe', blurring the by now familiar contours of 'our European home' – may boost and accelerate this tendency even further. The fast-fading sympathy and wilting sense of unity between the 'Wessies' and the 'Ossies' inside the reunited Germany, and the fear and alarm with which virtually all European Community countries have reacted to the prospect of massive Eastern-European migration after the collapse of the Berlin Wall, may well serve as intimations of the shape of things to come. We are not sure any more where Europe ends, nor how far we would like it (or allow it) to reach. The emerging ambivalence of the idea of 'Europe' surfaces, for instance, in Jürgen Habermas's recent confused voice of alarm: '*Europe* must make a great effort to quickly improve conditions in the poorer areas of middle and eastern *Europe* or it will be flooded by asylum seekers and immigrants' (italics added).[1]

As in the story of cultural assimilation which accompanied the modern nation-building efforts (a story which I have attempted to portray elsewhere)[2] – once the souls of the declared targets of the proselytizing mission have been won, and past infidels have been converted to become themselves the most dedicated preachers of the ostensibly universal creed, the prospect of victory tends to make the victors pause and recoil; they are now frightened by their own success, by the threat of being flooded and submerged by their new self-declared brethren in faith, clamouring for equal treatment and an equal share in the wonders life may offer.

For the last half a century, Europeanism was dangled before Europe's less happy neighbours on the other side of the Iron Curtain as synonym of the good life of which they were deprived because of that Curtain. In other words, as a privilege, but of a tempting, seductive kind thanks to the attached standing invitation to join in, to the promise of tomorrow's universality of bliss. But no privilege can survive its universalization. When the proclaimed obstacles to universality are finally removed, the moment of truth arrives. The Berlin Wall offered an effective barrier to the spread of the privilege called 'Europe'; it seemed to guarantee that the bluff would never be called. The collapse of the Wall could not but subject the idea of a single

---

[1] Jürgen Habermas, 'Citizenship and National Unity: Some Reflections on the Future of Europe', in *Praxis International*, vol. 12/1 (April 1922), p. 13.

[2] Zygmunt Bauman, *Modernity and Ambivalence* (Cambridge: Polity Press, 1992).

unified Europe to the most severe test to date. Now, paradoxically, it is the geographic periphery, and until recently the 'political outside' from where the most avid and dedicated advocacy is heard of the idea which the centre claimed to stand for and continues to be seen as standing for. It is in such spiritually distant places, from Warsaw to Tirana and Baku, that one hears political leaders of all shades of the political spectrum waxing lyrical about the beauties of a unified Europe and declaring themselves Europeans born and bred.[3] The old centre, on the other hand, recoils from the unanticipated success of its missionary message, and – more consequentially still – from the message its distant or next-door admirers have read into its practical achievement they admire and are keen to emulate. Are these people, indeed, all Europeans? Is Bulgaria part of Europe? Are the Turks Europeans, like us? Just how many spices can the soup called Europe bear and remain edible? With so many strangers inside the borders, what worth the whole dream of European identity? Just imagine a dozen more varieties of Greeks wanting to speak in the name of Europe . . . Paradoxically (or, perhaps, not that paradoxically after all) it is such elements in the centre as are today least enthusiastic about European identity, and lukewarm about the accelerating pace of integration (like the British Tory Eurosceptics) who most avidly promote throwing the gates of Europe wide open and keeping them open. The more bizarre peoples wrangle around the community table, the less, they hope, will be left of the communal spirit . . .

As it happens, it is not necessarily the old nation-state divisions and loyalties that will benefit from the present stresses of European integration. In the context of an economically and legislatively integrating continent, the old states are poorly equipped to manage economic and social policies within state boundaries; those among them whose political and economic elites are increasingly oriented toward supra-national networks are fast devalued as the focus of spiritual identity: the very role which the nation-states used to perform to such great effect at the time they combined legislative sovereignty, military self-sufficiency, economic management and cultural hegemony. Through most of the modern period of European history, nation-states did their best to condense the plural, diffuse

---

[3] The phenomenon is not at all confined, to be sure, to the countries of the defunct communist block. Compare the following statement: 'Malta is a European country by its culture and history. We feel ourselves Europeans . . . We truly believe in Europe.' (Eddie Fenech Adami, the Maltese Prime Minister, on 22 February 1992)

and centrifugal forces of ethnicity into unitary nationalisms and then make nationalist fervour synonymous with civic duty. As Carlo Schmid observed, 'es haben sich bei uns in Europa zwei Vorstellungen enwickelt, auf der eine seite das Reich, auf der anderen Seite der Staat . . . auf der einen Seite *Pax et justitia*, auf der anderen Seite *Pax et disciplina*'[4] The point is, however, that the nation-state, like no other unit before or after, managed to secure a lasting marriage between *Reich* and *Staat*, nationhood and statehood, between the *ethnic* and the *political* nation, now on the brink of divorce again. Today, one of the consequences of the ongoing erosion of nation-state sovereignty is that the forces of ethnicity are once more set loose, untamed and unanchored, free-floating and uncontrolled. Uncoupled from the burden of economic and social management to which it was harnessed in the era of the nation-states, roaming free in the thin air of emotions, ethnicity is, if anything, more potent a force today than it ever was throughout past European history.

There was a time, as well, when the nation-state could, for better or worse, supply the society it ruled with ethical guidance and a sense of unity and purpose; when it could underwrite a social compact of one form or another, by which – as the great prophets of modernity never tired of insisting – citizens agreed to sacrifice a part of their freedom and self-interest in exchange for living in a decent, just and civilized society. These times are over now, the long and tortuous ascendance of the modern democratic *polis* has come to a halt or at least has been interrupted – and it is not clear what the old and affluent part of Europe may offer its newly declared children and in what currency it is going to acquit itself of the self-incurred ethical debt. To quote Gregory Clark's worried musings:

> In the past, when our instinctive sense of social contract was operating, we in the West could trust our politicians to behave with some integrity and our citizens to relate to one another with honesty and responsibility. We could leave our doors unlocked and our children could walk the streets unharmed.
>
> Now, as all this disappears, we are trying to lecture other people on how to organize themselves, using a model that no longer has validity even for ourselves.[5]

---

[4]   Carlo Schmid, 'Verhältnis der Bürger zum Staat in der Bundesrepublik Deutschland und in Frankreich', in *Staat und Nation in Deutschland und Frankreich*, ed. Wolfgang Neumann and Berenice Manach (Lodwigsburg: Deutsch-Französisch Institut, 1977), p. 2.
[5]   Gregory Clark, 'The Lecture is Ringing a Bit Hollow', in *New York Herald Tribune*, 23 March 1994, p. 8.

In the past – still no more than half a century ago – only a few among the infinite multitude of ethnic distinctions could be seriously considered as potential foci for the condensation and separation of politically sovereign nations. Given the multiple, yet tightly linked functions of the nation-state, in order to entertain such a chance prospective nations had to pass the test of economic, social, and indeed military viability. At a time when the nation-states are fast shedding some of their traditional functions this test is no more required. We can repeat after Eric Hobsbawm that today 'there is no denying that "ethnic" identities which had no political or even existential significance . . . can acquire a genuine hold as badges of group identity overnight.'[6] Any group, however small and insignificant, can in principle bid for sovereignty, complete with the right to lodge valid claims with supra-state agencies, and virtually any group can get it, providing it makes its bid loud enough and assuming that no established or more powerful sovereign group is willing, or capable, of stifling its voice. If 'Sovereignty in Europe' is today a claim one hears from one end of the continent to the other, it is because of the fact that as long as the economic, social and a large part of political sovereignty, together with the worry of military defence, are ceded all over the place to the supra-state, all-European institutions, what is left of the traditional sovereignty of nation-states (and, most importantly, of their contractual and non-contractual obligations toward their subjects) seems to be seductively easy to hold and uphold: a prize with no penalty attached, a right without duties, taking without giving, pleasure without responsibility.

This puts the European Community, created and until now sustained as a compact of selected sovereign states, under one more tension still. The European Community has been formed by the governments of the states rooted in the nation-state tradition of enforced or induced *homogeneity*: in Jürgen Kocka's description, the practice of 'Reduzierung und Abbau von Unterschieden, Reduktion von Heterogenität, Homogeniesierung von einerseits regionalen Differenzen'.[7] The allegedly indivisible nations were born of that process of *homogenization*, which meant cultural crusades, the suppression of local languages and traditions, the imposition of unified curricula promoting a single common 'heritage'. Europe's member

---

[6] Eric Hobsbawm, 'Whose Fault-line is it Anyway?', in *New Statesman and Society*, 24 April 1992, pp. 24–5.

[7] Jürgen Kocka, 'Probleme der politischen Integration der Deutschen', in *Die Rolle der Nation in der Deutschen Geschichte und Gegenwart*, ed. Otto Büsch and James J. Sheenan (Berlin: Colloquium Vertrag, 1985), pp. 122–3.

states are jealous of their hard-won – more putative than real, and always open to contest – national integrity. They expect the Community to respect and protect such integrity. They retain in principle their long-standing interest in upholding the myth of one, unified nation, and are on the whole reluctant to admit the separate identity of any of their sub-populations. The greater, however, is the share of nation-state sovereignty ceded to the all-European agencies, the less is the chance that the nation-state-based identities will be successfully defended. Provinces and regions for whatever reason unsatisfied with the place allotted to them by the nation-states of which they are parts see no more any good reason to meekly submit to the state monopoly for sovereign rule; they sense in the all-European entity a sort of Court of Appeal, an address for the grievance to which the lesser political units closer to home refuse to listen, and thus a chance of redressing the incapacitating imbalance of strength.

Borrowing the established vocabulary of sovereignty claims, they discover or invent their 'ethnicity' which they want the European Community to defend against the next-door bullies. It is they therefore who – much like the new nation-states knocking at the Community door and asking to be let in – tend to be the most enthusiastic and dedicated addicts of the 'European idea'. One should not be surprised to find out that Basques, Catalans, Scots, Croats, or, indeed, Lombards may feel pangs of envy when Mary Robinson, the Irish President, declares that 'Since we entered the Community in 1973, we stopped defining ourselves almost exclusively in relation to Great Britain . . . This gave us a larger, more modern and just sense of our identity.'[8] After many years, Otto Von Bismarck's caustic comment sounds as if made today: 'I hear the word "Europe" falling from the lips of those who demand something which they cannot or are not ready to take by themselves.' And we must admit the prophetic wisdom of Michael Walzer's observation that 'if states ever become large neighbourhoods, it is likely that neighbourhoods will become little states. Their members will organize to defend their local politics and culture against strangers. Historically, neighbourhoods have turned into closed or parochial communities . . . whenever the state was open'.[9]

Some observers, most notably Eric Hobsbawm, consider the astonishing proliferation of 'nation-states' in the most recent period of world history as a sign not so much of the ultimate *triumph* of the

[8]   Interview in *Le Monde*, 26 May 1992, p. 14.
[9]   Michael Walzer, *Spheres of Justice: A Defense of Pluralism and Equality* (New York: Basic Books, 1983), p. 38.

'national principle', but – on the contrary – an outcome of the progressive *collapse* of the nation-state as the principal carrier of collective sovereign identities. Throughout the 'classical modern' era, up
to the cataclysm brought about by World War I, multi-dimensional
sovereignty (embracing first and foremost the grand triad of the
military, economic and cultural autonomy and self-management) was
inextricably woven into the nationalist idea; one may guess that it
was this link that made the institution of the nation-state so tempting
and so effective as the target and the reference point of collective
identities. 'Viability' was seen then to be the indispensable attribute
of the nation-state – and hence a territory too small or too weak to
cater for itself was not truly in the race; only large and medium-to-
large entities could consider themselves, and were considered by
others, as 'deserving' the nation-state status. Today, that criterion
seems to have been removed. And so we witness seemingly endless
fissiparousness of nationalisms, with ever new regional, linguistic,
denominational etc. differences being picked up by ever new prospective elites as distinctive identities powerful enough to justify a
separate state, or quasi-state, formation. To quote Eric Hobsbawm's
pithy statement,

> Any speck in the Pacific can look forward to independence and a good
> time for its president, if it happens to possess a location for a naval base
> for which more solvent states will compete, a lucky gift of nature such as
> manganese, or merely enough beaches and pretty girls to become a tourist
> paradise . . .
>   The majority of the members of the UN is soon likely to consist of the
> late twentieth century (republican) equivalents to Saxe-Coburg-Gotha and
> Schwarzburg-Sonderhausen . . .
>   If the Seychelles can have a vote in the UN as good as Japan's . . . then
> surely only the sky is the limit for the Isle of Man or the Channel Islands.[10]

The proliferation of units claiming a status similar to the one which
has been won historically by modern nation-states does *not* testify to
the fact that smaller and weaker entities can now reasonably claim or
strive for viability; it only testifies to the fact that viability has ceased
to be a condition of nation-state formation. Most significantly, it suggests – paradoxically – the *loss* of 'viability' in the old sense by such
large and medium-to-large state organisms as could claim to enjoy
the classical triad of sovereignty in the 'high modernity' era. The
overcrowded UN building does not augur the ultimate triumph of

---

[10] See Eric Hobsbawm, 'Some Reflections on "The Break-up of Britain"', in
New Left Review, no. 105 (1977).

the nationalist principle – but the coming end of the age when the social system used to be identified territorially and population-wise with the nation-state (though not necessarily, let us repeat, the end of the age of nationalism).The way in which the world economy operates today (and there is today a genuine *world* economy), and the extra-territorial economic elites who operate it, favour state organisms that *cannot* effectively impose conditions under which the economy is run, let alone impose restraints on the way in which those who run the economy would like it to be run; the economy is effectively transnational. In relation to virtually any state, big or small, most economic assets crucial for the daily life of its population are 'foreign' – or, given the removal of all constraints on capital transfers, may become foreign overnight, in case the local rulers naïvely deem themselves entitled to meddle. The divorce between political *autarchy* (real or imaginary) and economic *autarky* could not be more complete and seems to be irrevocable. Paul Valéry wrote not that long ago that 'les races et les nations ne se sont abordées que par des soldats, des apôtres et des marchands'. Though all three remain to a varying degree active, it is the traders who are active today as never before. This is precisely why the tiniest of populations may be gazed at hopefully by aspiring nation-builders as potential suppliers of the usual quota of ministries and embassies and professional educators. ('The fundamental reconstruction of the nation', as Fichte prophetically observed, 'is offered as a task to the educated classes.')[11]

Paradoxically, in the present era of cosmopolitan *economy* the splintering of *political* sovereignty becomes itself a major factor facilitating free movement of capital and commodities. The more fragmented are the sovereign units, the weaker and narrower in scope is their grip over their respective territories, the freer still is the global flow of capital and merchandise. World capital is no more interested in large, powerful, well armed states. The *globalization* of the economy and information and the *fragmentation* – indeed, a 're-parochialization' of sorts – of political sovereignty are not, contrary to appearances, opposite and hence mutually conflicting and incongruent trends; they are rather factors in the ongoing rearrangement of various aspects of systemic integration. Between themselves, the states police the orderly conditions in localities that increasingly become little more than transit stations in the world-wide travel of goods and money administered by the multi-national (more correctly: non-national, trans-national) executives. Whatever remains of economic management in state

---

[11] Johann Gottlieb Fichte, *Addresses to the German Nation*, trans. R. F. Jones and G. H. Turnbull (Westport, Conn.: Greenwood Press, 1979), p. 17.

politics is reduced to offering attractively profitable conditions (low taxes, low wages, frightened or pacified, docile labour, easy credit, high subsidies and low interest rates, and – last though not least – pleasant pastimes for all-expenses-paid travelling managers) that would hopefully tempt the touring capital to book a stopover in a given locality and stay there for a little longer than the refuelling of the aircraft demands.

The scramble for sovereignty becomes increasingly a competition for a better deal in the world-wide distribution of capital. This applies to both currently observed kinds of sovereignty claims: those coming from prosperous localities like Lombardy, Catalonia or Flanders, unwilling to share their boons and perks with poorer parts of the population who, as the state inexplicably insists, should be treated as brothers and sisters – as 'one nation' (The Slovenian and Czech Republics must cause insomnia among the leaders of the 'Northern League', showing what can be attained overnight if only the poorer brethren with their interminable clamouring for help were cut out, complete with the troubles they cause, in one fell swoop. The Czech Republic, for instance, can boast its economic miracle – 6 per cent growth expected in 1994, 3 per cent unemployed, nearly $7,000 GDP per capita – thanks to dumping its poor, the anachronistic part of its industry and its starved-for-credit agriculture to the graciously granted 'independence' of Slovakia – 7.6 per cent fall in GDP, 14 per cent unemployed, less than $5,000, and falling, GDP per capita); and those brought forth by impoverished localities like Scotland, objecting to what they see as too small a share in the wealth secured by the state as a whole. In both cases, the grievance is, at the start, economic. It is then followed by a frantic effort to collate and condense the scattered feelings of deprivation into the image of common fate and common cause; by a process of collective identity-building, to be used as effective cultural capital in the struggle for the 'devolution of state power'. A shared cultural identity is hoped to translate individually suffered deprivation into a collective effort at redress.

Significant cultural differences are at all times neither 'objectively given' nor can they be 'objectively obliterated' or levelled off. Cultural contents make a totality only in the form of a pool of tokens from which a volume of selections and combinations (in principle infinite) can be, and is, made. Most importantly, they serve as a raw material from which self-made identities are assembled; the truly significant cultural differences (those made visible, noticed, serving as orientation-points or labels for group integration, and jointly defended) are *products* of such identity-assembling processes. (As Ernest Gellner observed, 'For every effective nationalism there are several that are feeble or dormant. Those that go down are "objectively" as legitimate as the effective ones . . .')[12] It is the presence or absence of such processes, and their relative strength, which (always contentiously) elevates some dialects to the level of languages and reduces some languages to the level of dialects; which organizes the remembered or invented past in separate or shared traditions; which, in general, prompts imitative urges *vis-à-vis* some cultural tokens and imposes a ban on embracing the others. Indeed, as Eric Hobsbawm observed, the more defunct and ineffective is the past, the more it is 'liberated' for purely symbolic, mobilizing use.[13]

Identity needs tend today to be ever more acute (and more disjunctive than in the past) in the wake of the increasingly evident failure of the nation-states in their past role of identity-producers and suppliers. The identity-constructing function in which the established nation-states used to specialize may seek another carrier, and will seek it all the more zealously for the 'softness' of the available alternatives.

Moreover, the tools and resources the old established states of Europe deployed unscrupulously in promoting the 'one-state, one nation' principle are not available to the new, smaller and weaker political units entering an entirely different world in which one plays the sovereignty game by different rules. Cultural pluralism as a permanent condition of mankind, rather than a temporary nuisance and sign of backwardness, is the name of the game in which major players no more feel a missionary vocation nor feel threatened by variety of cultural taste and fashion. This new rendition of modern 'human rights' (previously translated as the right to be 'just human', to participate in universal 'human essence' – but today interpreted as, above all, the right to remain different) puts paid to the hope that one could get away with cultural crusades and other acts of oppression once normal and proper but today immediately denounced as criminal. To make things less promising still for the new 'sovereign states': with the growing number of sovereign units all over the place there is a virtual certainty that a minority inside one unit can call for

[12] Ernest Gellner, 'Ethnicity, Culture, Class and Power', in *Ethnic Diversity and Conflict in Eastern Europe*, ed. Peter F. Singer (Santa Barbara: ABC Clio, 1980), p. 260.
[13] See *The Invention of Tradition*, ed. Eric Hobsbawm and Terence Ranger (Cambridge University Press, 1983), p. 4.

assistance from another unit which happens to be its own 'sovereign state'; most minorities are majorities elsewhere. Most 'foreign populations' within the states are no more homeless or stateless, and so not politically powerless. (Recall how the assaults against 'local Turks' in Germany turned overnight into international conflict with the Turkish state.) One cannot really pretend that they are but lost sheep of the native flock and force them to rejoin the herd. Even less can one trample on their right to difference, or refuse political rights on the ground of that difference, without incurring the wrath of some nuisance-making neighbour and inviting sanctions from international bodies which would not allow the upstarts to do what the established had done in a past distant enough to be by now forgotten. With assimilation and enforced conversion no more viable or feasible, but 'human rights' still identified with the fiction of nation-state sovereignty, 'ethnic cleansing' is the name of the game for the new states who wish to become, just like their older examples, new nations.

When wringing our hands over the ethnic massacres in the territories no more smothered under the iron lids of the Pax Sovietica and Pax Titoica, let us remember that both the (now defunct) empires negligent of national sovereignty and the new self-proclaimed 'national states' vying to take their place operate in what C. A. Macartney already in 1934 called the 'belt of mixed population'; at the behest of the Treaty of Versailles, every state in that belt 'now looked upon itself as a national state. But the facts were against them . . . Not one of these states was in fact uni-national, just as there was not, on the other hand, one nation all of whose members lived in a single state' – an ideal starting point, in Hannah Arendt's words, to the 'transformation of the state from the instrument of the law into an instrument of the nation'[14] – and that means, more often than not, an instrument of national oppression, war and genocide.

With policies of enforced assimilation no more a viable prospect, the ideologies which presently accompany the strategies of the new tribalism and the associated policies of *exclusion* deploy, paradoxically,

---

[14]   Hannah Arendt, *The Origins of Totalitarianism* (London: André Deutsch, 1986), pp. 274–5. Arendt lays the blame unambiguously at the door of the League of Nations, fully dominated by old, well entrenched and secure states which at home made the identity of state and nation into a 'fact of life'. The Minority Treaty, which the League imposed on the new states born in the 'belt of mixed populations', 'said it in plain language . . . that only nationals could be citizens, only people of the same national origin could enjoy the full protection of legal institutions, that persons of different nationality needed some law of exception until or unless they were completely assimilated and divorced from their origin'.

the kind of language that was traditionally appropriated by the *inclusivist* cultural discourse. It is culture itself, rather than the hereditary collection of genes, which is represented by these ideologies as immutable: as both a unique entity which *should be* preserved intact, and a reality which *cannot* be significantly modified by any method of similar cultural provenance. Cultures, we are told, precede, form and define (each one in its own *unique* way) the selfsame Reason which previously was hoped to serve as the main weapon of cultural unification. Much like the castes or estates of the past, cultures may at best communicate and co-operate within the framework of the functional division of labour, but they can never mix, and they should not mix lest the precious identity of each should be compromised and eroded. It is not cultural *pluralism* and separatism, but cultural *proselytism* and the drive towards cultural unification that are now conceived of as 'unnatural', as an abnormality to be actively resisted.

No wonder contemporary preachers of exclusivist ideology disdainfully reject the racist label; they neither need nor deploy the argument of the genetic determination of human differences or the biological grounds of their hereditary continuity. And so their adversaries do not advance much the contrary case, the case of cohabitation and mutual tolerance, when they insist that the racist label fits. The true complexity of their task derives from the fact that the cultural discourse, once the domain of the liberal, assimilationist, *inclusivist* strategy, has been 'colonized' by the *exclusivist* ideology, and so the use of traditional 'culturalist' vocabulary no more guarantees the subversion of exclusivist strategy. As Julia Kristeva warned, for the first time in history we are doomed to live with our differences 'without any superior totality which embraces and transcends our particularities.'[15] We have not been in such a situation before, we do not know well how to act and what to expect.

The difficulty in warding off the ascent of militant regionalism and ethnicity stems partly from the ambivalence inherent in the European vision itself. In Henri Brugmans' words,

> L'Européen sait sans doute que la révolte régionale actuelle peut éventuellement dégénér en un nationalisme à dimensions réduites. Mais il sait ausssi que cette révolte se dirige aujourd'hui contre l'étatisme national, qui demeure l'ennemi numéro un de l'Europe . . . [U]ne nation politique . . . est une prison d'autant plus néfaste que ses justifications pratiques disparaissent.[16]

[15]   Julia Kristeva, *Étrangers à nous-mêmes* (Paris: Fayard, 1988), p. 290.
[16]   Henri Brugmans, *L'Idée européenne, 1920–1970* (Bruges: De Tempel, 1979), pp. 360, 39.

The other roots of the present weakness of the so called 'anti-racist' cause so poignantly felt throughout Europe lie in the profound transformation of the cultural discourse itself. Within the framework of that discourse, it has become exceedingly difficult (as they say – 'politically incorrect') to advance without contradiction (and without risking a charge of criminal practice) an argument against the permanence of human differentiation and the practice of categorial separation, an argument against confusing ethnic and political senses of the nation, and thus undermining political equality and universality in the name of ethnic egoism.

(This text is an edited and supplemented version of the Peace Lecture, delivered at Manchester University on 10 March 1994.)

8.3　An Epilogue: Threats and Chances, Old and New

(This is an edited version of "Alone Again: ethics after certainty," published by Demos, 1994).

Max Frisch

The great Danish theologist and moral philosopher Knud Løgstrup mused: 'It is a characteristic of human life that we mutually trust each other . . . Only because of some special circumstance do we ever distrust a stranger in advance . . . Initially we believe one another's word; initially we trust one another.'

Not so another great religious philosopher, Russian refugee and professor at the Sorbonne, Leon Shestov: '*Homo homini lupus* is one of the most steadfast maxims of eternal morality. In each of our neighbours we fear a wolf . . . We are so poor, so weak, so easily ruined and destroyed! How can we help being afraid! . . . We see danger, danger only . . .'

Surely, Løgstrup and Shestov cannot both be right. Or can they? True, they contradict each other, but don't we all get contradictory signals from what we ourselves have lived through? Sometimes we trust, sometimes we fear. More often than not, we are not sure whether to trust and disarm, or to sniff out danger and be on guard – and then we are confused and no longer sure what to do. Of which has there been more in our lives – trust or fear? The answer seems to depend on the kind of life we have lived.

Løgstrup was born and died in tranquil, serene, peaceful Copenhagen, where the royals bicycled the streets together with their sub-jects and when they finished the ride left their bicycles on the pave-ment, knowing that, because of the absence of thieves, the bicycles would be there when they needed them again. Shestov was hunted down and refused a university post by the tsarist regime for *being born* in a wrong faith, then hunted down and exiled by the anti-tsarist revolution for *professing* a wrong faith, then drank his fill from the bitter chalice of exile in a foreign country . . . The two wise men reported two stridently different experiences. Their generalizations contradicted each other, but so did the lives they generalized from.

And this seems to apply to all of us. We generalize from what we see. Whenever we say 'people are what they are', what we mean is the people we meet; people shaped and moved and guided by the world they and we together happen to inhabit. And if we say once that people can be trusted, and another time that they are wolves to be feared, and if both statements ring true or at least partly true, then it seems that what people are – or, rather, what they appear to be – depends, wholly or in part, on the kind of world they and we live in. Moreover, if what we think about each other reflects what we are, it is also true that what we are is itself a reflection of what we believe ourselves to be; the image we hold of each other and of all of us together has the uncanny ability to self-corroborate. People treated like wolves tend by and large to behave in a wolf-like fashion; people treated with trust tend on the whole to become trustworthy. What we think of each other does matter.

We would never know for sure whether 'people as such' are good or evil (though perhaps we will go on and on quarrelling about it, as if the truth could be known). But it does matter whether we believe them to be 'basically' good or evil, wishing to be *moral* or revelling in *immorality*, and consequently how we treat them. What matters even more is whether people are trusted with the *capacity for making moral judgements*, and consequently considered to be *moral subjects* – that is, persons *capable of bearing moral responsibility*, not just a legal one, for their deeds.

The story so far . . .

In 1651, at the dawn of what later came to be known as the modern era, Thomas Hobbes passed a verdict which was to guide the thought and action of modern legislators, educators and moral preachers:

> ... men have no pleasure (but on the contrary a great deale of griefe) in keeping company, where there is no power to overawe them all ... And upon all signes of contempt, or undervaluing, naturally endeavours, as far as he dares (which amongst them that have no common power to keep them in quiet, is far enough to make them destroy each other,) to extort a greater value from its contemners, by dommage ...
>
> Hereby it is manifest, that during the time men live without a common Power to keep them all in awe, they are in that condition which we called Warre; and such a warre, as if of every man, against every man ...

The message was straightforward: if you wish men to be moral, you must force them to be such. Only under the threat of pain will men stop paining each other. To stop fearing each other, men must fear a power superior to them all.

The corollary was another briefing: you cannot build on people's impulses, inclinations, predispositions. Their passions (that is, all passions except the passion for a better life, the one passion that lends itself to logic and reason) must instead be rooted out or stifled. Instead of following their *feelings*, people should be taught, and forced if need be – to *calculate*. In a moral world, only the voice of reason should be heard. And a world in which only the voice of reason is heard is a moral world.

Thus arose the great divide which was to become the trademark of modern living: one between reason and emotion, taken to be the substance and the foundation of all life-and-death choices: like those between order and chaos, civilized life and the war of all against all. In particular, the divide separated the regular, predictable and controllable – from the contingent, erratic, unpredictable and getting out of hand. Indeed, for every problem there is by definition one, and only one, true, reason-dictated solution, but a virtually infinite variety of erroneous ones; where reason does not rule, 'anything may happen', and thus the whole situation is hopelessly beyond control.

The moral world can only be, therefore, a *regular, orderly* world. (An 'orderly' world is one in which the probabilities of events are not random; some events are considerably more probable than others, while some others have virtually nil chance of happening.) *Moral* persons cannot be buffeted by erratic impulses; they can only be guided, consistently and in a systematic fashion – by laws, rules, norms, principles which clearly specify what in a given situation one should do and what one should desist from. Morality, like the rest of social life, must be founded on *Law*, there must be an *ethical code* behind morality, consisting of prescriptions and prohibitions. Teaching or coercing people to be moral means making them obey that ethical code. By this reasoning, 'becoming moral' is equivalent to learning, memorizing and following the *rules*.

Modernity came up with two great institutions meant to achieve that purpose – that is, to secure the prevalence of morality through rule-following. One was bureaucracy, the other was business. The two institutions differ from each other in many respects, and often are at loggerheads with each other, but they agree on one quite seminal thing: they are both bent on the eradication of emotions or at least keeping them off-limits. Since they are enemies of affection, they have both been hailed since their inception as incarnations of rationality and instruments of rationalization. Each embarked on achieving the same effect in its own fashion.

Bureaucracy has been described by its theorists, beginning with Max Weber, as the typically modern (and advanced) way of doing things; particularly, when a complex task needs division of skills and labour of many people, each doing but a part of the task and not necessarily aware of what the whole task consists of, all efforts must be dovetailed and co-ordinated so that the overall objective may be reached. The specifically bureaucratic way of running things is founded on a strict chain of command and an equally strict definition of the roles ascribed to every link in the chain. The global task, visible in full only from the top, is divided and subdivided as the command descends towards the lower levels of the hierarchy; and once the bottom level of direct performance is reached, performers are faced with fairly straightforward and predictable choices. Now, this ideal model can work properly only on the condition that all people involved in the work of the organization follow the commands they receive and are guided by them only. (Their actions are, as it is sometimes said 'rule-guided'.) And that means that people would not be diverted by their personal beliefs and convictions or by emotions – sympathy or antipathy – to their fellow workers or to the individual clients or objects of action. Everybody's action must be totally *impersonal*; indeed, it should not be oriented to *persons* at all, but to the *rules*, which specify the procedure.

This kind of action directed by a codified reason of rules is described as *procedural rationality*. What counts is following the procedure to the letter. What is more than anything else decried and punished is the twisting of the procedure to suit individual preferences or affections. No wonder; even the most painstakingly worked-out plan of complementary actions would not count for much, were personal emotions given a free run. Indeed, those 'affections' which co-workers in an organization are required to lock up in their closets before clocking-in stand for the choices which are erratic, rule-free, and hence impossible to predict and even less to control. Emotions come from nowhere and without notice; and when they come, it is virtually impossible to fight them back. One cannot commission emotions to order, neither can one send them away. Reason, calculation, memorizing the contents of the statute books, the most painstaking design – won't help here.

It is not just the wayward, 'centrifugal' sentiments that are unwelcome. To be effective, organization does not need affection of its members, nor their approval for the goals it genuinely or putatively serves and the task it performs. Were the members' readiness to fulfil their duty grounded in their enthusiasm for the declared purposes of their joint activity – their performance would depend on how they see the organization's loyalty to the ends it allegedly promotes; they would, so to speak, watch the hands of the givers of the command, measure each order against its ostensible purposes and real effects, and in the end may disagree with what they see as their superiors' genuine intentions and even disobey the orders. Thus, consent to the objectives of the organization one works for is not needed, let alone welcomed; making it a requirement would prove downright harmful.

To work effectively organizations need (and thus promote) only two kinds of affection: a 'do not rock the boat' kind of loyalty to the corporation and a readiness to fulfil one's duty (whatever the job one is told to perform, providing the command to perform it was 'legitimate', that is came from the right source and through the right channels); and loyalty to fellow members – the 'we are all in one boat' feeling, the 'I cannot let them down' attitude. These are the only two emotions 'procedural rationality' needs – and in order to secure them, all other emotions must be toned down or chased out of court.

The most prominent among the exiled emotions are moral sentiments: that resilient and unruly 'voice of conscience' that may prompt one to help the sufferer and to abstain from causing suffering. Conscience may tell one that the action one was told to take is wrong – even if it is procedurally correct. Or that a quite different kind of action is right, even if from the point of view of the binding procedure it is 'irregular'. And if the voice is strong and other voices which could muffle it are weak, the fate of the corporate action will now be at the mercy of the moral sentiments of the individual performers. Organizations defend themselves against such an eventuality in two ways.

The first is a phenomenon that may be described as *responsibility-floating*. Providing that the member of the organization followed the rules faithfully and did what his proper superiors told him to do – it is not he who bears responsibility for whatever effect his action may have had on its objects. Who does, then? The question is notoriously mind-boggling, as every other member of the organization also follows procedure and commands ... It seems, said Hannah Arendt, that the organization is ruled by *nobody* – that is, is moved only by the impersonal logic of self-propelling principles. This is not, however, the only problem – as to pinpoint responsibility is even more difficult because of the minute division of labour. Each member contributing to the final effects performs, more often than not, actions that by themselves are quite innocuous, and would not – could not – cause the effects in question without the complementary actions of many other people. In a large-scale organization most members do not even see (or hear of) the ultimate, remote and always oblique results that they helped to achieve. So they may go on feeling moral and decent persons (which they mostly are when hobnobbing with their near and dear) while helping to commit the most gruesome cruelties.

The second is the tendency to *adiaphorization* – to declare that most things which members of organizations are expected to do when in service are exempt from moral evaluation – are, so to speak, ethically indifferent, neither good or bad; only correct or incorrect. This does not mean contesting commonly held moral opinions – but to declare, bluntly, that categories of 'good' and 'evil' are neither here nor there when it comes to the implementation of organizational duties. The sole standards by which such duties can be judged are those of *procedural correctness*; if they pass this muster, there is no other test left to which they could conceivably be put. When 'ethics' appears in the vocabulary of bureaucracy, it is in connection with 'professional ethics'; the latter is considered breached when a member shows disloyalty to the organization (by leaking secret information, using his office for purposes not foreseen by the statute books, or otherwise allowing outside interests to interfere with discipline), or disloyalty to colleagues (charges of this kind are more often than not raised on the initiative of members who believe they have been given a rough deal, were offended or harmed; the language of ethics, notoriously less exact than that of the codified rules, is reverted to whenever defined competences are open to multiple and contentious interpretations).

All in all, the modern organization is a contraption designed to make human actions immune to what the actors believe and feel privately. Here, discipline is the sole responsibility which puts paid to all other responsibilities, while the ethical code spelling out one's duties toward the organization pre-empts the moral questions which could be addressed to the members' behaviour. In other words, the modern organization is a way of doing things that is free from moral constraints. Because of that, cruel deeds of a kind from which individual members acting on their own would most certainly recoil in horror can be in principle perpetrated by modern organizations. Even if this does not happen, though, one harmful effect is virtually unavoidable: people who come within the orbit of bureaucratic action cease to be responsible moral subjects, are deprived of their moral autonomy and are trained not to exercise (or trust) their moral judgement. They are cast in what the American psychologist Stanley Milgram called the 'agentic state' – in which they cease, at least for the duration, to be responsible for their actions and the consequences of their actions – and plug their ears tightly so as not to hear the voice of conscience.

If the *procedural* rationality is the constructive principle of organization – the *instrumental* rationality is what makes business tick. Here are the ends, here are the means; here are the resources, here are the effects one can achieve if one applies them wisely. Means are to be used to the greatest possible effect; there is no greater crime in the business world than the 'underuse' of resources, letting some assets which could 'work' and 'bring results' lie fallow and rust. How much the available means may bring in is the only question one can ask about their alternative uses. Other questions – moral questions prominent among them – are given short shrift in advance; they are dismissed on the grounds that they 'do not make business sense', the only sense business may recognize. (Doubts may be raised as to the truth of the last statement; do we not hear of 'ethical investment trusts' or 'green products'? Do we not read of companies carrying the torch of progress, bringing tomorrow's technology to today's people, or otherwise concerned with making our life better? We do; but mostly in such cases, speaking the language of morality itself 'makes good business sense' and helps to free the use of resources from political constraint; sometimes, as in the case of 'environment-friendly' consumer products, moral argument proves to be an excellent selling point.)

There is no denying that business, just like bureaucracy, is eager to spell out and to guard its own special kind of morality, sometimes called 'business ethics'. The paramount value of that ethics is honesty – which, as the small print shows, is mostly concerned with keeping promises and abiding by contractual obligations. Without such honesty, business cannot survive; by insisting that all sides to the

contract ought to be bound by the 'honesty' principle, business partners defend themselves against the danger of being conned or short-
changed. Even more importantly, though, they create for themselves
a relatively orderly, predictable environment without which instru-
mentally rational decision-making would be inconceivable. And yet, as
with any ethical code, 'business ethics' is as much about declaring certain kinds of conduct ethically imperative, as about making other
kinds of action, by commission or by omission, ethically neutral,
or not moral issues at all. The code spells out how far honesty must
reach and when one can say that s/he was 'honest enough'. Everything stretching beyond this boundary is of no concern for business
ethics; a businessperson has the right to consider himself or herself
perfectly within the moral duty while not worrying about them.

Modern times started with separating business from the household. Indeed, without such a separation the instrumental logic of
business would be forever contaminated, and cramped, by moral
obligations; inside the household, goods are given to people *because
of* who those people are – children, sisters, parents – and not *in order
to* attain the gains the giver hopes to achieve. To make 'business
sense', on the other hand, assets must be allocated 'to the highest
bidder' – not to those who may need them most, but to those who
are prepared to give most in exchange. Who the highest bidder is,
what are his credentials and entitlements (except his solvency, of
course), should not matter – lest the resources be not put to the best
use. In business there are no friends and no neighbours (though 'good
commercial sense' prompts one to pretend that there are). It helps if
the partner in a transaction is a complete stranger and remains such,
since only then may instrumental rationality gain the uncontested
ascendancy it needs; knowing too much of her or him may – who
knows? – beget a personal, emotional relationship, which will inevitably confuse and becloud the judgement.

But the logic of business which rules unfettered contemporary
markets breeds also oblivion and indifference to anything not relevant to the instrumental task at hand, everything extending beyond
the immediate space and time of action. In the poignant and perceptive
analysis of Geoff Mulgan,

> all markets bring very strong incentives to evade responsibilities; to pass
> costs on to the community and to devalue the future and what is left to
> later generations. Property rights foster care within narrow limits but only
> at the price of carelessness in relation to the rest of society, Moreover, the
> market's moral persuasiveness is corroded when almost any action can be
> justified as a response to 'market discipline' and when almost any provider

of an amoral product or service can claim that the real fault lies with the demands of the general public.

Moral devastation, not moral progress is the consequence of waiting for the 'deregulated' markets to 'bring out the best in people'; in Mulgan's words, 'selfishness and greed, and corruption in government and business, came to be the hallmarks of the neoconservative era.'

Like the *esprit de corps* of corporative bureaucracy, the spirit of business militates against sentiments, moral sentiments most prominent among them. Business interests cannot easily be squared with the sense of responsibility for the welfare and well-being of those who may find themselves affected by the business pursuit of greatest effects. In business language, 'rationalization' means more often than not laying off people who used to derive their livelihood from serving the business task before. They are now 'redundant', because a more effective way to use the assets has been found – and their past services do not count for much: each business transaction, to be truly rational, must start from scratch, forgetting past merits and debts of gratitude. Business rationality shirks responsibility for its own consequences, and this is another mortal blow to the influence of moral considerations. The horrors of inner cities, mean streets, once thriving and now dying communities orphaned by business ventures which used to keep them alive, but now – for the soundest and most rational of reasons – moved to greener pastures, are not victims of exploitation, but of abandonment resulting from *moral indifference*.

Bureaucracy strangles or criminalizes moral impulses; business merely pushes them aside. Horrified by the totalitarian tendencies ingrained in every bureaucracy, Orwell sounded an alarm against the prospect of 'a boot stamping on a human face – for ever'. An apt metaphor for the business variety of morality-bashing would be perhaps 'blinkers eternally preventing a human face from being seen'. The short-term consequences for people exposed to one or other of the two strategies may be starkly different, yet the long-term results are quite similar: taking moral issues off the agenda, sapping the moral autonomy of the acting subject, undermining the principle of moral responsibility for the effects, however distant and indirect, of one's deeds. Neither modern organization nor modern business promotes morality; if anything, they make the life of the stubbornly moral person tough and unrewarding.

Reflecting on the perpetrators' inability not just to admit, but to comprehend their responsibility for the Holocaust crimes (these people were, after all, merely following orders . . . There was that task to be fulfilled, that job to be done . . . They could not let their mates down . . .), Hannah Arendt, a most acute interrogator of the ethical accomplishments and neglects of the modern era, demanded that 'human beings be capable of telling right from wrong even if all they have to guide them is their own judgement, which, moreover, happens to be completely at odds with what they must regard as the unanimous opinion of all these around them . . .'

However nebulous such a demand may seem in the world dominated by bureaucracy and business, Arendt saw in it the last hope of morality, and in all probability the only realistic (however tenuous) strategy to recover for morality the ground from which it has been exiled. In the effort to meet that demand, 'there are no rules to abide by . . . as there are no rules for the unprecedented'. In other words, no one else but the moral person himself or herself must take responsibility for his or her own moral responsibility . . .

. . . and the beginning of a new story

The story so far has not been just about bygone times; the bureaucratic spirit of large corporations and 'business ethics' remain very much salient marks of our times and obituaries to the moral dangers they portend would most certainly be grossly premature. They are no more, however, the sole sources of the twin processes of 'moral adiaphorization' and 'flotation of responsibility' – both of which are still going strong, though taking somewhat new forms. There are quite a few new elements in the emerging human situation, which in all probability carry far-reaching moral consequences.

These new elements stem from the overall tendency to dismantle, deregulate, dissipate the once solid and relatively lasting frames in which life-concerns and efforts of most individuals were inscribed (analysed already in chapter 3). Let us repeat: jobs, formerly seen as being 'for life', are more often than not merely temporary and may disappear virtually without notice, together with the factories or offices of bank branches that offered them. Even the skills which the jobs required are ageing fast, turning overnight from assets into liabilities. Being prudent and provident, thinking of the future, become ever more difficult, as there is little sense in accumulating skills for which tomorrow there may be no demand, or saving money which tomorrow may lose much of its purchasing power. At the moment young men and women enter the game of life, none can tell what the rules of the game will be like as time goes by; what everybody can be pretty sure of is that they will change many times over before the game is finished.

The world, in other words, seems less solid than it used to be (or than we thought it to be). It has lost its apparent unity and continuity – when various aspects of life could be tied together into a meaningful whole, and what happened today could be traced back to yesterday's roots and forward to tomorrow's consequences. What most of us learn from our experience now is that all forms in the world around us, however solid they may seem, are not immune to change; that things burst into attention without warning and then disappear or sink into oblivion without trace; that what is all the rage today becomes the butt of ridicule tomorrow; that what is vaunted and recommended and hammered home today is treated with disdain tomorrow – that is, if still remembered; that, on the whole, time is cut into episodes – each with a beginning and an end but with neither pre-history nor future; that there is little or no logical connection between the episodes, even their succession looking suspiciously as though purely coincidental, contingent and random; and that, much as they come from nowhere, episodes go by and away without leaving lasting consequences. In other words, the world we live in (and help to bring about through our life-pursuits) appears to be marked by *fragmentarity, discontinuity* and *inconsequentiality*.

In such a world it is wise and prudent not to make long-term plans or invest in the distant future (one can never guess what the attractiveness of the presently seductive goals or the value of today's assets will then be); not to get tied down too firmly to any particular place, group of people, cause, even an image of oneself, lest one find oneself not just unanchored and drifting but without an anchor altogether; to be guided in today's choices not by the wish to *control* the future, but by the reluctance to *mortgage* it. In other words, 'to be provident' means now more often than not to *avoid commitment*. To be free to move when opportunity knocks. To be free to leave when it stops knocking.

Today's culture reiterates what each of us learns, joyfully or grudgingly, from our own experience. It presents the world as a collection of fragments and episodes, with one image chasing away and replacing the one before, only to be replaced itself the next moment. Celebrities emerge daily and daily vanish, only very few leaving footprints on the memory track. Problems commanding attention are born by the hour and slip away as soon as they are born – together with the popular concern they gave birth to. Attention has become the scarcest of resources. In the words of George Steiner, our culture has turned into a sort of a 'cosmic casino', where everything is calculated 'for maximal impact and instant obsolescence'; maximal impact, since the constantly shocked imagination has become *blasé* and to spur it on ever more powerful shocks are needed, each one more shattering than the one before; and instant obsolescence, since attention has limited capacity and the room must be made to absorb new celebrities, fashions, foibles, or 'problems'.

Marshall McLuhan is remembered for coining the phrase 'The medium is the message' – meaning that whatever the content of the message, the qualities of the medium that conveyed it is itself a message (though hidden and surreptitious), and as a rule more seminal than the content of the overt communication. One may say that if the medium that was the message of modern times was photographic paper, its equivalent for the new times is videotape. Photographic paper can be used once only – there is no second chance. But when used, it retains the trace for a long time to come – in practical terms 'forever'. Think of the family album, filled with yellowing portraits of grand- and great-grandfathers and mothers, innumerable aunts and uncles, all with a name attached, *all counting and to be reckoned with*, all adding their stones to the castle of the slowly accumulating family tradition, in which no part can be taken away or eradicated, in which everything is for better or worse – forever . . . And think now of the videotape, made in such a way as to be erased, and reused, and reused again: to record whatever may seem interesting or amusing at the moment, but keep it no longer than the interest lasts – after all, it is bound to wane. If the photographic paper oozed the message that deeds and things matter, tend to last and have consequences, that they tend to tie together and affect each other – the videotape exudes the message that all things exist by themselves and count merely until further notice, that each episode starts from scratch, and whatever its consequences may be they can still be erased without trace, leaving the tape virgin-clean. Or, to use a different metaphor for the difference between the two 'spirit of the time' messages, one may say that if the catchword of modern times was *creation*, the catchword of our times is *recycling*. Or again: if the favourite building material of modernity was steel and concrete, today it is rather biodegradable plastic.

What are the consequences for morality? Quite obviously, enormous. To take a moral stance means to assume responsibility for the Other; to act on the assumption that the well-being of the Other is a precious thing calling for my effort to preserve and enhance it, that whatever I do or do not do affects it, that if I have not done it it might not be done at all, and that even if others do or can do it this does not cancel my responsibility for doing it myself . . . As the greatest ethical philosopher of our century, Emmanuel Lévinas, puts it – morality means *being-for* (not merely being-aside or even being-with) the Other. And this being-for is unconditional (that is, if it is *to be moral*, not merely *contractual*) – it does not depend on what the Other is, or does, whether s/he deserves my care and whether s/he repays in kind. One cannot conceive of an argument that could justify the renunciation of moral responsibility – putting it into cold storage, lending or pawning it. And one cannot imagine a point of which one could say with any sort of moral right: I have done my share, and here my responsibility ends.

If this is what morality is about, it certainly does not square well with the discontinuous, fragmentary, episodic, consequences-avoiding life. Ours is the age of what Anthony Giddens perceptively described as 'pure relationship' which 'is entered for its own sake, for what can be derived by each person' and so 'it can be terminated, more or less at will, by either partner at any particular point'; of 'confluent love' which 'jars with the "for-ever", "one-and-only" qualities of the romantic love complex' so that 'romance can no longer be equated with permanence'; of 'plastic sexuality', that is sexual enjoyment 'severed from its age-old integration with reproduction, kinship and the generations'. We can see that to keep the options open, to be free to move, is the guiding principle of all three. 'I need more space' is the curt yet common excuse used by all those who do move away – meaning 'I do not wish others to intrude, also such others as I wished and thus allowed yesterday to intrude; I wish to be concerned solely with myself, with what is good and desirable for me.' Whoever seeks more space, must be careful not to commit him/herself, and particularly not to allow the commitment to outlast the pleasure which can be derived from it. S/he must therefore cleanse the acts from possible consequences, and if consequences do follow, then – and in advance – refuse all responsibility for them.

The life of modern man was frequently likened to the pilgrimage-through-time. The itinerary of a pilgrim is drawn in advance by the destination he wants to reach (which in the case of modern man's life is the ideal image of his vocation, of his identity) – and everything he does is calculated to bring him closer to the goal. The pilgrim is consistent in choosing every successive step, conscious that each step matters and the sequence cannot be reversed. Today's men and women can hardly treat their life as a pilgrimage, even if they wished to. One can plan one's life as a journey-to-a-destination only in a world of which one can sensibly hope that its chart will remain the same or little changed throughout one's life-time – and this is blatantly not the case today. Instead, the life of men and women of our times is more like that of tourists-through-time: they cannot and would not decide in advance what places they will visit and what the sequence of stations will be; what they know for sure is just that they will keep on the move, never sure whether the place they have reached is their final destination. Whoever knows that is unlikely to strike deep roots in any of the places and develop too strong an attachment to the locals. What s/he is likely to do is to treat each place as a temporary stay, significant only through the satisfactions s/he derives from it; but s/he must be ready to move again, whenever satisfaction diminishes or whenever greener pastures beckon elsewhere.

In other words, the 'I need space' strategy militates against a moral stance. It denies the moral significance of even the most intimate inter-human action. As a result, it exempts core elements of human interrelationships from moral evaluation. It *adiaphorizes* the parts of human existence which the adiaphorizing mechanisms of bureaucracy and business could not (or did not need, or wish, to) reach . . .

As in the case of the older forms of neutralizing moral evaluations and responsibility-floating, this is not a situation that can be rectified by moral preachers (not by preachers acting alone at any rate). Its roots lie deep in the life-context of contemporary men and women; it represents, one may say, a kind of 'rational adaptation' to the new conditions in which life is lived. These conditions favour some strategies while making other strategies terribly difficult to follow. The odds against taking a moral stance and sticking to it through thick and thin are formidable – all the socially generated pressures sap the emotional bonds between people favouring free-floating agents. Nothing short of changing the odds will regain for morality the areas now 'emancipated from moral constraints'. Everyone with ethical concerns had better take account of where the roots of problems really are and what is truly involved in the task of moral improvement.

The chances of moral togetherness

Michael Schluter and David Lee, shrewd observers of the moral plight of contemporary men and women, caustically commented on the way we tend to live today:

> We wear privacy like a pressure suit, Given half the chance we'll stuff the seat next to ours in a café with raincoats and umbrellas, stare unremittingly at posters about measles in a doctor's waiting room . . . Anything but invite encounter; anything but get involved . . .
>
> . . . [T]he home itself has grown lean and mean, wider families being broken up into nuclear and single-parent units where the individual's desires

and interests characteristically take precedence over those of the group. Unable to stop treading on each other's toes in the mega-community, we have stepped into our separate houses and closed the door, and then stepped into our separate rooms and closed the door. The home becomes a multi-purpose leisure centre where household members can live, as it were, separately side by side. Not just the gas industry but life in general has been privatised.

Separately side by side. Privatized. Sharing space, but not thoughts or sentiments – and acutely aware that in all probability they do not share the same fate either. This awareness does not necessarily breed resentment or hatred, but it certainly propagates aloofness and indifference. 'I do not want to get involved' is what we say more often than not to silence the inchoate emotions and nip in the bud the shoots of as deeper, intimate human relationship of the 'for richer and poorer, till death us do part' kind. Ever more ingenious locks, bolts and burglar alarms are the rage of the day and one of the few growth industries – not just for their genuine or putative practical uses, but for their symbolic value: inwardly, they mark the boundary of the hermitage where we won't be disturbed, while outwardly they communicate our decision: 'For all I care, outside could be a wasteland.'

The French film *La Crise* is a story of a few days in the life of a prosperous and self-confident lawyer who wakes up to find that his wife has left him and his boss has fired him, together with seven other prosperous and self-confident colleagues, in a bout of 'rationalization'. The hero is devastated; he visits one by one all his friends to share his grief and to find comfort. Each friend in succession meets him with similar griefs of his or her own: broken marriage, the evaporation of what seemed to be the safest job in the world, the cohesive world falling apart . . . The hero comes to realize slowly that no one listens to his story, preoccupied with the story of his/her own; in some scenes the conversation consists of two or three people repeating virtually identical lines, and the lines in each case report an experience uncannily similar to other experiences – yet the experiences are so impossible, apparently, to share . . . The dialogue is a collection of monologues, people talk with each other but not to each other; theirs is a mechanical co-ordination instead of sharing, the suffering coming from the same cause does not add up into a common cause against that common cause . . .

Of this deepening aloofness and indifference, some of the causes we have explored. Not all, though. 'Privatization of life in general' has long tentacles and reaches far and wide. Privatized life, like any other life, is never unremitting bliss. It has its measure of suffering, discontent, grievance. In a privatized life, however, misfortune is as private as everything else. Misfortunes of privatized singles do not add up, each one pointing as if in a different direction and each calling for different remedies. In our privatized society, grievances seem to point in widely divergent directions and even clash with each other; they seldom cumulate and condense into a common cause. In a shifting, drifting world – what possible benefit can an individual derive from joining forces with other pieces of flotsam?

Norbert Elias pondered on the lessons one might draw from Edgar Allan Poe's famous story of the three seamen caught in the maelstrom. In the story, two of the seamen died – not so much sucked in by the raging sea, as pushed down by their own paralysis born of despair and fear – while the third, having cast an alert eye around and noticed that round objects tend to float rather than being drawn into the whirl, promptly jumped into a barrel and survived. Good for him. But, since the time of Diogenes, barrels are notorious symbols of the ultimate withdrawal from the world, the ultimate individual retreat (in a barrel, there is no room for an-other . . .). Norbert Elias intended his commentary as a consolation: look, even in the midst of storm reason will point the way out . . . But note that the message which reason whispers in this particular storm is: each one of you, look for a barrel to hide in.

Recent years have been marked by the slow yet relentless dismantling or weakening of agencies which used to institutionalize the *commonality* of fate, and their replacement with institutions expressing and promoting the *diversity* of fate. The intended or unintended effect of the process is the recasting of the community (and communal action in general), from the pledge of the individual's security it used to be, into the individual's burden and bane; an extra load to carry, adding little to one's personal weal, yet something one cannot, regrettably, easily shake off though one would dearly like to. More and more, we confront the community, common needs and common causes solely in the capacity of taxpayers; it is no more a question of our shared responsibility for, and collective insurance against, everyone's mishap and misfortune – but a question of how much it will cost me to provide for those who cannot provide for themselves. *Their* claims testify to the fact that they are *spongers*, though – wonder of wonders – *my* (understandable . . .) wish to pay less into the kitty most emphatically does not . . . It is only natural that the taxpayer wants to pay less taxes. (Just as a beast of burden wants the burden to be smaller.) The outcome is, of course, that the quality of services collectively provided slides down a steep slope. And then everyone who can afford the price of a barrel buys one and jumps into it. If we can, we buy ourselves individually out of the underprovided, shabby schools, the overcrowded, undernourished hospitals, the miserly state old-age pensions – as we have already bought ourselves, with consequences which most of us belatedly bewail, out of the shrinking and wilting public transport. The more we do so, the more reasons we have for doing it, as the schools grow shabbier, the hospital queues longer, and old-age provisions more miserly still; and the fewer reasons we see to make sacrifices for the sake of those who failed to follow our suit. Were Marie Antoinette miraculously transported into this world of ours, she would probably say: 'They complain that the common boat has got rusty and no more seaworthy? Why would they not buy barrels?'

There is a point somewhere down the slope, now perhaps passed, at which people are no longer able to conceive of any benefit they could derive from joining forces: of any improvement which could come from managing a part of the money jointly, rather than individually. (For many years now, the burden of taxation, though showing no signs of lessening, has been shifted steadily from taxing income to taxing consumption; the trend is widely applauded and welcomed – as many people seem to enjoy the brief interlude of 'freedom' between cashing a cheque and signing another one.) The weaker and less reliable are the guarantees of individual security communally offered, the less justified and more burdensome seem the communal claims for joint effort and sacrifice. It is now more often than not a 'your value for my money' situation. And as the numbers of those who give money overtake the numbers of those deprived of value, the fate of the 'spongers' is sealed. Their claims and grievances have every chance of being voted off the agenda – freely, democratically, by the majority of the beneficiaries of our universal right to vote.

The neglect of the less fortunate is not, though, the only result. It can only come, as it does, together with the general fading and demise of the community spirit. If politics (things that are discussed and decided in the *agora*, where all those interested may congregate and speak) is about things of *common* interest and significance, who needs politics when interests and meanings keep steering apart? Interest in politics always had its ups and downs, but now we seem to witness a totally new strain of the electoral-apathy virus. Today's disenchantment seems to reach deeper than the old-time frustration with promises ill kept or programmes lacking in vision. It hits politics as such. It shows that the majority of the electors no more see why they should be bothered. In this privatized world, so little seems to depend on what 'they' say or even do out there, during these increasingly soap-opera-like performances at Westminster or in those smoke-clean rooms behind the thick and impenetrable walls of the mythical Whitehall . . . Almost everything of public significance has been, after all, privatized, deregulated and cut out of political control. The small print in privatization bills spelled out the end of politics as we used to know it: the kind of politics that needed to involve and engage its citizens.

In one of the most perceptive studies of the contemporary plight of democracy, edited by John Dunn, Quentin Skinner points out that the 'connection drawn by the ideologists of the city-republics between freedom and participation' is by now a largely forgotten lesson, replaced today by the insinuation that 'our civic liberties are best secured not by involving ourselves in politics but rather by erecting around ourselves a cordon of rights beyond which our rulers must not trespass', as if the two tasks could be attended to and performed separately . . .

We have heard recently quite a lot about the manifold 'citizens' charters' ostensibly aimed at recognizing and awakening the citizen dozing in each of us. The remarkable thing about the charters is, however, that they construe that citizen-sleeper not as a person eager to assume responsibility for issues larger than his private needs and desires, but as a consumer of services provided by agencies s/he has little right and no interest to examine, let alone supervise. Citizens' charters promote that image of the citizen by defining citizens' rights as first and foremost, perhaps even solely, the right of the customer to be satisfied. This includes the right to complain and to compensation. This does not include, conspicuously, the right to look into the inner workings of the agencies complained about and expected to pay the compensation – much less the right to tell them what to do and according to what principles.

There is a sort of a vicious circle, when increasingly privatized life feeds a lack of interest in politics, while the politics set free from constraints thanks to that disinterest is busy deepening the privatization, thus breeding more indifference; or perhaps this is a case of a Gordian knot so twisted that one can no more say where the string of determinations starts and where it leads to. The chances, therefore, that moral responsibilities eroded at the grass-roots level will be resuscitated by a moral vision promoted by the eroded institutions of the commonwealth, are slim. The odds against are enormous.

The new community?

Few if any grievances or hopes are nowadays addressed to the government of the country – not with much realistic expectation of being acted upon, anyway. No more is the government seen (as Neal Ascherson put it) as existing to 'shield the weak against the strong, to provide employment and redress regional imbalances, to prime the pumps which would eventually gush forth new industries and better educated citizens'. Like everything else, grievances and hopes have been privatized and deregulated. In Britain the tendency has been exacerbated by the ongoing devastation of the 'middle-range' institutions – local and corporative agencies of self-government. So much power has been taken away from the town halls, so little depends on what they do, so toothless have trade unions become after being barred from performing their traditional function of solidarity-forging, that a reasonable person seeking staunch defence, redress or improvement would rather look elsewhere. All in all, the new spirit is sceptical about the possible uses and benefits of acting together, joining forces, holding hands; and resigned to the idea that whatever you want to achieve, you had better look to your own cunning and ingenuity as the principal resources. Also the utopian visions of a better life are now, by and large, privatized and deregulated. Lady Thatcher might have committed a grave *factual* error when she said that there is no such thing as 'society'; but she certainly allowed no mistake as to the *objectives* her legislative efforts pursued. What the ill-famed proposition reported were the speaker's intentions, and the subsequent years went a long way towards making the word flesh.

But do we not act in solidarity – at least on occasion? Time and again we hear of people gathering to promote or defend a cause they seem to consider to be shared by them all. Without that 'sharing feeling' there would be no public meetings, marches, collecting of signatures. True enough. And yet more often than not common actions do not live long enough to precipitate solidary institutions and command stable loyalty of their participants – much as the participants enjoy the long-forgotten experience of helping each other and making sacrifices for each other as long as the common actions last and the 'common cause' remains common . . . Like other events, such collective causes burst into attention for a brief moment only and fade out to make room for other preoccupations. They give birth on the whole to 'single issue' actions, gathering around one demand people of most variegated persuasions, often strange bedfellows indeed, who have little in common apart from responding to a specific appeal. Very seldom do such 'single issues' manifest or enhance the sentiment of moral responsibility for common welfare. Much more often they mobilize sentiments *against*, not *for*: against closing down a school or a mine here rather than elsewhere, against a bypass or a rail link, against a Romany camp or travellers' convoy, against a dumping ground for toxic waste. What they would wish to achieve is not so much making the shared world nicer and more habitable, but redistributing its less prepossessing aspects: dumping the awkward and unpleasant parts of it in the neighbours' back-yard. They divide more than they unite. Obliquely, they promote the idea that different people have different moral entitlements, and that the rights of some entail the right to deny rights of some others.

Privatized existence has its many joys: freedom of choice, the opportunity to try many ways of life, the chance to make oneself to the measure of one's self-image. But it has its sorrows as well: loneliness and incurable uncertainty as to the choices made and still to be made being foremost among them. It is not an easy matter to build one's own identity relying on one's own guesses and hunches alone, but there is little reassurance coming from the self-made identity if it has not been recognized and confirmed by a power stronger and longer lasting than its solitary builder. Identity must be *seen* as such; the dividing line between socially accepted and merely individually imagined identity is one between self-assertion and madness. This is why we all feel time and again an overwhelming 'need of belonging' – a need to identify ourselves not just as individual human beings, but as members of a larger entity. That identification-through-membership is hoped to provide a firm foundation on which to erect smaller and feebler personal identity. As some of the old, once solid, entities underwriting and endorsing individual identities lie in ruins, while others are fast losing their holding power, there is a demand for new ones, able to pronounce authoritative and binding judgements.

We are being told repeatedly by the learned opinion of many social scientists, by the born-again enthusiasts of the 'pre-reflexive togetherness' they once assigned to the pre-modern and pre-civilized past, that 'community' is the most likely candidate to fill the gap. Modernity spent most of its time and a lot of its energy on fighting communities – those larger-than-life groupings into which people are born, only to be held inside for the rest of life by the dead hand of tradition strengthened by collective surveillance and blackmail. From the Enlightenment on, it has been seen as a commonsensical truth that human emancipation, the releasing of genuine human potential, required that the bounds of communities be broken and individuals set free from the circumstances of their birth. We seem to have come full circle now. The idea of community has been recovered from the cold storage where modernity bent on boundless humanity confined it, and restored to a genuine or imaginary past glory. It is on the community that many hopes bereaved by bankrupt or discredited institutions now focus. What had once been rejected as a constraint is now hailed as the 'enabling capacity'. What was once seen as an obstacle on the road to full humanity is now praised as its necessary condition. Humanity, we are told, comes in many forms and shapes, and thanks to communities, traditions and cultures the bequeathed forms of life are here to see to it that this be the case.

Social thought was always keen to repeat the stories told or merely thought of by the power-holders (or, rather, to make the humdrum bustle of the power-holders into interesting stories and moral tales), and to disguise the chronicle of the power-holders' ambitions and the (often shady) dealings that arose from them as descriptions of social reality, of its laws or its 'historical tendencies'. In the times of modern cultural crusades launched against regional, local or ethnic self-management, self-congratulating obituaries of communities filled social-scientific oeuvres. But powers eager to present their own particularity as human universality are today thin in the field, and there is naturally not much point in narrating their by-now faded dreams. New powers that took their place do not speak the language of universality. Quite the contrary, they appeal to what *distinguishes* one human collectivity from another; concerned more with defence than with an attack, they are ready to admit that the plurality of human forms is here to stay: no more a regrettable yet temporary flaw, but a permanent feature of human existence. And social thought, promptly and obligingly, changes its tune.

The argument about the supremacy of a supposedly 'natural' community in the life of the individual runs as follows: each one of us is born into a certain tradition and language, which decide what there is to be thought of before we start thinking ourselves, what we are to see before we begin to look, what we are to say before we learn to speak, what we are to consider important before we start weighing things against each other, and how we are to conduct ourselves before we start pondering the choices. Thus, in order to know what we are, to understand ourselves, we must fathom and consciously embrace that tradition; and in order to be ourselves, to keep our identity intact and waterproof, we must support that tradition with all our heart. In fact, we owe it our complete loyalty; and we ought to offer its demands an unquestionable priority whenever loyalty-calls in that society of multiple loyalties clash.

The argument, as it were, reverses the true order of things. Traditions do not 'exist' by themselves and independently of what we think and do; they are daily reinvented by our dedication, our selective memory and selective seeing, our behaving 'as if' they defined our conduct. The allegedly 'primordial' communities are *postulated*; and the meaning of their being 'real' is that many people, in unison, follow that postulate. The call to give the 'community of belonging' our prime and undivided loyalty, the demand to consider ourselves community members first, and all the rest later, is precisely the way to make community a 'reality', to split the larger society into little enclaves which eye each other with suspicion and keep their distance from each other. And because these communities, unlike modern nations well entrenched in the coercive and educational institutions of the nation-state, do not have many legs to stand on except the copying and replicating of our individual loyalties, they require in order to exist an unusually intense emotional dedication and shrill, high-pitched, vociferous and spectacular declarations of faith; and they scent in the half-hearted, lukewarm and undecided fringes the most mortal of dangers.

Hence another contradiction between the 'community narrative' and the true state of affairs it narrates. The siren-song of community is all about the warmth of togetherness, mutual understanding and love; such a relief from the cold, harsh and lonely life of competition and continuous uncertainty! Community advertises itself as the cosy, burglar-proof home amidst the hostile and dangerous city; it draws profusely, overtly or obliquely, on the very contemporary image of the sharp divide between the fortified and electronically protected homestead and the street full of knife-carrying strangers, the waste-land secure under the 'neighbourhood watch'. Community seduces its proselytes with the promise of freedom from fear and the tranquility of *chez soi*. But again, the reality is all too often the opposite. Given the endemic brittleness of foundations, community can ill afford anything but full and militant dedication to the cause; its self-appointed guardians are day and night on the look-out, searching for real or putative traitors, turncoats or just the not-fully-converted, half-hearted and irresolute. Independence is frowned upon, dissent hounded down, disloyalty persecuted. Pressure to keep the intended flock in the fold is unrelenting; the craved-for cosiness of belonging is offered as the price of unfreedom.

The overall effect of all this is another case of the by-now familiar tendency to expropriate the individual's moral responsibility. It is now the community, or rather the self-proclaimed wardens of its purity, who draw the boundaries of moral obligations, divide good from evil, and for better or worse dictate the definition of moral conduct. The paramount concern of their moral legislation is to keep the division between 'us' and 'them' watertight; not so much the promotion of moral standards, as the installation of *double* standards (as the French say, *deux poids, deux mesures*) – one for 'us', another reserved for the treatment of 'them'. True, unlike the depersonalized world of privatized individuals, the postulation of community neither promotes moral indifference nor suffers it lightly. But it does not cultivate *moral selves* either. It replaces the torments of moral responsibility with the certainty of discipline and submission. Disciplined selves, as we have repeatedly seen, are in no way guaranteed to be moral; while submissive selves can be easily deployed – and are deployed – in the service of cruel, mindless inhumanity of the endless (and hopeless) inter-communal wars of attrition and boundary skirmishes and the ruthless suppression of dissent.

Between hope and despair

We have come a long way in our search for the sources of moral hope, but remain, so far, empty-handed. Our only gain is learning where such sources are unlikely to be found. Bureaucracy and business were never famous as shrines of ethics and schools of morality. But little can be expected from entities meant to compensate for the harm they have done to the moral backbone of human selves. Back to the family? Privatization and deregulation processes reach deep into the heart of family life: even making unpaid policemen out of the parents, as proponents of fining parents for their children's misbehaviour want, would hardly stem the tide. Back into the community fold? Here moral responsibilities are more likely to be put into deep-freeze than resuscitated. More than two centuries after the Enlightenment promise to legislate for an ethical and humane society, we are left, each of us, with our own individual conscience and sentiment of responsibility as the only resource with which to struggle to make life more moral than it is. And yet we find this resource depleted and squeezed by the unholy alliance of tremendous forces.

This is not just the matter of concern for moral philosophers and preachers. However worried they may be, there is every reason for their worry to be widely shared. The dilemma we confront now has been expressed poignantly by the great German-American ethical philosopher, Hans Jonas: 'The very same movement which put us in possession of the powers that have now to be regulated by norms . . . has by a necessary complementarity eroded the foundations from which norms could be derived . . . Now we shiver in the nakedness of nihilism in which near-omnipotence is paired with near-emptiness, greatest capacity with knowing least what for.'

Indeed, the stakes are enormous. One of the most influential books published in the last decade was Ulrich Beck's *Society of Risk*. Beck's message, now widely approved of, is that our society becomes increasingly a risk-producing, risk-monitoring and risk-managing society. We do not so much move 'forward', as clear up the mess and seek an exit from the havoc perpetrated by our own actions yesterday. The risks are our own products, though unexpected and often impossible to predict or calculate. This is because whatever we do, we concentrate on the task at hand (this ability of close-focusing is, in fact, the secret of the astonishing achievements of science and technology), while the changes we introduce in the balance of nature and society in order to perform that task reverberate far and wide; their distant effects hit back as new dangers, new problems and thus new tasks.

What makes this already depressing plight near-catastrophic, though, is that the scale of the changes we inadvertently provoke is so massive, that the line beyond which the risks become totally unmanageable and damage irreparable may be crossed at any moment. We begin now to calculate the dangers of climatic change caused by pollution, or of the depletion of soil and water supplies caused by ever more specialized fertilisers and insecticides. We calculate, though not to any great effect thus far, the health risks arising from the trend to 'rationalize' the food industry and to make it more 'cost-effective'. But have we seriously started to count the dangers involved in releasing into nature artificially created viruses (each one, to be sure, with its specific, invariably praiseworthy, uses) or ever more ramified genetic engineering of the human species, aimed ultimately at introducing bespoke-tailor shops for human offspring?

Besides, very often we know the risks only too well, yet there is little we can do with our knowledge since the forces that push us deeper and deeper into increasingly risky territory are overwhelming; think for instance of the relentless saturation of the conflict-ridden world with ever more refined and ever less resistible weapons, or of adding each year hundreds of thousands of new vehicles to the blight of congested roads and traffic virtually at a stand-still we all, at moments of reflection, bewail. There is thus little ground to console ourselves that the same skills that make us powerful enough to produce awesome risks make us also wise enough to reflect upon them – let alone do something to limit the damage. The ability to reflect does not translate easily into the ability to act.

Even if the *mind* is perceptive and judicious enough, the *will* may prove to be wanting; and even if the will is there, the *hands* may be too short. We introduce our improvements (or medicines to heal the wounds left by the failed improvements of yore) locally; yet their effects may reach the nooks and crannies of the globe of which presence we are but dimly, if at all, aware. We act here and now, to deal with nuisances we feel today – and we act without giving ourselves enough time to think of, let alone to test, the long-term effects of our doings. But will we still be able to cross that other bridge when we come to it? And what sort of a bridge will it be? Think of the new wonder drugs which one after another burst into our dreams of happiness thanks to the ingenuity of scholars and promoters. Their so-called 'side-effects' are tested – sometimes over much too short a time, sometimes over a prudently longer period. The anti-conception pill has been taken by millions of women for over twenty years now, so we may say that we know the risks that come to the surface during this time-span. But do we really know what the human world will be like in, say, a hundred years from now, after several generations of women on the pill? And is there a way of knowing it? Or do we know the several-generation-long *social* effects of artificial insemination and *in vitro* conception?

These are serious questions; and the kind of questions we never had need to ask before. We seem to require now an entirely new brand of ethics. An ethics made to the measure of the enormous space-and-time distance on which we can act and on which we act even when we neither know nor intend it. The 'first duty' of such ethics, to quote Jonas again, is 'visualising the long-range effects of technological enterprise'. Such an ethics must be guided, says Jonas, by the 'heuristics of fear' and the 'principle of uncertainty': even if the arguments of the pessimists and the optimists are finely balanced, 'the prophecy of doom is to be given greater heed than the prophecy of bliss.' Jonas sums up with an updated (though – as he is quick to admit himself – far from logically self-evident) version of Kant's categorical imperative: 'Act so that the effects of your action are compatible with the permanence of genuine human life.' *If in doubt* – Jonas implies – *do not do it*. Do not magnify or multiply the risk more than unavoidable; err, if at all, on the side of caution.

The ethical self-limitation Jonas thinks we desperately need is a tall order. Following the 'heuristics of fear' would mean nothing less than resisting, withstanding and defying the pressures exerted by virtually all other aspects of contemporary living: by market competition, the ongoing undeclared war of redistribution between territorial and non-territorial units and groups, the self-propelling and self-enhancing tendencies of technoscience, our understanding of the life-process and collective living as a succession of 'problems' to be 'resolved' and our deeply ingrained dependency on ever more expert- and technique-intensive solutions to problems. Behind all those 'other aspects' stand powerful, well entrenched institutions which lend their impact an almost elemental power of 'natural forces'. Behind the new ethical imperative, on the other hand, stands only the diffuse feeling that we cannot go on like this for much longer without courting dangers of formidable, perhaps unprecedented, proportions. This feeling must yet find the institutional haven where to cast anchor. It is far from clear where are the forces likely to inscribe the Jonas-type principles on their banners – let alone forces powerful enough to make them victorious.

New ethics in search of new politics

Hannah Arendt, a most insightful observer and severe judge of our present human condition, wrote profusely and convincingly of the 'emptiness of political space'. What she meant was that in our times there are no more obvious sites in the body politic from which meaningful and effective interventions into the way our collective life is lived can be made. Partial, segmental, task-oriented, time-limited interventions – yes, of these we have no shortage. But more often than not they do not add up into any meaningful totality, they are, like everything else, fragmentary and discontinuous; quite often they clash with each other – and no one can with any degree of self-assurance claim to know in advance the possible outcome of such clashes. Such human interventions as are undertaken peter out in the intricacies of the opaque and impermeable social system, only to rebound later in a form reminiscent more of natural catastrophes than of deliberate human actions. On the other hand, it seems to be obvious that, due to the nature of choices we confront now, privatized initiatives and deregulated intervention simply will not do; they are, if anything, part of the problem, never the solutions. Evidently, some sort of co-ordinated and concerted action is imperative. And the name of such action is politics; the promotion of a new and badly needed ethics for the new age can only be approached as a *political* issue and task.

Politics, though, has many faces. The efforts of political scientists notwithstanding, politics remains what is called a 'hotly contested concept'. In the probably most widespread opinion, aided and abetted by daily governmental practices, politics is about making and unmaking laws and statutes, with the electors watching the effects and re-electing the law-makers if the effects are to their liking, or going for the competition if they are not satisfied. By this view, electors (and the lay members of body politics enter the picture as electors *only*) behave much as all sensible consumers do; they are, for all practical intents, 'consumers of political services'. If this is what politics is about, then the new ethics (or any other ethics for that matter) can be politically promoted solely through designing new legal rules – defining certain behaviour as criminal, penalizing other kinds of behaviour more severely than before, or encouraging still other kinds of behaviour through more alluring rewards.

Legislation may or may not evoke conduct of a desirable kind. What it is unlikely ever to achieve is to promote moral responsibility (as distinct from legal obedience) – the only soil in which the sought-after ethics can strike roots. Most importantly, even less likely is the prospect of the legislative effort following long-term ethical impera- tives rather than being buffeted, plankton-like, by calculation of immediate and short-lived electoral gains.

There is a certain resonance, a certain symbiosis between the way our country is governed and the way our lives are lived. Both – the action of the government and the activity of living – are cut into slices, often paper-thin slices; both are collections or successions of events, each of the events coming, by and large, unannounced and for no evident reason; in both, everything that happens, happens haphazardly and endures but until further notice; successive happen- ings arise as if from nowhere and fast sink into oblivion, to make room for other happenings; none of them seems to leave much trace behind.

We may say that the activities of government, like most of our life activities, tend to be nowadays *fragmentary*, *episodic* and *inconsequen- tial*. Politics has been split into a collection of happenings, one hap- pening unconnected with all the others, one brought into public attention mainly to erase from it yesterday's happenings. Today's triumph means sorting out the mess left by the deeds celebrated yesterday. One takes one thing at a time and forbids all thought of the bridges ahead. Scandals and inanities which burst into public attention have a salutary quality of effacing past scandals and inanities from memory. (Iraqgate helps us to forget the robbery of state pen- sioners; VAT on fuel overpaints the ugly stain of ever growing queues to the operating theatres; a televised auction of party leadership takes the eyes off the new tax bills; and the saucy details of some politi- cian's private life chase out of public attention everything else that may count.) Commitments are all until further notice, and eternal rights are as mortal as eternity itself has become.

A government that practises and promotes politics so under- stood likes its subjects as they come, with their shifting eyes and drifting attention, much as it waxes lyrical from time to time about glorious heritage and old family values. Subjects who live their lives as collections of inconsequential and forgettable episodes would do nicely, thank you, for the government whose policy is a series of inconsequential (and better to be forgotten) fragments. Episodic life chimes well with such politics and the vision of the world it emanates. Like the Australians their fourexes, such government would not give up such subjects for anything, and will do all it can to make them stay the way they are, or rather the way they are pressed and buffeted and brow-beaten (with government's blessing, conniving and devoted collaboration) to become.

And so it is a government that deregulates everything, so that nothing can be perceived as lasting and trustworthy, predictable, counted on and relied upon; that removes places where decisions are taken to where those affected by them cannot see them as decisions, but only as 'blind fate'; that wants the play of market forces to set the pattern for life, for life lived as play; that promotes the 'play your hand well' precept as the supreme standard of decency; that redefines the citizen, in theory and in deed, as a satisfied customer of a society made after the image of a shopping mall; that saps its subjects' trust in the world and in each other.

But this is also a government which holds high the life-mode of a shopping-mall stroller as the paragon of happy humanity and the good life, and by that standard disqualifies a growing number of its subjects – invalids, unemployed, deskilled, racially discriminated-against, single mothers – as inept and imperfect and unfit to improve on the ground of being flawed consumers ill able to afford frequent shopping-mall strolls. This is a government which in the name of episodic life of those who 'can afford it' draws an ever thicker line and digs an ever deeper ditch between those who can and those who cannot. This is a government which splits the society it rules into citizens defined as satisfied consumers and flawed consumers defined as flawed citizens. And this is a government which uses the harrowing plight of the second to frighten the first into satisfaction, and the shining paths of the first to seduce the second into self-deprecatory obedience. And yet . . .

The life of episode-juggling is not an unmixed bliss. Far from it. We are told over and over again that one must make the life of the poor ever more horrid in order to 'create jobs' – that is, to impoverish the jobless back into employment. This is at best half-truth. The other half of the truth is that one needs to make the flawed consumers ever more miserable in order to keep the proper consumers satisfied with their life of consumerism. Because the belief in bliss endemic to such a life is everything but 'trivially true', as is the idea that the more you consume, the happier you get. What about uncertainty, insecurity, loneliness? What of the future being a site of fear instead of hope? What of never accumulating anything securely, of being sure of nothing, of never being able to say with confidence 'I have arrived', 'I have done my job well', 'I have lived decent life'? What about seeing in the neighbourhood only a jungle to be warily and fearfully watched, in the stranger only a beast to hide from; what about the privatized prisons of burglar-proof homes? And is it really so pleasant to expend one's life on one-upmanship among people practising one-upmanship? Would you really choose such life given a choice? Summing up in his most recent book (*Le Dédale*) the lessons and the prospects of contemporary life, Georges Balandier stated what ought to be (though it is not) obvious: 'This individualism comes more by default than by choice.'

Life has not got to be like this. The space we co-habit may be well – consensually – structured; in such a space, in which many things vital to the life of each of us (transport, schools, surgeries, media of communication) are *shared*, we may see each other as conditions, rather than obstacles, to our collective as well as individual well-being. Much as the fragmented and discontinuous life promotes the waning of moral impulses, a shared life of continuous and multi-faceted relationships would reinvigorate moral responsibilities and awaken the urge to shoulder the task of managing – now truly common – affairs. Much as the life of episodes and the politics reduced to crisis-management prompt the exit from politics, the sharing of responsibilities would go a long way towards helping citizens to recover the voices they lost or stopped trying to make audible. As Steven Connor put it, 'it is only in the absolute putting of the "we" at risk that we realize the possibilities of our humanity.'

Can we do it? Will we do it?

Contemporary humanity speaks in many voices and we know now that it will do so for a very long time to come. The central issue of our times is how to reforge that polyphony into harmony and prevent it from degenerating into cacophony. Harmony is not uniformity; it is always an interplay of a number of different motifs, each retaining its separate identity and sustaining the resulting melody through, and thanks to, that identity.

Hannah Arendt thought that capacity of interplay to be the quality of the *polis* – where we can meet each other as *equals*, while recognizing our diversity, and caring for the preservation of that diversity as the very purpose of our meeting . . . How can this be achieved? (How can *we* achieve it?) *Through the separate identities stopping short of exclusivity*, of refusal to cohabit with other identities; this in turn requires abandoning the tendency to suppress other identities in the name of the self-assertion of one's own, while accepting, on the contrary, that it is precisely the guarding of other identities that maintains the diversity in which one's own uniqueness can thrive.

In his highly influential *Theory of Justice*, John Rawls presented the model of 'overlapping consensus', spelling out the assumptions under which the harmony between diversity and unity may be attained. This is how Richard J. Mouw and Sander Griffioen summarize his propositions:

> The core contention here is that while people come into the public domain from very different metaphysical/religious/moral starting ponts, once they have arrived they can agree to operate with the same intuitive ideas about what goes into a just arrangement. They can reach a consensus on such matters as the rule of law, liberty of conscience, freedom of thought, equality of opportunity, a fair share of material means for all citizens . . .

'They *can* . . .' The question is: would they? And will they? The citizens who used to meet at the public spaces of the *polis* managed on the whole to do it quite well. But they met there with the overt intention of discussing public matters, for which they, and they alone, bore responsibility: nowhere else would things be done if they did not do them . . . Whatever 'overlapping consensus' there was, it was their common achievement, not the gift they received – they made and made again that consensus as they met and talked and argued. In Jeffrey Weeks's apt phrase, 'humanity is not an essence to be realized, but a pragmatic construction, a perspective, to be developed through the articulation of the variety of individual projects, of differences, which constitute our humanity in the broadest sense.'

Albert Hirschman suggested that people may influence the affairs which concern them in two ways: through *voice* or through *exit* (not by accident Hirschman took as his model the actions undertaken by people in their capacity of *consumers*!): 'voice' stands for demanding changes in the kind of things done and the way they are done; 'exit' – for turning one's back on disliked things altogether and going elsewhere to seek satisfaction. The difference between 'voice' and 'exit' is, to put it bluntly, one between engagement and disengagement, responsibility and indifference, political action and apathy. We may say that if the present condition we are in needs people to make their voice audible, it is the exit that our political institutions, and the idea of 'citizenship' they promote, favour . . .

Indeed, this is what the conception of the citizen as a satisfied customer is all about. Leave decisions to the ones in the know, and they will take care of your well-being. As to yourself, take care of things close to your home: preserve *family values*. And yet we have seen that it is precisely the withdrawal into the walls of one's family (followed soon by further withdrawal into individual shells), losing from sight those intricate yet intimate connections between life in the family (or indeed individual life) and life in public spaces, private and public, biography and history, forgetting how much the latter determines the former – that constitutes the most grievous bodily harm which the present privatization and deregulation of human concerns has delivered and goes on delivering to the chances of moral renewal. Under closer scrutiny, the alleged medicine looks suspiciously like the disease.

It is all too easy to expose other people's hopes as not firmly enough founded, and their solutions as not realistic enough. It is much more difficult to propose one's own warrants for hope and one's own solution that would be immune to similar charges. This is not because of the shortage of imagination or good will – but because the present human condition itself is shot through with ambivalence, and any diagnosis seems to point in two opposite directions simultaneously – towards developments whose compatibility is far from evident. To put it in a nutshell: the chance of counteracting the present pressures towards draining intimate and public life from ethical motives and moral evaluations depends at the same time on more autonomy for *individual* moral selves and more vigorous sharing of *collective* responsibilities. In terms of the orthodox 'state versus individual' dilemma, this is clearly a contradiction – and promoting it seems like an effort to square the circle. And yet if any conclusions at all follow from our discussion so far, it is that *the contradiction is illusory*, and that the widespread uncritical acceptance of the illusion is itself a product of tendencies which need to be rectified and of the orthodox thought that mimicked them.

We have seen that all the designed and tried artificial substitutes for spontaneous moral impulses and the individual responsibility for the Other have failed, or worse: ended up disarming the ethical safeguards against the danger of the human thrust towards control and mastery degenerating into inhuman cruelty and oppression. We can now repeat with yet greater conviction the words of Max Frisch: at the end of our long modern march towards reason-guided society, we are returned, as far as the terms of our coexistence are concerned, to our old resources of moral sense and fellow-feeling, guiding us in daily moral choices.

For such a guidance, we have no indubitable and universally agreed codes and rules. Choices are indeed choices, and that means that each is to some extent arbitrary and that uncertainty as to its propriety is likely to linger long after the choices are made. We understand now that uncertainty is not a temporary nuisance, which can be chased away through learning the rules, or surrendering to expert advice, or just doing what others do – but a permanent condition of life; we may say more – it is the very soil in which the moral self takes root and grows. Moral life is a life of continuous uncertainty. To be a moral person takes a lot of strength and resilience to withstand the pressures and the temptations to withdraw from joint responsibilities. Moral responsibility is *unconditional* and in principle *infinite* – and thus one can recognize moral persons by their never quenched dissatisfaction with their moral performance; the gnawing suspicion that they were not moral *enough*.

On the other hand, a society that engages its members, as the *polis* did, in the difficult yet imperative task of caring for each other, and in running common affairs so that the common life could observe the standards of justice and prudence – such a society requires neither the disciplined subjects nor satisfaction-seeking consumers of socially provided services, but tenacious and sometimes obstinate, but always responsible citizens. To be responsible does not mean following the rules; it may often require one to disregard the rules or act in a way the rules do not warrant. Only such responsibility makes the citizen into that basis on which a human community resourceful and thoughtful enough to cope with the present challenges can be conceivably built.

Conceivably . . . And no more than that, since no guarantee can be given that such a community will indeed be built, and since there are no foolproof methods to make sure that it will. In fact, the only assurance are the relentless efforts of the builders themselves. What may help in this effort is the awareness of the intimate connection (not contradiction!) between the autonomous, morally self-sustained and self-governed (therefore often unruly, unwieldy and awkward) citizen and a fully fledged, self-reflective and self-correcting political community. They can only come together; neither is thinkable without the other.

Quoted works

Hannah Arendt, *The Human Condition* (Chicago, 1958)
Neal Ascherson, 'The British Problem', *Independent on Sunday*, 3 April 1994
Georges Balandier, *Le Dédale* (Paris, 1994)
David Campbell and Michael Dillon, *The Political Subject of Violence* (Manchester, 1993)
John Dunn (ed.), *Democracy: The Unfinished Journey, 508 BC to AD 1993* (Oxford, 1993)
Max Frisch, *Sketchbook 1946–1949* (New York, 1977)
Anthony Giddens, *The Transformation of Intimacy: Sexuality, Love and Eroticism in Modern Societies* (Cambridge, 1992)
Hans Jonas, *The Imperative of Responsibility* (Chicago, 1984)
Knud E. Løgstrup, *The Ethical Demand* (Philadelphia, 1971)
Richard J. Mouw and Sander Griffioen, *Pluralism and Horizons: An Essay in Christian Public Philosophy* (Grand Rapids, 1993)
Michael Schluter and David Lee, *The R Factor* (London, 1993)
A Shestov Anthology (Athens, Ohio, 1970)
Judith Squires (ed.), *Principled Positions: Postmodernism and the Rediscovery of Value* (London, 1993) [articles by Steven Connor and Jeffrey Weeks]

Index